BELIEF AND UNBELIEF IN MEDIEVAL EUROPE

JOHN H. ARNOLD

Hodder Arnold

A MEMBER OF THE HODDER HEADLINE GROUP

First published in Great Britain in 2005 by
Hodder Education, a member of the Hodder Headline Group,
338 Euston Road, London NW1 3BH

www.hoddereducation.com

Distributed in the United States of America by
Oxford University Press Inc.
198 Madison Avenue, New York, NY10016

Hodder Headline's policy is to use papers that are natural, renewable and
recyclable products and made from wood grown in sustainable forests.
The logging and manufacturing processes are expected to conform to the
environmental regulations of the country of origin.

The advice and information in this book are believed to be true and
accurate at the date of going to press, but neither the author nor the publisher
can accept any legal responsibility or liability for any errors or omissions.

British Library Cataloguing in Publication Data
A catalogue record for this book is available from the British Library

Library of Congress Cataloging-in-Publication Data
A catalog record for this book is available from the Library of Congress

ISBN-10: 0-340-80786-5
ISBN-13: 978-0-340-80786-6

1 2 3 4 5 6 7 8 9 10

Typeset in 10/12pt Sabon by Servis Filmsetting Ltd, Longsight, Manchester
Printed and bound in Great Britain by CPI Bath.

What do you think about this book? Or any other Hodder
Education title? Please send your comments to the feedback
section on www.hoddereducation.com.

For Peter Biller

Contents

Acknowledgements

This book attempts to look afresh at a broad area, and to the extent that it succeeds, I am indebted to the published work of many historians. I am most grateful for their scholarship, and I apologize for occasions when lack of space has prevented me engaging with their arguments to the full. For the most part I have met their work, and of course the primary sources that I have consulted, through the riches of the Institute of Historical Research, the Warburg Institute and the British Library; and I similarly thank those institutions for the invaluable services that they render to the historical profession. I was fortunate also to be supported by a small research grant for certain archival source materials given to me by the British Academy, who showed endless patience when various health-related complications delayed my ability to spend their money.

Many individuals deserve specific thanks. First among these is Susan Reynolds. The seeds for this book rest in her characteristically original and provocative 1991 article on medieval scepticism, which I first encountered when a PhD student at York. Its intellectual fearlessness, and deep sense of engagement with the lives of the medieval laity, liberated me to pursue the arguments presented here and in other work. I now have the great pleasure of knowing the author as well as her writing, and she did me the honour of reading and commenting upon several chapters of this book. I am hugely grateful towards her for that kindness, and apologize to her for any flaws in argument and style that remain despite her best efforts. I must also thank those others who have generously read and commented upon various chapters, whose knowledge and insight have been a huge contribution, namely Frances Andrews, Cordelia Beattie, Simon Ditchfield, Victoria Howell, Mark Knights, Sara Lipton, Simon Middleton and Andy Wood. Thanks also to Chris Wheeler, who first commissioned me to write this book and who supplied the title, and to those anonymous readers who commented upon the original proposal for the press. One memorably suggested that asking me to write it would be like 'asking Arnold Schoenberg to compose a Broadway musical'; I can only hope that I have gone some way to fulfilling such an intriguing proposition. I have also benefited from conversations with many people. Andrew Finch proffered many a helpful suggestion over a coffee in Norwich; Nick Terpstra allowed me to steal one of his stories, and helped me to understand the world of confraternities, as did my colleague John Henderson; Sarah Hamilton led me through some arguments about confession, and Sophie Page did similarly for magic; my old friends Katherine Lewis and Simon Ditchfield put me straight on various saintly matters; my friend and colleague Filippo de Vivo was a constant support, and an expert blasphemer, and Jan Rüger provided invaluable help eavesdropping on Hans Behem. Theo Riches, Trevor Dean and John Gillingham all rendered assistance at key moments, and Christine Caldwell, Shannon McSheffrey and Beth Williamson very generously allowed me access to their respective unpublished works.

Two final thank yous. The first is to Peter Biller, to whom this book is dedicated with great affection. I am grateful to him for all that he has taught me, from the various possibilities that inquisitorial registers proffer to the historian, to the delicate interpretive nuances that a good archival story presents. I would be surprised if every argument in this book met with his agreement, but I hope that he will see how deeply indebted it is to the example set by his own careful and diligent search for the lives and experiences of ordinary people in the medieval period. The second is to Victoria Howell. Life produced many sharp and painful edges during the period that it took to research and write this book. Without her love and support, it could not have been done. She has always been both healthy sceptic and supportive believer, for which I am grateful with all my heart.

J.H.A.
London 2005

1

Belief

Where, then, do we get the notion of belief from? From the term 'believe', and its inflected forms, in everyday English usage. Statements of belief are the only evidence for the phenomenon; but the phenomenon itself appears to be no more than the custom of making such statements.

(Rodney Needham, *Belief, Language and Experience*)

Belief is a very elusive concept: difficult to define, difficult to describe, and hence difficult to analyse. What we actually *mean* when we say we 'believe' in something is not completely clear. When we turn to other people's belief, the problem becomes magnified. How do we see something that, whenever we attempt to pin it down, dances away into greater complexity? Perhaps a way to start is to follow, metaphorically, the example of physicists. To study an elusive object like a subatomic particle, one needs a smoke chamber: scientists cannot see the particle, but they can see its passage, as something that has left a trace. Let us begin then by examining two traces from the Middle Ages, one the trace of a belief, the other – arguably – the trace of its absence.

The monk and chronicler William of Newburgh (*c.*1135–*c.*1198) believed, among various other things, in vampires. 'It is not easy, in faith, to accept this,' William admitted, 'except that in our present time there are sufficient examples and abundant evidence.' His *History of English Affairs* provides four tales of resurrected dead people (though he could have given more, he claimed), all set in the northern borders of England during William's lifetime. It is the final, bloodiest tale I want to relate here. In the town of Annan, in Dumfries, there lived a man of evil ways who, suspecting his wife of adultery, hid himself in the roof of their bedroom. Catching her in an adulterous embrace, he fell from the rafters and was mortally injured. Confused and distraught, he refused confession and the last rites proffered by the local priest, and so died unshriven. Soon after, his body arose from its grave to persecute the townsfolk. People dared not venture out between sunset and sunrise for fear of being assaulted by this monster, which wandered the streets accompanied by howling dogs and corrupted the very air with its pestiferous breath. Soon the town was disease-ridden and almost deserted, as people either fled or died.

The local priest, realizing the impending doom of his parish, summoned on Palm Sunday a meeting of wise and religious men to ask for advice. But while this gathering of clerics talked and feasted, two young brothers took it upon themselves to act. 'This monster has already destroyed our father, and will soon destroy us also, unless we do something about it,' they told one another. 'There is no one to hinder us: for in the priest's house a feast is in progress, and the whole town is silent as if deserted.' And so they set out to dig up the grave, armed only with a blunt spade. Having penetrated just a few feet of soil, they discovered the corpse, 'distended to enormous corpulence, its face red and swollen beyond measure. The shroud, in truth, in which it had been wrapped, seemed nearly torn to pieces.' Spurred on by anger, the brothers thrust their tools into the body, 'and from it flowed so much blood, that one understood it to have been a bloodsucker filled with the blood of many people'. Outside the village they built a pyre, and dragged the corpse to it. One brother hacked repeatedly at the body with the blunt spade until he was able to rip out the heart. This they tore to pieces, and the body was burnt. The contagion afflicting the village ceased, and the brothers returned to tell the priest and his wise men what had happened.[1]

Move forward almost exactly 300 years to 1491, and move south to Newbury. In that town Thomas Tailour, a fuller by trade, walks barefoot and bareheaded, carrying a stick. On his back is a bundle of faggots. Already that day he has visited the parish church, and on future days he will similarly make humble procession to several other churches, the monastery at Reading, and the marketplaces of Reading and Wokingham. When he reaches Newbury marketplace he will stand publicly and explain to the people the nature of his crime.

Tailour had been sentenced to this penance by the bishop of Salisbury, Thomas Langton. Brought before Langton in January, accused of various heresies, Tailour had confessed that he called people 'fools' who went on pilgrimage to the shrine of St James at Compostella in Spain, saying that 'it would be more merit to give a penny to a poor man than to visit him'. He had said that there was no point in worshipping images of saints (this also he had read in a book he possessed). He had disparaged the learning and righteousness of priests, shown contempt for the pope, and questioned the need for the sacraments of baptism and penance, saying that if you were born Christian, you didn't need the former, and if you died Christian, you didn't need the latter, so long as you asked God for mercy. Tailour also confessed that:

> I have held erroneously and before diverse men have argued and declared that when a man or woman dies in their body, then also dies their soul, for as the light of a candle is put out by casting it away or in other ways quenched by blowing or shaking it, so the soul is quenched by the death of the body.

Having abjured these heretical beliefs, Tailour was sentenced to perform his public penance; and furthermore, on every day of his life, to bow down before the crucifix and say the *Pater noster* (the 'Our Father' prayer) five times, the *Ave Maria* (the 'Hail Mary' prayer) five times, and then one *Credo* (the creed or statement of orthodox belief). Finally, on the feast of St James and on Good Friday for every year of his life he was to fast on bread and water. Were he to break this penance, or relapse into his heretical beliefs, he would be burnt to death. The faggots that he carried in penance were to symbolize this: like Christ bearing his cross to Calvary, Tailour was to carry his means of execution with him to Reading market.[2]

So we have two traces of belief: a chronicle account of supernatural evil, and a bishop's record of disciplining his flock. We know that religious belief mattered in the Middle Ages. It was the era of the great cathedrals, those imposing factories of prayer. It was the age of the crusades, inspiring thousands to charge east to defend the site of heaven upon earth. And it was the Middle Ages that produced intense and passionate mystical texts, such as Marguerite Porete's *Mirror for Simple Souls* (*c*.1305) and Thomas à Kempis's *Imitation of Christ* (*c*.1410), that record movingly intimate relationships with God. There are many traces of belief – of orthodox Catholic Christian faith – in the Middle Ages. It may seem obtuse to begin a book on medieval belief with two tales so far from the mainstream. Certainly, if I had started instead with an account of someone attending mass, or lighting a candle to a saint, or giving alms to the poor, we would be much closer to the notional 'centre' of orthodox medieval Catholicism. But this is a book about both belief and unbelief, and the relationship between the two. I am interested not only in centres but also in margins. As the preceding two tales attest, the Middle Ages were not a straightforward 'age of faith': certainly not (as William's vampire illustrates) in the sense that everybody pledged unproblematic allegiance to one clearly defined religion that excluded superstition and the supernatural. Nor even (as Tailour's trial shows) in the sense of everybody 'believing' in a similar general direction, even if not completely united on every detail. William's tale of the undead was not 'heretical' (a problematic term as we will see in a later chapter), but its depiction of death and the consequences of sin was far from run-of-the-mill. Tailour's beliefs – or rather, unbeliefs – were heretical, but may strike us as evidence for *doubt* as much as conscious dissent. William's tale was not, in any case, necessarily 'marginal', if by that we mean unorthodox or utterly unrepresentative. He himself emphasizes how frequently the dead return; and the elements of the tale, concerning death, blood, confession, resurrection, are all absolutely central to medieval Christianity. Tailour's rejection of the soul's immortality is (as far as we know) much less common, but his story is also embroiled with central features of medieval religion: the relationship between everyday life and the supernatural, the hierarchies of priest and laity, the concern with death and fate. Our two 'margins' in fact knit just as neatly to the centre as a more obviously orthodox example.

This book is about lay belief and unbelief in Western Europe between about 1000 and 1530. The two terms are obviously linked: if nothing else, unbelief may be understood to be the absence of something expected (such as the continuing existence of the soul, apparently missing from Thomas Tailour's thoughts). In fact, they may be the same thing: Tailour *believed* that the soul ceased upon death; he did *not* believe that it continued. Therefore, this book is going to consider both 'belief' (in the sense of orthodox Catholic viewpoints) and various things that we might call 'unbelief' (divergent, 'superstitious', heretical and sceptical viewpoints) alongside each other. This methodology has an added benefit. The repression of dissent produces evidence, such as Tailour's trial, that provides unparalleled access to the details of lay religion. Some elements of this evidence are particular to the context of heresy, but not all. Thus examples in this book are drawn not only from straightforward accounts of Catholic orthodoxy, but also from sources relating to heretics such as French Cathars and Waldensians, and English Lollards (Chapter 6 discusses these and other heretical groups, their beliefs and the Church's reaction to them, in greater detail). It is important to note that I am not using 'unbelief' simply as a synonym for heresy. There has been a long-standing tradition that claims that unbelief, in the sense of cynicism, atheism, irreligion and so forth, was 'impossible' in the pre-modern period; that prior to the eighteenth-century Enlightenment, nobody was mentally capable of thinking outside the accepted framework of religion. This is simply not true. It is not true for the early modern period, as more recent studies have shown. And it is not true for the medieval period, as Tailour's case, among others, would strongly suggest.[3] This is not to imply that the medieval laity were really all either pagans or humanists – they were not. But it is to emphasize that assertions of homogeneous conformity must be treated with suspicion; and to suggest that where we find 'heresy', it may veil intriguingly varied forms of dissent and divergence from the orthodox norm.

What else do our two initial stories tell us? What can we glean about 'belief' from their traces? One thing is a reminder about evidence (something I shall consider in greater detail below): William and Thomas are unusual first and foremost not because of what they believed, but because we have a *record* of what they believed. We know what William thought about the evil dead returning. We know what Thomas thought about the soul ending. For most people in the period – for the thousands upon thousands who lived within Christendom in the centuries considered by this book – we have no record of what they believed or did not believe. We need, therefore, to think about how we can make use of those traces of belief that have survived for us, and particularly to see whether certain less obvious traces may be hidden within the more apparent trajectories. For example, we might ask whether William's account allows us to see something of what lay people believed about the dead, as well as what one particular monk thought was worth recording. At the same time, we also need to be wary of sources and the traces they leave: in the case of Thomas's trial, we have a source that was attempting to 'set someone straight' about religion, make them conform by punishing them when they strayed. There are certain cultural patterns underlying how the bishop thought about Tailour's 'heresy' that may shape and inflect the surviving source in ways that are not immediately apparent. For example, the bishop understood himself to be prosecuting a heretical sect called Lollardy and appeared to have assumed Tailour to be part of that group. Whether we, as later historians, share that assumption will depend in part on how we read and interpret the surviving evidence.

We can also be reminded of change over time. The context of William's thoughts about walking corpses – the theological milieu of the late twelfth century – had rather different ideas about death, the soul, demons, the role of the Church and so on than in Thomas's time. Indeed, curiously enough, one would be hard-pressed to find vampire stories in late fifteenth-century England, or in fact for a long time after. Equally, it is tremendously unusual to have a record of the beliefs of a lowly labourer like Tailour – let alone beliefs as sceptical as Thomas's – dating from the late twelfth century (though not completely impossible, as later examples will show). Most bishops in William's period tended not to be terribly concerned about what an ordinary layperson like Thomas really thought about the mysteries of the faith. Or, at any rate, they were not worried about someone like Thomas expressing unbelief in the way that fifteenth-century ecclesiastics were bothered by it: twelfth-century bishops in England did not, for example, set up regular investigations into heresy in their dioceses. In contrast, in Thomas's time, the English Church thought itself under threat from heresy, and so Thomas was brought before the bishop on suspicion of belonging to a sect. The sources therefore also point towards certain changes in the relationship between the clergy and the laity: changes in what the former expected of (or worried about) the latter, and perhaps changes in how lay people viewed their priests and the authority they claimed.

Most importantly, despite their manifest differences, the stories also have some things in common. In their very different ways, both share concerns about death: about what happens upon death, the implications of this, and ways of talking about it. And both share concerns about community. In William's case, the question is how to protect the community from threat; with Thomas, the best way of caring for the poor of the community (furthermore, in a very different sense, his public penance sent a message to the community about misbelief and the price of transgression). Although the specific beliefs in each story differ greatly, they engage themselves with certain shared concerns. As we will see in later chapters, these concerns – the fate of the soul, the relations between kin and neighbours, among other matters – figure strongly throughout medieval Christianity. However, as we have already noted, William's and Thomas's responses to death and community do not fit with a received view of medieval Christianity. Neither story displays an unequivocally orthodox approach to thinking about these matters.

If religion – in the loosest sense of the organization of belief – responds to these deep-seated human concerns about life and death, we must note that it does so not in neat doctrinal patterns but in more complex ways. Hence, in thinking about belief, rather than assuming that we should automatically start with the doctrinal centre – the Catholic Church – and work outwards or downwards as belief is disseminated to the lay population, we also need to think about how belief operates within the social and cultural worlds of those doing the believing, and then consider how patterns of belief are organized and, on occasion, policed. Religion, whatever else it is, has a social existence, and beliefs are formed, expressed and acted upon within social contexts. For these reasons, the chapters in this book do not work chronologically, or follow a simple hierarchical structure from 'Church' to 'people'. Instead, the chapters focus on different themes, examining the reception of the Church's precepts, but also the working and functioning of belief in the world.

In analysing belief and unbelief, this book has three main aims. The first is simply to introduce the reader, from a fresh perspective, to the world of western medieval Christian religion. I have insufficient space here to be theologically encyclopaedic, nor can I deal with all aspects of religious practice, nor provide a detailed chronology for every area. However, the content and implications of faith will be glossed, and I have tried to indicate how themes changed over time. It is particularly important to note that this book is interested in the laity rather than ecclesiastics or theologians, and most of all in those ordinary people who were not monarchs, nobles or elite. My focus is upon their religion, their beliefs and unbeliefs, and where I deal with religious topics that tend not directly to involve them (becoming a saint, for example) I will still nonetheless primarily be interested in how the laity related to this topic (what they thought about, and did with, saints).

The second aim is to provide certain tools for thinking about medieval belief. In fact, this aim is closely linked with the first: if one comes to a new topic, it may be as useful to be shown *why* something matters as it is to be provided with a narrative or a chronology or a map. Narratives, chronologies and maps are undoubtedly helpful, but they are not always very interesting, and they can give a falsely calm and static impression of areas that are in fact highly contested. So, instead, we will set out to think about belief in conjunction with some conceptual tools and questions that can suggest ways in which one might connect the fairly abstract and difficult notion of belief with the more concrete social, political, economic and cultural worlds that it inhabited.

Finally, a third aim of this book is more argumentative. I want to suggest in what follows that, when studying medieval belief, we need to consider further the theme of power in relation to religion. There has been something of a tendency to see religion either as a static phenomenon – essentially a mulch within which other things occur – or else as a suprahistorical verity – something both innate to humanity and transcendental of its ruder elements. Both of these are, I would argue, mystifications: that is, they serve to place complex areas beyond analysis and argument. As we will see, religion is bound up with power relationships in a number of different ways. This is not to suggest that power is all that religion is about; and, as I shall outline further below, what I mean by 'power' is not the same as brute force or repression. But it is to insist that power – and the complex negotiations and resistances of those subject to it – is a theme we must take into account when analysing religion, faith and belief.

Ecclesiastical history to lived religion

Historians have written about religion and belief for a very long time, most frequently because of their own religious beliefs. Christian writers of the early Church produced histories of their religion – Eusebius's *Ecclesiastical History* (*c.* AD 325) for example – as a way of bringing greater authority to their faith at a time when the Church was subject to pagan Rome and in competition with other, non-Christian belief systems. Conflict similarly impelled the creation of histories a thousand years later: after the Reformation, when Christianity found itself split into Protestant and Catholic, both sides used written histories as polemical weapons. Catholic writers emphasized the longevity and tradition of their Church, in contrast with the novelty of Protestantism. On the Protestant side, history was used both to rebut this accusation (by, for example, claiming roots in a variety of medieval heresies) and to represent the Catholic Church as historically repressive and corrupt (pointing to trials such as the one endured by Thomas Tailour).[4]

To some extent, this competition between Catholic and Protestant historiography has never gone away. It is usually conducted in far more polite terms than those used by sixteenth- and seventeenth-century polemicists, and the ways in which historians' own faith may spur onward or inflect their histories have become far more nuanced and complicated than simply deriding the other side. Nonetheless, the foundations of modern religious history were built upon Catholic and Protestant argument in the late nineteenth and early twentieth centuries, and elements of this dialectic have continued today.[5] Even at the beginning of the twenty-first century – a far more secular time, in the West, than the beginning of the last century – the majority of historians writing on religion are themselves religious. Is this a problem? Not necessarily. Every historian comes to every kind of topic with certain sets of assumptions, beliefs and predispositions. The good historian uses his or her historical investigation as an opportunity to examine and engage with his or her beliefs, whether religious or secular – not to abandon them but not to be ruled by them either. Also, historians who have religious faith may approach historical religion with both a greater wealth of background information (a knowledge of Scripture, an understanding of certain rituals) and a greater sensitivity toward religious conviction as a motivation in and of itself. As the medievalist John van Engen has put it, 'historians of religious culture must take "religious man" seriously, just as economic historians take "economic man", or political historians "political man", seriously'.[6] By this he means, I think, that we should not automatically read religious actions as signs of something else. For example, if a nobleman made a gift of land to the Church, we should not reduce his motives to simple political functionalism (giving land as a way of declaring status and gaining ecclesiastical support) but should understand religious conviction (aiding the Church because of faith in God and a desire for salvation) as a serious motive in itself.

So an atheist historian like myself needs to be wary of discounting what seems unfamiliar or alien, for example, responding positively to Thomas Tailour's disbelief in the soul, but ignoring the elements of his faith (his ideas on giving to the poor) that place him as a medieval Christian rather than a modern sceptic. It is true that some historians have tended to discount the reality of faith, always reading it as a sign of something else rather than dealing with it in its own terms. Historians writing in Communist East Germany during the 1950s and 1960s, for instance, somewhat dogmatically followed (or were forced to follow) the analysis of medieval faith put forward by Frederich Engels, who saw Christianity purely as the ideology of the dominant class, and hence all occasions of heresy as expressions of class struggle.[7] The language of faith was thus read as 'really' being about economics and politics. In its extreme form this interpretation is unsustainable. Empirical work on medieval heresy has shown that the people involved came from many different ranks of society, in a variety of socio-economic circumstances, and cannot be represented as cohering as a class. More importantly, to analyse heretical ideas solely as 'encodings' of class conflict necessarily edits out other features and elements, such as different ideas about gender roles in religion, or concepts of moral conduct. However, we should not charge off in the exactly opposite direction. It is possible to suggest that religious activities can have material elements to them. To return to the brief example above, a nobleman's gift of land to the Church was *simultaneously* a social, political, legal and spiritual event.[8] Favouring one factor, whether secular or spiritual, over another misunderstands the interwoven nature of medieval culture.

Thus historians who have faith need equally to be wary of assuming a personal or cultural connection to that which appears familiar, without questioning its nuances and historical context. For example, there might be a temptation to treat the vampiric elements as irrelevant narrative colour, and to interpret William of Newburgh's tale as essentially demonstrating the need for confession prior to death, since it is the lack of the last rites, William implies, that caused the man to come back from the dead. But this would, of course, ignore William's insistence on the frequency with which the dead were returning, and the fact that the story inescapably *is* about a vampire; there are other ways of illustrating the desirability of confession, so why choose this one? Or, alternatively, there may be a desire to argue that stories like William's – and indeed Tailour's – are entirely marginal and peripheral to 'real' Christianity. This approach would suggest that such traces should be, if not ignored, then at least kept decently separate from the more important accounts of orthodox piety, and given much less prominence than matters such as going to mass, hearing preaching and praying to saints. There is a valid element to this latter critique: stories about vampires are less frequent, by a factor of many thousands, than sources recounting such things as attendance at church, the audience for sermons, testamentary practice. We will indeed spend time on these less lurid topics. Nevertheless, I suggest, a history of belief and unbelief must engage with those elements of faith that are less easily explicable and fit less happily with the core tenets of Christianity, as well as the notional 'centre' of Christian religion. One reason for this is that what one finds at the margins may tell us more about the way in which the centre *assumed* its central position. Another is that the margins, by the nature of the kind of evidence they produced, may allow us better sight of some of the beliefs, attitudes and ideas of ordinary lay people than the more normative texts produced by the centre.

One way in which the history of religion has changed over the last century is from a focus upon ecclesiastical history to what has been called 'lived religion'. Put crudely, the change is from the history of bishops and popes and the governance of the Church, to the history of the laity and the everyday practice of faith. The contrast is not entirely fair – people still write ecclesiastical history today, and some nineteenth-century historians were interested in lay belief – but it has a broad validity. Two factors have driven this shift in studies of the medieval (and indeed early modern) periods: changes in twentieth-century religion and changes in twentieth-century historiography. The religious element concerns the Catholic Church, particularly in France. In the 1950s, there were worries that industrialization and modernity had led to the Church failing in its pastoral mission to the rural laity. To combat this, a form of 'religious sociology' was developed that investigated the laity's experience of religion. Somewhat shocked by the lack of doctrinal knowledge and practice that this uncovered, in the following decade the Second Vatican Council (1962–5) implemented various reforms within the entire Catholic Church, many of which aimed to engage the laity more centrally with their faith. These developments resonated with various Catholic historians who had become increasingly interested in recognizing the place of the laity within the historical Church. Writers such as Etienne Delaruelle and William Pantin had already started to examine the position of the medieval laity, though perhaps mainly as people who were acted upon by the ecclesiastical machinery rather than as historical agents in themselves. In the 1970s, inspired by the techniques and questions of the religious sociologist Gabriel Le Bras, historians such as Jean Delumeau placed the laity firmly at the centre of their analysis, and wrote of *la religion vécue* – 'lived' religion. A further wave of French historians, led by Jacques Le Goff and his student Jean-Claude Schmitt, criticized the model of religious faith adopted by Delaruelle and others as still being too 'top-down', and began to develop more dynamic models of how religion was 'lived' by, for example, examining the growth of mercantile culture in medieval towns and how this fed into religious activities.

Here we meet the second factor, the wider changes in twentieth-century historiography. In all areas of historical analysis, there has been a move away from the elite history of events (whether it is of kings, popes, governments or ideologues) to a broadened sense of inclusion: the history of the working class, the history of women, the poor, the racially-oppressed and the marginalized. In France, the move was led by the *Annales* group of historians, in England, by those connected with the Communist Party Historians' Group. The desire, in the words of Edward Thompson, was to 'rescue . . . from the enormous condescension of posterity' those ordinary, everyday people who had nonetheless played a role in historical change.[9] This shift was felt also within religious history: the desire to present the laity as having an active role within the production of religion, and for some historians, such as Le Goff and Schmitt, to suggest that the religion of the laity and the religion of the Church were not in fact the same. As the American historian Natalie Zemon Davis advised, historians should stop 'evaluating lay piety primarily in terms of its deviation from one historical norm or religious ideal'.[10] Instead, they should analyse the meanings and uses of religion for the laity. The historiographical fruits of this included a reinvigorated interest in 'folklore', a greater focus on heresy, deviance and the margins, and an increased sensitivity towards religious diversity – including, particularly in the 1980s and 1990s, an interest and sensitivity towards gender and how it may affect religious life and thought.[11]

There has, however, been a further counter-reaction to these developments, concerned particularly with the apparent emphasis upon a repressive medieval Church and the suggestion that there was a huge disjuncture between orthodox 'clerical' religion and lay 'folkloric' faith. The American academic Gary Macy has asked, 'was there a "*the* Church" in the Middle Ages?' and suggested that there was not: in all kinds of ways, the edifice of faith was more complicated and confused than institutionally monolithic. What popes, theologians, priests, bishops, mendicants, monks and nuns all thought, wrote, hoped and understood about the Christian faith was far from one unified voice. Take, for example, the doctrine of transubstantiation: the belief that during the mass, the bread and wine were, in some sense, changed into the body and blood of Christ. The key qualifier is 'in some sense'. How *exactly* this happened was debated throughout the Middle Ages. One can find an inquisitor, Nicolas Eymerich, prosecuting two theologians in late fourteenth-century Spain for their views on the matter. What they propounded, however, was approved as perfectly orthodox in other parts of Europe. Talking about 'the Church' in relation to either example is to simplify, and perhaps to oversimplify.[12]

This critique is important. It forms a useful corrective to an image of medieval Christianity forged in the Protestant polemic against Catholicism mentioned above. This sense of the medieval Church as a repressive institution, demanding (and achieving) absolute conformity, still has a tendency to lurk today, at least in popular representations of the period. However, the critique of '*the* Church' has arisen more pointedly in response to a different historiographical trend, one springing from the changes in European historical enquiry discussed above. After the initial shift towards 'lived religion', wider changes in history writing (led by the French *Annales* school, influenced by anthropology) emphasized a focus upon *mentalité*, the cultural ideas and thoughts and feelings of a period. Certain historians – pre-eminently Jean Delumeau, Le Goff and Schmitt, but also Roberto Rusconi, André Vauchez and others – have suggested that we should not think of the Middle Ages as having one 'culture' but two, and indeed two cultures frequently in conflict or at least in tension.[13] The division is usually presented as being between ecclesiastical culture and lay culture, with the latter (particularly for writers like Schmitt) understood to be a 'folkloric' culture, embodying long-sustained practices and ideas originally quite removed from Christianity.[14] In this kind of model, the question posed is 'how and by what means did the Church "acculturate" the laity?'; that is, how did it impose its ideas and beliefs upon them? Sometimes, moreover, the binary divide has been presented as the gap between 'high' culture (understood to include both the Church and the lay elite, such as the nobility) and 'low' culture. This sense of division is influenced by a Marxist legacy, and also by the work of the literary theorist Mikhail Bakhtin (1905–75). Here, for historians such as the Russian medievalist Aaron Gurevich, the question posed concerns the ways in which low culture challenges, or operates independently from, high culture.[15]

From another perspective, cultural division has been understood as a putative tension between 'literate' and 'oral' cultures, or, in a more complex fashion, between 'Latinate' and 'vernacular' cultures. Historians such as R. I. Moore and Brian Stock have argued that the *litterati* – the literate elite – saw themselves as a group, and saw themselves in opposition to the *illitterati*, the general mass of people.[16] Some explanation of these terms is necessary. Medieval culture assumed that literacy was the preserve of the clergy, and not the laity; and 'literacy' meant a knowledge of Latin, not of vernacular languages. To read and write in the vernacular did not count as 'literacy', in this sense. The Latin word *litteratus* was often a synonym for *clericus*, a cleric or clerk. Furthermore, *illitteratus* (illiterate) was often used interchangeably with terms such as *rusticus* (rustic/peasant), *idiota* (halfwit) or *simplex* (simple person). In the English vernacular, too, 'clergie' could indicate learning and literacy in Latin, and 'lewed' meant both a layperson and someone without Latin literacy. This medieval idea of 'literacy' had a particular cultural charge. To describe someone as *litteratus* meant not only that they could read and write Latin, but that they would possess cultural authority through the wisdom they had gained in their studies. A *litteratus* would be expected to have a knowledge of Scripture, of patristic writings and of some classical authors. He (for it would overwhelmingly be a 'he') would also tend to have certain assumptions about the *illitterati*, the vast majority of the laity: not simply that they lacked literacy, but that they lacked the wisdom and insight that literacy supplied.[17] Thus, some historians argue, there is an essential cultural divide between the *litterati* and the rest, a divide grounded in the assumptions about language, knowledge, wisdom and power the literate elite claimed for itself.

Ignoring for the moment the confusing overlaps and differences between these positions, what would a 'two-cultures' (or 'high/low' or 'literate/oral') model provide in relation to our previous examples? To return to Thomas Tailour's confession, we might see Tailour's thoughts about the soul, expressed through the vivid metaphor of extinguishing a candle, as rooted in a kind of domestic, experiential, vernacular theology. Indeed, other cases of heresy tried in England in this period also show people using this kind of domestic, everyday language to express and give shape to their (heterodox) beliefs.[18] Bishop Langton represents the other side of the equation: an ecclesiastical authority who, via penances and the threat of burning, imposes clerical belief upon lay unbelief. Tailour was made to read out loud his abjuration of heresy and to recite orthodox prayers daily as part of his penance. And while Bishop Langton's register is written primarily in Latin – the language of authority and learning – Tailour's confession, and those of others that Langton tried, were written into the record in the English vernacular. An emphasis, perhaps, of the authority of *litteratus* over *illitteratus*?

However, as we have seen, for some historians the idea that one can identify a homogeneous ecclesiastical hierarchy and call it 'the Church' is unsustainable. Historians have also rejected what they see as the simplification of the 'folkloric' or 'lay' or 'oral' side of the equation. Eamon Duffy, for example, argues that there was no real division between the religion of the masses, the religion of the secular elite and the religion of the clergy in pre-Reformation England.[19] Other historians have objected that the beliefs, languages, thoughts and *mentalités* of the laity are much more varied than one 'culture', and should certainly not be identified with the more marginal views of people like Tailour. Furthermore, they argue, to divide clerical from lay culture is to ignore the fact that the clergy all started life as lay people, that someone like a poor parish priest almost certainly had more culturally in common with his parishioners than with the papacy, and that even the more elite clergy, who wrote books and treatises, spent a lot of time in close contact with the laity, preaching to them, hearing their confessions, for instance.[20] There does not, therefore, have to be a sense of an 'imposition' of clerical culture over lay culture: rather, a variety of clerics and a variety of lay people interacted throughout the Middle Ages, and it was through this inter-action that new cultural ideas emerged. In this line of argument, we might point to the fact that in William of Newburgh's tale there is no clear division between a 'lay' set of beliefs and a 'clerical' culture. William, the unnamed cleric and the lay townspeople would *all* appear to share a belief in vampires. They share a sense that a 'bad' death – one where business is left unfinished – is likely to lead to trouble. Perhaps the clerics and the laity bring slightly different under-standings of death and community to the event, but one could certainly claim that these interact. Finally, most critics of two-cultures models share either sus-picion or rejection of the theme of power in relation to medieval religion. Thomas Tentler, for example, commenting on a French collection of essays that drew upon two-cultures models, suggests that the desire to 'reduce' the interac-tions of religious institutions and cultures in the Middle Ages 'to a power strug-gle between hegemonic clergy and subject laity is to oversimplify'.[21] For Tentler, and others, the plurality of lay and clerical culture is more important, and the fact that some clerics were engaged in pastoral care – rather than, say, cultural domination – must be kept firmly in sight. Thus, in this view, what is important about Bishop Langton's treatment of Thomas Tailour is that he did *not* have him burnt: he wanted to save his soul more than he wanted to repress him.

The critique of the two-cultures model, and the questioning of 'the Church', raise important points. Most usefully, they provide a vital call for nuance in historians' analyses of religion and culture, and remind us how conceptions of the medieval Church, rooted in the religious conflicts of the Reformation, can still lurk within our contemporary senses of the past. However, the critiques them-selves present their own dangers. They have been partly informed by a traditional Anglo-American suspicion of French historiographical abstraction and 'theory'.[22] A problem here is that histories that eschew any kind of structural analysis of the past can end up presenting no more than a pedantic insistence on endless specificity: Thomas Tailour can tell us about nothing more than Thomas Tailour, William of Newburgh's tale tells us only about that particular time and place, and so forth. This, for me, is insufficient. More importantly, some critiques have misrepresented the nuances already present in the two-cultures analyses. Le Goff, Vauchez, Schmitt, Gurevich and others have all noted elements of interaction and diversity, among other things: to present the two-cultures model as utterly rigid is to misread it.[23]

We should also note that there were attempts to *assert* the unity and coherence of 'the Church' in the medieval period, often in an explicit attempt to limit diversity. For example, Hugh of Amiens, bishop of Rouen between 1130 and 1164, reported that heretics in his period challenged orthodox authority, saying 'You who propose to follow the "Church of God", tell us what it is, where it is, and why it is.' In response, Hugh and other twelfth-century churchmen set out to do just that.[24] The most important medieval ecclesiastical council, the Fourth Lateran of 1215, began its commandments with a lengthy and detailed definition of what it meant to be an orthodox Christian, and emphasized that there was but one unified Church, before turning to condemn contemporary heresies. Much effort, in dioceses across Europe, was put into implementing Lateran IV's vision in subsequent centuries. It may have been more a rhetorical 'the Church' than a concrete one, but through the development of preaching, confession, the parochial system, and so on, one might argue that ecclesiastics attempted to make it so.[25] Similarly, one can find a multiplicity of medieval writers drawing profound distinctions between their literate selves and the ordinary masses. They may themselves have overestimated the divide – and as a literate elite they represented but a fragment of all the clergy – but to ignore their sense of division would be to miss an important factor in medieval culture. Certainly these things were complicated, nuanced, multiform, and not reducible to monolithic, all-powerful or all-subjected cultures. But to correct a crypto-Reformation view of the medieval Church as all-powerful does not necessarily mean that we have to leap to the opposite conclusion.[26] The two-cultures model can certainly be applied too crudely, but the sense of cultural conflict or division has remained a useful concept for various medievalists.

And it is a concept that informs this book, not through an insistence upon rigid divisions between groups or cultures, but in a sense that examining cultural tensions is informative and important. For this reason, in the following chapters I do talk about 'the laity' and 'the Church', by the latter meaning principally both the higher clergy, theologians and popes who, by and large, set ecclesiastical policy, and the concatenation of administrative and liturgical mechanisms that organized Christianity across Europe. Neither term should be taken as a monolith, but they remain helpful generalizations. One's attitude and position partly come down to how the tools of analysis are conceived. Thomas Tentler, in the short passage quoted above, mentions critically the concept of 'hegemony'. His sense of the term is to mean something akin to 'absolute domination'. This we can clearly reject: the Church was not absolutely dominant.

However, there have been more subtle senses of hegemony developed within sociocultural theory, and indeed more subtle senses of power. The Italian theorist Antonio Gramsci conceived hegemony to indicate the means by which political elites managed to persuade the ordinary masses to accept their ideology, and he emphasized in particular the way in which elites might persuade ordinary people to embrace power and control *willingly*. Various later writers, developing this idea, have suggested that one could consider hegemony as a form of control that does not involve absolute dominance or brainwashing, but a more subtle manipulation of language and cultural norms to limit the domain of what is possible or conceivable at a certain moment in time.[27] Nor need such manipulation be a conscious plan on the part of those elites; it can simply be that the way in which they inevitably shape the concept of the world around them has powerful effects elsewhere. Most powerful are those cultural ideas that present a particular vision of society as either natural or God-given – which, in the Middle Ages, would include, for example, the very strong sense of society being divided into different social orders arrayed hierarchically.[28]

And what of power? What Tentler and others object to, quite rightly, is a sense of ecclesiastical authorities possessing some means of overwhelming *force*. This was not so; famously, the pope commanded no armies – or not directly, at any rate. Measures against heresy such as inquisition depended very much for their success upon the secular support they did or did not receive in particular localities. Priests did not command thugs who forced their parishioners to attend mass or recite prayers. However, as other theorists have suggested, 'force' is not the same as 'power'. Indeed, the presence of force – someone physically coercing another – could be seen as marking the point at which power has broken down. At its broadest, 'power' is what makes the world into its accepted (hierarchical, unequal) shape. In this sense, Michel Foucault, the French historian and philosopher, suggests that one should not think of power simply as something repressive or prohibiting. Instead, he argues, power can be thought of as something that, in order to get people to go along with it, also induces pleasures, needs, desires. Moreover, he argues, power should be imagined not as a straight line, one thing pushing at another, but as a field of relationships: a web of interactions and tensions that *pull* as much as push us into particular social, cultural and political hierarchies, and which is in flux rather than remaining static.[29]

I have become very abstract for a moment, so let us return once again to our opening examples to see what we can make of this. In Thomas Tailour's case, an obvious sense of power would be the repressive one: Tailour is being coerced into giving up his individual beliefs and accepting an alternative set of orthodox ones, under threat of violence. However, we also have an example here of how the use of force can indicate the failure of power. Imagine that Tailour were to remain stubborn, refuse to abjure, and thus get burnt to death. The bishop certainly has the power – the 'resources' we might say – to do this; but we already knew that the bishop was in a more powerful position than Tailour. Would not Tailour's stubbornness indicate how the bishop's power had *failed*? The bishop wants conformity, not death; to be driven to execute Tailour – to use force – would signal the defeat of the bishop's power over the other man's beliefs. The ability of the bishop to threaten Tailour is important; but much more subtle, and I would suggest effective, is the way in which Tailour's crime is managed. Through carrying out his penance – walking through those public areas, carrying the faggots, declaring his sin – Tailour would act as a more effective tool of power. His public penance tells the community about the boundaries of transgression, about the bishop's ability to punish – and, yes, to threaten death – but also about the Church's ability to forgive and to receive sinners back into the community. That, from a certain perspective, the bishop acts kindly or mercifully does not mean that he and Tailour are not in a power relationship, nor that acts of kindness (or, more properly, acts of spiritual care) cannot also be exercises of power. This is what a more sophisticated sense of 'hegemony' implies: when someone like Tailour dissents, his transgression can be redirected back into an underlying story of religious control and conformity. One might see similar mechanisms at work in William's tale. While the story tells of two laymen dealing effectively with a problem that is apparently defeating the clergy, the way in which the tale is framed – the need for confession and absolution before death – ensures that the story supports the underlying authority of the Church. One might say that the specific battle (how to deal with troublesome vampires) is relinquished, but the war (how to persuade the laity that they must turn to the clergy to manage death) continues. And most importantly, the field of discussion is arranged into a particular and persuasive shape, conjoining images of death, sexual sin and disease. The 'power' of William's story does not involve force: it is the subtle shaping of attitudes and mindset through the reiteration of such tales.

Let us turn, then, to some further conceptual tools. Although springing from different origins, the general trends in both European and Anglo-American historiography had an interest in the materialist analyses presented by Marxism, but also, by the 1970s, in the work of anthropologists. The role of the latter has probably had its greatest effect in the field of religious history, and it is worth reflecting briefly on its influence.

Anthropology, religion and history

The 'religious sociology' pioneered by Gabriel Le Bras in the first half of the twentieth century brought to bear upon the world of faith tools such as statistical quantification and serial analysis, and these methods have been used and adapted by historians. For example, historians have used statistics to examine the phenomenon of sainthood in the later Middle Ages, and also patterns of testamentary giving.[30] In contrast, the influence of anthropology has been more qualitative than quantitative, providing tools for the interpretation of religious beliefs and practices through 'reading' religion as a cultural phenomenon.

Probably the greatest debt that history owes to sociology and anthropology is the basic insight that religion is something that one *can* analyse, rather than simply describe. The pioneering work of Max Weber and Emile Durkheim has a huge importance here. The insistence by these writers on the centrality of shared cultural ideas (symbols, myths, moral codes) in not only affecting but maintaining social relations has been very influential.[31] Probably the most profound anthropological influence upon the history of religion came, however, in the 1960s and 1970s, from what was called 'structural-functionalism', and particularly, for medievalists, from the writer Victor Turner.

'Structural-functionalist' is an ungainly label, but not difficult to decipher. Let us take it in two parts. 'Structure' first: for Turner and others, religion (among other things) could be understood to have no *innate* meaning, but to produce meaning through its structural arrangement. Thus, for example, there was nothing innate about the idea of poverty being praiseworthy, but within a Christian milieu the structural pairing within the figure of Christ of poverty with kingship (Christ as poor, Christ as King) linked together low and high social concepts in a binary pattern. Therefore, poverty itself was not praiseworthy – but poverty arranged or represented within a particular cultural structure took on the aura of praiseworthiness (or, more accurately, became a resonant and useful symbol). This kind of analysis is a powerful tool: it gave Turner a way, for example, of examining something as apparently ethereal as holiness. By looking at the *structure* of symbolism and the ways in which it is deployed, Turner suggested that one could see someone such as St Francis of Assisi gaining holiness through undergoing a journey through structural patterns: starting out 'high' (Francis was born to a wealthy merchant family), becoming 'low' and entering what Turner called a 'liminal' period (Francis gave away his wealth, adopted the dress of a beggar), and then being reincorporated back into the community with a heightened charge of holiness and hence authority (Francis founded an order of preachers, and was canonized soon after his death). Thus the vast majority of poor people were not seen as holy, but only someone like Francis who had passed through this structural pattern. For Turner, these kinds of structures – particularly the passage through a 'liminal' phase (*limen* meaning 'threshold', and hence 'liminal' indicating the transitional quality Turner wanted to identify) – could be found in a number of different cultures, not simply medieval Christianity.[32]

Second, these structural patterns and movements had a function (the second half of the label): in essence, the production of community. Turner saw the movement of certain people through ritual structures as an essential part of community building; they provided a way of easing social tensions, and allowed people to fit their ideas and experiences of the world (involving all the things that were good or 'high' like wealth, power, and all the things that were bad or 'low' such as poverty, hunger, powerlessness) into a meaningful pattern. Thus rather than the gap between rich and poor leading to social conflict, the meanings invested in those qualities were made part of a larger structure by pairing them together, and linking them to other dyads: good/evil, black/white, high/low, male/female, and so forth. By 'linked' I do not mean that these pairs were all synonymous; clearly, they were not. Rather, I mean that the *pattern* of thought, the ways of thinking and feeling and acting within this kind of shape, resonated between the different pairings. Most importantly, it made (and perhaps continues to make) these kinds of value-laden pairings appear 'natural'. Thus, for Turner and others, they *functioned*, in that social groupings were able to operate more or less happily with their social divisions and tensions were deferred or transposed into this symbolic realm. To give a medieval example, the central rite of the mass – the production of Christ's body in the Eucharist (the bread and the wine) – can be read as a ritual that simultaneously re-enacts the 'social drama' of Christ's Passion, and involves the congregation in a set of liminal images: God is made into man and killed; believers eat God and are given eternal life. In this collective sacrifice and movement through 'high' and 'low' experience, the tensions and hierarchies of the social body are washed away, and all become part of one group. Thus, the mass, through the structuring of its symbolism, produces a feeling of community, and allows community to function.[33]

Another influential anthropologist is Clifford Geertz. In an essay first published in 1966, Geertz set out to describe 'Religion as a Cultural System' – all religion, whether that of western Christians, of the Azande tribe, or of the Javanese. Several of his points coincide with Turner's: most particularly that religions are there both to explain the hard bits of the world to us ('why has that building just fallen down on top of my mother?') but also to provide us with models for action ('how should I set about being a good person?'). More broadly, religion not only provides sets of symbols *of* the world (reflects to people how the world is) but also symbols *for* the world (how the world should continue to be; not, one should note, as a utopia but a model for how the continuing imbalances and inequalities of a world should continue to be borne). It does this through particularly charged ritual occasions such as (for Christians) the mass, baptism, burial and other such rituals, and also through the patterns that these moments set out for the more mundane passage of one's life. Thus religion both reflects the world – its chance elements, its passage and its social order – and also contributes to its *production and reproduction*. As Geertz puts it, 'Religion is sociologically interesting not because, as vulgar positivism would have it, it describes the social order . . . but because, like environment, political power, wealth, jural obligation, personal affection, and a sense of beauty, it shapes it.'[34] In this formulation Geertz gives us, therefore, another way of thinking about how religion is intimately connected with such things as social and economic organization, political hierarchies, and gender identities. Moreover, unlike Turner's functionalist model, which tends to presuppose a static and stable system, Geertz's analysis incorporates a sense of the tensions in the social fabric, the possibility of variation and dissent, and thus how society and culture may change over time.

Like Turner, Geertz sees religion as a system or arrangement of symbols. It is in thinking about symbols, however, that his influence has been most widely felt.[35] For Geertz, symbols can be thought to include not only those things that announce themselves as symbols (organized rituals like the mass, flags proclaiming this or that allegiance, images such as the Crucifixion) but also much less obvious and more mundane things, such as clothing and momentary gestures.

Indeed, he suggests, almost all human behaviour can be seen as symbolic action; it is symbolic because it carries with it meaning, in the sense that it allows non-verbal human communication and interaction. Think of those wise men in William of Newburgh's tale, feasting off-stage as it were, while the young men got on with their bloody retribution. Think of all the myriad movements, gestures, interactions involved when a group of people eat together. In a more directly religious setting, consider all the human activities *outside* the context of scripted rituals like the mass that nonetheless carry meaning: the respectful bow before a religious man, the glance turned to a shrine in passing, the simple act of walking through a graveyard while recalling that the land is sacred and not like other ground. Geertz's concept of symbols suggests that all of these activities (when they are visible to us as historians) are also capable of analysis.

What is most important to Geertz about the nature of symbols is their public, *lived* nature: that the symbolic meanings do not happen 'elsewhere' (whether in the subconscious or as part of some larger cultural structure, such as that imagined by Victor Turner) but occur within the warp and the weft of human interaction. An implication of this emphasis on the lived, transient, interactive quality of symbols is noted by Geertz, but is perhaps made more explicit by other commentators: that the meanings they carry or produce or communicate are unstable.[36] There is the possibility of misrecognition as well as recognition: the chance (to return to our feasting wise men) that a shrug of the shoulders and flex of the eyebrows intended to indicate 'this is a wonderful meal' is understood by another person to indicate 'is this meat safe to eat?' More importantly, when dealing with larger sets of symbols, such as those involved in the story of Christ's life, there is the chance that people will interpret them in different ways. For example, for one person the sense of Christ as an infant may suggest an attitude of preciousness and parental protectiveness towards him. For another, Christ as male child may indicate the idea of familial continuity. A third may see the element of divinity eclipsing all else in Christ, and thus (mis)understand the Passion narrative as a kind of trick or metaphor.[37] As we shall see in various chapters in this book, how people interpreted different aspects of religion could vary quite widely.

What should we take away from this brief excursus into elements of anthropological theory? Four things, I would suggest. First, that in trying to understand belief, we are trying to understand something that has an intrinsic relationship with social, economic, and political structures. We may not share Victor Turner's view of functionalism – we may not feel, for example, that 'community' is as seamlessly produced and sustained through ritual as he would suggest – but we can see that religious patterns of meaning have a close relationship to social patterns of meaning. Second, that in trying to decode or read the symbols through which religion is communicated we might think of 'symbols' as including all kinds of actions, interactions and so forth, not simply (although they are obviously important) the big, obvious ones like crucifixes or cathedrals. If we are interested in the laity, therefore, we can try to think not only about the kinds of symbols produced or performed by popes and bishops, but the small and passing symbolic actions undertaken by ordinary people as well. All of these will be part of religion, and implicated in belief. Third, in thinking about symbols, we also need to think about reception and interpretation. If we want to analyse what a symbol means, we need to analyse what it means *to* people in particular situations, rather than seeing it as completely abstract. Thus, at the most practical level, if someone preaches to a crowd, we must find ways of analysing not only what the sermon was intended to communicate but all the ways in which it could actually have been understood and received by the audience. As Natalie Zemon Davis has put it, we should not think of the laity as 'passive receptacles' being filled up by the message set out by the clergy.[38] The laity's experience of religion is more active and productive than that; and our job as historians is not to measure how well the clergy propounded their message, but to understand what different people made of it.

Fourth, we need to think about the *practice* of religion and belief, rather than automatically projecting it into a psychological or mystical or essentially 'other' plane. As noted above, historians from around the middle of the twentieth century began to focus upon 'lived religion'. However, as various critics have noted, for those earlier pioneers like Jean Delumeau, 'lived religion' was largely to be analysed in terms of its conformity or deviation from the clerical norm: whether or not the laity were doing what they were supposed to be doing. This is to imagine religion as a stable entity located in some 'other' place, and then to measure specific reality against this notional abstract – a point of view criticized by Geertz, Davis and others from a variety of perspectives. A key point here is how practice (formal or informal ritual, physical interaction, communal activity) is understood: not as something lower or subservient to interior, reflective piety; nor simply as an external sign that points to inner belief; nor as something necessarily static, automatic and lacking in motive force. To see practice (as a key element to lived religion) in these negative terms is precisely to fall prey to evaluating belief from a particular viewpoint: one that is clerical, elite, and arguably informed by post-Reformation spirituality. In contrast, Rodney Needham (whose work in this area provided the epigram to this chapter) has argued that there is no real difference – or at least, none that we can get at analytically – between belief, its expression in language, and its experience in lived reality. They are, to his mind, all the same thing, going on together, tumbling over one another, from moment to moment. Jean-Claude Schmitt has similarly suggested that:

> We must be careful not to reify belief, to turn it into something established once and for all, something that individuals and societies need only express and pass on to each other. It is appropriate to substitute a more active notion for the term 'belief': the verb 'to believe'. In this way belief is a never-completed activity, one that is precarious, always questioned, and inseparable from recurrences of doubt.[39]

We must, therefore, think about practice: either, at the very least, in the sense that, like Delumeau, we want to know if people did (and felt and thought and believed) what they were 'supposed' to do; or, if we follow Needham and Schmitt, in the sense that the thing we are interested in – belief – is actually *constituted* by practice, and hence is being performed and re-performed over and over again. In the former case, we might look to Thomas Tailour's trial for heresy as an indication that someone, at least, was not thinking what he was supposed to about the nature of the soul. (We would presumably then want to ask how many other people there were like Tailour, and probably answer 'not that many' – although, as we shall later see, he was not the only one.) In the latter case, we might ask instead *how* it is that other people did believe in the soul; what was it that led or prompted the sustenance of that belief, and how was it that Tailour thought differently. The former assumes that a set of religious ideas (the eternal nature of the soul) was stable and automatically available; the latter asks how this particular set of ideas was sustained. Both, however, point us to practice as an important area of consideration.

I have been dealing with rather a lot of abstract ideas in this section. If there is anything to the last point – the focus on actual practice – it suggests that, in exploring these ideas and tools further, we will be better served by dealing with specific examples in specific situations. Therefore, enough of anthropological theory for the moment: we shall meet it, explicitly and implicitly, in later chapters. Let us turn finally to a different matter, one always of concern to the historian: the nature of the surviving evidence.

The traces: historical evidence

Rodney Needham's book on belief was inspired, he tells us, while sleeping: he dreamt that he was speaking to one of the Penan people of Borneo, with whom he had lived and studied. He was trying to work out how to say that they 'believed' in a certain deity figure from their culture, and found, even upon waking, that he could not: the Penan language simply did not contain that kind of word. Nor, indeed, do the languages of various other non-European peoples; their relationship to their divine entities is expressed differently. For example, the Nuer people might say *kwoth a thin*, 'God is present' – that is, God is involved, implicated, a party to whatever is being done or discussed at that particular moment. For the Nuer there would be no way to say 'I *believe* in God'. It would be a pointless and senseless remark.[40]

What Needham noted, as an anthropologist, is that grappling with 'belief' is complicated by the act of translation from one culture to another. To understand truly what is meant by a particular expression – all its implications, nuances and resonances – involves a strong degree of immersion in that culture. The need for immersion is true also for the medieval historian. The cultural differences may not be as broad as between a European ethnographer and a Bornean tribesman, but there is a gap to be bridged nonetheless. However, as historians, we have a further complication: Needham could at least try to talk with his Penanese friend. The historian must deal with the surviving evidence – the traces, as I described them at the beginning of this chapter – and one cannot talk with evidence, or, at least, not in the same way that one can talk with a human being. We need, therefore, some tools and strategies for reading the surviving evidence, to get the most out of it that we can.

There is no overall lack of sources for the high and later Middle Ages. The archival holdings spread across Europe far outstretch the ability of any one scholar to assimilate them. In the field of religion, particularly from the thirteenth century onwards, the surviving evidence is vast, not simply because of an increased rate of survival, but because more written documents were being produced. In the wake of the Fourth Lateran Council of 1215 and the reforms that it set in motion, medieval ecclesiastics produced texts as never before: practical manuals on how to assign penance, theological manuals on sin and confession, commentaries on canon law, truly vast amounts of preaching material. From the late thirteenth century onwards, we see increasing numbers of works on spirituality and mysticism, devotional treatises, and other writings designed for reflection.[41]

However, there are some areas where evidence is much more sparse. Almost no medieval play survives in more than one copy, and given that we know from other sources – civic records and the like – that dramatic productions played a role in rehearsing religious stories before ordinary people, this is a frustrating loss.[42] The survival of material culture is also much more patchy; although a lot of architecture remains (churches, chantries, cathedrals and other such buildings), most of it is greatly changed from its medieval appearance. In particular, the smooth, white stone we tend to associate with gothic architecture would, in its own period, have been brightly adorned with wall paintings of saints and the like. Some of these paintings survive, but not many. Thus, our sense of another prime area of exposure to religious imagery has to work from highly fragmentary remains.

Most importantly, of the written evidence that does survive, almost none of it was created by lay people themselves. This is partly to do with literacy, which, of the kind necessary for the creation of religious texts, was very largely the preserve of the Church. Ordinary lay people also tended to lack the means to archive material. Written evidence survives for us today because someone in the past decided to store it and care for it. Cities kept archives about their civic business, for example, because their records could aid them in future legal disputes. Rulers stored records about government for much the same reason. In the area of religion, the Church (mainly in the guise of monasteries, universities, bishoprics and, of course, the papacy) preserved records for consultation and their own legal purposes. It is not simply the case that history is written by the victors: by and large, the *means* of history – the traces of the past – survive because of the archival mechanisms developed by dominant powers.

What does this mean with regard to our evidence? First, that the sources focused on belief are almost exclusively created by clerics dealing with lay people, rather than by lay people themselves. Both of our opening stories purport to tell us something about laymen (the vampire-killing brothers, the doubtful Thomas) but both were recorded by clerics. Second, with regard to the great outpouring of religious sources from the thirteenth century onwards, they are almost exclusively concerned with how the laity *ought* to be, rather than how they were. For example, as we shall see in Chapter 5, in the thirteenth century the Church produced a lot of material – statutes, manuals, treatises – related to the requirement that every Christian should confess to a priest at least once a year. We know a lot about what was supposed to happen. We know much less about what people actually did when they went to confession (as it was not supposed to be written down), less still about how often they actually went, and almost nothing about what they felt about confession. There is a kind of layperson-shaped hole in the middle of the evidence: we can feel our way all around the edges, and see where they were supposed to fit in, but for the most part we can not actually see *them*.

Thus a manual written for a parish priest, instructing him how to conduct confession, will say various things about lay people and belief; but these things will be normative – setting up expectations about what should happen – and to some extent idealized. Such a source is part of a process of shaping the laity, conducting the religious imperative of the 'care of souls' (*cura animarum*) in order that the layperson should be freed from sin and ultimately saved. And in the Middle Ages, salvation implied sameness: obeying the rules, conforming in behaviour, fitting into place. As noted above, the Church was not in fact homogeneous, and hence in reality modes of piety varied from place to place. But in conception, clerics emphasized conformity. A confession manual will therefore show us how the laity ought to behave, believe and confess. It may also provide evidence in the opposite direction: on the laity *not* believing or behaving correctly. For example, it may mention, when talking about the sin of sloth, that some lay people do not come as frequently to confession (once a year) as they ought. We might decide that this provides us with a more substantive, and less normative, insight into what the laity actually did. But one must still be wary. Our picture of some lay people not attending confession is given from a clerical viewpoint, and so the reason for non-attendance (the sin of sloth) is not necessarily the reason that the lay people themselves would have given. Furthermore, lots of confession manuals mention that lay people do not come sufficiently often to confession. Does this multiplicity of supporting evidence suggest that it reflects reality? Or does the repetition indicate that bewailing lay failure to make confession was something of a stereotype?

There are some sources that make more of a claim to represent what the laity – and sometimes individual lay people – actually did and believed. We might think of William of Newburgh's tale in this way. Although it is part of a chronicle account, the story of the Annan vampire looks quite a lot like another very common source: preaching *exempla*. These were short tales, purporting to be true, that would provide an 'example' to illustrate a particular moral point. Used to enliven and explicate sermons, collections of *exempla* were very common from the thirteenth century onwards. They frequently depict the activities of individual lay people, and thus have been used as a source of information about lay piety. Again, however, one must be wary. The whole purpose of an *exemplum* was to supply a didactic point, to show the audience a right and a wrong way of behaving. If one thinks of William's tale as an *exemplum*, an overall didactic point would be 'make sure you confess your sins before death' (as otherwise, like the vampire, you may not rest in peace). The 'reality' behind the story might, therefore, be squeezed into a more moral shape. We cannot tell what really happened in Annan – an outbreak of plague perhaps? – but we know that it was interpreted, at least in part, as a supernaturally-influenced event by the people of the town. Ascribing the cause of this evil to the lack of a death bed confession may have been how the priest and the laity thought about it at the time – or it may have been a pattern imposed, in order to give the story a moral, after the fact. The paths traced by *exempla*, and indeed by many other kinds of narrative source, frequently also involve more implicit cultural patterns or assumptions. For example, the fact that the Annan story begins with the adultery of a wife (who then disappears from the narrative) plays upon a deep-seated misogyny in medieval culture, which equated women with lust and a weakness for sin, and blamed women for men's spiritual downfall (literally, in this case). *Exempla* are therefore useful, as they at least claim to represent individual lay interaction with religion; but they still perform a kind of cultural work connected to the more didactic sources like confessors' manuals.

Other sources perhaps allow us closer access to real lay people. Take, for example, the confession of Thomas Tailour. Here we have a record that, although written down by a cleric, tells us what a layman said and thought. The gap between layperson and text is definitely smaller; instead of relying on what a priest told a monk about some lay people, as in William's chronicle, we have a layperson talking directly to a scribe. This kind of source, the record of an inquisition, is again something produced from the thirteenth century onwards. Inquisitions into heresy provide us with the interrogations of literally thousands of lay people from the thirteenth century, particularly from southern France. Records also survive for Italy and Germany, among other places; and in the late fifteenth century, the separate Spanish Inquisition began its work. In England, this kind of inquisitorial material was only produced after 1400, and the surviving records deal with smaller numbers of people, in the hundreds rather than the thousands. Aside from inquisition into heresy, there are other, less fraught, sources of this kind, for example, canonization proceedings, where inquisitors asked witnesses about miracles performed by putative saints. These are all valuable sources, but have their own patterns and pitfalls for the historian. They do not give us direct, unmediated access to the lay witnesses. Inquisitors had formulaic lists of questions that would shape their interrogation of suspects. Thus certain matters were asked about, and on others there is silence. In contrast to Thomas Tailour's confession, records of inquisitions in thirteenth-century France tend to say very little about what witnesses believed, and focus much more on whether or not they had met people named as heretics. Torture was a threat and all the words spoken were coerced to some degree. Deeper patterns of power mould the evidence, highlighting matters that fitted into the inquisitorial way of viewing religion and submerging other ways of viewing lay belief.

Nevertheless, this kind of record remains multi-vocal, permitting the historian to trace the shape of viewpoints other than those of the inquisitor.[43]

Tailour's record provides detail on his beliefs, but even here there are further ways in which the evidence has been shaped by the assumptions and culture of the bishop who interrogated him. The introductory gloss to his confession mentions, among other things, that he was in possession of a 'Lollard book', the one in which he had read that one should not worship saints. Lollardy was the name given to a heretical sect that the Church believed had sprung from the theological speculations of the Oxford don John Wyclif in the late fourteenth century. (A more detailed discussion of this and other heresies is found in Chapter 6.) It was the perceived threat of this heresy that led English bishops to keep an eye out for people such as Tailour expressing unorthodox beliefs. Thus Bishop Langton would have had certain expectations about him: that he would reject the power of priests (as he did), decry pilgrimage and worship of saints (as he did), and that his beliefs in these areas would have arisen through exposure to an underground network of Lollardy – as, perhaps, his ownership of this 'Lollard book' indicated. However, as some historians have noted, Lollardy could be in the eye of the beholder. Certain books that were theologically perfectly orthodox were, when found in possession of lay folk, described as Lollard or heretical.[44] And interestingly, Tailour's belief that the soul ended upon the death of the body does not fit with the beliefs admitted by other Lollards of the fifteenth century, and most certainly not with Wyclif's theology. How he came to this belief, and whether or not it made him a Lollard, are complex questions. The surviving source is sufficiently nuanced to give us a glimpse of this complexity but, because of the nature of its framing assumptions, it cannot solve it for us. Langton and his scribes shared certain assumptions about the way in which a lay person like Tailour came to unbelief: that heresy was a kind of poisonous infection, which could be spread through writing and preaching, rather than an innate doubt that could be arrived at from one's own questions – and these assumptions shape the surviving evidence.

Finally, there are a few kinds of sources which lay people had a stronger hand in creating. The most common of these are wills. For earlier periods few have survived, but there are many extant from the later Middle Ages. A will was dictated to a notary and clearly reflected the wishes of the testator. However, what one can and cannot glean from wills is complicated. They tell us something about the wishes of a person at a specific point in their life: its end. Unsurprisingly, therefore, wills frequently contain chantry bequests, asking that masses be said for their (soon-to-be-departed) soul. Specific bequests to particular religious foundations, such as a local monastery, might indicate a lifelong fondness for that particular site and mode of piety, but equally might show who the testator currently thought was the best bet at prayers for his or her salvation. Moreover, in various places there were specific requirements to leave a set amount or proportion of one's estate to particular religious orders, ecclesiastical buildings or other funds. These could be written in even if the testator had no particular wish to leave money in this way. Even the language of wills can be problematic. The will of one Petronilla Boys of Lownde, in Norfolk, made in 1460, specifies that 'firstly, I leave my soul to God omnipotent, to the Blessed Mary, and to all the saints'. Does this indicate something about the depth and direction of Petronilla's piety? It may well do so. But if (as is the case) almost every single will made in Norfolk around that time contains the same preamble, in exactly the same words, one suspects that it shows us more about the formulaic nature of scribal composition than anything personal. Later on in the will, Petronilla makes some specific religious bequests: two bushels of malt to the Guild of St John of Lownde, eight pence to the fabric of the church, a measure of malt to the church of St Michael at Yarmouth, money for a candle to be lit before the crucifix there and for a new handle for the movable cross that would be used in processions. These perhaps show us more of Petronilla's particular pious interests. There are other bequests of course, to family, friends and neighbours; wills are not only about piety, but also community, status and memory.[45]

Even when we have more personal and individualized sources, problems remain. The fact is that historical sources are not windows that open directly into the minds, hearts or souls of long-dead people. They are, rather, texts: traces of their passage through the world, inflected with all kinds of complicated cultural conformities. Take, for example, a tiny moment recorded in a southern French inquisitorial register. The witness, who had gone to visit a dying man who was receiving their version of the last rites from some heretics, recalled the sister of the recipient 'hitting her cheeks with her palms, not daring to cry out in grief until the heretics had got a long way away'. This might strike us as an unusually vivid moment of emotion, a piece of human reality that speaks directly to us over a gap of more than 700 years. However, from other evidence – images of mourners depicted on coffins – we know that hitting one's cheeks was a stylized motif that indicated grief.[46] The witness may, therefore, have been talking metaphorically (as we might say, 'he cried his eyes out'), or may have remembered strong grief by drawing on this particular cultural trope. The woman herself may well have actually hit her cheeks with her palms, but have done so because this was the culturally accepted way of expressing grief. There is no secure way of bridging these cultural gaps; we can only be aware of them and thus proceed with caution.

From fifteenth-century England, again from Norfolk, we have an autobiography of an elite townswoman called Margery Kempe who, in middle age, set out to become holy by leaving her husband, dressing in white, going on pilgrimage and spreading the word. Margery dictated her text, describing her life, her travels and her mystical experiences, to a scribe. It is a very personal piece of writing. Margery describes, for example, how she would weep and cry out uncontrollably in church. She disputed with church officials, and was accused of heresy. And she had visions of Christ, in one of which she imagines bedding down with him, and Christ telling her that they would sleep 'as man and wife'. This seems extremely, shockingly personal. But in fact, as ever, there are patterns here. The weeping and wailing can be found in accounts of the lives of other holy women. Disputing religion with men was something central to the life of the early Christian martyr St Katherine, someone to whom Margery had a particular devotion. And marital relations with Christ? Nuns today understand themselves to be 'brides of Christ', and Margery was not the only woman to imagine an intensely physical relationship with the Son of God. So once again, what a text like the *Book of Margery Kempe* gives us access to is primarily the cultural ideas, language and images of an age – not, necessarily, the individual (if, by that, we are imagining some unique and discrete entity).[47]

Are we therefore always trapped, as historians, into seeing nothing more than cultural patterns and norms? Can the traces left by the past – including others I have not yet mentioned such as bishops' registers, saints' lives, guild records, personal letters, family chronicles, conciliar statutes, papal decrees, books of hours – tell us only things about language and representation? No. The 'howevers' I have emphasized above do not have to be our end point. They are extremely important caveats, reminding us that any analysis we make on the basis of the traces must be cautious and provisional, and always involves an act of interpretation. The caveats should be carried forward throughout the book, though I will not labour the point in each chapter. But it should not prevent us from making the attempt to access lay belief and unbelief: to do so would be to give up the possibility of history. It should, however, encourage us to be smart in our analyses, and look for subtle tools to employ in our examination of past texts. Although, as we have seen, every kind of source tends to be shaped by cultural assumptions and languages, these are not absolute or so over-determining that no variation or nuance survives. In fact, very often there are tensions within and between the texts – particularly if they are the kind of text that co-opts the 'voice' of the laity for its own purposes. Think again about William of Newburgh's tale. In general outline, as I have noted, it affirms the importance of deathbed confession and absolution, and hence the importance of the ministrations of the clergy to the laity. The whole tale is recounted by the local clergyman, a man of 'honour and authority' as William describes him. But, as we saw, while the clergy have a feast and apparently fruitless discussion, the men who actually solve the problem by slaying the vampire are members of the laity. Whatever William's intentions in recording and shaping his tale (and indeed his friend the cleric's in passing it on to him), a degree of tension remains in the narrative over the relationship, and relative wisdom, between the clergy and the laity. Similarly, while Thomas Tailour's confession, abjuration and sentence formally display to us a layperson submitting to punishment before the religious authority of his bishop, the details of his confession indelibly record for posterity the fact that a layman *could* have independent thoughts about religious matters, and *did* arrive at an individual belief about the termination of the soul upon death. If we are interested in the beliefs and unbeliefs of the laity, these moments are precious to us. While still not giving unmediated access to the interior person – whatever we think that really means – they provide us with a more subtle and varied picture of the laity. This is where the patterns of culture break, and something more complex is revealed.

2

Acculturation

One day in 1319, Raymond de Laburat was travelling with Raymond Frézat, his parish priest, from the southern French village of Quié towards the town of Tarascon. As they walked, Raymond asked the priest, 'Can you tell me that one can find in any part of Scripture that God excommunicated anyone by His own mouth, or ordered any excommunication?' Frézat was silent, and gave no reply.

What lay behind Raymond de Laburat's question was twofold. He had heard, a long time ago, from a subchaplain called John, that there was no biblical basis for excommunication (the exclusion of someone from the mass, and hence from the community), and that clerics had invented it in order to have power over lay people. More pressingly, Raymond and various of his neighbours had been excommunicated for refusing to pay a tithe on lambs that the local bishop had insisted be collected in full. On account of this excommunication, Raymond and his neighbours were excluded from church – they had literally had the door shut in their faces – and hence from seeing the mass, something that had upset him greatly.

Raymond was not satisfied with Frézat's silence. He asked his question a second day, this time when they were walking to the mill at Quié. Again, the priest was silent, confirming Raymond's belief in what the subchaplain had told him many years before. Finally, in August of 1319, Raymond and the priest were sitting in Raymond's house and Raymond pressed the point again. 'And then the said priest replied to him that one found it written that the Hebrews had once made a great disturbance in church when God preached, and God had ordered that they be expelled from the church so that they could not disturb the sermon, and because of this, as he said, excommunication was invented.' Raymond had a further question: were the Hebrews men? Yes they were, replied the priest. And there, more or less, the matter rested.[1]

It is only rarely and in certain circumstances that we are party to such conversations. Had there not been Cathar heretics in Raymond's area he would not have been picked up by inquisitors as a troublemaker. That we know of his questions to the priest is therefore an unusual event; but *having* questions for one's parish priest may not have been so extraordinary. What we see in passing here (and with complexities to which we shall return) is something of the ordinary, day-to-day level at which the content and authority of Christianity reproduced itself. One can imagine – but usually cannot hear – a much larger, messier discussion over issues of faith, belief, law and practice throughout medieval Europe. The majority of the surviving evidence relates to the more formal channels of instruction and education, the means by which the Church propagated the faith. In this chapter we will look at three of these: sermons, images and texts. Two concerns underlie each area of enquiry. The first is to consider the means by which the laity were acculturated into Christianity. A little care is needed here over what precisely is meant. One sense in which 'acculturation' is used is as something close in meaning to 'conversion': changing the existing culture into something new. This is, arguably, a useful way of considering the spread of Christianity in the early Middle Ages.[2] But unless we are looking at the far north and east of Europe, by the twelfth century it is not at all the case that the laity were 'pagan' or that Christianity was a foreign import brought in by the clergy. On the contrary: the clergy and the laity lived in the same world, in part, shared the same general background, and Christianity was extremely familiar. It was, indeed, a dominant cultural force in medieval society. But it is precisely this familiarity and domination that therefore need to be considered. Dominant cultures are not passive, inert things. They produce and reproduce themselves, to ensure continued communication and (as I suggested in the previous chapter) maintain hegemony. The acceptance and support for Christianity by secular rulers did not, on their own, establish Christianity as a cultural force; it only provided the necessary grounding for the Church to do its work. Moreover, the content of Christianity changed over time. As we shall see, being a good lay Christian meant different things in the eleventh century and the fifteenth century. Thus we must consider how Christianity continued to spread its message within Christendom. In this sense, acculturation is seen not as a task achieved and completed, but as an ongoing project – the means by which successive generations of lay people entered into the Christian culture around them, and the particular, changing ways in which it embraced them.

The second area of concern is to think about Raymond de Laburat's side of the conversation writ large; to think, that is, about the lay reception of what the Church communicated. Raymond's doubts about excommunication were, apparently, either awoken or encouraged by the subchaplain John. His response, at a later date and in a different context, was to explore this area with his parish priest. But despite accepting what Frézat eventually told him, this did not constrain Raymond's future actions: he continued to protest against his excommunication and that of his neighbours, but now on the grounds of its injustice and misapplication in their particular case. If we take this small argument between priest and parishioner as standing in for the much greater encounter between Church and people, we are reminded that any tenet, image or message propagated to the laity would not simply be received in automatic, passive obedience.

The laity would *interpret* what they heard and saw (and occasionally read). Sometimes, perhaps even most times, their interpretation would fall in line with what the Church intended, and they would prove a receptive audience. At others, there would be a dialectic between Church and flock, as lay expectations about what the faith would or should supply might shape ecclesiastical message and policy. But at certain points – not, perhaps, always fully understood or even noted by the ecclesiastical authorities – lay interpretations could differ quite markedly from ecclesiastical intention. Thus our second concern has an impact upon the former, as a way of considering the limits of acculturation.

This question informs not just this chapter but the entirety of this book. For now, however, let us start at a more straightforward level. Let us, like Raymond de Laburat, ask some basic questions about the fundamentals of medieval Christian belief. The priest Raymond Frézat had presumably done some homework in order to answer his parishioner's persistent questions. Perhaps he had asked another priest, or his bishop, or had consulted a manual on canon law. In any case, he was finally able to supply what Raymond wanted: a biblical basis for a particular element of Christian practice. If we are interested in understanding the bases of medieval Christianity – the resources on which it drew – the Bible is obviously of primary importance. But as the nuances of the conversation between the two Raymonds suggest, the relationship between the Bible, orthodox Christianity, and the lived faith of the people was complex.

For a start, what one meant by 'the Bible' was far from straightforward. The modern English Bible (derived from the Protestant version authorized by King James I in 1611) consists of 39 books in the Old Testament, starting with Genesis and concluding with Malachi, and 27 books in the New Testament, running from the gospel of Matthew to the book of Revelation. However, the content and order were not the same in the Middle Ages, nor the same from place to place. For example, the gospel of St James, now counted as apocryphal, was sometimes included and sometimes not; the division of the books into chapters and verses only began in Paris around 1200; and although the most common Latin text (known as the Vulgate) derived from an early fifth-century translation by St Jerome, other Latin versions were also extant.[3] In addition to all of this, to have a complete collection of all the books of Scripture – everything from Genesis to Revelation – was far from common. Until the end of the Middle Ages such things would usually only be found in medieval universities, monastic foundations, and – as beautifully illustrated prestige texts – in royal courts. Much more common were texts containing *parts* of Scripture: the Gospels, for example, or the Psalms and Proverbs. Many of these would have been workaday copies, not lavishly illustrated or decorated, but for use by mendicant preachers and others. Parish priests, in fact, might well not possess a Bible or even part of one, but depended instead upon lectionaries – books of the relevant extracts – to provide the biblical readings needed for the mass. A mid-thirteenth-century inventory of books owned by the monastery of St Sernin in Toulouse and 64 of its dependent parish churches in the surrounding countryside illustrates the disjunction. In the monastery itself was a large library, including theological treatises, histories, and many Bibles, parts of Bibles and glosses upon the Bible. In the parishes, however, the picture was very different: most churches had at least three books, but these were usually service books, some collections of saints' lives and books of prayers. None of the 64 churches had a Bible.[4] It is not surprising that Raymond Frézat took a while to answer his parishioner's question.

In his answer, Frézat was presumably alluding to Christ's expulsion of the merchants from the temple (Matt. 21:12). This might, at a stretch, be taken as a biblical precedent for excommunication (although it would not have been the scriptural choice of most medieval theologians who most frequently pointed to a passage in Paul's letter to the Corinthians that describes separating the corrupting 'leaven' from the orthodox 'lump').[5] But, strictly speaking, Raymond de Laburat was perfectly right to suspect that excommunication was a later invention. Many of the rituals, practices and laws in Christianity had no direct biblical basis, but were later developments. It was possible to project justifications backwards, through particular interpretations of the Bible: for example, as the Church extended its control over marriage during the twelfth and thirteenth centuries, turning what was originally a social ritual into a sacrament, ecclesiastical writers could point to the gospel of St John for biblical authority, telling of Christ's presence at the marriage feast in Cana.

But, in fact, a fundamental principle of medieval Catholicism was that its faith was derived not only from Scripture, but also from later writings and decisions. To argue, as the fifteenth-century Wycliffites did, that one should rely solely upon the content of Scripture for one's faith was in fact a form of heresy. One might crudely describe the Bible itself as a collection of histories, laws and stories. The extra-biblical bases of Christianity can be similarly subdivided. First, there were a number of histories and treatises, written in the early centuries of the Church, such as Augustine's *City of God* (*c*.426). Through recounting and analysing the history of the Church, texts like these provided philosophical and theological speculation about God's plan and man's relationship to it. Other important texts contributed to the elucidation of God's plan, such as the seventh-century Isidore of Seville's *Etymologies* that provided interpretations of the origins and meanings of individual words, and Gregory the Great's *Dialogues* that reflected, among other things, upon the order of the universe. In addition, there were non-Christian works that influenced or became integrated into Catholic theology. Classical authors such as Cicero, Plato and, above all others, Aristotle were read and pondered by university scholars, particularly from the mid-twelfth century onwards (as various classical texts were 'rediscovered' and translated into Latin from the Arab sources that had kept them alive over the previous millennium).[6] In this same period, medieval theologians became extremely active, particularly centred on the University of Paris, producing a number of important and influential treatises, often attempting to apply theological principles to the social situation that they saw around them in a newly prosperous and populous city.[7]

Second, there were the laws that the Church made and continued to make, both at the highest level of the papacy and at more localized levels. For example, at the Council of Nicea in 325 clerics were ordered to abstain from sex, marriage or keeping mistresses. Of course, ordering something does not automatically make it so, and the command for clerical celibacy was reiterated many times over the next millennium, perhaps most forcefully (and arguably with greatest effect) in the twelfth century. It was never *wholly* accepted throughout Christendom – indeed, in certain places, such as northern Spain, even in the later Middle Ages the local communities seem often to have accepted priests having partners as if in marriage, as long as they lived without scandal – but it had become largely predominant by the thirteenth century. The most comprehensive statement of ecclesiastical law was provided in the twelfth century by Gratian's *Decretum*. This collection of past conciliar decrees, papal bulls and patristic writings provided for the first time a comprehensive attempt to make systematic the laws of the Church. Where past decrees differed, Gratian attempted to provide clarification through careful questioning and comparison. In the thirteenth century, the canon lawyer Raymond de Peñafort collated further papal decrees (mainly issued by Pope Gregory IX) and these *Decretals* were added to Gratian's work to form the *Corpus iuris canonici*, the 'body of canon law', which remained the fundamental basis for ecclesiastical law into the twentieth century.[8] However, although the *Corpus* was the central text of canon law, also important were local episcopal decrees and decisions that could vary from country to country and even from diocese to diocese.

Finally, there were stories: the great unspooling yarn of tales, parables, sayings, whether amusing, disturbing, moving or confusing, that wove Christendom's moral fabric. Stories began with the Old and New Testaments – Eve's seduction by the serpent, David defeating Goliath, Christ turning water into wine – but continued to be generated from the activities of later church men and women. The lives of saints were thick with stories: how St Margaret burst forth from the belly of a dragon, her virginal purity having protected her when swallowed by this symbol of evil; how St Julian conjured up a host of demons, looking 'like black Ethiopians', and then banished them with the sign of the cross; of St Marina, who lived in male disguise as a monk and patiently bore the false accusation of having fathered a child, the strange truth revealed only upon her death.[9] Miracle collections were a constant source of further stories, and bishops, monks and priests collected other remarkable events that they had witnessed or heard about: a talking bird who successfully invoked St Thomas of Canterbury to kill the goshawk that was hunting it; a fake, demonically-constructed corpse replaced for the body of a sick maiden, in order to fool her family into thinking her dead (her young lover discovered the truth, and thus won her hand in marriage); Renard the Fox attempting to catch a young bird by luring her into giving him the kiss of peace – this being a metaphor, as the Augustinian preacher Jacques de Vitry (*c*.1160–1240) noted, for churchmen who, under the cover of piety, attempted to seduce women.[10] Ecclesiastics traded these stories among themselves as useful kindling for the spiritual fires they had to stoke. Many of these became *exempla* for sermons; some, as we saw in the last chapter, ended up in chronicles.

There are several important things to note about these foundations of Christianity. First, they do not present one clear, straightforward message or set of instructions. There were, for Christians, some core tenets: that existence had begun as an act of divine creation, and would at some point end, leading to a Final Judgement; humanity was born in a state of sin, ever since Adam and Eve ate the apple proffered by the serpent; there was but one God; his son, Jesus Christ, came down to earth, was sacrificially crucified, and was resurrected; people possess souls, and will end up either in heaven or hell. However, beyond these fundamentals, there was a lot that was less clear and less fixed. What, precisely, was Christ's nature when he came to earth, human or divine or both? When would the Final Judgement come? What was the best way to gain salvation? How was one to understand the tripartite nature of God (the Father, the Son, the Holy Spirit)? The Old and New Testaments are inconsistent texts, and provide endless opportunities for exegesis. For example, Ambrose (d. 397), trying to establish the role of Mary Magdalen in the gospel accounts, noted with exasperation that 'some of the women are not aware [of Christ's resurrection], others are . . . One Mary of Magdala does not know, according to John, the other Mary Magdalen does know, according to Matthew. The same woman cannot know it at first and then not know it!'[11] Christianity, from its inception, was in a constant process of interpretation.

This meant, second, that Christianity was not static. The Church was formed in a period of persecution, and its Fathers had lived in desert lands, grappling with very different contexts of faith from those of their medieval descendants.[12] After the fall of the Roman Empire, it struggled to assert its dominion in Europe over the multiform pagan beliefs of the native peoples. A greater continuity with the Roman world was kept in the East, in the Christian Church of the Byzantine Empire; but Rome and the West had grown apart from Constantinople (modern Istanbul) and, in 1054, the division between the two churches came to a head. The tenets and theology of Christianity also moved. In the sixth century, St Augustine had argued against the possibility of there being any communication between the living and the dead, and hence rejected the idea that one need engage in elaborate burial practices.[13] By the high Middle Ages, the importance of communication between living and dead, and the Church's management of the rituals of death, were fundamental elements of orthodoxy. Sometimes writers were aware of these shifts. In the thirteenth century, authors pondering the biblical injunction 'Go forth and multiply' drew a distinction between its applicability in the early years of the Church – when there were not many Christians around – and its present applicability in the increasingly populous European cities. The world and the Church had changed, as they recognized.[14]

Third, and finally, one should not picture Christian faith, at any point in the Middle Ages, as simply a linear production line where theologians worked out its details, the papacy endorsed them, and the clergy passed them on to the obedient flock. There was indeed a Church hierarchy, formed by the papacy, influential theologians, famous preachers, the leaders of the great monastic houses and so forth. Below the papacy were the bishops, and a further hierarchy of deans, priests, deacons and subdeacons that stretched down into the soil of the parish. The elite frequently knew and communicated with each other, and there were doctrines conceived centrally and then promoted throughout Christendom. But the hierarchy had to work with the legacy of the Church Fathers, deal with the intrusion of new thoughts from rediscovered classical learning, mediate (or fail to mediate) between divergent theologians, and apply the Church's teachings to situations as divergent in social, economic, cultural and political terms as the highly developed city states of northern Italy, and the very rural kingdom of Norway (which had only been introduced to Christianity in the late tenth century). Moreover, in many ways the parish clergy shared much more cultur- ally and economically with their parishioners than with the episcopacy. For example, despite the hopes of diligent bishops, a thirteenth-century parish priest was not necessarily able to read Latin, and a fifteenth-century chantry priest would probably be poorer than many of the laity. Chasms of real life could sep- arate Parisian theological faculties and rural parish practices. Furthermore, ideas, customs and enthusiasms at a local level could also drive the edifice forward: the general idea of Purgatory – a place that was neither heaven nor hell – almost certainly arose from a popular, rather than an academic, context. The same was true of the feast of Corpus Christi.[15] At certain points and in certain areas, a top-down process was more apparent. In the twelfth and thir- teenth centuries, for example, the University of Paris was a powerhouse of theo- logical ideas, and there was a concerted effort to communicate their practical implications throughout the parishes. The Fourth Lateran Council of 1215 pro- vided a strong and fairly detailed outline for both conformity of belief and the mechanisms for its implementation. And actions against heresy in, among other places, southern France in the thirteenth century and England in the fifteenth century, brought the demands of orthodox conformity more clearly into focus.

The combination of all three factors is nicely illustrated by a problem dealt with at the Synod of Breslau, in Poland, in 1248. The council noted that 'The Germans who have emigrated to the dioceses of Breslau and Cracow complain that the bishops of those two dioceses wish to impose the custom, usual in Poland and Silesia, of not eating meat from Septuagesima [the third Sunday before Lent], whereas the German custom is to commence upon Ash Wednesday.'[16] A relatively small geographical difference split the interpretations of one of the central rituals of Christianity, the Lenten fast leading up to Easter. Particularly interesting is the conflicting role of tradition: the German immi- grants felt perfectly justified in complaining about a lengthier fast because it was not their custom. They wished to hang on to *their* version of Christianity. In the event, however, geography and episcopal authority won: the synod ordered the Germans to comply or be excommunicated. Some regularization – within dio- cesan areas, at least – was possible. But overall, despite the dreams of certain popes, bishops and theologians, Christianity was never entirely uniform.

So what things did Christianity share? I noted some core tenets above. Belief in Christ and his message of salvation was essential, as was the existence of heaven and an afterlife. As we shall see in the next chapters, the possibility of belief in some supernatural intervention in life and death was pretty much universal, even among those who doubted or rejected other elements of faith. The fact of morality and the need for a moral code – even if the details of that code would quickly become a matter for argument – were probably another core feature. Less positively, most Christians also knew what they were by what they were *not*: not Jews and not 'Saracens' (as they called Muslims). In not extending this tally further I am perhaps overcautious, too aware of those people charged with heresy (but still seeing themselves as 'good Christians') who would diverge in one way or another from other elements fairly central to Catholicism, such as the Virgin Birth, the general resurrection of souls, the power of the saints, the clergy's sacramental powers, and so forth. But part of this book's purpose is to try to see what links as much as what divides the heretical, the disbelieving, the superstitious with what is commonly described as 'Christian'. For that reason, the list is brief.

Perhaps more importantly there were a number of images, symbols and patterns of thought shared across western Christendom. We could think here of the image of the suffering body, most usually Christ's body during the Passion but also the bodies of earlier and later men and women martyred for their faith. Symbolic practices such as processions, pilgrimages and collective acts of sacrifice were also shared across Christendom. The tendency to conceive of things, both spiritual and temporal, in hierarchies was common to almost every variant of Christianity. Honour thy father and mother, honour the Lord thy God; hierarchy, faith and obedience were inseparable. Even those heretical sects that preached much greater equality, such as the Waldensians, in practice still recognized some divisions of status and ideas of obedience.

Most important of all was the very tendency to think symbolically: to see things as potential symbols that interlinked aspects of this world and the next, bringing together different registers of social and spiritual relations, different topographies of natural and supernatural space. Medieval symbolism overlaps with, but should not be reduced to, figurative language. 'The rose is the choir of martyrs, or yet again the choir of virgins. When red it is the blood of those who died for the faith, when white it is spotless purity. It opens among thorns as the martyr grows up in the midst of heretics and persecutors, or as the pure virgin blooms radiant in the midst of iniquity.'[17] In proffering this image, Peter da Mora, thirteenth-century bishop of Capua, was not simply suggesting a useful simile (that the rose was *like* the martyrs). He was providing a familiar symbol to illustrate two different kinds of sanctity (martyrdom and virginity), and, through the unity provided by a single symbol, show that different kinds of sanctity were at a certain level the same thing. Furthermore, the thorns of the rose gave an opportunity to link sanctity to its opposites – heresy and sin. Most importantly, he was doing all of this *at the very same time*. In writing it out, the symbol of a rose disassembles into a chain of associations; but for Peter all of these things were operating simultaneously. How was this? Because God had so ordered the natural world that a rose possessed all of these symbolic resonances;

at some level roses *were* linked to sanctity. The associations were not placed there by man but by God, and the theologian had simply brought them forth. The richness of Peter da Mora's symbol is the mark of an educated ecclesiastic, able to draw upon the possibilities of a number of different texts and registers to inform his analysis. But the sense of seeing and thinking symbolically – looking for what something, particularly something from the natural world, might mean beyond itself – was a pattern of thought that spread much more broadly across Europe and up and down the social scale.[18]

It may be in these vaguer tendencies that we can talk of 'medieval Christianity' as one phenomenon, one collective endeavour. But like the symbol of the rose, it is a unity that unfolds to reveal further multitudes. If we think, now, about what divided the Christian faithful, we would have to recognize that the highly literate, university-educated, theologically complex, socially elevated and exegetically rich world that Peter da Mora inhabited was not shared by the great mass of the laity. What, then, of those lower down the social and educational spectrum? What did the Church expect the ordinary laity to know, to understand and to believe?

The answer varies depending upon when and where we look, and perhaps upon whom we ask. Compare the following two instances. In 1172, an ecclesiastical council was held in Cashel in Ireland, on the orders (according to Gerald of Wales) of King Henry II of England who had just brought the country into his dominion. This was an important council, attended by many bishops, designed to unify the Irish Church with English ecclesiastical practice. What did it have to say about the ordinary laity? Five things: that marriage law (meaning the degrees of consanguinity) should be observed, that children should be catechized and baptized, that everyone should pay tithes, that everyone should make a will, and that everyone should confess prior to death and be buried in a Christian manner.[19] The focus is upon the core essentials of birth and death, and the material support of the Church. The statute on catechism does not suggest, in the way it is expressed, a very detailed process. It states that 'children should be catechized before the doors of the church and baptized in the sacred font of the church', which appears to indicate one single event. In the later Middle Ages, catechism could indicate instruction in the essential prayers and tenets of the faith; and after the Reformation, it was a much more sustained programme of education. However, thirteenth-century evidence on baptismal practice suggests that 'catechizing' meant, at most, teaching the child the Creed (on which, see below) and some simple prayers. In Cashel, however, it may simply have indicated exorcism: dispelling evil spirits from the child's presence.[20]

Compare this with the second instance: in 1281, the archbishop of Canterbury, John Pecham, issued a manual of instruction to parish priests, known by its opening words as *Ignorantia sacerdotum*, 'the ignorance of priests':

The ignorance of priests casts the people down into the ditch of error, and the foolishness and lack of learning of clerics, whom the decrees of canon law order to teach the sons of the faithful, is all the worse when it leads to error instead of knowledge . . . To remedy this dangerous situation we order that four times during the year . . . each priest in charge of a parish should personally explain or have someone else explain to the people in their mother tongue, without any fancifully woven subtleties, the fourteen articles of faith, the Ten Commandments of the Decalogue, the two precepts of the Gospel (namely the twin laws of charity), the seven works of mercy, the seven capital sins and their fruits, the seven principal virtues, and the seven grace-giving sacraments.[21]

The manual then proceeds to explain each of these elements in detail, so that no priest can excuse himself from obedience by claiming theological ignorance.

In contrast to the brief instruction ordered by the council of Cashel – essentially a ritual entry into the community of the Church – Pecham imagines a more sustained plan of education, with a reasonably developed content of Christian belief. We should note, however, that the stated context for the instructions is the failure of priests adequately to instruct their flocks. As it provides an explanation of the key theological points, it appears also to assume that some of the clergy themselves will lack this knowledge. Here is a gloss on what Pecham called for:

- The fourteen articles of faith relate to the deity: that God the Father, Christ and the Holy Spirit constitute an indivisible Trinity (the first four articles deal with this); that God created the heaven and the earth; that the Church is the only route to salvation (two articles on this); that Christ was physically incarnate on earth, the product of a Virgin Birth, died on the cross, descended into hell to free the righteous, was resurrected, ascended into heaven, and will return on the Day of Judgement at the end of time. The formal, prescribed statement of these points was known as the Creed (from its first word, *credo*, 'I believe').
- The Ten Commandments: no idolatry; no blasphemy; keep sabbath day holy; honour father and mother; no killing; no adultery; no stealing; no lying; do not covet a neighbour's house; do not desire a neighbour's wife or goods. These laws could be interpreted more symbolically in the Middle Ages: thus 'honour thy father and mother' was glossed by Pecham to include honouring people's social status and respecting secular and ecclesiastical hierarchies.
- The two precepts of the Gospel: to love God (and thus obey the preceding Ten Commandments from love not fear); and to love one's neighbour as oneself.
- The seven works of mercy: feed the hungry, give drink to the thirsty, give shelter to strangers, clothe the naked, visit the sick, comfort those in prison, bury the dead.
- The seven sins: pride, envy, wrath, sloth, avarice, gluttony, lust (we shall discuss these in greater detail in Chapter 5).
- The seven virtues: faith, hope, charity, prudence, justice, temperance, fortitude. (Temperance meant 'not to be swayed by earthly pleasures' rather than simply abstinence from alcohol.)
- The seven sacraments: baptism, confirmation, penance, the Eucharist, extreme unction (the anointing with oil, called 'chrism', immediately prior

to death), holy orders and matrimony. A sacrament was not simply a ritual, but one in which the power of God effected change through the hands of a priest: most powerfully and importantly in the Eucharist, as the bread and wine were changed into the body and blood of Christ; but also for example in marriage – if, Pecham says, it is contracted with a sincere spirit – where it bestows grace upon those being married.

Why the difference between Cashel and Pecham? Obviously, the specific circumstances for the texts differ. But there is a broad context of change: prior to the twelfth century, the Church's expectations of the laity were relatively minimal. In the centuries following the fall of the Roman Empire, as Christianity slowly moved across the West, it was enough to wean lay people away from the old pagan rituals. Bishops might also try to encourage a kind of 'public welfare': caring for the poor and the sick, refraining from field work on Sundays.[22] From the eighth century, some ecclesiastical councils called for simple versions of the Creed to be taught to the flock. But essentially, the salvation of the laity was something undertaken on their behalf by the Church, particularly through the prayers of monks. When the Church thought about 'the laity', it primarily thought about the warrior class: how to get them to support the Church materially, how to persuade them to observe certain rules, how to prevent them from usurping clerical property and privilege. It was not until the twelfth century that the Church began to consider seriously whether the general mass of the laity should be more actively involved in their salvation; not until the thirteenth that it began, systematically, to put effective mechanisms in place to educate and mould the laity as it desired. And arguably it was not until the later fourteenth century that these mechanisms really began to bear fruit, in terms of a more individual and personal lay spirituality.

Various wider factors prompted these developments, including the twelfth- and thirteenth-century growth of cities, and an accompanying rise in wealth, population and education; the growing power of non-noble laity in local and even national politics; and shifting relations between secular rulers and the Church. However, one key event lay between the earlier and later sets of instructions: the Fourth Lateran Council of 1215. At this great gathering, convened by Pope Innocent III, a template for Christianity was laid out that sustained the Church until the Council of Trent in the sixteenth century. In its opening decrees, Lateran IV expanded the defining statement of Christian faith and, among many other things, stated clearly that all lay people should come annually to make private and individual confession, that each parish should be provided with a priest, and that he should be given sufficient income from the parish to support himself, that the people of the parish should receive preaching to instruct them in their faith, and that parish priests should be up to the job of caring for the souls of their flock.[23] Across Europe diocesan councils set about promulgating these new measures. In England and France in particular, the bishops emphasized the need to explain the requirements in simple terms to parish priests, so that they could pass them on clearly, in the vernacular, to their flocks.[24] As we shall see in later chapters, Lateran IV did not invent all of these new demands and activities, but rather produced an authoritative statement that codified disparate currents from the previous century. It was, nonetheless, in the thirteenth century that these new concerns with faith were brought to a wider audience. Regional implementation of Innocent III's plan varied in speed and comprehension: English bishops were enthusiastic and relatively quick, whereas in some rural parts of Italy the process was much more tardy.[25] Overall, however, western Christendom engaged with the reform programme, or 'the campaign of interior reconquest' as André Vauchez has called it, referring both to the 'interior' of Europe (rather than the 'exterior' holy lands), and the 'interior' selves of the laity.[26]

Pecham's *Ignorantia sacerdotum* should probably be seen as an example of thirteenth-century 'best practice': the aspirations of a reform-minded and thoughtful bishop, hoping to bring his Church up to the mark. Not all commentators demanded or hoped for quite as much. The most commonly reiterated requirements called for the laity to know the *Pater noster* and *Ave Maria* prayers, the Creed, and how to make the sign of the cross (probably accompanied by reciting 'In the name of the Father, the Son and the Holy Spirit').[27] Just the two prayers alone are found repeated over and over again as the basic requirements of religious knowledge throughout the medieval period. It may seem like a fairly slender basis for faith, although it arguably communicates the essential seeds of the Christian message: God, salvation and intercession. However, we may also wonder what being taught these prayers really implied: being taught their theological implications, being taught how to recite the sounds they made, or being taught something in between?

A text on confession written by Bishop Robert Grosseteste some time between 1235 and 1250 suggests asking if a layperson 'knows the *Pater noster*, the Creed, and such kind, and whether in the language of the Church [i.e. Latin] or his own'.[28] This indicates the possibility – in some parishes – of learning by rote in a language foreign to the laity. This may in fact have been fairly common: in the twelfth century we see the Creed being recited by the laity, perhaps in Latin, during mass, with the priest enjoined to explain what it meant at various points in the year.[29] In the early thirteenth century, there were specific statutes passed ordering priests to teach parishioners the Creed in their vernacular tongue.[30] But this may have taken a long time to become universal. In the late fourteenth century, an English sermon by John Mirk mentions in passing that 'each priest is held by all the law in Holy Church to expound the *Pater noster* to his parishioners once or twice in the year', and instructs the laity that 'it is much more useful and of greater merit for you to say your *Pater noster* in English than in such Latin as you do. For when you speak in English, then you know and understand well what you say.'[31] Learning the prayers in Latin does not preclude retaining knowledge of what they meant, if the parish priest was diligent in his glossing: for example, one can remember that *Pater noster* means 'Our Father', even if one does not know whether it is *Pater* or *noster* that means 'father'.

Mirk's sermon points simultaneously to the continuing practice of ritual recitation without particular comprehension, and also developing attempts in the later Middle Ages to encourage the laity into a more reflective faith. The two may have run side by side, but with something of a class division: as we will see below, well-off families in the fifteenth century could well expect to own psalters and other texts, containing this and other prayers and hence encouraging private, domestic reflection upon their meaning. In contrast, the 1472 statutes of Heytesbury hospital, aimed at the poor and indigent inmates, simply say that if a patient did not know the *Ave*, *Pater noster* and Creed, he was 'to do his besy labour to cunne say hit perfitely'.[32] To 'say it perfectly' here implies rote memorization. Something similar is implied by an *exemplum* told by the great Tuscan preacher Bernardino da Siena (d. 1444). A stupid usurer complained to his priest that he could not remember the Lord's Prayer. The priest sent him a succession of beggars to borrow grain from him, each beggar introducing himself as a part of the text: 'I am "Our Father"', and 'I am "Who Art In Heaven"', and so forth. The priest then told the usurer to recite who owed him grain, in the order that they had borrowed it. By saying their 'names', the layman was able to say the prayer. Bernardino glossed the tale for his audience: 'Thus I say to you, if you cannot manage to learn the Creed or any other prayer, use tricks similar to those of this priest . . .'[33] Of course, memorization could be seen as a precursor to reflection; but it is interesting, nonetheless, to see fifteenth-century examples from both England and Italy that indicate adults who did not know the basic minimum. This is not to suggest that they were any less 'Christian' because of it. But it is to note that what constituted belief for these people, contrary to the pedagogic instincts of churchmen, was not essentially to do with the contents of prayers or the tenets of faith.

In southern France in the early fourteenth century we find the inquisitor Bernard Gui making a passing statement about good orthodox practice, which he called 'the general rules of life'. He expected that a layperson would make confession three times a year, abstain from labour and go to hear mass on Sundays and feast days, would shun divination and magic, and avoid usury (lending money at interest) and theft.[34] Context again is important: Gui was writing a manual on how to catch heretics, and had the lack of good behaviour in his mind – hence, perhaps, his focus on not doing bad things (usury, theft, magic). More subtly, given that Lateran IV had encouraged confessing three times each year but only actually demanded that it be done annually, Gui's emphasis on thrice-yearly confession may indicate an inquisitor's enthusiasm for the chance of monitoring people's orthodoxy (confession providing an opportunity, among other things, for a priest to see whether his parishioners were conforming). But overall, Gui's 'general rules' remind us that what the Church more commonly wanted from the laity was not a deep knowledge of doctrine but conformity of behaviour.

So what things were lay people expected to do? We shall look, in Chapter 4, at the practical contributions that the laity made in their parishes. Here, I will focus on more universal aspects. First, as we saw at the council of Cashel, there were the key rituals that accompanied certain stages of life: being baptized, preferably as an infant; having the priest solemnize one's marriage; and receiving, on one's deathbed, the last rites. Second, there were annual rituals: fasting during Lent; making confession of one's sins, and then receiving communion at Easter; celebrating particular saints' days at different points of the year. Third, there were more regular demands: principally attending mass at the parish church on Sundays and feast days, but also participating in other regular festivals or rituals. We should note that these activities comprised the bulk of the Church's demands upon the laity: the demand to do certain things (and not do certain other things), rather than the demand to know all that much.

This emphasis upon practice rather than theology is important, and somewhat complex. As we will see, being a good Christian was as much about what you did as what you knew. It is important not to mistake this for simplicity. The doing was not necessarily a veneer of conformity or empty ritual; it was, rather, belief *as* embodiment and enactment. But we also need to consider this from the Church's viewpoint. For optimistic ecclesiastics, conformity in behaviour would, it was hoped, lead to inner faith. Medieval thought, in many different areas, saw close connections between outer appearance and inner reality. When the two were apparently at odds (as when outer piety concealed inner heresy), it was most upsetting. In other situations, however, there was a sense in which the opaque inner world could be affected by disciplining the outer reality. Ascetics could cure lust by, for example, sitting in freezing cold streams or rolling in briar patches; such practices did not just take one's mind off sex, but through protracted use could entirely dispel lust from the inner heart.[35] In a parallel but more modest way, encouraging the laity to obey certain rules – such as not working on feast days – could help to bring their souls closer to God. The outer could reform the inner. And if, less optimistically, this process did not succeed, conformity of behaviour at least avoided public 'scandal' – scandal being something likely to disrupt the faith and potential salvation of others.

All of these activities, these doings of religion and faith, were extremely important, and I shall explore them in greater detail further on. For the rest of this chapter, however, I want to return to matters of doctrine, law and story; and to consider the routes by which lay people received instruction, and how they responded to that instruction. One of the most intriguing features of Raymond de Laburat's conversation with his priest is the enquiry 'Were the Hebrews men?' The immediate implication of the question was to check that what Frézat told him was applicable to his own particular situation; that the Hebrews (ejected from church as if excommunicated) were men *like him*. The bigger implication leading on from this is almost dizzying in the glimpse it provides of a potential chasm between ecclesiastical culture and lay comprehension. Were the stories in the Bible, the central messages about Christ, God and salvation, actually applicable to the here and now, or were they just interesting tales of distant lands and foreign people? Did they *apply*?, Raymond seems to ask. This was, one must remember, a quite devout layman who was very upset at being excluded from seeing mass in church. How many years had he been listening to sermons and been instructed about Christ and the apostles – and perhaps seen all of this as essentially distant from his own faith?

Preaching

Henry was a tall man, with a shaven head, ragged beard and fierce eyes; and it was said that when he looked at your face he knew your sins. He is sometimes now called Henry of Le Mans, but when, in 1115, he strode barefoot out of the winter gales into that particular French town, he came from no discernible place – except, perhaps, stepping directly from the pages of the Gospels. He came to Le Mans to preach and, impressed by his holy appearance, the local bishop Hildebert granted him licence to do just that. Hildebert himself had business in Rome, but a portion of the local clerics and many of the laity came to listen. They were not disappointed: 'he roared pronouncements like an oracle. It was as if legions of demons were all making their noise in one blast through his mouth.' The clerics wept, the people wondered, and 'by his speech, even a heart of stone could be moved to repentance'.

But repentance was not the only effect. Whether through a desire for reform or a more aggressive anticlericalism, Henry's words led the people of Le Mans to shun the clergy. Three clerics were allegedly tumbled into the filth in the street gutters. When Hildebert returned, he found a mob who rejected his benedictions screaming 'We don't want your blessings! Bless filth! Consecrate filth!' Seeking out the man who had turned the city upside down, Hildebert discovered Henry to be but a lowly deacon, who did not even know the order of words for the morning service and could not sing a simple hymn to the Virgin Mary. And so, apparently chastened (according at any rate to the very hostile chronicler), Henry left for pastures new.[36]

The story of Henry at Le Mans, although extraordinary, tells us some interesting things about medieval preaching, and also the problems it poses for historians. There had been preachers throughout the Christian era, and monastic preaching (including, on occasion, to lay audiences) was common in the early Middle Ages. But it was Henry's era, the twelfth century, that saw the beginnings of a great upsurge in activity. The expansion of preaching to the laity – preaching as a regular and essential part of the lay religious experience – reached its apogee in the thirteenth century, when the energetic mendicant orders began to spread the word across Europe. Its roots, however, lay in the previous century. People like Henry (and others, such as Peter de Bruys, Robert of Arbrissel, Arnold of Brescia and Norbert of Xanten, to name but a few) were received enthusiastically as a new phenomenon; or rather, the return of a very old phenomenon, the apostolic wanderer, dressed simply and penitently, come to inspire the people to devotion. Henry and the others were condemned as heretics, not for the theological content of what they had to say, but for the challenge and threat they represented to the Church. One might consider the last in this unfortunate line to be the merchant Waldes of Lyons who, in 1173, was suddenly inspired to preach the virtues of voluntary poverty and gathered a mass of followers. Waldes had no desire to challenge the Church, but by continuing to preach when 'unlicensed' (that is, lacking the permission of the local bishop) he and his followers were declared heretical. After Waldes, the Church learnt its lesson: the next inspired penitents, Francis of Assisi and Dominic of Caleruega, were embraced, licensed, and set on the road to leading the greatest preaching movements of the age.[37] As St Francis and St Dominic their deeds lived on, and the orders that they founded, the Franciscans (or Brothers or Friars Minor) and the Dominicans (or Brothers or Friars Preachers) had an enormous impact upon Christianity. The Church jealously guarded the power of preaching. A synod at Eichstädt from around 1280 condemned what was probably preaching within Beguine communities: 'Certain laity are holding secret conventicles and arrogating to themselves the office of preacher, leading simple folk astray.'[38] The Beguines were groups of laity living quasi-monastic lives, following penitential piety but without taking vows or following an ecclesiastical Rule. For some senior churchmen they were a wonderful example of lay piety, but for others a worrying phenomenon of independent and undisciplined religiosity. Thus, at Eichstädt, it was the power of preaching to sway lay devotion that the Church wished to channel and protect.

In focusing on preaching to the laity we should note, then, that a willing audience was already in existence. As Henry's story illustrates, the twelfth-century laity appeared hungry for it. People were excited by this charismatic man (the chronicler alleges that matrons and adolescent boys could not keep their hands off him, in a mixture of pious awe and lust). His sermon was a public event, held outside, with Henry on a platform to address the crowd. His speech was, the chronicler admits, 'remarkably fluent' and extremely effective: when it 'entered the ears of the mob, it stuck in their minds. Like a potent poison, it penetrated to the inner organs . . .' Here we have a rare picture of how a particular sermon was received and the effect it had upon its audience.

But what was the content of his sermon? We do not exactly know. We *might* surmise, from other documents that refuted his 'errors', that it questioned the power of the priesthood, asserted that there was no need to build or worship in physical churches, and doubted that an unworthy priest could produce Christ's body in the Eucharist. It may, in Le Mans, also have dealt with social problems such as prostitution, as Henry seems to have arranged for 'unchaste' women to leave their old lives and get married, forgoing the need for dower or dowry.[39] But we do not know for certain. Here lies one of the problems with any discussion of preaching: finding evidence for both the sermon and its performance is extremely difficult. In Henry's case, we have one picture of performance and reception – albeit a picture distorted by the feverish antipathies of the source – but we are not told much about the content of the sermon. More often the case is reversed: a vast number of sermon collections survive in manuscript, yet very little evidence for their performance and reception remains. And, of course, the manuscript records of sermons are (with a few exceptions) notional rather than actual sermons; the relationship between what is written and what was actually said has long been debated, without any firm conclusions being reached.

What can we say, then, about medieval preaching? First, that the kind of preaching presented by Henry was an unusual and special sort of sermonizing, which perhaps goes some way to explain its popularity. Most preaching took place in a more prosaic and familiar context: by the thirteenth century, in the parish church and its immediate environs. Earlier, one might expect some regular preaching to the laity from a local monastery or cathedral. The Benedictine abbot of Bury St Edmunds monastery in the late twelfth century used to preach 'in the Norfolk dialect' to the people, for example.[40] As we saw, the Fourth Lateran Council emphasized the importance of the parish priest preaching to his flock. In some places, this was almost certainly already the case; in others, it may have taken time to become established.[41] Evidence, as ever, is patchy and tells us more about what was desired or commanded than what actually happened. What we can say is that by the end of the thirteenth century there was an expectation that preaching would happen in the parish.[42]

The usual context for a sermon was on Sunday, inside the church, as part of the mass. It appears that the congregation were expected to sit down, though it is less clear whether they would be seated on benches or on the ground (pews did not appear in England, for example, until the fifteenth century). On occasion, the sermon could take place outside – in the churchyard or village square – and preachers' pulpits were sometimes made of wood so that they could be moved around as required.[43] Whether these outdoor sermons were reserved for particular occasions, or were incorporated into the mass, with the congregation moving out of church and then returning, we cannot know. Coming and going during the mass seems less likely, but not impossible. There is also evidence that outdoor sermons were delivered at particular occasions or events. The Dominican preacher Humbert de Romans (d. 1277) advised that 'provided you can get sufficient hearing, a sermon can be extremely useful at tournaments, because a lot of people attend who are very much in need of instruction'.[44] This may, however, have been more of a nice theory than a regular practice. One area where we can see the actual practice of preaching in greater detail – because of the questions that inquisitors asked about it – is that of sermons given by Cathar heretics in southern France. It is dangerous to draw a direct comparison, as there was pressure on these preachers to operate clandestinely but, at a rough estimate, in the first half of the thirteenth century about one-quarter of Cathar sermons were delivered outside, in cemeteries, town squares, woods and so forth, usually to quite a large crowd of people.[45]

Not all preaching was conducted by the priest. Peripatetic preachers known as *questors* or pardoners, raising funds for particular foundations such as hospitals, might visit a parish and be allowed to deliver the sermon, then beg for alms from the congregation. Mendicant friars could arrive in a parish to deliver sermons, a more common occurrence over the course of the thirteenth century. Humbert de Romans advised his brethren that if a friar 'wishes to preach in some parish in which he is not known personally, nor is his Order known, he should explain straightaway what he is and what his Order is, so that people will not mistake him for a man who is preaching to collect money'.[46] These were still sermons incorporated into the regular parochial pattern. One could, however, have extraordinary sermons such as those encouraging people to go on crusade, those begging divine reprieve from the horrors of plague, the penitential sermons preached by Bernardino da Siena around Tuscany – or, indeed, the sermons given by Henry at Le Mans.

What about content? The vast manuscript evidence is predominantly comprised of model sermons. These can vary from a brief template outline, to something so structured and refined that one may suspect that what is notionally a 'sermon' is in fact being used as a genre for written composition and was never intended for oral delivery. There is some evidence of preachers recording their words after the event, but these are late medieval and often problematic. A few English preachers in the 1420s seem to have written down their sermons, but in the context of trying to ward off suspicions of heresy by being able to produce proof of their words. Towards the end of his life, Bernardino da Siena translated vernacular transcriptions of his sermons into Latin and inserted learned references.[47] Fortunately the vernacular originals of Bernardino's sermons, recorded by a listener, still survive. This probably gives us the closest access one could hope for to the actual presentation. But it is an extraordinary rarity, and the words are those of an extraordinary preacher. It is debatable whether we can use Bernardino, who persuaded the Florentines to toss their vain belongings onto civic bonfires, as an index for the practice and effectiveness of most medieval preachers.

Direct evidence of content is thus problematic. One can, however, gain a sense of the expected patterns of regular preaching from the various sermon collections produced and reproduced in manuscript. Many model sermons, from the thirteenth century onward, were written in Paris and then spread more widely through Europe. The themes they emphasized were humility, contrition and charity. Larger sermon collections usually followed the annual pattern of the missal, and thus presented certain biblical themes to be expounded on particular days; but still, large degrees of regional variation are found between manuscripts.[48] Collections structured around saints' days, such as John Mirk's *Festial*, were also prey to local variation, dependent upon which saints were honoured in a particular parish. A sermon collection attributed to the twelfth-century bishop Maurice de Sully survives in two versions, Latin and French, apparently for use in parochial preaching. The vernacular version spends much more time glossing biblical and theological details, possibly indicating the way in which a good preacher might make a model sermon accessible to a lay audience.[49] We also have various handbooks for preaching that provided general advice on content. In the fourteenth century, Richard of Wetheringsett said that sermons should include most of what Pecham had set out in his *Ignorantia sacerdotum* and 'matters of error, what should be avoided, what performed'. These sermons were presumably to be spread across the year, forming a programme of instruction for the laity. Model sermons containing a portion of these elements can be found in the fifteenth century. Some parish priests may have possessed small copies of synodal statutes, in the form of a *quire* (small booklet) to aid them. A late medieval monastic sermon criticizes uneducated preachers who produce sermons when their only authority is 'an olde quaier with a fewe custummes or a few statutis', indicating both that expectations of sophistication were rising in the fifteenth century, and conversely (through the stereotype it presents) that a fairly basic programme of instruction still constituted regular practice.[50]

But not all sermons were expressly didactic. There is ample evidence of votive sermons, perhaps performed particularly on holy days and in processions, giving thanks for things as varied as fine weather, protection from pestilence, or for the king's successes in war. Archbishop Richard Fitzralph of Armagh (d. 1360) kept a sermon diary, noting the general content of some of his preaching:

> And all the matter of the rest of this sermon was the matter of the two preceding sermons, namely, concerning those who tithe falsely, against whom we have published statutes . . . Further, against those who impede the judges of church courts from investigating . . . Further, against those who hinder women from freely making their wills, or Irishmen [doing likewise] . . . This sermon dealt with others too, against whom Statutes were framed at the last General Council, a little while ago.[51]

Fitzralph's sermons seem more a part of discipline and legal discourse than religious education, and were perhaps tied to particular local troubles. In a more pointed example, the holy woman Margery Kempe of Lynn noted that a local Franciscan preached against her, 'not expressing her name, but explaining his opinions so that men understood well that he meant her'. The sermon was directed at Kempe because her attempts to behave as a mystic were causing tensions within her home town. It raises the possibility that sermons could include this kind of oblique but personal address. Another example comes from a sermon given by a Cathar 'Perfect' (one of the heresy's priests) addressing a small group including an inquisitorial spy called Arnaud Sicre, in whose evidence the event is recorded. The Perfect raised the matter of 'false prophets' mentioned in the Bible, interpreting these as those people who would betray Cathars to the inquisitors. And he added a particularly pointed gloss: 'O Arnaud, take care that you are not a false prophet!'[52] In these two very different contexts we see how sermons could play a part in the policing of a community.

What, then, of those people listening to these sermons? Gaining access to audiences is difficult. As with most things, our sources present partial and problematic accounts. Were the women listening to Henry at Le Mans so inflamed by his words that they stroked his feet, buttocks and groin; or was that a nasty bit of invention by the hostile chronicler? In thirteenth-century France, Stephen of Bourbon presents the opposite idealization, claiming that noble women donned the clothes of paupers in order to follow mendicant preachers around incognito, so desirous were they to hear their sermons.[53] Even in less extreme cases, whether positive or negative, the historical evidence more often gives us access to an idealized audience rather than a particular reaction. For example, many sermon collections from the late twelfth century onwards were divided into *ad status* ('to state [of life]') sermons: that is, different sermons written with particular social groups in mind. Thus Alain de Lille's twelfth-century *Art of Preaching* (reproduced throughout the Middle Ages) includes sermons to soldiers, to cloistered monks, to married folk, to widows and to virgins.[54] One can imagine that certain kinds of sin were more likely to beset some groups than others: adulterers, for example, must perforce be married. Alain's idea of audience is one divided partly by occupation and partly by a kind of social geography of sin. Whether a preacher would truly find audiences thus arranged is doubtful. Alain's division of female lay audiences corresponds neatly to the commonplace trinity of maiden, wife and widow, a map of womanhood drawn very much from a male, clerical perspective.[55] Thus the *ad status* divisions are notional rather than actual: they present sermon compilers' ideological pictures of society. Audience reactions, within these pictures, were either presented as dutifully contrite (the sermon having brought them to recognize their sins), or else misbehaving in a way that allowed the preacher to make a didactic point. Thus, for example, Jacques de Vitry records an *exemplum* of a preacher who promised absolution to members of each trade and asked them to stand up in turn as he blessed them. Last of all he asked 'the usurers' to stand up, thus shaming his audience, as none would stand up to admit it but all had done it.[56]

The *ad status* distinctions are not the only way in which preachers divided up their audience. Perhaps the most important notional division was between literate and non-literate: or rather, *litterati* and *illitterati*, which, as we have seen, indicated a particular gulf in learning, wisdom and comprehension. Alain de Lille argued against preaching scripture to the *illitterati*, because 'if it's dangerous for wise men and saints, it's extremely dangerous for the ignorant'. In the thirteenth century, Thomas de Cantimpré criticized overly intellectual preachers who 'perturbed' listeners by raising unnecessarily difficult theological questions. Domenico Cavalcanti, writing around 1333, condemned preachers who wanted to glorify themselves by failing to preach 'useful, necessary things' and instead talked of 'subtleties, new-fangled ideas and their own philosophies', which placed their simple lay audience 'in doubt and error'.[57] These examples perhaps illustrate concern about lay reactions to certain kinds of theological ideas, but the literate divide could also lead to more subtle thoughts about how audiences listened. Thomas of Chobham, a thirteenth-century theologian, argued that 'we should explain the truth by natural similitudes when we have to convince the infirm mind of something in sermons', implying (alongside intellectual arrogance) a technique for communicating more effectively. Humbert de Romans noted that 'people find exemplary anecdotes more moving than mere words; they are also easier to grasp and make a deeper impression on the memory, and many people find them more enjoyable to listen to, so that the sheer pleasure of them attracts some people to come to sermons'.[58] Thus *exempla* were seen as a useful tool for educating the *illitterati*, because they could be enjoyed as stories and because they were memorable. One might think here of the Lincolnshire tale of a man who preferred to go hunting rather than spend Sunday at mass with his more pious wife. He came across a devil in the shape of a giant hare and shot at him with his bow. The devil, however, disappeared and the arrow, rebounding, hit the man and pierced his clothing but not his skin. Shocked, he went penitently to church.[59] This is an easily memorable tale, with an obvious moral for the audience. Francesc Eiximenis (*c.*1327–1409), who wrote an *Art of Preaching* based on his experience in Spain, also thought about how audiences might be aided in remembering what they had heard. He, like others before him, emphasized that brevity was likely to get a point across better; keep it short, and keep it funny, as later advice would put it.[60]

But preachers also had to take care with *exempla* and other entertaining elements. Humbert de Romans advised that 'implausible stories should never be told' (a suggestion not always adopted in practice by his contemporaries) and that stories with some basis in fact were preferable. If the preacher was making up a story, he should make this clear to his audience. Alain de Lille said 'preaching should not contain jesting words or childish remarks' or overly poetic or rhythmical passages, as 'such preaching is theatrical and full of buffoonery, and in every way to be condemned'. We can presume that while some would follow Alain's advice, what he condemned was also practised – and hence that certain sermons were, essentially, entertainment. John Wyclif, the late medieval English reformer and heretic, indeed criticized the friars for preaching for money and for 'preaching to the people fables and falsehood to please them'. A thirteenth-century author commented that audiences would recommend skilful preachers to one another as a form of entertainment, but were slow to put their words actually into practice.[61]

More subtle thoughts on audience reaction, perhaps based upon long experience, can also be found. Alain de Lille describes 'playing' an audience:

> When the preacher sees that his hearers' minds are moved, and that they weep freely, and that their expressions are downcast, he should hold back a little – but not too much, for as Lucretius says, 'Nothing dries up faster than a tear.'[62]

His imagined audience here is still, perhaps, somewhat idealized (and somewhat monastic); but a later example seems rooted in direct experience and gives a sense of how preaching texts formed a network of shared stories and techniques. Robert of Basevorn (writing *c*.1320) explains that:

> The preacher . . . ought to attract the mind of the listeners . . . This can be done in many ways. One . . . is to place at the beginning something subtle and interesting, as some authentic marvel . . . [For example] one could adduce that marvel which Gerald [of Wales] narrates in his book . . . about the spring in Sicily [where] if anyone approaches it dressed in red clothing, immediately water gushes forth . . . Another way is to frighten them by some terrifying tale or example, in the way that Jacques de Vitry talks about someone who never willingly wanted to hear the word of God; finally when he died and was brought to the church . . . [the image of the crucified Christ] pulled His hands from the nails . . . and plugged His ears.[63]

Apart from emphasizing the utility of *exempla*, Robert's advice to fellow preachers indicates the different ways in which such tales could be used, and a set of expected audience reactions that are less idealized than the earlier examples we have seen. Some surviving sermons give another sense of how the preacher could tailor his work to his audience. Peregrin, a Dominican preacher active in late thirteenth-century Poland, compiled a popular collection of sermons of which some 350 manuscripts are still extant. His preaching addresses the lay audience very directly, establishing a sense of community between preacher and congregation. The sermons on marriage display particular nuances: at different points the men and the women of the congregation are addressed separately, there are moments of pretend dialogue, and Peregrin recounts personal thoughts rather than high theology. He relates the abstract ideal of marriage to specific problems that occur within the actual partnerships of his congregation.[64]

I have emphasized the imagined audience thus far, but other material perhaps gives us more direct evidence. We can certainly find evidence for the desired response to sermons. A witness at the canonization proceedings of Vincent Ferrer said of his preaching mission in Brittany in 1418–19 that Ferrer taught children the *Ave* in French and how to make the sign of the Cross, that people gained greater respect for Sundays (ceasing to hold markets then), and that 'a great number refrained from blasphemy, perjury, fornication and many other crimes that they were accustomed to commit' because of his efforts. Various late-medieval wills show people leaving money to support preaching, presumably indicating their enthusiasm for it. Margery Kempe noted in her autobiography that she had learnt about Scripture in sermons. A Pyrenean shepherd, Pierre Maury, knew from sermons that he should not take communion while in a state of sin, as 'one would do better to take a hot iron into his mouth'. Perhaps the most representative example of successful parochial preaching comes from the canonization proceedings of the Breton priest Yves of Kermartin. A witness said of his regular sermons, 'after he had begun to preach to the local people, they became twice as good as they had been before, as everybody said in the area'.[65] The sense of a communal appraisal – and its sweet vagueness over the community's moral improvement – is perhaps indicative of the ordinary state of affairs, whether or not the particular parish priest happened to become a saint.

However, we can also glean information about more problematic audiences. There are numerous references to people speaking and gossiping during sermons, and the excuses they made: 'Me must speke to hym that spekyth to me'! So common was this that a frequently repeated *exemplum* tells of devils who collected in sacks all the idle words that people spoke in church – the usual punchline being that they ran out of sacks. If not talking, the audience still might not be listening: a sermon by Jacques de Vitry says 'Do you want me now to talk to you about worthy womanhood? I'm going to say something instead about that old lady whom I see asleep over there. For God's sake, if anyone has a pin, let him wake her up!'[66] If awake, they might not stay there: Arnaud de Savinhan, in trouble with the inquisitor Jacques Fournier in 1319, tried to excuse his theological idiosyncrasies by explaining that on account of the demands of his trade (he was a stonemason), although he went to mass he never stayed for the sermon, and thus he was understandably confused about orthodox belief. Arnaud was far from alone in wandering off, and Caesarius of Arles used to shut the doors of the church after the Gospel reading to prevent people exiting prior to the sermon.[67] On occasion, audience absence might be reactive: when Bernard of Clairvaux (1091–1153) was preaching against heresy at Verfeil in 1145, he directed his sermon against the local nobility, who promptly left the church followed by the rest of the laity. Bernard pursued them and preached in the square; the nobility went into their houses. Bernard continued his sermon to the people still present, but those inside started beating their doors and making such noise that eventually the great Cistercian preacher gave up, and simply cursed the town. Less politically-fraught contexts could also affect audience attentiveness. An anonymous cleric from Béthune in the early sixteenth century noted that 'after Easter no one pays any more attention to [sermons] than to overripe herrings'.[68] Thus during Lent, in the lead-up to Easter confession and communion, people were keen to hear about sin and salvation; but once Christ's sacrifice had been re-enacted, there were better things to do.

The audience was far from passive; the laity made choices: about when to go, when to listen, who to listen to. In the early thirteenth century, we see a few people who went to listen to both Waldensian and Cathar heretics preaching, one man explaining that he wanted to see which were better. Among the small group of Cathars clinging on in early fourteenth-century Languedoc, the laity still made judgements about the quality of different preachers: '[Bélibaste] does not know how to preach', said one: 'When you hear Pierre and Jacques Autier preaching, it is a glory, and they know well how to preach.' Such decisions must doubtless also have been made about orthodox preachers. And sometimes the audience were very active, to the point of joining in. A friar in East Anglia, preaching the call to crusade, was interrupted by a member of the audience who had actually been to the Holy Land and who tried to dissuade his fellow parishioners from heeding the preacher's propaganda. Archbishop Stephen Langton, preaching at St Paul's Cross on Psalm 27 – 'In God hath my heart confided, and I have been helped; and my flesh hath flourished again' – was challenged by a member of the audience: 'By the death of God, you lie! Never has your heart confided in God, nor will your flesh flourish again!' There was a stunned silence, then the audience jumped on the unruly challenger. In Paris, a man scorned the message of mendicant friars, pointing out to the rest of the congregation that 'if [what they preached] were true, we will all be damned!'[69] Less aggressive interruptions are also recorded, with the audience asking for specific examples or further explanation of the preacher's theme.

Various historians have argued that medieval sermons constituted a form of 'mass communication', and even that the model sermons churned out from Paris, and recopied throughout Europe, provided a uniform message as strong as that later provided by print.[70] Some caution is needed here. It is true that preaching formed one of the main channels of communication between Church and people, and in that sense can be described as 'mass'. But parallels with print are problematic. While sermon collections could be reproduced in whole or part literally thousands of times, there is still a large gap between text and performance. Indeed, it is important to remember that preaching was *always* a performance, always in some sense 'theatrical'. It might not be a very good performance, it might have become dull from familiarity, it might alternatively set one aflame with enthusiasm – but it was always an oral communication between the preacher and the congregation, not the textual traces to which we now have access. As a performance, it was active, protean, liable to both disaster and success; and these factors were probably more sensitive to the quality of the preacher than the text. The cultural authority of print, in the sixteenth century and beyond, worked through very different mechanisms, less tied to an individual voice. Moreover, while preaching was undoubtedly the broadest method of medieval communication, the idea of 'mass media' tends to have, lurking behind it, certain assumptions about the passivity of the audience – that such media can 'programme' their beliefs. As we have seen, audiences were active things, active through laziness, absence and confusion as much as in their moments of enthusiasm and rapture.

Bernardino da Siena asked his Italian audience,

> What would become of this world, I mean of the Christian faith, if there were no preaching? . . . How ever should you have known what sin is, if not from preaching? What would you know of hell, if there were no preaching? What would you know of any good work, or how you should perform it, if not from preaching; or what would you know of the glories of heaven?[71]

Sermons were the most important conduit of doctrinal information between Church and laity. But let us take Bernardino's rhetorical questions at face value. How else did people know about the faith that claimed them?

Images

Our modern encounters with medieval art and architecture are misleading. We meet finely-wrought pieces in art galleries and museums, behind glass, arranged to illustrate the movement of technique through time. Walking through the nave of a medieval cathedral, we breathe in the hushed, cool space, and perhaps imagine a foreshadowing of heaven. Individual drawings from the margins of a thousand manuscripts are pinned out, like butterflies, on the covers of academic books, or animated by the television camera's lens, or printed onto tea-towels and souvenir bric-a-brac.

None of this captures a medieval experience of images, particularly not the experience of the general laity. They would rarely if ever have seen manuscript illustrations, because these textual images were the preserve of monastic and high secular culture. Most people would have seen only a few pictures regularly. They would probably not have compared, or even been aware of, different 'schools' of artistic endeavour, and the creation of images was understood in far different terms from our post-Renaissance sense of Art and Romantic ideas of 'the Artist'. Makers of images were, for the most part, engaged in artisanal labour rather than 'Art'. Medieval cathedrals and (more importantly, since most people would see the cathedral but infrequently) parish churches were not serenely whitewashed, but frequently alive with light, with colour and with sound. Moreover, many images in churches and elsewhere were not the skilled altarpieces and frescoes now beloved of modern audiences, but so-called 'primitive' art, depicted through much simpler techniques – but nonetheless powerful for their medieval viewers.[72]

For the vast majority of medieval people, it was here, in the parish church, that they most frequently met religious art. Two-dimensional images covered the walls, painted directly onto the plaster. The rood screen that separated the nave of the church (where the congregation sat) from the choir (where the priest made the Eucharist) would be similarly adorned. If the parish was wealthy, or contained a wealthy benefactor, there might be a stained-glass window. And three-dimensional art – carved wooden statues, also brightly painted, inside the church and stone relief outside the church – depicted Christ, Mary and the saints. In front of these statues, people lit candles, laid gifts; sometimes they touched them, for the good favour it brought. For most of the laity, then, the experience of art was largely public (or else a private moment snatched in the public space of the church), was cocooned within the collective liturgical rhythms of the year, and was clearly didactic in intent and interactive in experience. For a few rich people, a more private appreciation of art might pertain: small figures or (in the late fourteenth and fifteenth centuries) private altarpieces might be meditated upon within the home (and textual images also – the books of hours, which we will meet in the next section). But even these apparently private images were most likely understood and interpreted by their owners within a liturgical framework, as that annual cycle of ritual meaning did not end at the door of one's house.[73]

So what was the function of this art? How was it 'read' at the time? A sermon by Bishop Gerard of Arras-Cambrai (1013–48) states that 'the less educated and illiterate in the church, who cannot understand written biblical texts, form a mental impression of them through the painting's delineation'. Similarly, a twelfth-century English psalter says 'The picture is for simple men what writing is for those who can read, for those who cannot read see and learn from the picture the model which they should follow. Thus pictures are, above all, for the instruction of the people.' Later examples can also be found: Jean Gerson (1363–1429), in a letter accompanying his didactic *Threefold Work*, asks that 'this teaching is written in books and is made available in pictures . . . in public places such as parish churches, in schools, in hospitals, and in religious institutions'.[74] Thus one predominant ecclesiastical view (its origins in a much earlier letter written by Gregory the Great (d. 604)) was that art acted like a book for the *illitterati*, cut off as they were from texts and learning. However, as Lawrence Duggan has argued, it is difficult to see how visual images by themselves could allow the accumulation of new knowledge. A picture of a woman standing next to a wheel would not, in itself, communicate the story of St Katherine and her tortures. In fact, Gregory may not have meant that art could teach anything new, only that, like preaching, it could 'edify', or 'build up', the existing faith of the audience.[75] The basic aim of medieval religious art, then, was to remind its audience of what it had been told through preaching and other instruction. This was, in itself, a powerful tool. In the late-medieval English poem *Dives and Pauper* the poet 'reads' the symbols of a picture to remind his audience of the story behind them:

> Saint Katherine is painted with a wheel . . . in token of the horrible wheel which the tyrant Maxence ordained to rend her limb from limb. But the angel destroyed them, and slew many thousands of the heathen people, and so they did her no harm. She has a sword in the other hand in token that her head was smote off with a sword for Christ's sake.

The image acts as a powerful mnemonic device, triggering the recall of history and doctrine.[76] Indeed, what distinguished an orthodox relationship to images from idolatry was that the art should act upon one's memory, to summon up the subject depicted. As John Mirk explained to a lay audience, 'just as a man does worship to the king's seal, not for love of the seal, but for reverence of the man that owns it', so one worships the crucifix and other images, not for themselves, but for what they signify: Christ's sacrifice.[77]

But the comparison with books indicates also the cultural prejudices of literacy: the assumption that only the *litterati* were cognitively capable of forming adequate mental pictures of what they heard, whereas the illiterate laity would need external, concrete aid. For example, rebutting Lollard criticism of images, Mirk goes on to state that: 'there are many thousands of people that could not imagine in their hearts how Christ was crucified if they did not learn it by looking at sculpture and painting'.[78] In fact, the claim that the laity were unable to 'imagine' unaided was demonstrably untrue. As we shall see in later chapters, some lay people had their own mental images of, for example, the afterlife that were based upon what they had heard preached, but which nonetheless diverged from orthodox artistic depictions. Perhaps this was recognized by the Church: Bernardino da Siena's sermons refer repeatedly to the images that adorned the churches and public spaces of medieval Florence. The preacher sought thus not only to guide their immediate interpretation but to shape also their future reception.[79] We should note, therefore, that religious art was not simply an aid but a tool: an attempt to condition and influence the particular impressions made upon lay minds. Images were linked to power.

Some links between visual artefacts and power were quite direct, where buildings, paintings and objects announced the authority of particular people or institutions. One can think here of Norman churches stamping their lesser mark, alongside the muscular castles the conquerors built, in the post-1066 landscape of England. Or of mosques, captured and reconsecrated in thirteenth-century Spain and arrayed with images of the Virgin Mary (an act of idolatry for Muslims), symbolically proclaiming Christian domination over the 'Saracen' faith.[80] The great and imposing cathedrals – Reims, Chartres, Canterbury, York – sang out the power not only of God but also of those ecclesiastical and secular potentates associated with their construction and operation. As individual donors and patrons became increasingly visible in the art they commissioned – their figures appearing in altarpieces (the famous Wilton Diptych, showing a young Richard II facing the Virgin and Child, flanked by saints), stained-glass windows (Henry II and Eleanor of Aquitaine, at the foot of the Crucifixion, in Poitiers cathedral, *c.*1170), and frescoes (the wife of a wealthy donor being presented to the Virgin, *c.*1376, in Padua's cathedral) – the simultaneous function of religious art to display piety and prestige was made more visible.[81] An elite style of decor-ation that illustrated extreme piety developed around the thirteenth-century French monarchy, epitomized by the royal palace chapel of Sainte-Chapelle in Paris, built by Louis IX and consecrated in 1248. The chapel was made to look like a gigantic, jewel-encrusted reliquary (the ornate boxes in which saints' relics were stored), suitable to house the 'Crown of Thorns' Louis had acquired from the East.[82] The ability of the wealthy to sponsor the creation of art should not, in a medieval context, be understood as simply showing off wealth: it was, rather, a demonstration of the appropriate, pious way of spending money, as part of charitable duty rather than personal pleasure.[83] Nevertheless, it did also act as a demonstration of wealth and social status, and by linking oneself to particular images – a national saint, for example – that status could be further enhanced.[84] Such expenditure, on a much lesser scale, also pertained far down the social strata, as parishioners provided liturgical objects – chalices, candlesticks, crosses, and so forth – for their local church. This does not contradict the point about expenditure and social status, but rather reaffirms it: just as much as at higher levels, the finely graded socio-economic distinctions within the parish could be represented in such provisions.[85]

There were also, however, more subtle links between art and power than the display of economic hierarchy. One was to affirm orthodox belief in the face of threat. The façade of the church at Saint-Gilles in Provence depicts the Last Supper, the Crucifixion, and angels fighting dragons – all of which, it can be argued, was designed to counter the heretical ideas of Peter of Bruys, who was burnt there around 1133. The early fourteenth-century carvings on Orvieto cathedral have been seen as statements of joint civic, clerical and divine author-ity directed against Italian Cathars.[86] This was certainly the purpose of the various images placed in Italian churches and monasteries of St Peter Martyr, a Dominican inquisitor killed by Cathar supporters in 1252. These propaganda images could be contested: one onlooker, in 1311, said contemptuously that St Peter had not been martyred for the faith, but rather killed in a fight over a woman.[87]

Images certainly played a role not simply in reminding the laity of their faith but also in channelling their devotions. The broad move, across the high Middle Ages, from depicting Christ as King (and therefore, in some senses, transcendent) to Christ as suffering man (emphasizing his bodily nature), was doubtless con-nected with the increased emphasis upon the sacrament of the Eucharist and Christ's true presence in the Host.[88] The parish church itself would usually have a three-dimensional depiction of the Crucifixion, flanked by Mary and St John, above the rood screen that separated clergy from people: a simultaneous emphasis of Christ's humanity, Godhead, and the cleric's role as intermediary. The screen itself grew from a low and quite permeable structure in the eleventh century to something increasingly grand and opaque by the later Middle Ages. Beyond it, the priest would handle those precious items that the laity had paid for, such as the pyx (the store for sacramental wafers) and the chalice (for communion wine). Thus images and objects, and the way in which they were presented, could teach the more implicit elements of religion, such as the hierarchy between clergy and laity and the drama of sacramental theatre. Art was not always didactic directly through its visual content, and although one can link the subjects of wall paintings, for example, to medieval sermon stories, some historians have questioned whether a parish priest would really have referred to these images during preaching.[89] In certain churches the images were not easily visible to a lay audience. In Berry, a region of central France, of 19 churches only seven had any decoration in the nave, and only four on the wall that faced the congregation; 14, however, had decoration in the choir and apse, directly visible to the clergy alone. It has been argued that the narrative arrangement of the paintings – the particular combination of biblical figures they depict – emphasize the mediating role of the clergy between God and man. The laity in these churches would therefore not be able to see the visual details of the murals, but would be aware of their general message, and that the clergy were in a privileged position both spatially and spiritually. And they would be able to glimpse dimly Christ in majesty, in the distant apse. Thus the paintings in Berry – and hence perhaps elsewhere – carve up the space of the church, emphasizing the differences between the clergy and the laity. The clergy are presented as interpretive intermediaries, and as the bestowers of sacraments. Moreover, the character of visual depictions act to make a man-made narrative appear God-given. What is social and disputable is thus, through the medium of images, tacitly transformed into the divine and immutable order of things.[90]

All of this is, however, to make certain assumptions about how such art was read. Again, I have dealt thus far with the imagined audience. Modern art historians may not in fact be in the best position to try to reconstruct an average, lay response to medieval pictures because, although a medieval layperson might have had a wider scriptural frame of reference than a modern audience (though this is more assumed than proven), both the detailed deciphering and sensitive responses to art that modern critics undertake are rooted in their specialist training and personal sympathies. Michael Camille argues that 'when people at the end of the thirteenth century looked around them as they stood in the nave of Amiens cathedral, they were neither seeking to label architectural components, nor deciphering symbols. They were the enraptured witnesses to a new way of seeing.'[91] Perhaps. Certainly, unless they were craftsmen looking for employment, they probably did not stand there thinking 'that's an archivolt and that's a jamb' or 'what a lovely bit of tempera'. At the times when they were most likely to visit a cathedral – at Easter, on pilgrimage, as part of a procession, or while doing public penance – the context might well engender the kind of heightened, transcendent sensibility Camille evokes. Equally, however, if they lived in the cathedral town and it was therefore a familiar building, they might not take much in at all, other than a general sense of 'cathedral-ness'. Moreover cathedral-ness, as Camille and others have also pointed out, was not necessarily a positive, communal symbol but could also be riven by social tensions. It might, indeed, act as a reminder of the violent protests against the economic costs of such buildings, as had occurred in Amiens, Laon, Lincoln and Coventry in the thirteenth century, or of the occasions when disputes over jurisdictions and rights provoked citizens to assault the very fabric of the cathedrals themselves, as had been the case at Reims in 1233 and Norwich in 1272.[92] In any case, the kind of beauty and awe situated in cathedrals was the exception rather than the rule. For the vast majority of lay people, the kinds of religious images that more commonly surrounded them were much simpler: things like the sign of the cross, carved on bedsteads, cradles, doorways, even on loaves of bread. These simple icons of Christianity saturated the fabric of late-medieval everyday life, and were again reminders of activity – crossing oneself, for example – more than signs for veneration or contemplation.[93] Evidence from fifteenth-century wills shows a good degree of devotion to – or affection for – statues of saints found in parish churches, but with bequests often directed towards one *particular* saint or image, rather than the whole panoply of artistic representation.[94]

Can we get any closer, then, to lay responses to images? We are dependent, as is often the case, on passing references from a variety of sources. Some responses were, as intended, pedagogic. The fifteenth-century *Tale of Beryn* satirically depicts pilgrims visiting Canterbury Cathedral, and 'poring' over the stained-glass tableaux, attempting unsuccessfully to decipher the narratives they contained. Comedy aside, the problem must have seemed plausible to the *Tale's* audience. Moreover, it shows two interesting features about their expected reactions. One is their attempt – also unsuccessful – to work out the heraldry of the glass's donor, a reminder that religious iconography also conveyed social messages. The other is their desire to 'mourn' upon the story – that is, to use it as a focus for emotional, affective piety (albeit somewhat counterfeit, in the *Tale's* satire).[95] On other occasions, images appear to have engendered a particularly rapturous spiritual response: at Easter 1305, a 'terrifying cross', created by a German craftsman and costing the vast sum of £23, was placed in a London chapel, and people 'flocked in crowds' to see it. As various writers have suggested, this was probably a *Gabelkreuz* (fork cross, in a Y-shape, rather than the usual +), rendered 'horrible' either by its unusual design or its violently realistic depiction of the suffering Christ. It was, in any case, banned by the local bishop who thought that the 'undiscriminating populace' might 'imperil' their souls by worshipping it. As Paul Binski points out, the bishop probably also wanted to remove a rival to a great crucifix at St Paul's, the financial offerings to which went towards the cathedral.[96]

As is often the case, we catch our best glimpses of actual practice when someone is doing something wrong and thus gets reported. A thirteenth-century inquisitorial register records a woman saying to a neighbour while in church,

'Pray to the Almighty. Don't pray to the cross or other images because they are without value.' So, presumably, a normal thing to be doing in church was praying to the cross and the other images in the expectation of some benefit; as, indeed, the following attests:

> One morning, Priest Arlotto was walking through the church of Santo Spirito in Florence, and he saw a woman who was heaving deep sighs and saying her prayers devotedly before an image of Saint Nicholas of Tolentino. She had been praying and gesticulating in that manner for perhaps one whole hour and she seemed spellbound.
>
> Priest Arlotto went to her, seized her by the head, and turned her in the direction of an image of the crucified Christ that was nearby; and he said 'Can't you see, you foolish woman, that you are making a big mistake? Address your prayers to Him who is master and can help you better than his pupil.'[97]

This tale, of the pious Florentine priest Arlotto Mainardi (1396–1484), gives a slightly different inflection both to 'proper' and 'actual' practice: the former here emphasizing Christ's importance over local saints (although perhaps more basically asserting Arlotto's authority in correcting the old woman), the latter showing us a depth of piety when someone was petitioning an image.

Given that the function of the tale is outwardly didactic and inwardly hierarchical (Christ has dominion over saints in matters of intercession, priests have dominion over parishioners in matters of theological interpretation), it might also have expressed another common worry, and possible reality: that lay people confused the image with the saint. As a late-medieval English commentator put it, writing against images from a Wycliffite perspective, 'Some simple people believe that the images themselves perform the miracles, and that this image of the crucifix is Christ himself or the saint that the image is representing.' Pilgrims might stroke and kiss the statutes at shrines and 'mak[e] vows . . . to come next year again, as if [the statues] *were* Christ and our Lady'.[98] I shall examine attitudes to saints more closely in the next chapter; for now, one might note that such lay 'confusion' may not have been remarkable, given first, that certain decorative objects – reliquaries – did actually contain saints' body parts, and were thus supposed to impart their power or *virtus*; and second, that there were various orthodox *exempla* of statues that came to life. A popular tale tells, for example, that a Jew set a statue of St Nicholas to guard his goods, but he was nonetheless robbed. Furious, he physically beat the statue, demanding that Nicholas do something. The saint appeared before the robbers covered in blood and explained to them his predicament, prompting the return of the goods – and the conversion of the Jew to Christianity.[99] We saw earlier the story of the crucifix that covered its ears to a sinner's pleas. These are fictional tales, but they may have engendered the kind of lay response that bothered our Wycliffite writer. Alice Hignell of Newbury, questioned on suspicion of Lollardy in 1491, admitted that she had called people 'fools' who offered a candle (another usual practice) to the statue of St Leonard; and had further ridiculed them, and images, by saying that if she saw St Leonard blow out a candle then she would offer one to him.[100] Her taunts speak to her understanding that her neighbours saw the statues as, in some sense, animate.

Such fragmentary evidence remains either expressions of expectation or of failure. Here again we see a largely imagined audience and attempts to shape its responses. The laity's interaction with imagery was often a case not of 'reading' (and being theologically instructed) but of *doing*: giving gifts, lighting candles, praying before statues, and so forth. In these interactions the image was, at best, a conduit to the real object – the saint – and this will be discussed in the next chapter. One might argue that many of the 'heretical' rejections of images throughout the Middle Ages were driven as much by resentment at their disappointingly inanimate nature as by any theological point about idolatry. For example, from the peasant Leutard who 'seized and broke to bits the cross and image of the Saviour' in 970 to Alice Hignell who imagined having all the church's images in her backyard, 'having an axe in my hand to hew them to cook my meat and to make my pot boil', to indeed the iconoclastic spasms of the Reformation, the desire to shatter and burn was fuelled by anger at the images themselves as much as at the putatively idolatrous viewers.[101]

The images *may* sometimes also have worked, as every churchman from Gregory the Great onwards hoped they worked, by prompting and edifying lay people in a more reflective piety. When certain kinds of images (such as the 'cards figured and painted with images of the saints' sold by a pedlar in late fourteenth-century Bologna) were taken into the more private space of the home, perhaps they were used as objects for meditative religiosity.[102] The very occasional evidence we can find for lower-class bequests for the provision of paintings and statues suggest strands of affection for art – though often still tied up with aspects of social status such as guild membership and commemoration.[103] Undoubtedly the nexus of preaching, liturgy and imagery supported each other, and images formed an important part of the Church's acculturation of the laity. But we should note that real, as opposed to imagined, audiences did not always read or interpret in the way they were supposed to. Eudes de Chateauroux recalled how, as a boy, he had been unable to decipher a stained-glass window. A nearby layman had explained to him that it depicted the story of the Good Samaritan – and that the point of the tale was that lay people cared more for the poor than priests did. William Fornier told inquisitors in 1273 that he suspected his neighbour Bernard Demier of heresy. Why? Because William had seen Bernard in church, looking at the images of the saints. And Bernard had said 'it was today, just as in olden times, that the good men were persecuted by bad men', and that the Franciscans and Dominicans were those spoken of in the Gospels where it said 'Attend to false prophets'.[104] Thus, at one level, the images in Bernard's church did their designated work: they reminded him of the torments of the martyred saints and prompted him to think of the Bible. At another level, however, they backfired – because, for Bernard, it was the Cathar 'good men' that he associated with the saints, and the inquisitorial friars with their persecutors. Images can work in the service of power – but they are open to various readings.

Texts

There is a certain stereotype of the Middle Ages (a Protestant, Reformation stereotype in origin) that sees the Church as the sole owner and controller of religious texts, keeping the laity in a world of orality and ignorance. This stereotype contains a small grain of truth, I as argue below, but is for the most part unsustainable. Religious texts, including the Bible, were available to some members of the laity throughout the period. As we have already seen, 'literacy' had particular inflections of meaning in the Middle Ages, literacy in Latin above all else. However, a wealth of vernacular texts existed, not only on secular topics (such as romance literature and troubadour poetry) but also on religious themes, including vernacular translations of the Bible. Thus, in thinking about texts as a channel for religious instruction, we need to consider a number of different ways in which people might relate to books.

It is very nearly impossible to say what proportion of medieval people were literate, not least because defining what 'literacy' is causes various problems. For example, being able to read and being able to write are two different skills – and were treated as such in the medieval period. We might take the ability to sign one's name as an indication of literacy, and indeed this has been used by some historians as a suitable index. But a signature might be the only writing of which a person was capable, or might indicate a kind of functional literacy, directed toward the needs of business or law, that would not imply any facility with religious texts. With these large caveats, recent work on medieval literacy has tended to assert a greater degree of familiarity with texts than previous scholars had supposed, and if we are interested principally in those who might have owned, and read, religious books, we can sketch the broad outlines of an answer.[105] First, it changes over time: many more people read books, owned books, could afford and were accustomed to books in the fifteenth century than in the eleventh century. They could afford them because, with the increased use of paper during the thirteenth century, books became much cheaper. In the high Middle Ages, book ownership among the laity was essentially restricted to the nobility. By the late Middle Ages, both the nobility (by now a larger group) and the upper ranks of the urban mercantile bourgeoisie were commonly book owners. But there is also regional variation: in northern Italy, in Languedoc, in some other major northern cities and in Scandinavia, vernacular literacy rates, however reckoned, were high even by the thirteenth century, such that in some Italian cities the majority of the adult population may have been able both to read and to write in their vernacular tongue.[106] This is much less likely to have been the case in other parts of Europe. However, even the totally illiterate had access to some texts: during the Sunday sermon the priest mediated elements of written culture to the congregation, and one can catch sight of other instances where a literate reader allows a non-literate audience access to writing. Margery Kempe, for example, had religious works read to her by a priest. Certain heretical groups in the eleventh and twelfth centuries seem to have had a small number of literate people who read out a holy text to a larger, non-literate group.

Later dissenters did similarly: as William Wakeham confessed to the bishop of Salisbury in 1437, 'I, with other heretics and Lollards, was accustomed and used to hear in secret places, in nooks and corners, the reading of the Bible in English, and to this reading gave attendance by many years.'[107]

To which books, then, did lay people have access? Vernacular Bibles existed from the early Middle Ages, and were quite common by the fifteenth century. The merchant Waldes in the late twelfth century commissioned two priests to translate Scripture for him into the vernacular, and in about 1199 the bishop of Metz wrote to Pope Innocent III to tell him that a 'multitude' of lay men and women were meeting to study and preach to each other French translations of the Gospels, among other works.[108] We can see from a variety of thirteenth-century references that Cathar preachers in Languedoc had copies of the New Testament (or parts of it), and by the second half of that century some of these were in the vernacular.[109] These examples may appear to link vernacular Bibles with heresy, but this is not the case. The real link is to *enthusiasm*; Waldes, for example, wanted desperately to read the Gospels for himself because he was so inspired by what he had already heard. Plenty of orthodox examples exist: the so-called 'St Louis Bible', another French translation made between 1226 and 1239, was copied into over 100 manuscripts in the following century. Thirteenth-century Italian translations also existed, apparently without engendering any ecclesiastical disapproval.[110]

It appears to have been enthusiasm also that first spurred the development of a vernacular religious literature beyond Scripture itself. Female religious recluses – those who had taken a vow to remove themselves more fully from the world – appear to have formed the initial target readership for thirteenth- and fourteenth-century vernacular devotional works. These texts were written by male clerics to be instructional and inspirational to the women: small collections of the lives of female virgin martyrs, for example, or works such as the *Ancrene Wisse* that aimed to guide their spiritual life.[111] Further devotional, sometimes mystical, works followed such as Raymond Llull's *The Book of the Lover and the Beloved*, Thomas à Kempis's *The Imitation of Christ* and the anonymous *Cloud of Unknowing*. These texts, directed toward a particularly devout, contemplative, mystical – and therefore probably quite restricted – readership form one strand of vernacular literature. Another thread, aimed at a wider audience, developed in the wake of the pastoral reforms of the Fourth Lateran Council. In an effort to aid priests to fulfil their duties towards their flocks, various manuals were produced in or translated into vernacular languages. Although originally written for the clergy, these works slowly migrated to a lay audience. Thus collections of sermons can be found in lay hands by the late fourteenth and fifteenth centuries, presumably designed for reading at home, either to oneself or one's family. For example, a Sunday Gospel collection known as the 'Mirror' was translated into Middle English from a thirteenth-century Latin text. It invites, 'When ye have will for to read, draweth forth this book', indicating that the author expected a domestic context for its use. In 1357, Archbishop Pecham's constitutions (which we met earlier) were translated by a Yorkshire monk into English for clerical use, thus potentially rendering them directly available to a lay audience. Works on the vices and virtues, the nature of sin, or the liturgy of the mass became increasingly available in vernacular languages in the later Middle Ages. Indeed, a late-medieval English text comments that, 'There be so many books and treatises of vices and virtues and of diverse doctrines, that this short life shall rather have an end for any man, than he may manage to study them or read them.'[112]

These vernacular translations could sometimes slightly alter elements of theology, as they translated concepts as well as words. For example, the sin of sloth was understood, in academic thought, to be a state of mind, namely a 'boredom with good' as Thomas Aquinas defined it. Vernacular treatises, however, tended to focus on actions rather than thoughts – the failure to *do* certain things, such as attend mass – and hence 'sloth' shifted its meaning a little, such that it became more akin to laziness than ennui.[113] A final kind of text, one both instructional and devotional, became the most popular and common in late-medieval Europe: the book of hours. These texts, sometimes lavishly illustrated if created for a noble owner, were works of liturgy, containing prayers and services. A few early examples can be found in England from the thirteenth century, and by the fifteenth century they were extremely popular across Europe. Aristocratic houses often owned several, and less lavish books were found in merchant families and even, occasionally, in artisan households. When printing first began producing larger numbers of texts, books of hours were among the first best-sellers.[114]

These form the main lines of contact between laity and religious texts, but there are further elements. A number of secular texts could contain significant amounts of religious information or instruction: the thirteenth-century *Lancelot-Grail* romance cycle, for example, contains lengthy passages devoted to explaining to knights and kings what being a good Christian ruler involved, and encouraging devotion towards the Eucharist. In fact, Arthurian literature marks a process of change and development: whereas, for example, Chrétien de Troyes's twelfth-century *Conte du Graal* depicts the Grail as its central symbol, in Gerbert de Montreuil's thirteenth-century continuation to this romance, the Grail is replaced by the 'marvels' of confession, repentance and absolution. Vernacular literature, aimed primarily at the courtly elite and (by the later fourteenth century) upper bourgeoisie, could be a convenient vehicle for encouraging lay religiosity. We should not see it simply as a kind of clerical propaganda: Jean Gerson, chancellor of the University of Paris, in fact grumbled that 'the French passion for romances had accustomed people to all sorts of fabulous and superstitious beliefs'.[115] But the intertwining of religion and secular literature need not be as direct: the sophisticated works of Dante and Chaucer are, among many other things, concerned with faith. More prosaically, conduct books from the fifteenth century frame their secular concerns about living decently within a general framework of Christian piety, as one might well expect. All of these texts were produced within a Christian culture, and they embody and reproduce that culture even when not deliberately setting out to propagate it.

A late fifteenth-century English text, the *Myroure of Oure Ladye*, enjoins that 'when you read by yourself, without a teacher's assistance, you should not be too hasty and read too much at once. Rather, you should linger over the text, and sometimes read a passage over again twice or three times or even more often, until you understand its meaning clearly.' Just as much as 'literacy' had a particular medieval inflection, so too did 'reading'. The ideal of reading was to be literally 're-formed': by internalizing the written words (the biblical metaphor of 'eating' the book was sometimes used), the reader was changed. Their behaviour would change for the better, and their inner heart would change also; the text would *shape* them according to its pattern for a better way of life. As Hugh of St Victor (1097–1141) put it, our memories are moulded by the words and deeds of others 'like wax', and this in turn shapes our moral life.[116] That, at any rate, was the ideal.

But as the *Myroure* also makes clear, there was a difference between reading with a teacher's help, and reading on one's own. Reading alone, and silent reading, were fairly rare until the late Middle Ages. Far more common was reading conducted in a group, whether primarily for fun or for pedagogic purposes. As Joyce Coleman has pointed out, such 'aural' reading was not in any sense replaced by silent, individual reading: it remained an extremely popular way of enjoying texts into the early modern period – and, indeed, is still enjoyed by both children and adults today.[117] What the *Myroure*'s advice also betrays, though, is the concern that the reader should not 'get it wrong' in their engagement with the text. The medieval cultural divide of Latin and vernacular literacy had a further implication about cognition and comprehension: learned *litterati* were supposed to know things '*explicite et distincte*', meaning that they could explain and defend theological tenets to others. Those without learning were expected only to 'know' in a simple, unquestioning way.[118]

The difference underlines, once again, the construction of a cultural hierarchy between a clerical elite and a lay general populace; but its gently patronizing superiority has a darker shadow, in the fears that ecclesiastics sometimes held about the laity, texts and learning. I mentioned above a letter sent by the bishop of Metz to Innocent III in 1199, concerning lay people who were reading vernacular religious texts. The reason for the bishop sending the letter was that such a phenomenon bothered him deeply. Innocent, in fact, was quite happy with the existence of these vernacular Bibles (though not happy with the suggestion that the laity might be preaching, a job that was reserved strictly for clerics). As I have established, it is not true that the medieval Church kept the laity from all religious texts. It is fair to say, however, that lay access to texts could, in some circumstances, be a source of concern. Texts were powerful, symbolic, an embodiment of authority, law and wisdom. A famous story depicts St Dominic confronting Cathar heretics, and challenging them to place their holy texts upon a fire, with the Bible being similarly subjected to this trial by ordeal. The Cathars' books burnt, whereas Dominic's book leapt up from the flames.[119] The story thus encodes a wider battle between different scriptural interpretations (Cathar and Catholic) as a physical battle of books – and, indeed, suspect books could themselves be tried and burnt, much like human dissenters. To display control of a text – to act as the mediating reader to a wider audience, or to make claims about what a text authorized – could bring one into competition with the Church. Just a few decades after the Metz letter, the Church was banning scriptural translations in southern France, calling for any such books to be handed in for burning. In England, Archbishop Arundel issued directives in 1407 that banned Wycliffite translations of the Bible, and required licences for any further vernacular versions.[120] In both situations, fears over heresy and the struggle for religious authority had partly focused upon the meaning of texts, and the Church's ability to control the laity's relationship toward them. But ecclesiastical legislation did not always achieve its aims: as we have seen, French texts did circulate in Languedoc. Similarly, although only one licence for a vernacular Bible was issued after Arundel's Constitutions, over 250 fifteenth-century English manuscript Bibles existed, and their ownership was clearly not restricted to Wycliffite dissenters alone.[121]

Analysing outbreaks of heresy in the eleventh and twelfth centuries, Brian Stock has argued that there is an element of truth to the Church's fears: that the combination of texts and laity could foment dissenting groups. Stock's argument is subtle. He does not mean that by gaining access to new knowledge, lay people chose to challenge orthodoxy. His analysis is, rather, that religiously enthused sects, in the eleventh and twelfth centuries, tended to form around an individual or small collection of leaders who structured the behaviour of the group (and its sense that it was a group) on the basis of a text, usually the Gospels. The leader or leaders drew their symbolic authority from the fact that they were the mediators of the text to the rest of the group; thus it was the idea as much as the content of the central text that mattered. For example, a religious sect was discovered in Arras by the local bishop in 1025. The adherents explained that they were followers of a certain Italian called Gundulf, who had instructed them in the principles of the Gospels and enjoined them to practise these principles 'in word and deed'. But these beliefs included unorthodox elements: rejection of baptism, marriage, the Eucharist, confession and penance, and the belief that one should venerate only the martyrs and the apostles, and not any other saints. The group were conscious of the fact that they were different and set apart from the society around them, but were arguably not intending to challenge the Church. Their sense of group identity and authority was drawn from this *idea* of a legitimating text, made available to them by the charismatic Gundulf. Stock describes such groups as 'textual communities': around the nucleus of a charismatic and literate individual, a larger social group is formed, structured in their behaviour by the principles of the (mediated) text, structured in their social reality by the image of the text that binds them together.[122]

Others writers have taken this idea of a 'textual community' – a group formed around a book or books – and developed it into a wider, looser sense of how texts might bind readers together in certain ways. Felicity Riddy, discussing female book ownership and the gifting of books in late-medieval England, has found that groups of nuns and groups of devout gentlewomen 'not only over-lapped but were more or less indistinguishable' in their shared textual interests. The readership for books in the Middle Ages was very often a collective reader-ship, in both a literal and a more symbolic way. Just as monks had communal readings (at mealtimes, for example) in their monasteries, so aristocratic audi-ences would have vernacular literature read to them as a group. Joyce Coleman notes that such an event could produce 'a deep affirmation of the group's sense of self and togetherness . . . united in a feeling of sorrow or exhilaration'.[123] This is perhaps to imagine the strongest moments of textual community – the coming together to be uplifted by a particular work, feeling bonds between both text and audience. Other circumstances within which texts were read might posit a dif-ferent kind of community, one less simultaneous and more theoretical. For example, William Bryn, chaplain of St Stephen's church in Norwich, had the fol-lowing recorded in his 1477 will: 'Item, I give to the church of St Stephen my *Golden Legend* [a collection of saints' lives] to be kept in some desk in the choir for them that will read it and learn.' Keeping the book in the choir – an area of the church theoretically restricted to the clergy – probably indicates that Bryn intended a clerical audience, but the wide sense of potential parish readership he suggests is interesting. Some evidence appears to indicate more restricted circu-lation: a fifteenth-century English tract defending Bible translation asserts that 'Lords, ladies and other gentles have, and may lawfully have, in their chapels mass books and portable breviaries, bibles, and books of holiness and God's law to occupy them . . .' This refers to the private chapels that the late-medieval gentry sometimes owned, and seems to depict, alongside its defence of vernacu-lar theological literature, a much more private, domestic space for religious reading. The two overlap in the 1487 will of Sir Edmund Rede, who clearly had a very large library. He left numerous books, religious and secular, to various relatives, both male and female; and a breviary to the vill of Sandelfe 'to remain in the said vill whenever they happen to require it'. Wills occasionally show us books owned by non-nobles also, from the later fourteenth century onwards – for example, in 1348 Nichola Mockyngg, the wife of a fishmonger, left a missal and a portable breviary to her parish church – and these again present the pos-sibility of more domestic reading practices.[124]

These different contexts for reading invite further questions on how the audi-ence for a book interpreted what they read or heard. Clear evidence, as ever, is difficult to find. As literary critics have long argued, while texts encourage certain interpretations, their meanings are never fixed and the reader plays a key role in producing meaning. We might return again, here, to St Dominic's competition with the Cathars over whose texts would burn and whose float free of the fire. Dominic's book was the Bible; but in fact it is almost certain that the Cathar text would also have been biblical, most probably part of the New Testament. The same book had different meanings for Dominic and for his foes. In a less fraught example, we could think of how Margery Kempe related to the texts she had heard, particularly the lives of female mystics. One can argue that most late-medieval religious works addressed women in ways designed to constrain them

religiously and socially – to make them compliant and docile, chiefly by emphasizing the inherently sinful nature of woman and her need for guidance and
instruction within a male-ordered social hierarchy. In Kempe's case, however, the
stories of female spiritual experience that she heard inspired her to quite radical
action: leaving her husband, going on pilgrimage, doing her best to 'spread the
word' while just keeping herself from being accused of preaching (a task usually
forbidden to women), and of course eventually producing her own spiritual
autobiography.[125] Readings could diverge from the explicit meaning of a text in
less challenging ways also. One interesting sub-genre of religious literature is pilgrimage guides, particularly those relating to the Holy Land. On the face of it,
these appear to act as guidebooks for fellow pilgrims, but their more common
use was probably a textual substitute for undertaking actual travel.[126] Thus a different kind of 'textual community' is formed – a loose, notional link between
those who had really gone to Jerusalem and those who had travelled there in their
imaginations.

The most precious evidence for how lay people responded to books is provided by the rare moments when lay people produced texts themselves. There
are two fascinating fifteenth-century examples of this, both notebooks or 'commonplace' books. One was compiled by an unknown bourgeois of Frankfurt
between about 1470 and 1482, the other in the 1470s by Robert Reynes,
a reeve (overseer) of the village and manor of Acle in Norfolk.[127] In both cases,
the men had apparently written down what was of particular interest to them:
prayers, extracts from sermons they had heard, snippets of history, medical
cures, charms, and so forth. Both men, interestingly, use a mixture of Latin and
vernacular. In both cases, there are a few elements that appear to have been
copied from other books, namely saints' lives. This would suggest that both
Reynes and the unknown Frankfurtian had access to a wider library of material, presumably borrowed for the purposes of copying from another reader –
perhaps the parish priest, or perhaps a wealthier or more bookish neighbour
or relative. So we can see, in both a civic and a rural context, non-noble (albeit
fairly wealthy) laymen having some kind of access to texts, and being sufficiently educated and familiar with literacy that they wished to create their own
texts for their own use. But what is also notable is how much of what the two
authors record is more oral than literary: many extracts from sermons, many
exempla, many poems and mnemonic devices and ditties and sayings. Despite
their desire to make written notes of things of interest and importance, the
sources that surround the two men are perhaps more things heard and seen
than things read.

This may give us the best picture of the place of religious literature in the lives
of the medieval laity. It had a greater presence by the fifteenth century than in
earlier times, particularly among the upper reaches of society, but by this stage
also within reach of civic bourgeois and rural officials. It played a greater role
than older historiographical pictures of a purely oral and illiterate Middle Ages
would suggest. But it was still, however, much *less* important for the majority of
people – even those able to read and write – than the sermons they heard, the

poems they knew, the sayings they remembered. One of the verses recorded in Reynes's book reflects upon the priorities here. A knight was sent to school:

> He was put to the books to learn to spell and read
> His ABCs, the Our Father, Hail Mary, and his Creed.
> But when the Hail Mary was his lesson,
> He would learn nothing else for any reason,
> But Hail Mary always in his mind he kept,
> And said it with his mouth, except when he slept.
> And so these words Hail Mary he never forgot,
> No matter where he went, no matter what he wrought.[128]

So firmly does this prayer entrench itself in the knight's mind that when he died a lily grew on his grave, 'And on every leaf was written Hail Mary'. Thus the bestowal of grace after death permits his spoken prayer finally to become writing. Oral prayers and literate text intertwine in the theme of the poem, just as much as they do in the evidence itself – a written version of an oral performance. There is, however, a clear hierarchy: literacy is the desirable aim, but available only to the few; oral memorization is the suitable, and admittedly powerful, tool for lay illiterates. But, considering this poem's presence in a commonplace book written for his own interest by a layman, we might also remember that, as we have seen, every element of teaching, preaching, writing, art and so forth is *interpreted* by the lay audience – and sometimes taken in different ways from those intended by the Church.

Other mechanisms

In this chapter, like a mendicant friar using multiple *exempla* to repeat a core message, I have made constant refrain to two themes, in various different contexts: the importance of activity and practice, as much as reflection and comprehension, in lay religion; and the possibilities of lay interpretation of the ecclesiastical message of sin, salvation and obedience. These two elements are brought together in a further mode of communication: religious drama.

Plays on religious themes appear to have arisen in the tenth century (and perhaps earlier), and were initially performed by members of the clergy. Given that the medieval liturgy of the mass was itself quite dramatic, drawing a clear line between clerical ritual and what we might call theatre is difficult.[129] In the twelfth century we find plays that, while still closely linked to the liturgy, may have been performed outside the actual space of the church, as part of the wider festal celebrations. Once again, these events may not have been seen in quite the way that we understand drama. For example, Philippe de Mézières's *Feast of the Presentation of the Blessed Virgin Mary* (1372), which looks to modern eyes very much like a full-scale play, was described by its author as 'a certain solemn celebration with various representations adorned with most devout speeches, new actions and signs'.[130] Towards the end of the fourteenth century we find in

England the large-scale civic drama commonly known as mystery plays or the Corpus Christi cycle. These famous pieces of liturgical theatre enacted biblical scenes (often adapted very freely from their source), and covered events from the entire span of sacred time, from Lucifer's fall to the Day of Judgement. They would usually be performed at the Feast of Corpus Christi, a movable feast that signalled the end of the Easter cycle of fast and celebration. Large-scale drama, independent of the Church, also existed in other parts of Europe, though not in quite the cyclical form of English craft plays.

All such plays clearly had instructional potential. For example, a missionary bishop in Livonia noted in 1204 that 'a most well-organised *Play of the Prophets* was performed in the centre of Riga, so that the heathen might also learn the rudiments of the Christian faith through the evidence of their own eyes'.[131] Seeing any part of the life of Christ enacted in the church or in the marketplace would have surely formed a nexus of doctrinal communication with preaching and medieval art; although, as with those media, questions of audience interpretation are important. Drama, just like preaching, is a performance; any surviving text shows us only the skeleton of a play, and it is impossible to say how each individual production put flesh upon those bones. In the high Middle Ages, when ecclesiastical authorities took a role in the organization of plays, one may assume a fairly strong correlation between their message and other modes of acculturation. Late-medieval drama was more commonly under civic control, however, and it can be argued that this fostered a more unstable dramatic culture that could express critiques of authority and more unconventional pious enthusiasms, alongside doctrinal orthodoxy.[132] However, for several reasons, reference to drama in this chapter is brief. There is simply not that much of it until the late Middle Ages: prior to the fourteenth century, less than a dozen vernacular plays survive.[133] Moreover, when the genre, or the surviving evidence, expands in the later fourteenth century, what we see is primarily (though not exclusively) an urban phenomenon which, though important, does not have the universality of preaching or images. More positively, as a third reason, civic drama is as much to do with guilds and the performance of community as with the performance of doctrine. We will therefore meet it again, in this guise, in Chapter 4.

By the late Middle Ages, religious plays were usually performed by the laity. This fact is a useful reminder of the permeability of the division between clergy and laity that is both evoked and interrogated by this book. With preaching, we can talk of 'the clergy' speaking to 'the laity', and can be confident that, apart from certain heretical instances, the boundary lines were firmly drawn, and the imagined mechanism of doctrinal instruction built into a clear hierarchy of authority. With images and texts the relationship is less clearly marked, but implicit nevertheless. It might thus appear that it was primarily through these media that the laity were acculturated (in the sense discussed at the start of this chapter) into medieval Christianity. But such a conclusion does not tell the whole story. It ignores the most important – but frustratingly opaque – mechanism for the transmission of culture.

'Are you ignorant of the Creed? . . . Have you been negligent in teaching to your godchildren the Creed and *Pater noster*?' These were questions posed by Cadwgan, bishop of Bangor, in the confessor's manual he wrote in the 1230s. John of Bromyard, author of an influential fourteenth-century preaching manual, admonished laymen to repeat the sermon that they heard in church to those members of the household who had been unable to come to church. Various statutes from thirteenth-century church councils indicate that it was the responsibility of parents to bring their children to church on Sunday, and their aid in religiously instructing their children was thus implied. Reginald Pecock's *The Donet* (*c*.1443–9) enjoined parents to teach their children 'our belief and God's law'. In fifteenth-century Spain, Fernando del Pulgar wrote a letter trying to persuade inquisitors to act less harshly toward those deficient in faith, on the grounds that 'there are in Andalusia ten thousand girls, between ten and twenty years of age, who, from birth, have never left their homes and have never heard or learned any doctrine save that which they have seen their parents perform inside their homes'.[134] This is the missing mechanism: the domestic pedagogy of the household, and the local community around it. St Paul's letter to the Corinthians asserted that 'The unbelieving husband is sanctified through his believing wife' (I Cor. 7: 14), and the power of the household to educate people into the faith remained strong throughout the Middle Ages. It is visible in unorthodox contexts, too. In southern France and northern Italy, families were understood by inquisitors to have a key role in fostering and transmitting heresy, as we will see further in Chapter 6. Michael Clanchy has argued that the increasing use of liturgical books within the household 'was the foundation on which the growing literacy of the later middle ages was built', emphasizing the role that aristocratic and upper bourgeois women played in using books of hours to educate their children; and, interestingly, other historians have found evidence that such books were more frequently handed on through the female line in a family.[135] The faith of the family was not destiny: one finds many examples of people who diverged from their background. Nevertheless, the household was the most important site in which people entered the Christian community.

But this is not to suggest that every mother taught her child the Creed, the prayers, the virtues and vices, and so on. As we have seen, there is good evidence for thinking that this was not so. The acculturation of which I speak here is not indoctrination into a specific programme of theological dogma. It is, rather, the entry into the wider realm of symbols, narratives and practices that are largely shared across the breadth of medieval Christianity, orthodox and heterodox. A conservative modern viewpoint tends to recuperate this process into a super-ficially ecumenical view – that medieval Christianity was a broad church – while simultaneously coding certain elements of this culture 'conformity' and ignoring or rejecting what does not seem otherwise to fit. But this position misses the great variety of medieval belief and practice, a heterogeneity born precisely from its local and domestic cultivation. And it fails to see – as we *have* seen in this chapter – the potential for dissent, confusion and argument that is engendered *within* acculturation, as each specific narrative, practice or element of doctrine is received and considered by its lay audience. What is learnt in the household, at the mother's knee, is probably never forgotten. But that does not mean that it is never discussed or questioned. We opened this chapter with a conversation, Raymond de Laburat arguing with his parish priest. This is just one small whisper, a zephyr carrying the gentlest murmur, of a far larger discussion conducted in the houses, marketplaces and fields of medieval Christendom.

3

Intercession

Early in February 1270, in the north Italian city of Ferrara, Domenico de Capodistria sat chained up in a prison cell. He had been accused of the crime of murder – falsely accused, he later told the local bishop's officials – and was awaiting execution. While he was sitting there,

> a man, formerly blind, came into the city square singing out about certain miracles which were ascribed to the blessed Armanno, near the palace where he [Domenico] was imprisoned, to which [preaching] the people of the area came running from all directions. And Domenico, seeing and hearing this through a certain window, imme- diately vowed to God and to the blessed Virgin Mary that if he could be freed from this danger by merit of the blessed Armanno, he would fast for all of that week and visit the grave of the blessed Armanno. And thus fasting and praying that night before the day when he was to be executed, whilst praying greatly through fear of death, he began to sleep in such a way as if half asleep. And then it seemed to him that a certain pale and lean man came to him saying these words: 'Get up and leave this place', and immediately he awakened and found himself in the city square without the shackles which had held him in prison, without the aid of any other person.[1]

The bishop was interested in Domenico's testimony because what had occurred was clearly a miracle: an act of intercession for this poor (but wrongfully arrested) sinner, enacted through the power of God contrary to the normal course of nature, facilitated by appeal to an intermediary figure – the late Armanno Punzilupo of Ferrara – who appeared to have become a saint.

Domenico's intercessor aided other people also. A woman called Adelasia swore that she had 'bad and painful eyes' and difficulty in seeing, such that if she wished to see the Eucharist when it was elevated during mass she had to raise her eyelids with her fingers. However, she had knelt before Armanno's grave and kissed the ground and prayed there – and her eyes and her sight had improved. Quite a while later, in 1280, another woman, Bonaventura, told of how she had been possessed by nine evil spirits since the previous Easter. They had shook her and struck her 'and made her speak foully and shamefully', and she could not sleep or eat – until her father and her husband took her to Punzilupo's grave, and she was cured.[2] Prompted by the enthusiastic cathedral canons in Ferrara, many other people attested to Armanno's posthumous powers, most of the miracles being cures for various kinds of ill health.

All of this was, in a sense, far from extraordinary. A major role for saints across medieval Christendom was to intercede, to step in as a powerful protector on the petitioner's behalf, saving them from illness, protecting them from evil spirits, undoing the harsh turns that fate had set against them. This is not to suggest that for Domenico or Adelasia or Bonaventura the experience of God's grace rendered through Punzilupo was other than miraculous, wonderful, and a very special favour gratefully received. But it is to note that these petitioners had certain expectations, drawn from the culture in which they lived, that led them to make their pleas for help. They had, in their troubles, at least some sense that intercession might be, if not expected, then at least possible. This wider cultural context – the shared belief in intercessors and their powers – also shaped the ways in which those petitions were made; or, rather, the ways in which they were relayed to the ecclesiastical officials who wrote them down. Domenico prayed to God and Mary, from whom the power originated; promised pious acts in recompense (fasting and visiting Armanno's grave); and emphasized that his escape was unaided by any other person (thus asserting it as a miracle rather than just the saint adding luck to a common-or-garden jailbreak). Adelasia and Bonaventura not only visited Armanno's grave but touched it, which was a very common tactic for those suffering physical infirmity.

In this chapter we are going to meet three interlinked medieval phenomena: saints, holiness and intercession. In each case, I shall try to draw out the variety and complexity hidden behind each of those terms. Saints, as we shall see, came in several different guises and were situated in a number of different contexts. Intercession prompts thoughts about the range of problems for which medieval people begged aid, from things quite familiar to us today (healing physical illness), to the more unusual (freedom from prison) and the highly unfamiliar (possession by demons). Looking at how these and other threats were faced, I shall also argue that the routes by which one might seek aid were varied – and did not all lead in the direction that the Church wished. First, however, we need to think more about holiness itself. We must do this not in the manner of the medieval witnesses we have just met – attesting to holiness, providing proof of its presence, assessing its quantity – but as historians. This means thinking not only about the cultural context of holiness (the ways in which it was described, symbolized, understood) but also the social workings of holiness: how it functioned, the roles it played, the structures it inhabited, and how these elements may have changed over time.

Being holy

There are few things more persuasive than dying for one's faith. Given that Christianity has always frowned upon suicide, such a sacrifice also requires the presence of someone else prepared to put one to death. In the early centuries of the Christian Church, the Roman authorities (among others) were happy to oblige. Thus, the vast majority of early saints were martyrs. These brave souls – huge in number, if we include each of the unnamed 'eleven thousand virgins' who were killed by the Huns for being too successful at making converts to Christianity – frequently died after torture or the threat of torture. In later times, their torments functioned as mnemonic devices, easily depicted visually to recall the specific saint and their experiences: St Katherine and the wheel with which she was threatened; St Sebastian and the arrows that pierced him; St Margaret and the dragon that swallowed her. The tortures were key elements to these stories, but whereas in the later Middle Ages the point was often taken to be the patient acceptance of bodily torment, for early audiences – and some medieval ones – it was more often a case of demonstrating God's power to protect one from suffering. Thus Katherine's wheel was shattered into a thousand pieces (in some versions flaying her tormentors) *before* she was broken upon it, and thus Margaret emerged safely from the dragon unharmed.

There are various key ideas attached to these early saints – a commitment to virginity for both women and men, or a learned eloquence in defence of their religion – but the overall message was the strength of Christianity. This strength came from God (a singular God, triumphing over all the little gods of the Romans and the pagans) but manifested itself through particular individuals. And thus (here the message, now and forever after, became a little blurred) the individuals were powerful also. While alive, the holy men and women were often known as 'Friends of God'. The concept of 'friendship' here implies a formal and structured relationship. Through lengthy ascetic practice, a few extraordinary individuals had brought themselves close to God, such that they could act as a conduit for the prayers and entreaties of the wider, more sinful community. These late antique and early medieval holy people were important both in terms of providing access to divine powers – healing sickness, protecting crops, cursing enemies, prophesying the future – and also in more human terms, as they negotiated on behalf of their flock with secular powers. The holy man was, in his idealization at least, the epitome of the 'good patron': someone who interceded on behalf of the poor and the weak with those forces – God, emperor, fate, nature – that usually ruled their lives with casual harshness. It may well be that the practice, dimly glimpsed through the carefully framed propaganda of posthumous hagiography, may not have always held up to these high standards. Material wealth donated by secular powers tended to accumulate around these extraordinary individuals, and the gravitational pull of the status quo must have affected their ability to act quite as the ideal model would have it. But when that happened, it was the specific individual that was at fault, not the model itself: one had to look to someone more ascetic, more removed from the secular world, and hence more holy.[3]

The greatest guarantor of continued holiness was therefore death: having died, nothing could stain the garb of purity. And so the powers of intercession persisted, and indeed increased, after death. As Christianity became an established religion and the threat of persecution faded, these powerful individuals continued their work of attesting, through their holiness, the efficacy of their faith. But they also became players in the more complex world of early medieval politics. At the geographical borders (mainly north and east) of Christendom the world could still be crudely divided into Christian and pagan, the latter both enemy and potential convert. For the most part, however, the threats were within Christendom, between the different, competing warlords and kings who carved up the landscape of western Europe. Here, saints became protectors, of both communities and individuals, and protectors to be ranked in a certain sense alongside other protectors: they were powerful lords, deployed against other powerful lords, for the benefit of the local community.[4] Unsurprisingly, those who became saints in this period were overwhelmingly those who had been protectors in life, namely princes and bishops. A further change accompanied this pattern. Whereas in the early centuries after Christ there was a strong balance between living holy people and dead holy people, the emphasis was now shifting. The highest form of holiness – the ability to intercede with God – was increasingly being discovered in powerful individuals only *after* death. Relics (pieces of dead men and women) became far more popular and important. The bones of the holy dead not only retained their power but seemed to magnify it; and these relics were so important, so desirable, that they were not only traded but often stolen, as one community attempted to appropriate the power of a saint from another. This practice continued into the high Middle Ages. Bishop Hugh of Lincoln (d. 1200), while visiting Fécamp Abbey in France where relics of Mary Magdalen were stored, much to the displeasure of his hosts chewed off a piece of her arm in order to bring it home. He was only one among a number of pious cannibals.[5] Note that the relics moved from one ecclesiastical site to another: the ordinary laity had access to the intercessory power only through the mediation of monks and clergy. This was a different form of interaction with the divine from that promised by the earlier holy men and women. It has rightly been described as an 'institutionalization' of piety – although, as we will see, this does not cover all the tactics taken by the laity in their search for intercessors.[6]

Turning to the high and later Middle Ages, we must remember that the extant saints were still predominantly made up of these early martyrs and powerful figures, forged in the fire of the early Church and the harsher world it inhabited. How were people to relate to those early heroes? Should they attempt to continue the same tradition, albeit in a changed world, or see them as testament to a different time and place? The choices made affected the productions of holiness in the eleventh to fifteenth centuries. Saints continued to be created, though in far fewer numbers, and the elements that went into making a holy person – and then a saint – were part of a long history. It is possible to outline some broad, shared elements to sainthood across the span of the later Middle Ages. There was always, for example, a complex relationship between diffuse lay enthusiasm and papal authority. Saints were undoubtedly popular, and in the high Middle Ages the Church put effort into promoting individual saints and promoting papal involvement in confirming their ultimate sanctity. Formerly it was the episcopate who declared the sanctity of the holy dead in their locality. In the twelfth century, the papacy began to assert its authority over such declarations, as part of a wider efforts to extend papal power. Gregory IX enshrined this privilege in canon law in 1234, and formal methods for investigating and canonizing a saint developed during the thirteenth century. For a saint (*sanctus*) to be a saint, he or she had to undergo a kind of posthumous inquisition, where evidence from witnesses was initially gathered locally and submitted to the papal curia, and if found sufficiently persuasive, a deeper investigation then was authorized. The evidence from this second enquiry would be weighed and sifted, and eventually papal judgement passed on whether or not the candidate had qualified. The witnesses we met above, attesting to Armanno Punzilupo's miracles, were part of a preliminary investigation aimed at prompting formal proceedings. The whole process quickly became both lengthy and expensive for the locality promoting a potential saint. Only 33 people were canonized between 1198 and 1431, and another 38 reached papal investigations were but were unsuccessful. However, the category of 'blessed' (*beatus*) became recognized as meaning someone not papally canonized but acceptably worshipped as a saint nevertheless. Furthermore, there were many more popular saints, 'local' saints or *beati*, who remained unrecognized but tolerated – usually – by the papacy and the episcopacy.

Let us look a little more closely at how someone became a saint (in the broadest sense) in the high Middle Ages. Armanno had died on 16 December 1269, and miracles seem to have started soon afterwards. Before his death, though not a priest or monk or apparently in any kind of ecclesiastical orders, he was known as a good man, a pious man – perhaps even a holy man. Rainerio, a chaplain in Ferrara, told of how for two years before his death Armanno had frequently come to him to make confession, 'and he devoutly and reverently presented himself to me on bended knee, just as a man who looks very sad and contrite for his sins'. As various people noted, he used to go around Ferrara collecting bread and alms to give to prisoners. Giving comfort to those in prison was one of the seven works of mercy, as noted in the last chapter, and it may have been Armanno's association with this activity that encouraged the imprisoned Domenico to pray to him for assistance. And, as the opening statement to the dossier of evidence supporting his sanctity asserts, Armanno was 'faithful and chaste, humble, submissive, compassionate, kind-hearted and simple, of truly dove-like simplicity'.[7]

There were various ways in which one could become a saint (in the loose sense, including local saints and *beati*). One could live an unusually holy life in the service of the Church, like the great preacher Bernard of Clairvaux. Very occasionally one might get martyred, as Thomas Becket famously was. Or one might meet some other death that garnered public sympathy, such as dying while upon pilgrimage. Or, increasingly, one could live an exemplary life and thus provide something of a model for others, for example, Omobono of Cremona (d. 1197), a layman canonized by Innocent III as an encouragement to the laity, although his cult only gained popularity many decades later. This is perhaps where Armanno, as presented in the evidence we have seen, fits into the wider picture: he embodied pious practices of good living – sexual continence, social charity, spiritual obedience – that the Church wished to encourage the laity towards. And there was, in fact, a rise in the number of lay people canonized from St Omobono onwards, with an accompanying rise in the proportion of laywomen among them, such that some historians have talked of a 'feminization' of sanctity in the later Middle Ages – although one should be wary of placing too much emphasis on what are quite small numbers of saints.[8]

One can trace a broad change over time in these paths to sanctity: in the early Middle Ages, as we have seen, the saints were almost all powerful men, extending their protection from the next life. Their holiness had consisted of rendering good service in their allotted roles, and demonstrating very great virtue, usually understood as manifesting itself by giving service, wealth or protection to the Church. Their sanctity was more often a fact discovered after their death than an obvious element of their life. From the late eleventh century on, however, new enthusiasms in holiness and sanctity appeared: potential saints, on the whole, embodied penitence in their mode of life, embraced poverty and lived humbly.[9] The shift was broadly paralleled by an accompanying change in the image of Christ: from Christ the King, a ruler in majesty, as the early Middle Ages had it, to Christ the man, suffering in expiation, preferred by the later Middle Ages. This broad change could perhaps be linked to changed socio-economic factors: as Western European society expanded, urbanized and increased in wealth during the twelfth and thirteenth centuries, the ideal of sanctity moved from that of powerful protector to something more delicate. The sociologist Emile Durkheim argued that religious asceticism was the symbolic form of a wider essential element to a more complex society: the ability to organize society depended upon self-restraint and the acceptance of individual sacrifice.[10] This is an interesting theory, but depends upon seeing asceticism as something embraced across the social spectrum. In fact, it would appear that medieval urban societies usually had a few particular figures who conducted ascetic practices for the benefit of the wider community. An increase in material stability allowed one to appreciate better the penitential suffering of the holy few; and the drama of their suffering could act to mitigate the increasingly complex hierarchies of wealth, status and power that urbanization provokes. Thus a pious mendicant is a useful figure, helping to make relative the quotidian suffering of the involuntary poor.

One might also see a tendency for sanctity to differ between northern and southern Europe. In the north, cults continued to form around bishops, kings or other leaders in the later Middle Ages, with a greater tendency for clerical or social elites to present the populace with a holy person for their veneration. The sanctity of these saints was revealed after death, and a northern saint was essentially a dead body that did miracles. Where we find more ascetic saints, often female, they were intimately connected with royal power: Elizabeth of Hungary

(d. 1231), for example, was Landgravina of Thuringia, and despite being piously impoverished (she was disinherited by her brother-in-law) her posthumous canonization had strong support from various European princes. Hedwig of Silesia and Margaret of Hungary were similarly bolstered by royal supporters.[11] In the south, and particularly in Italy, a saint often came from more modest social origins such as an artisan or merchant, had lived an ascetic life of penitence and renunciation, and their posthumous sanctity was in a way an extension of their lived holiness.[12] Epitomizing this group was St Omobono, mentioned above; and one could also see the more famous St Francis, who started life as the son of a merchant, in this way.

So how did this renewed link between lived holiness and posthumous sanctity now operate? The latter could be seen to act as a retrospective guarantee of the former, not just for the individual but also for those who lived similarly. When, for example, the Franciscan friar Thomas of Pavia wrote a *Dialogue on the Deeds of the Saints of the Friars Minor* in the 1240s, he was not simply creating a gentle work of memorialization, but a useful and quite pressing piece of propaganda. The Franciscans had been granted papal recognition only in 1209, and their way of life was still criticized by many. Producing and publicizing Franciscan saints was an effective way of bolstering their brand of holiness.[13] There was more than one way of living a holy life, and the mechanisms of holiness also had a history. In the early Middle Ages, the holy withdrew from society, retreating into the desert and the wild places. At least, that was the idea. There is an extraordinary seventh-century monastic settlement off the south-west coast of Ireland on an inhospitable island known as the Skelligs: domed beehive-like buildings huddle precariously upon sharp knuckles of rock that thrust up from the sea bed. This appears to embody the most extreme form of withdrawal.[14] But for survival, even these hardy monks necessarily kept close contacts with the mainland; and through the geographical drama of their home, theirs was a very *public* withdrawal, a visible reminder to those ashore of their piety. The pattern repeats itself many times. In the early Middle Ages, through gifts from secular patrons, monasteries became and remained huge landowners and there was a cycle of economic expansion followed by spiritual reform. In the eleventh and twelfth centuries, a variety of new styles of monasticism developed, all centred on a reforming notion of eremitical withdrawal; but again a 'withdrawal' that was fairly notional and symbolic, and which in any case was quickly swamped with wealth and secular connections as soon as it found success.[15] In the thirteenth and fourteenth centuries, a few extremely devout women desired to follow the example of the early desert Fathers, but finding themselves in highly urban environments had to improvise by contemplating desert images, imagining the desert as an internal space, or like the widowed noblewoman Umiliana de' Cerchi in 1241 claiming the tower of the family *palazzo* 'as her own private desert retreat'.[16] This creation of a private space of withdrawal is epitomized by the anchorites and anchoresses, such as Julian of Norwich, who walled themselves up in cells (usually attached to a church) in an effort to become 'dead to the world'. But even these great feats of exclusion from society were, in practice, more permeable: people would frequently come to visit anchoresses in order to ask their advice or to gain their blessing. A thirteenth-century guide for anchoresses, the *Ancrene Wisse*, explicitly recognizes that their lives must balance withdrawal into spiritual contemplation with practical interactions with the world that surrounded their cell.[17]

What was true for anchoresses was doubly true for ordinary monks. Although early models of monasticism imagined dividing the communities into monks who would engage themselves in prayer and 'seculars' who would deal with the laity and the practicalities of running the monastery, the theory was far removed from practice.[18] An *exemplum* recorded by Jacques de Vitry recognized the problem, and skipped a nimble path through it. A knight, desiring a pious life, left his riches and joined a monastery. His abbot, seeing that he was successful in the secular world, sent him off to market to sell the old asses of the monastery and buy younger ones. But at market, when asked about the quality of his live-stock, the ex-knight refused to dissemble and admitted that the beasts were worn out. When he returned home without having made the sale, the other monks were angry with him, but he responded 'I relinquished many asses and great pos-sessions in the secular world, and I refuse to lie for your asses and injure my soul by defrauding my neighbours!' After that, it was agreed that they would not send him to market any more. Jacques de Vitry did not explicitly gloss the tale, but two morals, delicately counterpoised, appear to present themselves: that relin-quishing secular wealth is a worthy and pious thing that monks would do well to remember; but that monasteries do also sometimes need new asses, and must act accordingly.[19]

But if the desert retreats of the early Church Fathers continued to provide one model, there were other developments. The new mendicant orders, formed in the early thirteenth century, presented a mixture of monastic contemplation and pastoral action within the world. Their template was not withdrawal but Christ's ministry to the people. From the late eleventh century onwards, the emphasis upon rules – the monastic rules above all, but other self-imposed rules also – constituted not simply the context for living piously but an actual embodi-ment of holiness. To live in a scrupulous and law-abiding way could itself be a path to holiness. In the thirteenth, and particularly in the fourteenth and fif-teenth centuries, there was a growth in mystical piety. This was a very different kind of holiness, which claimed, somewhat perilously, to tap into a direct con-nection with God, expressed in arcane and poetic language, sometimes mani-festing itself through bodily feats and wonders such as eating only the Eucharist or levitating.

Over this period there was also a growing degree of ecclesiastical control. The Fourth Lateran Council (1215) limited the proliferation of different monas-ticisms by banning the formation of any new rules, and of course the Cathars and the Waldensians were placed beyond the pale. Various saints were promoted by the papacy against the Cathars and other heretics: Omobono, Dominic, Francis and Peter Martyr among others. But some groups were more complex. Jacques de Vitry put a lot of effort into promoting the Beguines (lay groups who independently followed a quasi-monastic lifestyle), and particularly the mystic Mary d'Oignies whose *Life* he wrote, as an orthodox alternative to the Cathars. However, not everyone trusted the Beguine movement, and by the fourteenth century parts of it were being prosecuted for heresy. The Franciscans ran into trouble in the later thirteenth century as part of their number (the Spiritual Franciscans or Fraticelli) attempted to cling to the extreme vows of poverty originally set out by Francis, but in so doing discovered, to their cost, the boundary between 'reform' and 'heresy'. Other groups, such as the female religious who pursued pious poverty in thirteenth-century Italy, were shaped and organized by the Church – ordered, for example, to cloister themselves. As Luigi Pellegrini remarks, 'the ecclesiastical authorities tended to merge distinct religious realities into a single and easily controllable institutional channel'. Those, such as the north Italian 'Minor Sisters', who were not regulated found themselves condemned by the papacy in the 1240s for scandal and deceit: 'in order to extort people's good faith they go barefoot, wearing the habit and belt of the nuns of Saint Damian'.[20]

Mysticism was also policed: the Beguine writer Marguerite Porete was condemned and burned in 1310 for her treatise *A Mirror for Simple Souls*. However, while she was being tried and executed in Paris and her book burned, copies of the work circulated in perfectly orthodox contexts and were enjoyed long thereafter as a powerful mystical text.[21] In the fifteenth century Jean Gerson, chancellor of the University of Paris, wrote a tract *On Distinguishing True from False Revelations* that set out a method for ascertaining whether mystical visions should be believed, or condemned as demonical deceptions.[22] This perhaps gives us the best sense of how power worked in this area: not so much the occasions of outright violent repression (such as the Albigensian crusade called against the Cathars in 1209), but Gerson's attempt to monitor, order and police a form of holiness.

What led people to attempt holiness, or at least to set themselves on the path towards it? Given that those in monastic orders or similar vocations never constituted more than a very small proportion of an area's population, their motivations are not a major concern of this book.[23] Up until the twelfth century, in any case, 'motivation' was not a meaningful question for most monks, as they would have started their lives as child oblates, brought up to their vocation with no choice in the matter. For those entering religion later in life, a mixture of individual enthusiasm and social pressures can be discerned. Some, like Francis of Assisi or Waldes of Lyons, clearly experienced an epiphanic conversion that prompted a radical change of life. For others, such as those noble daughters surplus to requirement in southern France, entering the religious houses of the Cathars (or later the orthodox alternatives set up to halt this tendency) was part of a family strategy concerning property, marriage and inheritance. One finds a similar pattern in later times: as the Venetian nobility tightened their grip on their 'pure' hereditary class in the fifteenth century, the numbers of noble women placed in convents – and hence safely out of the marriage market, where they might succumb to a 'lower' social match – grew substantially.[24] However, the example of the Cathars reminds us that pious enthusiasm was also present: the numbers of Perfects (perhaps several thousand at the highest point in the late twelfth century) were not simply produced through social pressure but also because some people desired the life that their faith proffered. Like other groups of lay people, such as the Humiliati and the Beguines, who lived in quasi-monastic communities but without following a monastic Rule, the Cathar phe-nomenon primarily attests to fervent piety. Indeed, just like the holy men of late antiquity, one name given to the Cathar Perfects was the 'Friends of God'. For Cathars, Waldensians, Beguines and others the language of holiness was famil-iar: an ascetic lifestyle, restricting diet, clothing and property; the practice of chastity, gender-divided communities; and – once again – a notional withdrawal from the world.

The literal withdrawal undertaken by recluses and anchorites was much more common for women than men: in both England and Italy, for example, about two-thirds of recluses were female.[25] Here we may wonder whether the experi-ences of gender had an effect. Although confining oneself may seem to indicate a loss of power and freedom, it perhaps had a liberating effect for those few women who pursued it, freed as they were from the demands and dangers of the patriarchal society around them. But, of course, one may argue the reverse, seeing recluses as an extreme form of medieval misogyny, cutting women off from the world. In the case of the Beguines, we may wonder whether the com-munal existence of all-female, semi-religious groups who supported themselves through teaching and labouring, might have represented for some women a par-ticularly tempting combination of accessible piety and freedom from male gov-ernance. In fact, the definition of a 'beguinage' seems to have blurred in the later Middle Ages to include what were essentially small groups of women, newly arrived in towns and cities, providing each other with mutual support while operating at the margins of the labour market.[26] It is a truism of medieval studies to note that religious and social motivations cannot be easily separated; but it is important to see that in some areas the demands of economics and civic politics made certain social and cultural choices much more attractive. A lone, poor woman is vulnerable; a group of women, engaged in pious activity, less so.

If one restricts the question of motivation to the most extreme forms of holiness – the attempts to approach or achieve sainthood – alongside the more ineffable desires affecting the human heart, one can note, once again, the large degree of continuity between social structures and sanctity. As Brigitte Cazelles suggests, holiness is bound up with status, as part of the 'medieval articulation of order [where] access to God is proportional to one's position in the hierarchy of the Christian community'.[27] Sanctity could be a good and logical career move. It was also something for which models not only pre-existed but proliferated. As we have noted, recurrent patterns were provided by the early Church Fathers and by Christ. However, the very process of recording and publicizing medieval saints – the various *Lives* that were written, the preaching material for use by parish priests and mendicants, the religious imagery produced for churches, and so forth – meant that further templates became available. Taking the example of mystical piety, by the fifteenth century there were numerous texts that not only recounted the experiences of mystics but proffered a model on how to do it oneself. Part of the attraction of being holy, for those few who attempted it, was surely to be like the other holy people of whom one had heard or read.[28]

By the time that someone like Margery Kempe (daughter of an important mayor, and member of the merchant bourgeoisie) felt like attempting holiness, there were numerous models and patterns available for imitation.[29] Compare, for example, two northern European saints: Agnes of Bohemia (d. 1282) and Nicholas von Flüe (1417–87). Agnes was daughter of the king of Bohemia, and she spent much of her childhood betrothed to various nobles while being shuffled around from convent to convent. Eventually promised in marriage, against her objections, to the Holy Roman Emperor Frederick II, she rebelled: she became extremely pious and ascetic, began wearing a hair shirt beneath her jewelled robes, and a girdle studded with iron points to rend her flesh. Eventually the pope intervened on her behalf and she was freed from her unwanted suitor. In 1236 she founded the first convent north of the Alps associated with the Franciscan order, took the veil, and retired there followed by a hundred other noble girls.[30] Without wanting to diminish the honesty of Agnes's piety, we can note several ways in which her social and cultural context helps to make sense of it: Elizabeth of Hungary (mentioned above) was her first cousin, and hence perhaps an available role model. Punishing her flesh with a hair shirt had a particular resonance, given that she was attempting to escape from marriage: it emphasized that she wanted to be free from bodily needs and desires, something that would be impossible within an aristocratic marriage, which would demand the production of an heir. The betrothal broken, she removed herself to a convent, thus signalling clearly a withdrawal from the games of dynastic politics which her actions had upset. In all, her extreme piety clearly provided her, as very little else would have done, with the necessary cultural capital to effect an escape from her ordained fate.

St Nicholas von Flüe – popularly known by his fellow Swiss as 'Brother Klaus' – provides quite a contrast. He was born into a family of small farmers and his father held a minor official post in the canton. He was brought up, by his mother, as a member of the 'Friends of God' – not, this time, the early Christian holy men or the Cathar Perfects, but a late medieval group of pious laity spread across Germany, Switzerland and the Netherlands who sought closeness to God through strict living and constant meditation. Nicholas fought in two wars for his region, and was appointed magistrate, judge and then governor of the canton. He married and had ten children, the eldest of whom went on to become governor, too. At the age of 50, Nicholas completely withdrew from political life and went to live as a hermit in a valley, subsisting on a minimal diet. People began to come and visit him, to ask advice and to bring gifts. After a while a chapel was set up, and there would be an annual procession at Lucerne in which he took part. In 1481, during complex high political negotiations about the political division of Switzerland, it was suggested that Nicholas be asked to mediate a solution between the opposing parties. This he did, saving much potential conflict, and upon his death he was honoured throughout Switzerland as a saint (although he was only formally canonized by the papacy in the twentieth century).[31] Although Nicholas's holiness had a very different shape from Agnes's, we can see how it, too, grew out of a particular set of social, cultural and political circumstances. His position as a civic leader flowed seamlessly into his sanctity, and his very withdrawal from the world in old age facilitated his last great political act. Nicholas, like Agnes, became ascetic; but his restricted diet and rejection of worldly trappings were much less a sudden and dramatic break from a privileged background than the culmination of a mode of life that he had been brought up in.

Thus we can see that there are numerous different ways of being holy, which nonetheless share a number of recurrent images or practices. Inversions are common, of status or gender: the son of a rich merchant like Francis (or Waldes before him) might give away his wealth and embrace poverty. A strong strand in Cistercian rhetoric used maternal imagery for holy and authoritative people; most strikingly, by St Bernard of Clairvaux to describe his own role as abbot.[32] As I suggested in Chapter 1, following the analysis of Victor Turner, these inversions can be seen as processes of liminality, enacting the symbolic removal from society, and ritual debasement, which then permit the reincorporation of the holy person back into the social group, with added kudos and authority. Such inversions are only possible from certain starting points: one cannot enact symbolic poverty if already poor, one cannot depict oneself as feminized if already a woman. Nevertheless, certain key signs were put repeatedly into play: dressing in an ostentatiously impoverished way, with plain clothes and sandals or even going barefoot; adopting ascetic and disciplined dietary practices; meditating or praying repeatedly; and generally enacting either apostolic or penitential behaviour in public places. A most extreme example would be the flagellant movement, which that first sprang up in the later thirteenth century and reached its apogee when the Black Death swept across Europe in the mid-fourteenth century. The flagellants made public procession, dressed in robes, hooded and masked, scourging themselves with flails in bodily penitence for the sins of mankind.[33]

But this was an unusually severe and pretty rare kind of piety, and one not encouraged by the Church as its extremity and intensity could be hard to control. More common was the apostolic holiness adopted during the twelfth century by figures like Henry of Le Mans, whom we met in the previous chapter, and developed by the Cathars, Waldensians, Franciscans and Dominicans in the thirteenth century. The orthodox and heretical groups were engaged in a kind of battle over the ownership and meaning of these apostolic symbols: despite their differing theologies, all adopted similar dress, modes of life, attitudes of piety.[34] As early histories of the Dominicans make clear, the Cathar Perfects were a real threat because of their clearly displayed holiness (glossed as 'false piety' by the mendicant commentators) and their pastoral energy and courage: 'the heretics never stop risking their very lives to travel round houses and towns to lead souls astray' remarked Humbert de Romans. The best defence was to imitate them: 'use a nail to drive out a nail' advised Diego of Osma, according to Jordan of Saxony.[35] An early Franciscan account relates that the friars who went on the first missions to France and Germany were repeatedly mistaken for Cathars, partly because of language problems (not knowing German, the friars answered *Ja* to every enquiry, including 'are you people heretics?') but mostly because their dress and behaviour made them look to the local bishops suspiciously like Perfects.[36] In fact, there is evidence that some lay people saw Waldensians, Cathars and Dominicans as essentially the same kind of thing: holy people, who might help to save one's soul. The apostolic imagery of mendicancy was powerful even when not in competition with heretics. When Franciscans and Dominicans entered Brittany, it was their learning, their preaching and their symbolic use of poverty that helped them to gain local secular support.[37]

Lay enthusiasm for apostolic imitation, whether by mendicants or heretics, allows us to see a little more clearly, from the wider social perspective, the relation between the rare and powerful holiness of saintliness and the more run-of-the-mill attempts at heading in the general direction of holiness found in the average monastery. As we have seen, monasticism experienced waves of reform, as new movements invigorated by apostolic fervour broke free from old 'corrupt' ways – only, through the very success of their message, to become quickly endowed with wealth, land and power. Monasteries needed men who could get a good price for old asses in the marketplace. These men, who in theory set themselves apart from the world in order to move closer to God, nonetheless found themselves very much part of the world. For many of the ordinary laity, their main experience of monks would not be as otherworldly 'friends of God', but as landlords or businessmen. In certain ways – dress, diet, sexual continence – monks and nuns (and indeed priests, whom I shall discuss further in the next chapter) were set apart from the world that surrounded them. But it was only a little way apart; and in a society that was innately built upon social differentiation – between complex social strata, genders, allegiances and orders – the 'apartness' of monasticism was only one subdivision among several. The situation may have been similar with heretical holy men and women: the Cathar Perfects were often also very much part of the community, involved in labour and money.[38] However, we might argue that it was precisely *because* monks were, in practice, so tied up with the secular world that the liminal imagery and rituals discussed above continued to perform the cultural work of signing *certain* men and women as particularly 'holy'. What the laity prized about poorly dressed, humble, holy men and women was partly their rarity.

We may say that holiness had certain prerequisites – a particular mode of life, symbolic practices, charitable activities – but that it was the wider hand of communal approval that brought it to fruition. Armanno Punzilupo, one might therefore have thought, could have become a saint. He had the qualifications: a pious and exemplary way of life, a variety of suitable miracles performed after his death and the support of the cathedral clergy. That he was not canonized is not hugely surprising. As we saw, very few people made it over all the legal hurdles in the Middle Ages. But in Armanno's case there was a bigger, and more intriguing, problem. In June 1270, a Dominican friar called Arasino, from Pergamo, attested that he had asked a passing merchant what the news was from the places he had visited. 'Good', replied the merchant: 'because a saint has appeared at Ferrara' (meaning the recently deceased Punzilupo). 'That's not impossible', mused Arasino. The merchant replied, 'Your brothers [i.e. other Dominicans] and the Minorites [Franciscans] are not pleased, because they suspect him of heresy.'[39] Armanno Punzilupo had apparently been not a saint but a Cathar.

This, at any rate, was the opinion of other witnesses interviewed by Dominican inquisitors, in a rebuttal of the miracle evidence. They alleged that Punzilupo had been friends with Cathars, talked with Cathars, received Cathars into his house, and had both been given and had given others the Cathar rite of the *consolamentum* (a ritual purification). If this was true, Armanno was not merely a supporter of the heretics, he was himself a Cathar Perfect. Other witnesses made further allegations: that Punzilupo had insulted the Dominicans, particularly when they went to lead a convicted heretic to the stake; that he only rarely went to church, took no counsel from churchmen and said bad things about the clergy; and that on Easter day (or so the witness had heard from neighbours) Armanno used to take a great big loaf and cask of wine and use them to feed many people, and when it was eaten he would say 'Why do those ravening wolves say that the body of Christ cannot be consumed? Behold: we have eaten up a great big loaf and cask of wine!' Lady Bengepare, another witness, said that many Cathars made jokes about the matter, and had said 'How can those of the Roman Church now say that we are bad men when they have made one of us a saint?'[40]

How indeed? One may have suspicions about this case: many of the witnesses the Dominicans dragged up against Armanno (including Bengepare) had themselves been convicted of heresy, and therefore might be open to coercion, and some of what they alleged was clearly contradictory and confused. The hostile witnesses were also, on the whole, markedly upper class, which may mean that the struggle over the cult was implicated in other civic politics in Ferrara. No witness actually ascribed specific Cathar sayings or beliefs to Armanno, only association with them. However, there was clearly some problem with the man – perhaps his antipathy towards the mendicant orders? – or else there would have been no reason for the Dominicans to get involved in the first place. Quite where Armanno's religious sympathies lay will never exactly be known, and his case, like many others, shows us that heresy is essentially a quality in the eye of the beholder. More interestingly, it also emphasizes that holiness was similarly ascribed – a quality imparted to a saint by others.

So we must also, as Armanno's case illustrates, consider holiness in relation to power. The posthumous squabble at Ferrara shows once again that an orthodox holy man and a heretical preacher could look remarkably similar; from the point of view of their audiences, they embodied in fact the very same mode of holiness. We cannot, as historians, decide Armanno's 'guilt' or 'innocence'; nor, I would suggest, does such a decision get us very far. What we can do is note that the wider use and effects of holiness – what was really at stake in the ascription of holiness and sainthood – were very much to do with the factional power in the immediate community and the desires of the wider ecclesiastical authorities. As we will see, his case was far from the only occasion when a person was celebrated by one social group as a saint, but rejected by another.

Regarding holiness

In 1397, a Dominican called Marcolino of Forli died and his mendicant brothers prepared to bury him. Alerted to Marcolino's passing by a child, a crowd of local artisans gathered and declared that he was a saint. Marcolino, they said, had been kind to children, gave to the poor, healed wounds (using herbs, but this was just a modest cover for his innate powers the patient later said), and had recited 100 *Paternosters* and 100 *Ave Marias* every day. For mostly the same reasons, the Dominicans thought Marcolino had been a rather foolish and eccentric man; an ill-educated simpleton who knew only the most basic prayers, someone who tended to doze off during mass ('No, he was rapt!' protested the crowd), and definitely not saint material. At any rate, the Dominicans buried Marcolino. But the next day a crowd returned and opened up the grave, and found that a sweet smell – the odour of sanctity – issued from his corpse, encouraging them in their devotions.[41]

The conflict over the sanctity of Armanno Punzilupo was, as far as we can tell, connected to political factions within Ferrara and disagreement between the local cathedral canons and the mendicant friars. In Marcolino's case we have an example of a different and arguably broader disjuncture. The Church's attitude toward sanctity was complex, as outlined above. Many medieval saints were local and had at least some popular support. In the eleventh and twelfth centuries the papacy encouraged these developments, institutionalizing its role in the canonization process of the thirteenth century. By that period, however, the Church also began some attempts to rein in the expansion of lay enthusiasm, and to direct the message of sanctity. For the Church, the point about a saint was his or her completion of a spiritual journey: through living an exceptionally good life, the saint had ascended to sit in heaven with God. Miracles – performed *by* God *through* the saint – were, although impressive, essentially a by-product of that spiritual excellence. Moreover, sanctity had a collective shape: the miracles that saints performed (or, at any rate, that were recorded by the Church) were usually the miracles that Christ had performed, raising the dead, healing the sick and so forth. Artistic depictions of saints and their works were deliberately repetitious, asserting visually the collective conformity of sanctity.[42] In addition, from the thirteenth century onwards the Church wanted saints to act as exemplars to the laity. Most people could not hope to emulate the extraordinary piety of the saintly, but could be encouraged at least to set out along the path.[43] As the anonymous poet of a thirteenth-century vernacular *Life of Saint Paula* tells his audience,

> This mirror [the poem] is for the souls.
> Ladies should contemplate themselves in it.

For they can learn a lesson—
Those who are attentive—
From how Saint Paula led her life,
Avoiding covetousness and envy,
Pride, concupiscence and avarice
And conquering every vice through her virtues.[44]

A French noblewoman, listening to this poem, could not hope to imitate Paula exactly, as Paula had lived a very hard life of fourth-century austerity. Nor might the lady expect to conquer *every* vice at all times. But she might see Paula as an example of the kinds of pious activities and modes of self-discipline to which she should aspire. However, this kind of text – and perhaps the call for self-improvement it contained – were very much restricted to the upper echelons of society. What troubled lay people more usually sought (and were encouraged to seek) from a saint was a mixture of intercession and a vague moral guidance. A thief called Jacob, imprisoned and fearing execution at Millau in Provence, decided that 'because he had heard that the Magdalen sought forgiveness with God for her sins, having made a mental vow, he turned to her for intercession so that just as she had obtained forgiveness for her own sins, she would thus seek forgiveness for him'.[45] There is a whispered promise of self-reform in Jacob's petition, but buried pretty deeply within the more pressing plea for saintly assistance.

There were also other ways in which saints could be imitated or used as models, not quite in alignment with the Church's central message of moral discipline. Katherine Lewis has argued that St Katherine of Alexandria, who had outwitted the pagan philosophers of the Emperor Maxentius in learned disputation, could be interpreted as a model for female wisdom and education. Fifteenth-century evidence of people praying to Katherine for knowledge shows a mixture of intercession and exemplar, as 'one prays to St Katherine in order to become like her'. The evidence of late-medieval English household manuscripts provides further examples of St Katherine as a model of educated, maidenly behaviour. Moreover, because Katherine experienced a mystical marriage to Christ, there is evidence that some laywomen prayed to her in order to secure for themselves a good husband.[46]

As the struggle over Marcolino's body indicates, however, there could also be a more serious disjunction between clerical and lay ideas. In this specific case, as Vauchez notes, the lay idea of sainthood 'was ascetic, caring and thaumaturgical [magic performing], whereas for the Dominicans a saint was first of all a dignified and cultured person, brilliant and effective on the pastoral plane'.[47] Other contrasts in other cases can similarly be found. Clerical witnesses in canonization proceedings tend to stress the saint's spiritual efficacy, whereas lay witnesses talk more of miracles and the protection that the saint offered in this present world.[48] Indeed, the papacy frequently, but largely unsuccessfully, tried to persuade those attempting to have a saint canonized that it was better to have good evidence of one or two specific miracles rather than a myriad collection of healings and such like. Where the laity were impressed by the life someone had led, it was (as with both Armanno and Marcolino) most often because of the charity that they had shown towards others. This was, of course, an area where clerical and lay views overlapped – but were still not identical. For the Church, the charity a saint enacted was very much an element for imitation. For the laity, the saint's charitable activities and post-mortem interventions were in a continuum: here was someone powerful who *cared for them*.

There could also be further differences of emphasis on what made a saint. The specific case of martyrdom might be expanded by the laity into death that had been in some sense dramatic or unjust. A number of children supposedly murdered by Jews were seen as martyrs – around a dozen of them, from William of Norwich (d. 1144) to Lorenzino Sossio (d. 1485). These deaths, and their anti-Semitic stories, were long remembered and occasioned great devotion. To their number we could add those Cathars, Waldensians, Beguines and even Lollards who were executed for their heresy. Their persecution and deaths seem to have impressed various lay people, including some who had no particular allegiance to their 'sects', and occasionally they were suggested to be saints.[49] There were also flurries of sanctity around those who died in political revolt. Around 1196, after William Longbeard's execution for leading an insurrection in London, the chain in which he had been bound was allegedly used to effect a cure and people made pilgrimages to the place where he died – until royal soldiers were sent to put a stop to this. Simon de Montfort, who led the barons' revolt against Henry III of England in 1264, was also credited with a number of posthumous miracles, until once again royal prohibitions intervened; and similarly Archbishop Scrope, executed for treason by Henry IV in 1406, enjoyed a brief cult.[50] It is not that every violent death occasioned sainthood, but that such a death had the *potential* to acquire sanctity in the eyes of others. In the case of William Longbeard and Simon de Montfort, this potential received an extra push from the high political context of their actions. Similarly, the anti-Semitic poison squeezed from the deaths of William of Norwich and his unhappy brethren was, at least in part, the doing of monks, engaged in their own cultural and political struggle.[51] The making of a saint, then, could involve a curious collision between elite and popular ideas, politics and desires. Sometimes these elements coincided, as one might see with St Thomas Becket: his cult heavily promoted by the papacy in an assertion of its authority over secular power, but the glamour of martyrdom also encouraging a large popular cult. But this does not mean that all parties therefore automatically shared exactly the same set of ideas about sanctity. Even where lay and clerical ideas came closest – in Italy, where the laity shared the papacy's sense that sanctity led on from a pious, ascetic, holy way of living – the example of Marcolino illustrates the gulf that could still open up in interpreting that life.

There was perhaps a further, subtle divergence of ideas over the miracles that saints performed, and their nature. As noted above, the theological position was that miraculous interventions – healing a dying child, freeing a prisoner, and so on – were the work of God, channelled through the particular saint invoked. Saints were, indeed, God's elect; chosen at birth to be His instruments (it was a hagiographical commonplace that the saint demonstrated precocious holiness as a child) their posthumous powers came from the especially close relationship they had with the deity. We can recall, from the previous chapter, the priest Arlotto Mainardi instructing his female parishioner to address her entreaties to Christ rather than the local saint. But the laity tended to associate the miracles more directly with the saint. One might thus try out a variety of saints in the search for aid. A witness for the canonization of Archbishop Philip of Bourges in the mid-thirteenth century said that he invoked the cleric only after having first unsuccessfully appealed to Giles of Rocamadour, Veran of Jargeau, the Blessed Virgin Mary, Stephen, Radegund and Philip's uncle William of Bourges – an interesting mixture of local and international, recent and ancient saints.[52] In another case, a knight giving testimony at the first canonization trial of St Thomas Aquinas (d. 1274) in 1319 gives a further reminder of what the evidence does not generally show us. This knight explained that he had experienced paralysis in his right arm for about a year. In 1316, he happened to be travelling toward Rome and came into the general area where Thomas was buried. Ever since he was a child he had been told that Aquinas was a man who had lived a holy life, and thus, he said, 'it had crossed his mind that perhaps the merits of the holy man might help to cure his arm'. Accordingly, he diverted his journey, found where Thomas was buried, made a prayer for help and lay flat upon the grave. 'And at once he felt his arm grow stronger. For a while a kind of numbness remained about the joints . . . but this too vanished by the end of the same day.'[53] The cure itself is unremarkable, much like a thousand others. What is interesting is the fact that the knight was clearly trying out Aquinas as a possible cure for his troubles. He knew that Thomas had been holy during life; perhaps, therefore, he could now do miracles. We may imagine quite a number of other occasions when people tried out someone they knew as holy, in life or in death; but if they had no success, no historical evidence would be generated. Moreover, there is ample evidence from miracle stories of people who first went to doctors for assistance, and only approached a saint having had no joy from conventional healing. One did not necessarily petition a saint without first exploring other courses of action, and as we shall see in Chapter 6, some people did not seem at all impressed by saints and disbelieved in miraculous aid. The phrase 'the cult of saints' may, because of modern resonances to the word 'cult', suggest a credulously devout kind of piety, rigidly fixed upon a particular intercessor. The truth is very different: individual saints were available resources, used by some people in certain circumstances, but rarely to the exclusion of other avenues of assistance.

The fact that the physical remains of saints, around which shrines were constituted, were understood to have the strongest healing powers (emitting a kind of 'holy radioactivity' as Ronald Finucane puts it) encouraged an association between the individual saint and his or her miraculous powers. Not only the body, or body parts, of the saint, but the things he or she had touched, the water in which their corpse had been washed, the very mortar of their tomb could carry the power to heal. Despite the fact that the saints' powers came from their elevated position in heaven, there was a strong sense in which they continued to reside in a specific physical place. Jean de Joinville tells a story of a shrine to the Virgin Mary at Tortosa in Cyprus (where, he claimed, the very first altar was erected in her honour). A madman was taken to the shrine for healing, but the devil inside him cried out 'Our Lady is not here! She is in Egypt giving help to the King of France and the Christians' who were currently on crusade.[54] The devil was lying, but for the lie to be plausible illustrates the point: Mary, like any other saint, was sometimes presumed to inhabit some specific geographical space at a particular point in time. As we saw in the last chapter, people also tended to conflate the physical image of saints with the saints themselves, asking statues for help, punishing or even ritually humiliating them when they failed to intercede. In Germany, for example, an image of St Urban was dumped in the mud if he failed to provide good weather for the harvest.[55] Through the power they embodied, images helped to widen the possible circle of miracles, effectively multiplying the incarnations of the saint, so that in the later Middle Ages more cures and interventions were effected at some distance from saints' shrines.[56]

This sense of negotiation with the individual saint is strengthened by the bargaining with which people engaged in seeking aid. Saints did not work for free: one had to do a little something for them, even if (like the cured blind man Domenico heard from his prison cell) it was only to publicize the saint's powers. As one witness in the canonization process of Clare of Montefalco put it, 'I ask you by your virtue that you free me from this pain, and I promise you, if you do this, I will tell a hundred people.'[57] Most usually a vow was made, involving a future gift: heal me, and I'll give you this coin, or these candles, or another votive offering. Frequently people gave the saint's shrine images of the afflicted area that had been healed: wax feet, arms, buttocks, or (for other kinds of miracles) the chains from which they had been freed, the noose from which they had been spared. In a set of miracles recorded soon after the death of Louis of Anjou in 1297, almost 90 per cent involved conditional promises: 'Lord Geoffrey Richau had gout in his left arm for more than a fortnight, and suffered greatly. He made a vow to Saint Louis that *if* he obtained liberation [from his illness] from him and from Lord Jesus, he would bring him a wax arm.'[58] Vauchez has compared these vows to vassalic acts of homage, but one may wonder whether the bargaining quality of the vows indicates a more contractual, businesslike relationship.[59] This would certainly seem to have been the saint's perspective in the case of a cure effected by Thomas Becket for a priest called Robert. The intercession had been made after some pious parishioners had made a vow to the saint for their priest. After the cure, Becket appeared to Robert and asked him why the vow had not been fulfilled; Robert replied that he had not made any vow. 'Certainly you did not vow, but since another made the vow on your behalf, payment lies upon you', replied the saint. If the debt was left unpaid, penalties could come into force: a boy was healed of his leg ulcers by Nicholas von Flüe, but his parents failed to pay the money for the wax votive offering they had promised. One of the ulcers grew back, so violently that it began to push apart the bones in the boy's leg. Upon payment of the debt, the wound healed.[60]

Louis IX of France (himself later canonized) indicated an alternative model of interaction: 'It is the same with the saints in Paradise as with the counsellors of kings . . . whoever has business with an earthly king seeks, in effect, to know who he holds in high regard and who, having his ear, is able to approach him successfully.' Perhaps, then, kings and nobles petitioned saints as at a royal court; whereas, for the general laity, other models of negotiation – the market or the manor – were more apposite. A sermon by John Mirk suggests that the saint to whom one's parish church was dedicated was exactly like the (idealized) temporal lord of the manor, defending his tenants from their enemies.[61] Various fifteenth-century prayers address saints in similar, or even more domestic terms: St Barbara is described as 'my honourable mistress'; a devotee declares herself to be human god-daughter to Mary Magdalen; a testator calls upon 'my own helpers and providers of succour in this my great need'.[62] Certainly different saints moved in different social circles: a very local saint like Godric of Finchale (d. 1170) worked miracles mainly for ordinary people, whereas Thomas Becket more frequently intervened for the clergy and upper classes.[63] The tales of saints inflicting violent punishments against transgressors (promoted by the clergy from the early Middle Ages onwards, in an effort to instil some fear and respect for church property in rapacious landowners) also encouraged the laity to think of them as somewhat capricious, powerful individuals who needed handling with care – perhaps not unlike local secular lords.[64]

The comparison with secular powers can perhaps be extended further. One can think of a layman having access to, and being beholden to, his local lord, who has jurisdiction over the local community and most immediately represents order and justice. All of this was, of course, in theory: individual lords could be oppressive, unpleasant and a threat to the community – or could simply be absent and unavailable much of the time. In any case, dealing with such an individual involved familiar but ritualized interactions (at a local court, or through acts of submission and homage) and payment, but was perhaps ameliorated by some recognition of the interdependencies that existed between landlord and tenants. On lucky occasions, a villager might even feel that his lord was a friend to him and his household – where 'friendship' implied a formal attitude of benevolence. But in addition to the local lord there was, for some people, a greater magnate who might be worth approaching; or a competing authority such as a local bishop or abbot; or a representative of state authority such as a judge. One might appeal to such a figure if the local lord was not providing the requisite aid. And for many, there was also the king or prince, the final, secular court of appeal. Dealing with these more distant individuals was a different matter, involving a greater degree of symbolic submission, greater expense and a greater imaginative projection of their care for the community – that someone so grand as the king might feel love for one's insignificant village.

Thinking (in these very broad and idealized terms) about the potential negotiations with secular powers – with *benefactors*, literally 'those who do good (to you)' – gives us a map that we can helpfully apply to saints. Saints are benefactors, but can also be liabilities who need careful handling, as can be seen on the various occasions when saints blind, paralyse, or even kill those who doubt their powers or blaspheme against God. One appeals to them via familiar rituals, indicating one's subservience and indebtedness, and frequently money or other payment has to be rendered. Most importantly, different saints operate at different levels: local saints, like local lords, are the most immediate presences. One rubs along with them much of the time, and they are often perhaps the first benefactor to whom one turns. For example, people making wills in the fourteenth-century Toulousain, like every medieval testator, left money to saints. The patterns of bequest, however, were very localized: 'each village produced its own type of comportment, a model of piety and charity'.[65] One might name a son after the local saint, hoping that some of their power and fortune would rub off on the child.[66] There is a lot of evidence that people saw certain saints as essentially members of the local community, with particular responsibility to their 'neighbours'. For example, the *Life of Wulfstan* tells of a disabled man in hope of a cure waiting for several days at Wulfstan's shrine; eventually he complained to the saint 'Was I not born and raised on the land of your church? You cure foreigners and strangers daily, but not your special servant.' A Cornish man, a tenant of the canons of St Stephen, suffering from a painful eye infection, talked to the saint (to whom, the text notes, he had usually spoken 'as a friend'): 'O blessed Stephen, Stephen! Long time have I laboured in thy service; yet now, I think, in vain. For if I had served the Earl of [Mortain] . . . so faithfully as I have long served you, he would have enriched me with many gifts; but you, to whom I have committed myself and my whole soul and all that I possess, give me now over to torture!'[67] Fortunately the saint appeared to him that evening and healed the eye, restoring their former amity. Evidence from Sweden illustrates the way in which the existing cultures of sanctity were interpreted by this relative latecomer to Christianity. The author of a *Life* of Nicholas of Linköping, written in 1414, notes that 'each region or even each city or parish should venerate with special honours its own patron [saint] . . . France honours a cult to Denis, England to Thomas, Sweden to Siegfried. And we too, in our diocese of Linköping, ought to venerate our father Nicholas and redouble our efforts to have him canonized . . .'[68] Having a local saint was something that marked out a place *as* a place.

But as the Linköping author indicates, there are also higher courts of appeal than the local, saints who have a much wider constituency, such as Thomas Becket, Katherine of Alexandria or Mary Magdalen. These saints were promoted by the Church and were venerated across most of Europe. People knew them to be international figures. And above them all was the Virgin Mary, the most powerful of all intercessors. Shrines to the Virgin existed all over Christendom, and the majority of medieval English churches were dedicated to her. The power of these superstar saints came from a mixture of popular enthusiasm (just as most kings had popular enthusiasm projected onto them, perhaps primarily for the idea of transcendent justice they embodied) and ecclesiastical propaganda – for it was around figures like Mary Magdalen and the Virgin that mendicant friars, among others, would weave their cultural work. Thus, in interactions with the saints, we have a mixture of the local and the international: the parish church, its dedicatee, the images and statues it contained; and pilgrimage sites, such as Canterbury (Thomas Becket), Compostella (the apostle James), and of course Jerusalem (Christ's empty sepulchre among other sites). There is also a chronological element complicating this spatial variation in sanctity. The widespread worship of universal saints largely developed from the twelfth century onwards, with Marian devotion growing much greater after the mid-fourteenth century. The later Middle Ages also saw more saints being associated with *particular* powers: St Margaret for protection during childbirth, St Clement for saving sailors from drowning, St Sebastian to ward off plague, to give but three from a host of examples.[69] Chronology may also have affected the sense of closeness and familiarity that people had with particular saints. Guilds dedicated to individual saints (discussed in greater detail in the next chapter) became markedly more important and common in the later Middle Ages. So too, for the gentry and upper bourgeoisie, did private chapels and statues, manuscripts or paintings intended for domestic contemplation. Petitioning a saint, via a statue that one had in one's very own home, must have facilitated a different sense of contact than when in church with one's neighbours. Poorer versions of this kind of domesticated icon may sometimes have been available for the less well off, in the form of pilgrim badges (commemorating passage to a particular saint's shrine, although sometimes obtained by people who had not actually performed the pilgrimage), or, in a more unusual example, the thousands of strips of paper depicting scenes from the life of St Catherine of Siena, distributed in that city in the early fifteenth century in order that people could take them home to venerate.[70]

To sum up: holiness is a quality bound up with cultural attitudes, mechanisms of assessment and social behaviours. There is no value in historians indulging (as they have sometimes done) in judging the extent or truth or merit of a medieval person's piety, holiness or sanctity. Our job is, rather, to understand how such valuations took place within different historical contexts. What we have seen most frequently is the repeated use of a set of images – poverty, bodily suffering, penitence – that place people at a certain symbolic distance from the rest of the community. Although there were ways in which people could interact with and even imitate saints and other holy people, holiness mainly set one apart. For ordinary pious lay people, the closest that they usually came to these areas was when approaching death and hoping for salvation. The Cathars had a ritual, the *consolamentum*, which they performed to make someone into one of their holy men or women, and also for a dying believer in order to 'purify' him or her and thus ensure the salvation of their soul. If the sick person in fact recovered, it is clear that the community considered them to have been 'changed' by the ritual, as if they had partly stepped out of this world, and that there was pressure for them to continue with the ascetic lifestyle of the sect's elite rather than returning to their secular life. In exactly the same way, Robert Mannying's fourteenth-century instructional poem *Handlyng Synne* notes a popular belief about extreme unction: 'But many one thus hope and say / Anoint him not unless they should die / For if he turn again to life / He should lie no more by his wife.'[71]

Becoming holy (which, in the sense of moving closer to God, most lay people hoped they would experience upon their deathbeds) meant crossing a kind of boundary.

This sense of the holy – pre-eminently the saints, but also those who while living might conceivably become saints – as 'different' is balanced, as I have argued, by the ways in which saints continued to remain part of the local community. I have made a number of different comparisons for the laity's relationship to the saints: as patrons, lords, kings, exemplars, friends, neighbours. The point is not that one of these metaphors best describes the relationship, but rather that they *all* do – in different times and places, in different petitionary contexts, and with different individual saints. The holy dead certainly shared essential qualities – theologically they were closer to God and, perhaps more importantly for the laity, they had thaumaturgic powers – but this did not render them homogeneous, any more than living holy people were homogeneous. To meet, when alive, Marcolino of Forli must have been a very different experience from meeting Louis IX of France, although both had a reputation for holiness in their lifetimes. After death, when both became for a certain audience 'saints', perhaps something of those differences persisted. God, and for much of the Middle Ages Christ, were very distant, powerful, and literally awe-inspiring beings. Saints were a way of domesticating that power, making it accessible, attainable, negotiable. Federigo Visconti (d. 1277), archbishop of Pisa, talked in a sermon of touching this power: 'Truly blessed are those who actually saw the blessed Francis himself, as I did, through God's grace. I saw him, and with my own hand I touched him, in a heavy press of people in the great piazza at Bologna.' In the *Golden Legend*, and various later dramatic reworkings, a midwife who disbelieves in Mary's virginity has her hand withered as she tries literally to lay hold of the Godhead.[72] The supreme being was too powerful to touch; but the holy radiation of the saints permitted a greater degree of interaction. Let us now consider how people set about using that power, and where else they looked for it.

Using holiness and magic

If one asks what people wanted from the saintly and the holy, the most obvious answer is salvation. People wanted to know that when they died, and when their loved ones and relatives and neighbours died, they would go to a good place. 'First I bequeath my soul to our lord God Almighty, maker of heaven and of earth, praying and beseeching our lady Saint Mary . . . and all the company of Heaven to pray for me to our Lord Jesus our saviour'; 'Bless us, Good Christians, grant us God's blessing and yours. Pray God for this sinner that he may be delivered from an evil death and brought to a good end'; 'I bless you Lord for Mary Magdalen, for Mary of Egypt, for St Paul, and for St Augustine. And as you have shown your mercy to them, so show thy mercy to me and to all that ask thee mercy of heart.'[73] These entreaties come respectively from the preamble to a London grocer's will, a common greeting to Cathar Perfects by their followers, and a prayer by Margery Kempe. The petitions come from different contexts, and conceal very different views of God and the next world; but they share the same desire for salvation. From around the twelfth century onwards, the Church increasingly wished the laity to see salvation as something for which they had to work, albeit aided, guided and policed by the clergy. This is explored further in Chapter 5. For the laity, however, other ways of understanding salvation could be more attractive. The Cathars, for example, held out a clear and relatively easy promise: die within our sect and you will be saved. In practice, this meant receiving the *consolamentum* upon the deathbed. Theologically, the *consolamentum* and orthodox extreme unction were very different; but structurally, as a ritual activity, and perhaps in the minds of the lay recipients, they were not so far apart. Indeed, certain Cathar adherents received both the *consolamentum* and the orthodox last rites, perhaps in an effort to ensure salvation.[74] That people could imagine having both rituals suggests that the attitude one can see towards the *consolamentum* in inquisitorial records might tell us something of how they felt about extreme unction (where we otherwise lack this kind of evidence). If so, it was clearly seen as an important rite to them, but also as a kind of final trump card, clearing misdeeds and sins in one fell swoop, guaranteeing passage to the next world.

On occasion the papacy encouraged a similar promise about the power of the saints to offer a complete remission from all penance that sin demanded. This was the case with crusading indulgences, proffered at the outset in the late eleventh century and thereafter, heavily promoted by preaching, and clearly an attraction to some who went East to fight.[75] In 1300, the pope announced that in that special year every Christian could receive a plenary (full) indulgence, remitting penance for sins both confessed and unconfessed, if they visited various holy sites in Rome. As the chronicler Giovanni Villani (*c.* 1276–1348) tells us, one of the biggest attractions to the massed hordes in the city was the public display on every Friday and feast day of the *sudario*, the cloth with which St Veronica had mopped Christ's brow on his journey to execution, which allegedly bore the imprint of his face. The Jubilee was a great success, and was repeated in 1350. No Jubilee was planned for 1400, but a number of the laity had other ideas: 'On this day [20th August 1399] the Girdle was shown at Prato and many people dressed in white . . . went to see it . . . so that according to what I have heard there were more than 20,000 people in Prato.' What Luca Dominici reports here was the beginning of a movement known as the *Bianchi*. Following an alleged appearance to an Italian peasant by the Virgin Mary, calling for mass penitential pilgrimage for mankind's sins, thousands of lay people across Italy and from elsewhere converged on Rome. 'On this day [3rd October] there arrived certain pilgrims, men and women, dressed in white with white staffs; they were going to St James . . . From Rome there arrived a letter [saying] that it was full of *Bianchi* to the extent that it couldn't hold them; there were great shortages and the Pope showed the *sudario* every day.'[76] This was a great outpouring of lay piety – but it is worth considering the particulars of its appeal. What the papacy got from the Jubilee (and perhaps found getting out of hand in 1399) was a strong, clear association between itself, the city of Rome, the most powerful of saints and relics, and the promise of intercession. For the laity, the attraction was clear: guaranteed salvation, drunk straight from the well.

We should not, however, use the extraordinary events of 1300 or 1399 – or for that matter the earlier crusades – as a straightforward guide to regular lay piety. A feverish massed pilgrimage to see a cloth that had touched Christ's very face, and the promise of complete redemption, were not the same things as ordinary devotions to a local saint. If they were, the jubilees would not have been so wildly successful. As Jacques de Vitry noted in the early thirteenth century, 'people are more willing to promise things and make devotion to God in times of need and affliction', sometimes later forgetting their moments of pious enthusiasm.[77] On a much less dramatic scale, we should also be careful what we extrapolate from the relationship with holiness and the desire for salvation conducted at the deathbed, or recorded in wills. Most people do not live on their deathbeds, or, even in the Middle Ages, with their deathbeds constantly in mind. Salvation was extremely important, but most important at a particular moment: near the end. Before that point, people had other needs from their saints, and their living holy men and women. Miracles were the most dramatic example, and healing miracles the ones most frequently attested in the sources. About 90 per cent of recorded miracles were cures, frequently from illness and injury, occasionally from death itself.[78] We must, however, be wary of what the evidence tells us. As noted above, the template of Christ's miracles in the New Testament tended to shape the types of miracles that ecclesiastics were happy to record: raising the dead, healing paralysis and blindness. Complex ideas developed about what precisely constituted a miracle and these informed canonization investigations. For example, a miracle had to be against nature, meaning, in practice, that medical intervention must first have been sought, but without avail; or that the recipient sought the cure only on their deathbed. As Laura Smoller has shown, by the fifteenth century (and perhaps earlier), the laity had been taught by the very process of investigation – the questions asked by the canonization inquisitors – that a miracle must conform to a particular model in order to qualify.[79] It is important to note that medieval people did not customarily ascribe 'the miraculous' to everything beneficial that happened or that they did not understand. They, like us, drew a distinction between the 'natural' and the 'supernatural'; but the boundary traced – in, for example, the miracle stories – was different from our own. Cures rarely occurred instantaneously at the saint's shrine, but (particularly from the fourteenth century onwards) were more frequently experienced at a distance, with the saint invoked and a pilgrimage then undertaken in thanks. In fact, as Sharon Farmer has shown, there was a class element to this picture. For the bourgeoisie and nobility, saints worked at a distance; for the poor, one was more usually present at the shrine.[80]

The use of saints, and indeed living holy people, to produce healing miracles existed alongside a variety of medical techniques and practices, and these were not necessarily in opposition. In an interesting conjunction, one Cathar supporter told inquisitors that Guillaume Bernard d'Airoux (a Perfect and practising medic) had 'with God' healed his illness.[81] We saw above that Marcolino of

Forli healed a patient using herbs. In the context of Marcolino's disputed sanctity, the patient said that the herbs had been a modest cover for the Dominican's powers – but we might wonder whether, before the argument blew up, it was precisely the combination of herbs *and* holiness that had been appealing. One might see miraculous cures as part of a spectrum of medical interventions, the more extraordinary tip of a larger iceberg which for the most part involved a largely unremarked linkage of health and holiness.[82] In the late thirteenth century an inquisitorial witness named Arnaude de Cordes reported a conversation between herself and a friend, wherein both women had admitted that they wanted to go to Lombardy with the Cathars. The conversation took place in the church of St John in Maurdanha, where Arnaude had gone to keep a vigil after she had recovered from an illness.[83] Apart from noting the intriguing fact that a keen Cathar supporter was nevertheless giving thanks – presumably to a saint – in her parish church, we also catch a glimpse of a more routine votive practice. Arnaude had been sick, but then recovered; and so she went to church to say 'thank you'. Such interactions do not make it into the records of canonization proceedings or miracle collections, but are almost certainly more reflective of common practice. Diana Webb has noted that 'miracle stories . . . have little or nothing to say about pilgrims who neither sought nor experienced a miracle, who must surely have been in the vast majority'.[84] To that multitude, we might add that even larger number of folk who went no further than their parish church. A cure, or any other intervention, only becomes a miracle after the fact; is only recorded as a miracle if an ecclesiastical authority is attempting to build or defend a cult; and perhaps is only *experienced* as a miracle if certain contextual frameworks (the sermons heard in the parish, or the presence of canonization inquisitors, or the enthusiastic promotions of cathedral canons) are there to prompt such an interpretation.

If we return to the question with which I began this section – what do people want from the holy? – a further answer broadens the picture. Although salvation is the most obvious answer, and 'healing' the most common miracle, the best response is much more diffuse. The saints made the rains come, made the sun shine, kept the soil rich, diverted floods and winds and storms, made the harvest bountiful, the market favourable, the land peaceful, the city prosperous, kept one's enemies at bay and, in short, made life bearable. This is not to suggest that the saints *alone* did these things. Any study of such quotidian sanctity has to recognize that people clearly also saw the value in, for example, good husbandry, collaborative soil preparation, crop rotation, storing food, forming defensive militia, launching collective legal actions against rapacious landlords and so forth.[85] But, to the minds of many, the saints assisted; it was not necessarily a matter of deciding between the two (although, as we shall see in Chapter 6, some people did think differently). The saints provided their aid not through any sequence of specific, spectacular miracles, but in a more low-key, continuous provision of good fortune. This general hum of beneficence was punctuated by similar but more individual acts more clearly visible to us. A priest cures spring storms by getting folk to worship the Virgin Mary on Saturdays. A woman gives a halfpenny to St Gilduin and a halfpenny to a poor man, in hope of securing a good bargain in the marketplace. A witness at the canonization trial of Thomas Cantilupe noted that 'people say that since the bones of Lord Thomas have been brought to the cathedral of Hereford, the harvests have been more plentiful, the waters have borne more fish, and the animals have produced more young'.[86] Patron saints of Italian cities were expected not only to perform particular wonders to impress a wider audience but also to display a 'day-to-day concern for their constituents'.[87] Holy people were bound into the fabric of the local community in such a way that their very presence brought 'good fortune' – a necessarily vague and all-encompassing concept. In the later thirteenth and early fourteenth centuries, when Cathar Perfects were thin on the ground in southern France, a number of believers stored bread blessed by the heretics, keeping it as something that the holy men had touched and which might carry their goodness with it.[88] This perhaps ameliorated worries that some supporters had about the absence of their holy men, that the land itself was not as agriculturally as productive since they had left the area.[89] In the village of Montaillou and its neighbouring settlements, nail parings and hair cuttings were kept from a deceased family member in order to preserve the good fortune of the household.[90] This was perhaps the most domestic end of a spectrum of practice, the other pole being holy relics.

If we allow our gaze to broaden out from the diverting spectacle of miracles, a wider realm of assistance and fortune, an extended thaumaturgical landscape, can be seen. The saints, and the holy, provided one kind of supernatural power. For the Church, this was usually the only acceptable non-natural intervention. But for the laity (and indeed for many individual members of the clergy) other magic was present in their lives, in a number of different ways. It was into this wider terrain that the saints were, at points, located. Thus pilgrimage took place not only to saints' shrines, but also to springs, woods, wells and other sites deemed to be invested with a kind of power. Such unofficial pilgrimage sites had been banned by the Fourth Lateran Council, but we catch brief glimpses of them thereafter. In the mid-thirteenth century, for example, the inquisitor Stephen of Bourbon encountered a shrine in northern France dedicated to a dog. The hound had valiantly defended a young child from a snake, but had subsequently been unjustly slain by its master who had mistakenly assumed that the dog had attacked the infant. The dog was honoured 'as a martyr', and sick children healed at the well where the dog's body had been buried. In 1290, Bishop Sutton of Lincoln wrote to the archdeacon of Oxford to forbid, on pain of excommunication, the veneration of a well 'commonly called St Edmund's'. A similar 'holy spring' that had healing powers was placed under episcopal investigation in a parish in Bridgwater. People in fifteenth-century Italy took their children to a spring for purification – until Bernardino da Siena, denouncing it as devil worship, stopped the practice. As Diana Webb notes, we probably see only a fraction of what was originally there.[91]

Nor was petitioning a saint the only method that people used to address life's other problems. One might pray to a saint for a successful marriage, but one might also use a love potion to try to ensure that a prospective husband stayed faithful, or perhaps consult a soothsayer concerning a proposed marriage.[92] When neighbours were summoned by inquisitors in thirteenth-century Languedoc, some Cathar supporters consulted soothsayers on what would transpire, nervous that they would be betrayed, despite the fact that fortune-telling was as foreign to Cathar theology as it was to Catholic.[93] Prophecy, often conducted by holy women and often used by secular rulers, might be said to be the more acceptable sibling of soothsaying and divination.[94] Saints were often invoked to produce rain, and some living holy men – Bernard of Clairvaux and Bernardino da Siena, for example – were able to do it also. Other methods might be sought: Burchard of Worms recorded, in the eleventh century, a ritual wherein women gathered local girls together, stripped one naked, and led the group out of the village in procession. Having located a particular kind of herb, the naked girl was to dig it out with her little finger. The others, with sticks in their hands, would then chase her to the nearest stream, sprinkle her with water and chant incantations for rain. The girl was then led, walking backwards, home to the village. A real folkloric ritual, or a monk's fantasy? Procedures similarly arcane are recorded for much later periods. An account from seventeenth-century France described how, in time of drought, the old people of the village chose a young, virginal girl who was led to a pool, undressed and then plunged into the water to purify it. More recent accounts from eastern Europe tell of a girl, dressed only in leaves and flowers, dancing and singing her way through the afflicted village. At each doorway, the villagers would throw water over her.[95] Various confession manuals advise asking whether confessants have consulted diviners, done sorcery to locate missing objects, performed incantations to purify their house, or having regarded something with lascivious eyes 'done sorcery or incantations for this kind of thing' – more bluntly, 'if he has done sorcery in order to have women'.[96] There were some professional magic doers, such as Alison, a woman active in Languedoc during the 1240s, who treated illness and did fortune-telling by casting molten lead (though this, she told inquisitors, was only to get money and not because she believed in it). One John Smith of Sleeford, around 1417, publicly asserted that one was allowed to do conjurations and the casting of lots, not least because it had worked for St Peter and St Paul. Matteuccia Francisa, a woman of Todi tried in 1428, cured illness, removed curses, made contraceptives and did love magic.[97] But much of the time magic, spells, incantations, charms and healings were things that all kinds of people did, just as all kinds of people prayed, made votive wax offerings, visited shrines, and so on.

The warp of Christian religion and the weft of what we would now call 'magic' were part of one cloth, for most of the laity. As the Church persuaded people that the objects and words of its divine services were powerful – the Host, chrism, candles, prayers – so there developed attempts to make use of these powers in extra-liturgical settings. An early eleventh-century ritual for blessing a field used the *Pater noster* prayer as a magic incantation. A thirteenth-century confession manual connects sorcery and sacrilege, 'as when things are foolishly stolen from church to do divinations'.[98] A fifteenth-century German manuscript, probably compiled for the good running of a domestic home, contains a cure for menstrual problems: write words from the mass ('By Him, and with Him, and in Him') on a piece of paper and lay it upon the woman's head.[99] The strong instrumentality of such practices is not simply a characteristic of magic: it is part of a wider spectrum of the laity's relationship to religion and the things that religion supplied. Which is not to say that the clergy were not also involved: although canonists and theologians were generally opposed to what they saw as superstitious practices, individual clergy often used such techniques alongside their flock. From a lay perspective it may have been difficult to discern the line between the aid provided by saints and the clerical blessing of fields and livestock, and the aid produced through magical use of sacramental objects.[100]

It may also have been that attitudes shifted over time. In the early Middle Ages, there was a willingness to supply the instrumental aid the peasantry required through liturgical means, in order to establish the power of Christian rituals and relics.[101] From the thirteenth century there was a greater tendency for clerics to condemn magical practices, and this, during the fifteenth century, hardened into the kinds of attitudes leading to witchcraft prosecutions, although large-scale witch-hunts were not a medieval phenomenon, belonging mainly to the late sixteenth and early seventeenth centuries. But condemnation could vary in its tone. The worst kinds of magic were those that maliciously attacked the health of livestock or human beings, or which, regardless of purpose, worked by invoking demons who would fulfil the necromancer's will. These practices could be strongly denounced by the Church, though the evidence for the latter kind of magic – necromancy – suggests that it was an almost entirely clerical practice. Other tones, however, could be adopted, such as fourteenth-century advice to parish priests to warn their parishioners that magic arts and incantations could not help sick men or animals – a warning, that is, that the magic would not *work*.[102] In Poland, in 1454, we see a mendicant friar criticizing a noble woman for making medicinal use of water and wine blessed with a fragment of the True Cross, distributed by the abbey of Lysiec. This, the friar said, was magic, an opinion that placed him somewhat at odds with several centuries of European-wide devotional practice, but perhaps an indication of how clerical ideas varied.[103]

To capture something of the complex interweaving of attitudes and beliefs found in this area, we can look in a little more detail at a specific case from the early fourteenth century. Geralda de Codines was summoned before Bishop Pons de Gualba of Barcelona at the monastery of St Cugats, having been publicly defamed of sorcery and divination in her parish of Subirats. Under questioning, she admitted that she had done conjurations and invocations to help cure sick people. Geralda was certainly not the only magic-worker in the diocese of Barcelona: the episcopal visitation that had first brought her activities to light also found other accusations of sorcery, all made against women, mainly older and unmarried or widowed. Geralda herself was at least 35 and possibly older, but was young enough to be carrying a child at the time of her trial, although no husband is mentioned. These magic-workers were very popular. One priest

reported that 'some of his parishioners at some time or other rushed off to
Marchesia, a female *divinatrix . . .* whom, it was said, all the land hurried to
visit'. Geralda explained her techniques to the bishop. She would invoke God
and the saints, she said, by saying the *Credo, Pater noster* and *Ave Maria* followed by a conjuration which began 'I conjure you by each drop of blood,
I conjure you in whole, I conjure you by God and by lady St Mary and by the
male saints and by the female saints . . .' To make conjurations to heal animals,
she would again recite the *Pater noster* and *Ave Maria* prayers, and would use
her little finger and index finger to make the sign of the cross over the tail of the
animal being treated. She knew a third conjuration too, a bit of nonsense verse
concerning a king with three daughters.

The invocationary use of Christian prayers and ritual were both common in
medieval magic and completely comprehensible: we can see how close the
healing 'conjurations' were to regular prayers to God and the saints for intervention and assistance.[104] But her third, nonsense conjuration was clearly a bit
different: she stressed that 'if she happened to use it, it would be for good purposes', rather than, implicitly, to do anyone harm. In thinking about why
someone would go to seek aid from Geralda and her ilk, we have to recognize
a complex mix of factors. Part of what she did was to deploy perfectly familiar
orthodox ritual, invoking the same powers of intervention that a thousand
shrines would have endorsed. Part also, however, was a more arcane knowledge
that marked her out as a specialist. Further questioning from the bishop elicited
another, intriguing element. Geralda did in fact possess some technical medical
knowledge, which she said she had learnt some 30 years ago from a foreign
medic, being able to diagnose different kinds of malarial fever from the colour
and consistency of a patient's urine. This technique was common medical practice, with no supernatural element, as was Geralda's proposed treatment for
malaria: to confine the patient and fetch other doctors.

The bishop was quite lenient in his punishment, ordering that at Christmas,
Circumcision (1 January) and Epiphany (6 January) Geralda was to stand in
church bareheaded next to her priest, while he explained to the congregation
that no one was to believe in her powers or to ask her for medical help.
Furthermore, she was to visit a local church and there say one hundred *Pater
nosters* and one hundred *Ave Marias* every day for one year. A century or so later,
Geralda might have had a much worse fate, as the image of the witch hardened
into something darker and more demonical.[105] But at this point in time, the
bishop – who clearly shared with Geralda the sense that the common prayers did
one good – was willing to accept that she had acted more or less in good faith,
although she was to cease her activities. In fact, as a further interrogation a few
years later proved, Geralda did not desist. Many ill people came to her 'especially for judging their urine' (so she said); she had not wanted them to come,
but they had come anyway. After consulting with some physicians, the bishop
permitted her to continue diagnosing urine and counselling the sick, but to practise no other medicine. Perhaps to encourage the bishop in the sense that she was
on the right side of the line, Geralda also told him of another magic-worker

called Axa, a Saracen woman who made conjurations with rope (another common magical technique) for evil purposes and to steal things.[106] Clearly the circumstances mean that we are not getting a straightforward account from Geralda; but in persuading the bishop of the existence of 'good' magic-workers like herself, and 'bad' magic-workers like Axa (conveniently not a Christian), we can see a further way in which the complexities of magic, religion and the powers of intervention blurred and overlapped. Having had Geralda's more arcane powers denounced to them by their parish priest, we might imagine that her fellow parishioners would feel more nervous about consulting with her in future. But we can also see that, from the perspective of a layperson suffering from sickness, distinguishing between Geralda with her invocations and medical knowledge, and the healing powers of whichever local shrine was deemed to have the most powerful saint, would be mainly done on grounds of efficacy rather than theology. Geralda might cure, with a mixture of prayer, diagnosis and conjuration; the saint might cure, through invocation or after a short pilgrimage. Both would need some kind of payment, the latter usually in the form of a wax votive offering. It was not that the two were indistinguishable; but that what they *did* was much the same in the end. And the next time one fell sick, who knows which might prove the more effective?

I have highlighted the ways in which these interwoven strands of power and the supernatural were instrumentally useful to the laity. But I do not want to give the impression that it was just the ordinary laity who made instrumental use of such things, nor that this attitude should be seen as 'impious'. There were in fact many other less spiritual ways in which the holy were useful to a range of social groups. Saints were, for example, a very good and very important source of income. The Fourth Lateran Council had banned the exhibition of relics for payment, but local conciliar statutes reworked this injunction so that it excluded 'customary' ritual displays for pilgrims.[107] A successful shrine could mean big money for the religious foundation involved. The local neighbourhood could also benefit, as the chronicler Villani noted regarding the pilgrims who attended the 1300 Jubilee: 'all were adequately provided with victuals, both horses and people, and with great patience and without disturbance or dispute, for I was there and I saw. And from the offerings made by the pilgrims great treasure accrued to the church and to the Romans; all were made rich by their takings.'[108] Secular society did not always benefit, however, and could in fact experience pilgrims as a burden rather than a blessing. In 1106 Abbot Artaud was killed at Vézelay during rioting against dues and services imposed in connection with the newly-built church there. Violent protest continued in subsequent decades, as townspeople objected to the abbey forcing them to provide accommodation without payment for the pilgrims who came to visit the church at Easter and on the feast of St Mary Magdalen.[109] By and large, however, saints meant business, and both Church and people benefited.

The opportunity of pilgrimage itself also had other benefits. Some pilgrims were inspired by intense piety, and perhaps experienced the effort and hardships of travel as an opportunity to undergo a kind of liminality, and thus to perform a kind of holiness themselves. We might see Margery Kempe, who travelled to Santiago, Rome and Aachen, in this light; similarly, the Prussian mystic Dorothea of Montau who, all but one of her children having died, began a life of strict religious observance with a pilgrimage to Aachen in 1384. She went on subsequent pilgrimages, enduring various hardships, but coming closer to God through her suffering, leaving the condition of wife and mother behind her. But Dorothea and Margery were exceptions, not the rule. The majority of pilgrims were young men, who had the time, fitness and freedom to undertake them.[110] Most pilgrimages were not great lengthy treks to glamorous and far distant shrines, but local affairs undertaken within a single diocese. And they were, for many, communal and social events. William Thorpe, tried in 1407 as a Lollard heretic, provided a picture of the pilgrimages he detested:

> every town that they come through, what with the noise of their singing and the sound of their piping, and with the jangling of their Canterbury bells and with the barking out of dogs after them, they make more noise than if the king came there alway with all his clarions and many other minstrels.[111]

Local pilgrimage was also an opportunity for a mixture of piety and pleasure, as Bishop Grandisson makes clear in 1361 when condemning the unauthorized cult that had sprung up around a deceased parish priest in Cornwall. Local people and others came to keep vigils and give offerings, but also, particularly on Saturday evenings, 'victuals and other goods are carried to them at those times, and in the manner of a market are sold. Under the cloak and pretext of this there are feasting, drinking, and shameful meetings, and some so illicit and nefarious that it is not fitting to speak of them.'[112] This kind of joyful, somewhat excessive communal activity is not the only social element to pilgrimage, however. A satirical text, *The Fifteen Joys of Marriage* written around 1400, tells us more:

> And here they are, arrived at Le Puy in the Auvergne, not without difficulty, and they make their pilgrim devotions. God knows how crushed and pushed about the poor husband is in the middle of the crowd in order to get his wife through! Here she is, giving him her girdle and her beads so that he can touch the relics and the venerated statue of Our Lady with them. God knows that he is well jostled, that he gets some good elbowing and is nicely buffeted! Furthermore, there are among the women there with them some rich ladies, maidens and bourgeoisies who are buying beads of coral, jade or amber, and rings and other jewels. So his wife must have them like the others; sometimes, there's no money, but nevertheless he's got to get them.[113]

Beyond the mocking misogyny we can see that pilgrimage could be part of social display, bound up with status and honour. Going on pilgrimage was an effort and a cost, and it marked the important nexus between social status and Christian piety. A weaver called Pierre Sabatier, trying to persuade an inquisitor of his good standing in 1318, said that he paid his tithes, gave alms to the poor and went on pilgrimage; in fact, he emphasized piously, he had confessed his sins at Monxoy, the last staging post before Compostella.[114] Through emphasizing such activities, he hoped to divert suspicion from any awkward opinions he might have previously expressed.

Thinking about social status leads us to another way in which holy people were useful. In late antiquity and the early Middle Ages, holy men had played a particular role as social mediators, to act, from their position as extraordinary people 'outside' the normal bonds and behaviours, as peacemakers. They were, in theory at least, able to arbitrate for the greater good without falling prey to the tensions and temptations of kinship or politics. This ideal may have been no more than a fantasy, bolstered by the propagandistic nature of the sources recording their lives; but it was a useful fantasy nonetheless.[115] Similar functions can be found in the high Middle Ages. Cathar good men, for example, resolved a number of conflicts between southern French noblemen, and Waldensian brothers played a similar role in Alpine villages; the hermit Godric of Finchale, among other things, acted as a mediator in various social situations; and we have seen Nicholas von Flüe perform this role at a national level.[116] The liminal processes through which holiness was often achieved – being taken outside the community through illness, poverty, abandonment of family, wealth, clothing and so forth – left available a mechanism for the holy man (and occasionally woman) to stand at a certain useful distance from social tensions. The holy person or saint could act as a kind of 'supplement' to the mechanisms that governed social life – law, honour, violence and so on – providing a particular kind of intervention.

Valerie Flint has analysed certain miracles associated with Thomas of Cantilupe (d. 1282), which illustrate the point nicely. Several concern accidental deaths of children – a girl pushed into a fishpond by a little boy, a boy crushed beneath his father's ox-cart – and the problems that arose because of the strict English laws pertaining to the king's coroners' inquests. Upon finding a body, the discoverer was supposed to raise the hue and cry, and was then held until someone would stand pledge for him (that is, assume responsibility for his freedom) so that the chief witness was available for the king's officers. And the body was not to be moved until the officials had arrived – even, in theory, if this took several months. Thus, in the stories told, the deaths of the children were concealed or ignored, the discoverer not wanting to have to submit to custody; but the saint (who in life had been bishop of Hereford and connected to the royal court) brought the children back to life, thus resolving the problem. Another miracle involved a woman called Christina who had sold her pigs at market, including an extra pig that had joined her herd long before but had never been claimed. Despite this, she was accused of theft and was sentenced to death. She was hanged, and the body then brought to the church of St Martin to be buried. However, her children having 'measured' her to Thomas (that is, made an offering of a piece of thread, perhaps a candlewick, the length of her body), Christina revived and explained that the saint had grabbed her feet and held her weight while she was on the gallows.

As Flint argues, these tales illustrate the perceived problems with royal justice – its harshness and inflexibility – and the saint's role in ameliorating these problems.[117] We should note, however, that the relationship between saint and king is not oppositional, but supplementary: in proffering confession, pilgrimage and saintly intervention, Thomas Cantilupe provides passing remedies that permit the system to function essentially unchanged.

Finally, saints and holy people were a highly useful source of symbolic power for secular elites. Henry V, for example, used a triumphal pageant entering London after the victory at Agincourt to associate himself with St George, St Edward, St Edmund, and Christ: a complex connection of military and masculine sanctity, England and Christian community. In addition to these very manly saints, however, Henry also showed devotion to St Birgitta and founded, at great expense, Syon Abbey in her honour. Nancy Bradley Warren argues that what the Birgittines gave the king was a kind of 'incarnational politics': their religious observances focused upon the Virgin Mary and her important *maternal* role in the transmission of salvation. Henry's claim to the throne of France (which he was currently pursuing) depended upon the recognition of a female role in the royal lineage. Thus St Birgitta and Syon helped to bolster Henry's image and claims to legitimacy.[118] In France itself, following the great posthumous success of St Louis, the Capetian monarchs had expended considerable effort in continuing to associate their royal line with sanctity, attempting to present most members of the family as saints or potential saints.[119] Associating oneself or one's position with sanctity was not restricted to kings or the nobility: St Anne, mother of the Virgin Mary, was celebrated in late-medieval England and elsewhere as a symbol of familial sanctity, associating the bourgeois household with holiness and the social status it conferred.[120] As we will see in the next chapter, the guilds and confraternities dedicated to saints proffered similar ways of using holiness within social contexts for less elevated folk.

Conclusion

On the abbey church at Vézelay there is a thirteenth-century carved lintel which depicts a procession of peasants, hunters, fishermen and others coming to render tithes. Opposite them are pilgrims from far distant places who have come to receive hospitality and make their oblations. The image is one of order, community and sanctity; and as such, it presents a lie. As outlined above, Vézelay experienced sustained tensions over the activities of the abbey, its control of the pilgrimage site and the demands of hospitality for pilgrims.[121] The carving is not simply an idealized representation of a rather different reality – it is, rather, part of an attempt to shape that reality to an ideal. The saints and the holy possessed a particular kind of power in medieval society, and like all powerful players they were caught up in the political games of their localities and the wider social order of their societies. As Paul Haywood notes, the images of piety, order and power associated with the cult of saints should not be read as a straightforward representation of how medieval society worked: 'This aspect . . . is probably better understood as a projection of how certain sections of the élite felt social life *ought* to be conducted – of the kind of loyalty, obedience, and efficiency they hoped for.'[122] As we have seen, however, the ways in which the laity interacted with saints – and with the other means of intercession they perceived – could in fact vary greatly from this dominant image of order. And as I will demonstrate in Chapter 6, some people disdained saints entirely and had no investment in supernatural intercession.

Holy people, while living, operated within society. The liminal rituals that many underwent did not place them utterly beyond the social arena, as if they had already escaped into the next world. Instead, such rituals positioned them in a particular, symbolically privileged relationship to the social body. And after death, from the perspective of the living, the next life continued to be implicated in the secular world. Saints' cults were hugely malleable. Consider, for example, the case of St Werner of Oberwesel (d. 1287). The young Werner was allegedly murdered by Jews, one of that small, sad pantheon of anti-Semitic martyrs. Miracles began at his tomb and the local populace responded by enthusiastically massacring the local Jewish community. Over the next 200 years an uneasy balance was struck between popular, and recurrently anti-Semitic, devotion to the cult; and sporadic ecclesiastical enthusiasm, tempered by an uneasiness about the common people's interpretations of the saint. In 1428 a large number of witnesses were interviewed concerning Werner's miracles, as part of proceedings for canonization. But in the same year the inquisitor Heinrich Kalteisen wrote a tract challenging Werner's claims to sanctity on the grounds that, according to his own legend, he had been disgracefully working for Jews on Maundy Thursday; and given his youth, he must surely have died with some shameful sins unconfessed. The fifteenth-century canonization witnesses were clearly very proud that Werner had been a vineyard labourer, born of peasant stock, just like them; but this element was a later embellishment, as the earliest sources gave no information on his background or trade. Indeed, it can be argued that Werner was not immediately associated with anti-Semitism, but that this element arose soon after, perhaps even to justify the Jewish massacre that had taken place for other reasons. Just prior to the Reformation, the cult spread to France where, over the course of time, it lost its anti-Semitic association and Werner came to be the patron saint of vinedressers.[123] What actually happened to Werner can never be known. His history shows us very clearly, however, the ways in which saints embodied the changing cultural projections of society; and, indeed, the competing projections of different *parts* of society.

The thaumaturgical aspect of saints – their ability to perform miracles – is perhaps what now makes us suspect that people related to them as 'other' and 'apart' from society. But the evidence concerning non-saintly magic reminds us that the confused area where magic, healing and intercession blur together was extremely broad. That saints worked miracles, healed people, found things, protected communities and enriched the fields, marked them out as powerful; but not necessarily as utterly 'other'. In the same way, the localism so often surrounding saints' cults is not simply a thing to remark, as further evidence that the medieval Church was not a uniform monolith. Rather, it shows us again something of how saints were considered: as one powerful benefactor, part of a hierarchy with other potential benefactors – lord, bishop, parish priest, sooth-sayer, holy woman, hermit, healer, divinatrix – in the locality. One sought inter-cession and assistance from a variety of sources. Belief was more a matter of allegiance than indiscriminate credulity.

4

Community

Each year in fifteenth-century Bologna, on the Rogation days that led up to Christ's Ascension into heaven, the priests and the citizens of the city would make procession. Carrying a beautiful statue of the Virgin Mary, they walked from church to church in the city, traversing its parishes. First came the artisanal companies and confraternities, each marching with his fellows; then the clergy, in their own hierarchical order; and finally the image itself, carried with great honour. Each evening the statue was placed in the hospital of St Maria della Morte, run by the leading confraternity. While the Madonna rested, her subjects would feast together. On the third day, the Madonna was set down in the Piazza Maggiore – the symbolic centre of the city – before eventually being returned to the confraternity's shrine, where it was kept under lock and key.[1]

Such an event was far from unique. Annual processions were, particularly by the fourteenth century, a common facet of civic life across Europe, and smaller-scale processions can be found in towns and villages as well as the great cities. Historians have long seen these practices as an essential expression of medieval community: the whole social body joined together under the unifying symbol of (in this particular case) the Madonna. It is an attractive picture, mixing piety and festivity, social order and communal celebration, the physical space of the city and the collective emotions of its populace. Such a depiction emphasizes an apparent order and stability to medieval communities; processions like the one at Bologna are thus sometimes explained as a natural and joyful expression of these inner qualities.

But consider another moment of community. On 18 September 1363 at the parish church of Malling, a married man called John Newland was called before the consistory court for having committed adultery with Denise Penyes, a single woman. He confessed his sin, and in punishment was beaten three times around the marketplace and three times around the church, further swearing to avoid Denise's company in future under penalty of a 40-shilling fine. Denise herself did not initially respond to the court citation, placing herself under threat of excommunication. Some days later she turned up, confessed, and was also sentenced to public flogging.[2]

The punishment of sexual sins by church courts is also commonplace. John and Denise's case was just one of 65 recorded in this particular document, and the pattern of transgression and punishment is found pretty much wherever records of ecclesiastical tribunals survive. The cases of adultery and fornication may not involve a very large proportion of each local population. But as most of those prosecuted were given the same public penance of being flogged around the market and the church, their presence would have been very visible within each community – as visible, in their own way, as the annual procession at Bologna. I present this case here firstly as a rather crude reminder that community was not always happy, unified and celebratory, but could also be oppressive, coercive and regulated by rituals of violence and public shame.

This fairly obvious point may lead us to further reflection. What we mean by 'community' is not clear-cut. Like 'belief', it is a word that is used very often, but reflect upon far less. Miri Rubin has suggested that medievalists tend to employ the term 'community' without considering its different possible theoretical underpinnings as a concept; it is tempting to see it simply as obvious and natural.[3] But to view community as 'obvious' leads us away from some important questions about it: who is included and who excluded, and for what explicit or implicit reasons? Where are the borders (geographical or conceptual) of a particular community, how are they mapped and how are they policed? How conscious of their collective identity are the community's inhabitants? Do people belong to just one community, or can communities overlap? What 'makes' a community? In recent years some medievalists have started to explore these and other factors, from a variety of viewpoints.[4] In this chapter, I shall consider a variety of means by which religious belief and practice played a role in the production and maintenance of community. The way in which I have subdivided what follows is clearly not the only available framework, and the topics included could easily be placed into different contexts. In the choices taken below, I have sought to emphasize the sense of community as process and activity, rather than as something innately ordered and static. From this perspective, practices like the public performances outlined above (and, indeed, the texts that record them) are seen not as straightforward reflections of community, but as essential elements in its production.

A theologian might posit salvation and moral order as the most important functions played by religion. For a social historian, however, religion's role in creating and sustaining community is arguably its most powerful feature, particularly if we are looking at religion from the perspective of the general population. This is not to suggest either that salvation did not matter to the laity, or that theology does not consider community among its topics. Indeed, the central medieval Christian virtue was *caritas*, 'charity', a concept that for medieval people incorporated a strong sense of community and order. However, the particular emphasis that I am placing upon community as *process* suggests that we should not treat it as a kind of by-product of religious activity, nor as the basic mulch in which religion grew. By not taking community for granted as a concept – not treating it as 'natural' and therefore beyond question – we may better understand how it was produced, and how it was situated within cultural discourses of belief.

Asking questions of our two opening communal events certainly reveals more about them. The church court (known as a consistory court) that sentenced John Newland and Denise Penyes was one mechanism by which local communities were policed, its most obvious complements being the various secular courts of law to which lay people were subject. The role of the Church in social regulation is clearly important here: the authority of the court came from the local bishop, and the moral code of conduct it enforced was propagated by the Church. We shall explore further some ways in which religion policed and ordered communities later in this chapter. For now, let us simply note that ecclesiastical law was not a completely top-down interaction. John and Denise were almost certainly presented to the court by their neighbours; the evidence doesn't show us this explicitly, but it is clearly so in other similar cases, and it is difficult to imagine any other way for this kind of case to reach episcopal officials. Hence, although the official framework was ecclesiastical, the process of policing sexual misdemeanours was, at least in part, communal. Had John and Denise's liaison not displeased at least some in their locality, they would not have been brought before the court.

And what of the procession at Bologna? The story here is what lies behind an apparent show of unity, and the mechanics by which rituals were constituted. Almost all religious processions were linked into the cyclical rhythm of what has been called 'the ritual year', the annual pattern of feasts, fasts and celebrations (discussed further below). Placing a communal celebration into this cycle lent it the aura of timelessness, part of the gentle and endless rise and fall of the seasons: it has been thus many times before, the ritual murmurs, and it will be thus many times again. Thus through the manipulation of space, time and memory do custom and ritual attain their authority. But in fact the procession at Bologna had a quite recent date, and an interesting genealogy. In 1433, a period of heavy and continuous rain was ruining the fields of the *contado* (the rural area upon which an Italian city depended for its sustenance) and famine threatened. The civic oligarchs ordered a three-day procession of clerics, confraternities and lay people through the city, in an attempt to petition God to improve the weather – but to no avail. A five-day procession was then attempted, but without success. So they tried an eight-day procession. Still it rained. Then, in desperation, someone suggested that they should do what the Florentines did: make appeal to a particular image of the Madonna, held in the town of Impruneta, who was generally understood to be very good at controlling precipitation. (We can note in passing the tendency to conflate an image with a saint, and the specialization of particular intercessionary powers.) Taking this statue, and again making procession, the city's prayers were finally answered. Bishop Albergati, the local potentate, then seized the opportunity to associate a newly-invigorated Marian devotion with the oligarchical confraternity he supported, and declared the procession an annual event. The lay members of the confraternity took the leading roles in organizing the ritual thereafter, over the complaints of the cathedral canons who felt that they should be in charge. The canons continued to protest this state of affairs well into the seventeenth century.[5]

So our picture of Bolognese communal unity and piety began its life as a practice borrowed from another city, using an image belonging to a third locality. It was originally directed toward a specific supernatural task, and turned into an 'annual tradition' as part of a power play in civic politics. Moreover, it continued to be a cause of division and dissension within the city, as much as unifying activity. Neither custom nor community, it would thus seem, are quite as simple as they first appear. If one scratches the surface of other processions or collective rituals, similar complexities can often be found. This does not mean that the procession of the Madonna at Bologna was not a communal event, nor that its origins render it 'fake' in contrast to some other 'authentic' processions. All such rituals must have their origins somewhere. But it does mean that the way in which such an event produces a sense of community is complex, and sometimes fraught; and that the overt claims that a ritual can appear to make about its timelessness and naturalness are fictions, deployed to bolster its strategic purposes. As we shall see throughout this chapter, the various means by which community was brought about were frequently more complex than they first appeared, and often bound up with power relations. Community is neither simple nor static. It is something wrought.

Collective activity

Let us look first of all at things that people did together, as a group, as part of their religion. The most immediate framework for such activity was the parish. This subdivision of Christendom developed from the late eighth century on, partly through the building of local churches, but more importantly in the slow extension of sacral power (the ability to baptize, for example) from cathedrals and minsters to parish churches. By the thirteenth century, the parish was simultaneously an administrative unit for ecclesiastical power, a defined geographical space, and a communal entity. Very few new parishes were created in Western Europe after the mid-twelfth century, and so by the later Middle Ages parishes had well-established identities.[6] The rather organic feel that this can give to parishes should not, however, obscure the ways in which their formation and definition were bound up with questions of power and governance. The initial development of the parochial system in the early Middle Ages was part and parcel of the Church's relatively recent position as a major landholder. It had become both 'lord and neighbour', and inescapably more involved in the local communities. A key drive to the definition of parish boundaries was the formalization of the tithing system (explored below) which, as essentially a form of local taxation, demanded that clear lines be drawn in order that no one pay twice or not at all.[7]

So what defined a parish? There was no fixed size, either geographically or demographically; it was simply an area that possessed a church, cared for by a priest./Sometimes a parish would coincide with a manor, sometimes with a village, sometimes they would overlap. In central Europe, where Christianity arrived only in the eleventh century or later, parishes and parish churches were created alongside governmental *castra* (fortified structures with accompanying settlements). Those people who lived away from a *castrum* would have to travel to it to find a church and a priest. Most of the countryside in Hungary, for example, was not covered by any parish boundary until the late Middle Ages.[8] Most European towns had multiple parishes, jostling side by side. Ideally the priest would be resident in the parish, but there were examples of multiple residence or non-residence. This occurred because each church provided a benefice (an income) and, like every income-bearing job in the Middle Ages, benefices were sometimes deployed as gifts within political economies. Although the priest was under the authority of his local dean, and above him the bishop, the right to 'present' a priest for appointment could belong to non-ecclesiastics, usually the local landowner, who might be a lay lord or might be a monastic foundation. There is some evidence in Italy and Germany of local people electing their priest (who would then be 'confirmed' by the local bishop), although this is not found in France or England.[9] These factors must have affected, in different ways in different places, how the parish functioned and how the priest related to the parish community.

For the sake of simplicity let us for the moment imagine a rural parish, its boundaries coinciding with those of the village, equipped with a resident priest. Immediately, we must recognize that we are looking at a community that is simultaneously religious, economic and social. From the perspective of the laity, the parish brought with it certain obligations and certain benefits. Of the former, the most pressing was the tithe: the portion of income and produce handed over to the church in order to provide the priest with his benefice. This was generally understood to be one-tenth of a household's income, though this notional rate might vary in certain ways: if someone's flock produced only seven lambs in spring, for example, the seventh should be given to the priest. Artisans would be more likely to make cash tithes, and this may have been common in towns, but in rural parishes the tithe was usually a literal portion of the goods or livestock themselves. Parishioners were also asked to make oblations (gifts) at particular points of the year, typically Christmas, Easter and the day of the saint to whom the parish church was dedicated. A portion of revenue could also be due to the church on the sale or transfer of lands, and from the estate of a deceased parishioner. And as a less regular expenditure, parishioners were expected to pay for the upkeep of parts of the church (usually the nave and the bell tower), to fence and weed the churchyard, and to supply various necessities such as bells, crucifixes, chalices, missals, vestments, processional banners, books, candles and the font.[10]

Were these onerous demands? A notional one-tenth, perhaps negotiable in size, is not a massive exaction, although it was quite high in comparison to secular taxation. Most of the statutes regulating tithing include exceptions to be made in the case of poverty. However, it was not the only taxation incumbent on the laity: households would also be trying to meet the dues demanded by their local lord or city government, and on occasion royal taxes as well. As Christopher Dyer has shown for England, the income levels of most rural households – even among the higher echelons of the village – provided very little surplus in most years, and many would be impoverished when harvests failed.[11] At such times, tithing may have been more demanding; but, of course, the parish priest would be sharing in the ill luck and perhaps therefore one should not assume an automatic sense of grievance. It is clear from clerical admonitions that partial payment was the more common problem, giving 'the worst part' of one's stock as Robert Mannyng put it.[12] A variety of tithe and other monetary disputes in the register of Bishop Oliver Sutton give a flavour of regular points of argument. Here, in the early 1290s, we find the rector of Aylesbury in dispute with lay people from a neighbouring village, who had pastured their sheep at Aylesbury but then refused to pay any tithe on them. At Hagworthingham, the parishioners were ordered to contribute to the cost of building a belfry for the local church (Sutton here was actually chasing up the dean, who apparently had not previously bothered to pursue the issue). More intriguing than these cases of avoidance is a letter instructing a dean to pursue action against three parishioners who were accused of having 'conspired' to prevent the payment of oblations known as maynport; and a letter to the dean of Framland to warn, and excommunicate if necessary, those people preventing the rector of Kettleby from collecting the tithe on hay.[13] These two instances may indicate some organized rebellion against a particular clerical tax – but they might be more to do with a dispute between the local lord and the priest, the lord attempting to disrupt or appropriate parish finances.

What does seem to have caused resentment, however, is when particular ecclesiastical demands conflicted with the expectations of the local community. Raymond de Laburat, whom we met at the start of Chapter 2, had been excommunicated along with his neighbours for failing to pay a tithe on lambs. They had also resisted providing a large Easter candle for the church. There was no clear revolt against tithes in principle, but rather against these particular exactions. At heart was an assertion of a local way of doing things, which came into conflict with the bishop's (and, as it happened, the inquisitor's) sense of ecclesiastical right. Raymond asserted the fluidity provided by local practice: that, for example, the parish should make the best candle that they could, rather than a candle of a particular weight and size. He also turned to the authority of custom, arguing that the tax on lambs should be paid 'as my father paid it'.[14] These grounds of argument are important, revealing again the strength and power of locality in the laity's relationship with religion. Where we find other evidence for clear resentment at income gathered by churchmen it is again usually in situations where the exactions were seen as exploitative and unnecessary. A document from the early 1250s, recording complaints made by Toulousan citizens against different priests, illustrates certain recurrent issues: demands for money for burial, demands for money in advance before blessing marriages, and even demands for payment before baptizing ill children. Similar complaints can be found in visitation records, and the complaint was usually that what was supposed to be a customary gift – a small amount after the blessing of a marriage for example – had been turned by the priest into a formal charge for his service. The chaplain of St Sernin, for example, was alleged to have refused Vital de Aycio communion, telling him that because Vital had not offered any pennies in oblation at mass, he was not going to offer him the body of Christ – a very clear transaction![15]

The purpose of tithes was to provide for the fabric of the church and the income of the priest. One could say, therefore, that in contrast to the occasional royal tax spent on foreign wars tithing provided a local service immediately visible and accessible to all. The church was a place of communal gathering. The priest provided services to the community that he and only he could perform: the sacraments of baptism, communion, marriage and the last rites. If he was any good at his job, he visited the sick, distributed alms to the poor; he preached to his flock, providing instruction but perhaps also entertainment; he may (perhaps more from the fourteenth century onwards) have provided a small degree of education to the local children. And he heard confessions and provided penances; which is to say, he tried to save the souls of his parishioners. These were the goods that tithing bought. With a diligent priest – perhaps interacting and aiding his parishioners in further ways, not obvious in the historical record – one can well imagine that the transaction was not much resented. A lacklustre priest, or a priest trying to change local practices in ways the community disliked, might be more likely to provoke resistance. And as we shall see in Chapter 6, in some circumstances of harsh lordship or economic crisis, tithes could become a key point of dispute and even revolt.[16]

Objections might be raised to the quasi-commercial, transactional way in which I have described tithing and the care of souls here. Although sixteenth-century reformers may have objected to the 'selling' of salvation, such concerns were focused particularly on the huge inflation of indulgences (time off from Purgatory, bought from the Church for cash) found only at the end of the Middle Ages, and not on the general business of supporting the ecclesiastical framework. This 'corruption', as the reformers saw it, should not be projected back throughout the medieval period.[17] Nor should one see the priest as ruthlessly exacting large sums of money from the locality. Priests could be as poor or as wealthy as their parishioners, and some of the very large number of unbeneficed priests were perhaps among the least well off.[18] However, this does not remove the fact that, in aggregate, money flowed from the laity to the clergy; and hence there is evidence that some medieval people saw their contributions as providing them with a certain sense of possession. Raymond de Laburat, for example, decrying the exclusion from church brought by excommunication, apparently rallied his disgruntled neighbours by shouting 'We made the churches and we buy all that is necessary for the churches, and the churches are ours . . . !' By the fifteenth century, the formalized duties of churchwardens and similar lay offices that had developed in some areas would surely have furthered these feelings of ownership.

Ownership might well be felt for what was an important communal building. An example from Gützkow, in what is now eastern Germany, is suggestive. The unconverted local inhabitants, in 1120 or so, paid a considerable sum of money to build a pagan temple. As their area came under Christian rule, the new local bishop wanted to destroy this monument, but the townsfolk begged him to convert it instead into a church.[19] Keeping a valuable communal building mattered more than the fine points regarding religious adherence. As we see throughout Europe, both church and churchyard had many uses beyond the liturgy. The Synod of St-Hippolyta in Austria in 1284 forbade the selling of wine and other goods, or the use of the church as a grain store – except when it was absolutely necessary. Similarly, around 1258 the bishop of Bath and Wells banned the laity from building booths or stalls in the churchyard, or holding markets or 'dishonest games' there. William of Pagula's *Oculis sacerdotis*, a popular manual for parish priests in the fourteenth and fifteenth centuries, says likewise and adds prohibitions against holding legal courts or dances and other festivities in the churchyard.[20] A charter from mid-thirteenth-century Picardy records an agreement between the village of Domvaast and the local abbey over the rebuilding of the parish church. Among other things, it was agreed that the church could be built in such a way as to serve as a refuge, 'not so as to be able to fight against their lord, but to defend themselves' – an agreement that raises several interesting possibilities.[21] Many more examples could be found, and a spread of evidence shows that parishioners made use of this communal resource in a variety of ways.[22] *Handlyng Synne*, Robert Mannying's fourteenth-century instructional poem, warns people that they may commit sacrilege if they hold 'carols, wrestlings or summer games' in the churchyard, or perform plays or singing when the priest is conducting mass.[23] What clerics particularly sought to discourage, therefore, was the disruption of services and activity that might pollute the sacred space of the cemetery. Many of the prohibitions include a fear that secular activities such as markets might lead to violence: if blood was shed on holy ground, it had to be reconsecrated by the bishop with holy water. There is a degree of struggle here between ecclesiastical and secular views. A fifteenth-century story encodes the wider fears of 'polluting' the space of the church through lay activity: a couple having sex in church were stuck together by God mid-copulation. The homily is glossed 'And therefore here is an example that nobody should do any such filth in church, but should keep it clean and worship God therein.'[24]

This chapter began with a particular communal activity, the Rogationtide procession at Bologna. This was far from the only annual gathering that medieval communities performed. As mentioned above, pattern of services, celebrations, rituals and feasts punctuated the calendar year, and in rural areas (where the vast majority of the medieval population lived) these were intertwined with the cycle of agricultural duties. Let us join the turning wheel at the beginning of the winter season, usually marked by Michaelmas (29 September). Communities would plough, sow winter corn, move cattle from summer to winter pasture. On Hallowe'en, the night before the feast of All Saints (1 November), bonfires would be lit and games played. The period of Advent, starting on Martinmas (11 November), was supposed to be marked by giving up meat and fasting on soup and fish (although the poem *Gawain and the Green Knight* satirically suggests that soup was not so bad if one was given 'two helpings of each'; and neither was a choice of baked, boiled, grilled, stewed and spiced fish, particularly when taken with wine).[25] This fast was broken by the slaughter of animals for the Christmas feasts, and the beginning of a brief respite, in rural areas, from agricultural labour. In the 12 days following Christmas, plays and entertainments were put on. These included mock processions involving 'Lords of Misrule' in secular settings, or 'Boy Bishops' in religious ones: youths 'elevated' to power for the day, usually making procession to collect money from the locality. Records of boy bishops are found at all English cathedrals in the later Middle Ages and also in some parishes. There has sometimes been a temptation to read such diversions as acts of cultural rebellion, inverting the usual hierarchical order of society. More notable, however, is the mocking of age rather than class: certainly in cities, the 'Lord of Misrule', although a youth, was still drawn from the familial ranks of the ruling oligarchs.[26]

The Christmas period came to an end on 7 January with the resumption of labour. This day frequently saw ploughs being blessed either inside or outside church, and there is also some evidence of a non-clerical ritual: 'leading of the plough about the fire, as for good beginning of the year, that they should fare the better all the year following' as the fifteenth-century poem *Dives and Pauper* describes it.[27] Candlemas, on 2 February, saw another communal event as people went in procession with blessed candles and then enjoyed a feast. Ash Wednesday marked the beginning of Lent – the period of fasting leading up to Easter, and hence a movable period – and the days before Lent were again a time for feasting and celebration, a carnival (*carne vale* meaning 'farewell to meat') in preparation for the privations to come. Palm Sunday had another procession to church, with branches or 'palms' being blessed in memory of Christ's entry into Jerusalem. Easter itself was the most solemn and important liturgical moment in the year. Every layman and laywoman would be expected to make confession and, thus purified, partake of Christ's body in the form of the consecrated Host. In England, another, rather less solemn ritual came soon after Easter week: Hocktide. On two days, first the men and then the women would chase and attempt to tie up members of the opposite sex, and those that they captured had to pay a 'fine' – donated to the parish – to be released.

May Day (1 May) was another key moment of festivity. Games would be held, including the election of youthful may queens and kings, and the blossoming of spring celebrated by bringing foliage and flowers into houses. May Day was definitely a sexy occasion; Robert Mannyng warned that garlanding women with flowers and gathering them together 'to see which was fairer' was sinful and lecherous. Rogation days (linked in timing to Easter, so also movable) were the Monday, Tuesday and Wednesday leading up to Christ's Ascension into heaven, and were again fasts prior to feasting. As in Bologna, civic processions could mark this holy occasion. Similarly, in parishes it was often a time for 'beating the bounds': going on procession with the parish priest to bless the fields and note the boundaries of the parish. At every boundary marker – an old tree, a stream, a stone, a bridge – the children on the procession would be smacked, or knocked against the object, to secure the borders in their memory and hence in the future life of the community. Particularly from the fourteenth century onwards, the feast of Corpus Christi (again movable) was marked by further communal processions, and in towns these frequently became the high-point of civic self-representation, marked also by the performance of plays.

Midsummer (24 June) came as the last of these celebrations, and was another occasion of games, bonfires and other events. A tradition seen across Europe was to set light to a wheel which was then pushed down a hill or mountain. Late-medieval and sixteenth-century evidence interprets this dramatic symbol as both the sun falling and the wheel of fortune turning. Lammas (1 August) was seen as the notional end of summer and transition into the fecund autumn season. On Lammas ('Loaf Mass'), ordinary bread was blessed in church and people feasted on the first fruits from the fields. Harvest, now beginning, was the busiest time of year. It is unmarked by formal feasts or rituals, but was probably one of the most communal periods as most of the locality would be working together in different ways to bring in the produce. At the end of harvest, we find Michaelmas again – and thus the year begins once more.[28]

It is very tempting to present this cycle of ritual as something as timeless and unchanging as the seasons themselves, and hence a reflection of medieval society's bucolic stability. It is certainly the case that the pattern of the agricultural year, from ploughing to harvest, was enmeshed in the ritual cycle and its changing tasks were, in broad terms, marked by various of the celebrations. Certain of these – particularly those at the summer and winter solstices – doubtless had their original roots in pre-Christian pagan practices. But one can present too organic a picture, where the browns and greens of the land and its demands obscure the more vibrant hues of human experience. While the seasons and their associated tasks persisted, the individual people undertaking those tasks did not. Boys whose heads were knocked while beating the bounds grew up into young men who chased girls during May Day. The girls who tied up young men on Hockday became mothers who decorated the house at Christmas. The role of the individual, and hence his or her precise place in the schema of ritual celebration, changed during the course of their life. Moreover, people were not static: they might move village, and the new location may have brought fresh rituals. Far from all English villages, for example, had boy bishops. Different locations would have celebrated particular saints' days – the saint to whom the local church was dedicated, for example – and in some places these celebrations might be more important to the community than some of those notionally shared across Christendom. People moved from place to place, particularly in harder times from the countryside to the town, bringing their rituals with them, but perhaps also changing them in the process. Thus something that looks particularly rural and bucolic – the fecund celebrations of May Day, for example – had an active life as a ritual in towns and in elite courts, not just in country parishes.[29] In later medieval towns, the civic authorities could play a major role in organizing ritual celebrations and devotions, including their timing: in 1340, for example, the town of Poggibonsi in Italy switched the feast day of their local saint Lucchese from 28 April to the first Sunday in May.[30]

Moreover, recent work on medieval festal culture has argued that these kinds of rituals can express or permit different things in different contexts. The gathering up of foliage for Maying appears to be one of the most collective and celebratory of rituals. But in 1311, it was precisely this practice that became the focus for dispute between the monks of Pontoise and the commune of Chambly. The monks had been given ownership of a local wood by Louis IX back in 1261, and had allowed the lay people to gather flowers and green boughs from it in May. This had been done peacefully for years, but on two days in 1311, very large groups – 500 one day, 1000 the next – stripped the wood of timber and other resources. This was clearly more than overenthusiasm for the festival, as royal officials summoned by the monks attempted to forbid the group from further gathering on the second day, only to be overwhelmed by force of numbers. It is likely, therefore, that the commune, through its excessive exploitation of the wood, was attempting to score a political and economic point over the abbey; hence the regular practice of Maytime festivity provided, in this context, an opportunity to express discontent.[31] A slightly different perspective comes from Louvain in the thirteenth century. In this town in the Netherlands in 1210, the bourgeoisie gained the power to elect their own leaders annually rather than have officials with decade-long jurisdiction imposed upon them by the local duke. These elections were traditionally held on 24 June – the feast of St John the Baptist, or Midsummer. In Louvain, the process of election was marked by strident music-making and popular festal celebrations. It may be therefore that one of the symbolic themes associated with Midsummer – the turning wheel of fortune that brings down the power of the highest and raises up the lowest – helped to express the town's democratic gains over the region's potentates.[32]

Nor is it very helpful to overemphasize the 'pagan' element to celebrations, if by this we mean to suggest that an utterly different religious tradition continued to lurk beneath Christianity. There was no hidden religion, in the sense of a self-consciously oppositional faith. What might appear to be quite unChristian elements, such as leading the plough about the fire for good fortune at the beginning of the year, was functionally similar to other practices – blessing the plough or the fields, for example – where the sacramental power of the priest was more clearly central. It is true that at various points in time, the Church criticized certain festivities. In 1244, for example, Robert Grosseteste, bishop of Lincoln, writing to his archdeacons regarding various clerical abuses, noted that 'the clergy, as we have heard, make games which they call *miracula*, and other games which they call the bringing-in of May or of Autumn, which the laity call "scot-ales"'.[33] Several thirteenth-century Dominican *exempla* condemn the dances that young men and women engaged in on feast days, preferring, as the preacher saw it, 'a worldly day to the day of God and the saints'.[34] But these are not outright rejections of 'folkloric' culture: Grosseteste's explicit concern was for the behaviour of the clergy, not the laity, and the Dominican preachers decried dancing because they thought it could engender lust. A lurid story from *Handlyng Synne* tells of Christmas carollers who disturbed the mass. The priest cursed them to dance uncontrollably for the following 12 months. In an effort to save his sister, one man grabbed her arm, only to have it come off in his hands and his sibling dance on. Burying the limb, it three times shimmied out of the grave.[35] The story (and Mannying knew that it was a tall tale) emphasizes a gap between raucous secular behaviour and righteous Christian worship, but once again it is the fact that the carollers disrupted the service that seals their fate, rather than a blanket condemnation of lay celebration, dancing or singing.

One may see differences between lay festivity and clerical holy day, but they are differences of emphasis rather than utterly separate worlds. It is not that lay people held their own celebrations instead of ecclesiastical ones. They had *both*, and hence clerically-sanctioned communal celebrations and more secular games and feasts overlapped rather than competed. From the perspective of certain moralists and reforming bishops, the division between sanctioned ecclesiastical celebrations and uncouth secular festivals might have seemed both abundantly clear and a matter of some concern. But from the perspective of the laity themselves, it is likely that no clear line was drawn: whether processing to church with candles or organizing May kings and queens, the feasts were moments of collective organization and interaction. The religious and secular worlds were enmeshed, not least because of the religious nature of the calendar itself. In England, for example, accounts were usually settled on Michaelmas, Christmas, Lady Day and Midsummer. At Carlton, in Nottinghamshire, an annual ploughing competition (used to share out the common land among the competitors for the coming year) was held on the day after Epiphany (6 January), attended by the lord, the parson and all the free men of the village.[36] For those men taking part, would anything separate their competition and subsequent celebrations from the preceding Christmas rituals? Moreover, as financial and administrative burdens upon the parishioners increased over the later Middle Ages, so too did their sense of rights and involvement in the church and the liturgical celebrations.[37]

These events in the parish worked, in a variety of ways, to sustain community. They did so not least because they were necessarily collective activities: collaboration and group endeavour were built into their very foundations. Keeping to the calendar was itself an act of community: Jacques de Vitry tells of a town where one old man, who had memorized the dates of all the festivals, would on those days put on a pair of red shoes and walk around in public, thus alerting his neighbours to the fact that it was a holy day and they should abstain from labour.[38] The feasts and festivals were part of collective memory, which was an important cement for binding folk together. During the Rogation days' processions, memory, space, the sacred and the secular all conjoin: the parish would attend mass at church early in the morning, and then walk the fields to bless them, hoping to ensure a good harvest. They marked out the geographical borders of the parish, beating the bounds. Having fasted over the three days, the community feasted together in celebration. A sermon that John Mirk wrote for the occasion emphasizes how important it was to join in, suggesting that failing to contribute was as sinful as not attending mass. He follows this injunction with a picture of those 'fiends that float in the air' who, upon hearing the thunder of the spring storms, fall to earth and cause mischief:

> They make argument between neighbours, and manslaughter from this; they start fires, and burn down houses and towns; they raise up winds, and blow down houses, steeples and trees; they make women to overlay [accidentally smother] their children; they make a man kill himself, hang himself or drown himself in despair . . .

The demons' deeds are all, in one way or another, attacks upon the fabric of the community – largely blameless crimes that nonetheless rend apart people's lives. To ward off these effects, Mirk says, one fasts and then goes upon procession, and the procession is like Christ leading his troops into battle.[39] One can imagine how this rallying cry could make parishioners feel, in that ritual moment, very much part of one group with mutual interests at heart.

But another English sermon gives us a slightly different picture of what that Rogationtide procession might be like: 'do not go in procession', it admonishes, 'talking of nice tales and japes . . . as you walk; or to backbite [gossip about] your other Christians. Nor go more for pomp and pride of the world than for to please God.'[40] Collective ritual *could* produce feelings of fraternal affection and charity, but, as we shall see further below, they could also express tensions and hierarchies. Parishes, villages, towns and cities were not always unified groups, and were certainly not equal societies. Some ordinary lay people could feel a sense of ownership over their parish churches; but, particularly as the structures were extended and rebuilt in the fourteenth and fifteenth centuries, more divisive gradations may have entered as richer members of the parish endowed certain chapels or windows. As Andrew Brown has noted, one must be wary of statements ascribing efforts to 'the whole parish community' (as the documents sometimes put it): it was probably always a wealthy minority who put most in, and thereby advertised their status.[41] Nor were people's pious affections necessarily limited only to their own parish. A leatherworker called William de Altarippa left, in his will of 1243, gifts to various churches of the Knights Templar both in Toulouse where he lived, but also in villages far to the north and to a monastery to the south. The area of the bequests of this man of fairly modest means covered 90 kilometres. Similarly, the early sixteenth-century will of Annis Laci left money to the church where she and her husband were buried, and to the church where she was born, and to another church in Cambridge.[42] The sense of religious community began in the parish, but was not necessarily bounded by it. Let us now turn, therefore, to other ways in which community was produced, delimited, maintained and policed.

Exclusions

Bishop Pons de Gualba of Barcelona, whom we saw questioning Geralda the witch in the previous chapter, spent a good deal of time in 1303 making episcopal visitation to his diocesan parishes. The procedure was for the bishop to arrive with his retinue, receive anyone who was being confirmed, administer tonsure to anyone going into holy orders, and then to summon a few lay people – always men, and presumably senior members of the parish – to report under oath on the moral doings of their neighbours. Most often this would result in a fairly lengthy list of complaints about the misbehaviour of the parish clergy, and to a lesser extent the laity, with a strong focus upon fornication and gambling. On 9 July, however, Pons fetched up in the parish of St Maria da Pinu. Here the normal pattern was broken: the six lay witnesses 'knew nothing', they said, of any misdeeds among the clergy. But they did have some more pressing complaints. There were several adulterers and fornicators in the parish, which was perfectly common, but also some prostitutes and brothels, which was not. Moreover, they alleged the following:

> Item they said that Na Hanon, Jewess, and her daughter are public sorcerors, such that publicly they come to Christians to do sorcery and of this they are very much defamed . . .
>
> Item they said that Jews made many dwellings and homes in certain houses . . . that greatly overflowed causing much danger to the souls of the neighbouring Christians.
>
> Item the Jews of Barcelona had bored through the wall in various places, through which openings and other ways they brought women into their houses and there was much pimping and larceny and other dishonesty.
>
> Item they said that the Jews and Jewesses, under cover of certain goods that they carried for sale, entered the houses of Christians and there carried on pimping and many bad and dishonest things.
>
> Item they said that Jews made themselves breakers of marriages, which was most dishonest and pernicious.
>
> Item they said that [the Jews] did not wear their hoods or their cloaks when moving amongst Christians as they are supposed to do.[43]

In terms of medieval anti-Semitism, this is a relatively restrained example. Much more explicit expositions of hatred for Jews could be evinced from other evidence across Europe, and moreover evidence of intimidation, violence and murder rather than just accusations. But the parishioners' lurid fears are interesting nonetheless, in that they illustrate a number of elements in medieval Christian animosity toward Jews and the role that this played in the production of community.

A powerful tool in making community is exclusion. Exclusion draws lines, divides and so describes the world. By pointing at what we claim we are not, we assert who we are. Hate is thus a useful tool, erasing or silencing any lurking sense of connection to the one pointed at. '[The Holy Spirit] hates them and I do too. /And God hates them and I hate them / and the whole world must hate them', sang Gautier de Coinci of the Jews in thirteenth-century France. He wrote his verses within a monastic milieu, but his vernacular texts reached a much wider lay audience.[44] That hatred had several functions: then, as nowadays, blame for the woes inflicted by society, economics and chance could be placed onto the outsider. The ugliness imputed to the outsider implies beauty for oneself, and both qualities are understood to indicate inner moral status of good and evil. And ugliness reassures that it is their fault that they are hated; they clearly deserve it and draw hatred upon themselves. Social theorists, drawing upon psychoanalysis, often describe these processes as the construction of an 'Other', against whom one's 'Self' is positioned and thus made whole. This basic mechanism is clearly present in the Barcelonan visitation. The houses of Jews should be kept away from Christians, the parishioners tacitly suggested, and Jews should not use trade as an excuse to enter Christian dwellings. Jews, it is implied, carried out apparently innocuous tasks (selling goods, on this occasion) as a cover for their true, repellent nature; and for this reason they should wear clothes that clearly marked them out as different, so that Christians could avoid them. These demands had first been made at the Fourth Lateran Council in 1215, which ordered Jews to wear distinguishing badges on their clothing, and mandated other requirements excluding them from Christian society.[45] Similar ecclesiastical legislation can be found in various local councils: 'We forbid any Christians, men or women, to work for Jews in their houses or presume to dwell therein, and we order that Jews be compelled to wear visible signs by which they may be distinguished from Catholics'; 'Jews . . . are not to live intermixed with Christians, but should have their houses contiguously in one place in the city or town, such that the habitations of the Jews are always separated by a wall or ditch from the common habitations of the Christians'; 'Jews . . . are to carry a sign of cloth . . . sufficiently large and of different colour to their clothing so that they can be seen and recognised.'[46]

This anti-Semitism did not begin in 1215. Some historians argue that 1096 is a key date, marking the bloody passage of those who, while heading East to fight for Jerusalem, decided to slaughter Jews along the way, as the Jews were more convenient 'enemies of Christ'. Others have suggested that this violence, though appalling for those on the receiving end, was not unusual for the time and marked no particular watershed in relations that were always liable to turn nasty.[47] It is clear, however, that animosity against Jews increased over the course of the later Middle Ages. As I mentioned in the last chapter, stories appeared in England and France in the twelfth century of children murdered by Jews in mimicry of the Crucifixion, the first and most famous being William of Norwich in 1144. These tales were repeated long after, in preaching *exempla* and in works of literature (including Chaucer's *Canterbury Tales*).[48] Germany, and to a lesser extent Spain, produced tales of Jews stealing and then abusing the consecrated Eucharist. Sometimes this was presented as a Jewish attempt to disprove the Eucharistic miracle, but frequently – and contradictorily – as a desire to re-enact the tortures inflicted upon Christ's body by biblical Jews (as the medieval Christians saw it).[49] In the thirteenth century, under the aegis of the papacy and of Louis IX of France, copies of the Talmud were burnt in Paris and elsewhere.[50]

Pogroms occurred across Europe, often making Jewish communities choose between forced conversion to Christianity or martyrdom. Between April and September 1298, for example, thousands of Jews in Röttingen, Würzburg, Nuremberg and other German towns were slaughtered by a cohort of Swabian noblemen. Finally, there were the expulsions, first from cities or landowners' domains, and then from kingdoms: from England in 1290 (never to return until Cromwell's Protectorate), from Sicily in 1292, from France in 1306. In Austria in 1419, at a time when German soldiers were heading East to fight Hussite heretics in Bohemia, there were rumours of Jews desecrating the Host, and forming alliances with the heretics (who did not believe in Christ's presence in the Eucharist). The following year there were mass arrests of Jews, who were imprisoned in Vienna. Some killed themselves in prison, some converted. Those remaining were burnt to death by the banks of the Danube in March 1421.[51]

Thus Christian society, particularly from the twelfth century onwards, put a good deal of effort into demonizing the Jews. The stories were repeated for centuries, and did not diminish after the expulsions but, if anything, grew worse. Artistic depictions of Jews were not content with recording the imposed signs on their clothing, but further marked them out as 'Other' by giving them hooked noses, dark skin and even horns.[52] The stories and images are important because, as we can see from the Barcelona case, storytelling about Jews was a key element in sustaining anti-Semitism and thus keeping them apart from Christian community. The parishioners talking to Bishop Pons were literally 'telling tales', alleging vague and unnerving practices – holes in walls, breaking up marriages – against 'the Jews' as an undifferentiated group. One strand in past historiography has sought to explain, in whole or in part, animosity against Jewish groups by reason of their own actions, particularly by the association of Jews with moneylending. But this approach is wrongheaded, for at least two reasons. First, although moneylending was a major activity for the very small Jewish community in England – not least because they were forbidden to engage in most other commercial activities – this was not always the case elsewhere, and Jews in fact did many different trades.[53] We can see this, in passing, in the parish of St Maria above: clearly some Jews sold things, as the claim regarding their entry into Christian houses states. Second, blaming the victim for his or her own oppression diverts attention away from what functions such social hatred plays. For while there was undoubtedly a good deal of popular ill-feeling toward Jews of the kind displayed in Barcelona, the more lurid stories of Host desecration and child murder only became programmes for action when given force by social elites. As Miri Rubin notes, the violent atrocities committed against the Jews depended in large part upon the efforts of preachers, inquisitors, bishops and civic officials who nurtured and sustained the narratives of hatred.[54]

Preaching, in particular, played a very important role in sustaining and disseminating stories about Jewish evil. The mendicant orders are prominent here, and the collections of preaching *exempla* that they and others collated for European-wide usage all contain at least some stories of Jewish plotting.[55] The explicit point of such tales was to assert the presence of Christ's body in the Host, and to emphasize the power of Eucharistic and other miracles to lead Jews to conversion. But the implicit message that they spread was more hateful. Thus it is important to see these stories not as straightforward reflections of popular belief about the Jews, but as performing the cultural work of producing, sustaining and feeding those beliefs. Moreover, this general mutter of suspicion and dislike could play a strategic role in other contexts. Actions against the Jews in thirteenth-century England, including their eventual expulsion, played a role in wider political struggles. Simon de Montfort, leading a baronial rebellion against Henry III in 1264, made attitudes toward the Jewish population (whom he had long persecuted) part of political propaganda, as a foil to claims for national self-interest and unity. Henry followed suit, and Edward I after him, leading up to the eventual expulsion of all Jews from England.[56] Thus anti-Semitism could be part of political strategy. Similar activities can be found within popular politics also, such as the uprising known as the Shepherd's Crusade of 1320. This involved attacks on Jewish communities in France, but as part of a protest against royal power, in the context of a period and place where Jews were seen as fiscal agents of the state.[57]

We may wonder whether the Barcelonan parish accusations are similarly directed toward a particular strategic goal, albeit one more local. What is notable is the recurrent harping upon sexual fears: the repeated suggestion of sexual contact between Jewish men and Christian women in each other's houses, and that the Jews were 'breakers of marriages'. Desire to prevent Jews and Christians having sex was not new, having lain explicitly behind at least some of the ecclesiastical legislation requiring Jews to wear distinguishing signs of their Jewishness. But it is an unusual feature in this set of episcopal visitations, appearing in no other parish. What is then striking about St Maria da Pinu is that the parishioners also complained about the presence of brothels: 'they say that Maria de Ulmo, who lived by the house of Eymeric Bos, was a public whore and moreover procured others for libidinous purposes', 'they say that next to the oven den Thio is a public brothel and there are there at least ten whores', 'Item, Raimund Speciar always sustained and sustains in his own hostel low and venal women commonly known as whores', 'they say that Bernard de St Eulalia held publicly a brothel and gambling den, and was a pimp'.[58] While accusations of fornication and concubinage were common in every parish's visitation – here as throughout Europe – concerns about brothels and prostitutes were not. Clearly the parish witnesses felt themselves to be living in a red-light district. The accusations against the local Jews might therefore be part of a tactical response: if one wishes to get the authorities to do something about prostitution, suggesting that it leads to a kind of interfaith, sexual melting pot is a cunning tactic.[59]

Implacable hatred was not universal, and the images of absolute Otherness work to cover up the actual quotidian quality of Jewish/Christian relations. As we shall see in Chapter 6, sporadic evidence from inquisitorial registers shows some Christians suggesting that the Jewish faith was as good, in its own way, as their own. The ecclesiastical legislation flowing from Lateran IV that forbade contact between Jews and Christian servants, and vice versa, makes sense only if such contact was actually a feature of medieval life; and medieval servants were a much less subservient part of the household than their nineteenth- and twentieth-century equivalents. The very complaints of the St Maria parishioners illustrate how close Jewish and Christian communities were.

Thus the processes of exclusion that worked to define and delimit community could render a very distorted picture of real social life. Jews were not innately 'outsiders' to medieval society. It was the *process* of exclusion that pushed them 'outside' at certain points of time, only actually leaving medieval communities when physically expelled from various countries. Before that point (and in the places they remained, such as Spain and northern Italy) they were intimate members of medieval communities. It was their very familiarity that permitted religious ideologies to make use of them as 'Others', mapping what was Christian by pointing to what was Jewish in the stories woven by *exempla*.[60] In their appropriation by that cultural mechanism, they were not alone. Certain other groups were held at a curious double-distance from the community: both held 'apart' as different, dangerous or hateful, and kept close as useful markers of community's limits. Prostitutes, for example, in the later Middle Ages often also had to wear distinguishing clothing and live in certain restricted areas. They were also seen as a necessary evil, providing an outlet for male desire that might otherwise lead to worse sexual crimes.[61] Lepers, in a different fashion, were held in a liminal position; often literally, as the leper houses to which they were confined were frequently built at the perimeter of cities.[62] Again, the leper had a use for Christian community: guided by Christ's actions in the New Testament, giving alms to lepers – or even, for the very devout, caring for them bodily by washing their feet – was a way of performing particularly pious actions. More negatively, given that what constituted leprosy was medically hazy – 'leper' was as much a cultural as a medical category, often diagnosed by collective opinion – the revulsion and threat of infection it encoded could be deployed in the unofficial politics of parish life. For example, in 1413 one Simon Daniel alleged that many people in Whitstable were 'afraid to drink the beer of . . . Christine [Colmere] because she was strongly infected and inflicted with the disease of leprosy'.[63] We know of Simon's words only because the man to whom he spoke, John Sanden, strongly disagreed and did not think Colmere was leprous. It is impossible to tell what exactly lay behind the slander, if slander it was. But accusing someone of activities or afflictions that would make them socially outcast – leprosy, homosexual behaviour, heretical speech – was a tool in the armoury of local dispute.[64]

Each of these groups, by standing on the boundaries, thus provided a way of delimiting the centre of Christian community. Or rather, the 'centre' was *produced* by positioning these groups at the social margins: by saying that such-and-such a thing is 'outside', one marks tacitly what is inside. Religious tenets underlay each exclusion: the 'stubborn blindness' of the Jews who rejected Christ's divinity, the 'fallen' state of public prostitutes, and for the lepers, the combined elements of biblical precedent and the long-standing belief that their disease was the result of (and just punishment for) sexual sins.[65] But exclusion was not only a matter of drawing a line between who was in and who was out.

More complex processes also pertained. For example, those condemned as guilty of heresy were held at a particular distance from society, forced to wear badges, like the Jews, and facing public punishments – such as we saw given to Thomas Tailour at the beginning of this book – that marked them out as separate. But unlike the Jews or the lepers, or probably even the prostitutes, most of these sinners would eventually be reincorporated back into the community. If they were stubborn or 'relapsed' back into heresy after abjuring it, they would be burnt at the stake – the ultimate exclusion. Heretics were only one kind of sinner, marking the outer limit of misbehaviour. We saw earlier in this chapter the case of Denise and John, condemned for adultery and beaten around the parish church and marketplace. This was a little and brief exclusion from the bounds of community; there were many gradations between their penance and public execution. People who were excommunicated might be excluded, very publicly and ritually, from the parish church during Lent. Kept outside the door of the church, they were literally 'liminal' (on the threshold) of community. The medieval Church was, among other things, a body of law and a system of courts. Parts of this legal system were a resource for the laity to draw upon, in the settlement of marriage disputes for example.[66] In other areas, it was a more top-down system, regulating moral behaviour and prosecuting cases of sexual misbehaviour, slander and other infractions. Episcopal visitations were just one part of this system. One should not overplay, however, the degree of control that church courts brought to bear, at least prior to the later fifteenth century. Earlier records indicate many people failing to attend the court and avoiding their penance, and episcopal registers make frequent use of blanket excommunication decrees because the bishop lacked any information about the identity of the particular malefactors brought to his attention.[67]

There was one final group whom we should note, who were in a rather different position: Muslims – or 'Saracens' as medieval Christians called them. Islam, which had risen to control most of the Middle East and North Africa by the tenth century, was for much of Christendom a distant and somewhat fantastical threat. Tales told of the horrors committed by Saracen warriors were luridly frightening. The call to go East and fight on behalf of the Pope and Christendom was certainly known across Europe as, particularly in the twelfth century, the Church organized large, concerted preaching missions to gain support for crusading. Apart from the knightly classes who controlled the military pilgrimages, ordinary lay people clearly knew the stories of Saracen atrocity. Some were inspired to take up the cross. In 1275, a villein called Richard Burton paid his lord thirteen shillings and four pence for licence to sell his goods in order to head off to the Holy Land, and his was not the only example.[68] But people like Richard were the exception rather than the rule. The primary role that 'Saracens' played in the lives of most of the laity was not as an enemy that one would meet in real, physical combat, but a famed and mysterious enemy across the seas, whose hostility marked the overall boundary of Christendom itself.

This last statement must be tempered, however, by the recollection that in certain parts of Europe – Sicily and Spain – a large Muslim presence had coexisted

with Christians for several centuries. Modern historiography is divided on the
question of whether, particularly in Spain, the overarching narrative should be
seen as *reconquista* or *convivencia*: that is, Christian 'reconquest' of Spanish lands
from Muslim control or, conversely, a largely harmonious coexistence of knock-
ing along together more or less peaceably. For many ordinary Christians it seems
likely that the latter was the case, for economic and logistical reasons as much as
anything else. And one can find some evidence for not just coexistence but friendship. For example, a Pyrenean shepherd called Pierre Maury, who travelled back
and forth across the mountains with his flock in the early fourteenth century, knew
a number of Saracens in a village called Flix, near Tarragona. One of them, a
boatman, even offered to protect his friend Pierre from a stranger who was
looking for the shepherd, by beating the man up.[69] Bonds of friendship could
bridge what were supposed to be vast religious and cultural gulfs.

The mechanisms of exclusion and the construction of certain groups as
'Other' were an essential element in the production of community. Their power
comes from the reassuring lie that they whisper: that the world is easily divisi-
ble into 'them' and 'us'. Those curious holes in the walls of Barcelonan Jewish
houses through which, the St Maria parishioners alleged, Christian women were
somehow spirited could, however, been seen as a tacit recognition of the permeability of communal barriers. Jews and Christians *did* sometimes sleep
together; and, perhaps more importantly, eat together, work together, talk
together and even live together. Nearly a century later, after many Jews in northern Spain were forced to convert in 1391, ever harsher legislation and exhorta-
tions to separate Jews from Christians were enacted. The king of Aragon, for
example, wrote to towns in 1393 demanding more obvious badges for Jews to
wear, and hats also, to keep them separate. In the second decade of the fifteenth
century, Vincent Ferrer (later canonized) preached that 'he will never be a good
Christian who is neighbour to a Jew'. What drove these anti-Semitic demands
forward was the belated realization that the creation of thousands of *conversos*
(converted Jews) had utterly blurred the line between Jew and Christian. A crisis
point was reached – and fed into the creation of the Spanish Inquisition –
because of the large numbers who had changed identity all at once.[70] But the fact
of blurring had long pre-dated these events. The ordinary laity could undoubtedly dislike and attack other groups, as we see from the fact of various pogroms
to the milder, inchoate complaints at the St Maria parish visitation. The overarching drive toward definition, exclusion and control, however, came from the
top down, from secular leaders and religious preachers.

Ordering society

Thomas Brinton, in a sermon written for other bishops in 1373, drew the
following image of the social body:

> heads are kings, princes and prelates; eyes are wise judges and true counsellors; ears
> are the religious; the tongue, good doctors; knights are the right hand, ready to

defend; merchants and faithful workmen are the left; citizens and townsfolk are the heart, placed as it were in the middle; the feet are farmers and labourers, as it were supporting the whole body firmly.[71]

There is nothing terribly unusual about this image: picturing society as a body had long been common, and in the twelfth century John of Salisbury made it a central metaphor in his influential work of political philosophy, the *Policraticus*. Numerous late-medieval manuscript illuminations depict 'the body politic' in similar ways. The specific ascriptions could alter from invocation to invocation: for Brinton, the left hand represents merchants and artisans, whereas for Salisbury both hands stood in for soldiers and merchants did not figure at all. But the repetitious centrality of the body to medieval society is undiminished by such variations.

It is quickly apparent that Brinton's picture is hierarchical. The king is at the top and the labourers are at the bottom. Other classes of people are arranged according to taste (and since Brinton was a bishop, in his picture religious people are much closer to the top than the ordinary laity). It is also *reciprocal*. That is, the 'organic' links between different parts of the hierarchy mean that each element must do its job for the whole, or else the body in its entirety will fail. John of Salisbury emphasized this: the feet (the labourers) cannot tell the head (the monarch) where to walk, as they do not have the head's vision; equally, however, the head cannot tell the feet to do things that feet cannot do. Each man (women are notably absent from the image) has a proper place and an appointed task; thus, the image implies, community functions organically, each person allotted a place in the hierarchy but contributing toward the whole. The body is clearly a very useful symbol, the epitome of what is 'natural', but actually highly mutable in its meaning.[72] It was also an image with many sacred resonances, because of the importance placed upon the presence of Christ's body in the Eucharist. A chain of metaphors bound together the Christian community with Christ's flesh, with the body politic, with the bread and wine in the sacrament of the altar. It is perhaps thus unsurprising that we find that the feast of Corpus Christi (first celebrated in Liège in 1246, but only established more widely after 1317) was a major occasion for communal celebration, and for the practice of rituals of community. In the German city of Würzburg, for example, celebrations of the feast in 1381 took the form of a procession. Following mass, different groups from across the city – clergy from each parish and college, masters and apprentices from the guilds, representatives of Würzburg's geographical quarters – gathered in the cathedral and then processed through the marketplace to the bridge crossing the River Main, and then around the city walls to other gates and important sites. If the procession had tied a thread to the cathedral and unspooled it as they marched, the end result would be a cat's cradle that knitted together disparate parts of the city: cathedral stitched to marketplace, parish churches to the cathedral, the quarters of the city to each other, the whole locality to the bishop and the town council.[73]

Corpus Christi became one of the most important feasts of the later Middle Ages, and similar processions can be found across Western Europe. Celebrations of a smaller scale, but also symbolically charged, occurred in rural villages as much as in larger towns. In many cities, from the late fourteenth century on, plays or pageants were performed as part of the celebrations, often enacting scenes from the life of Christ. Cities and towns often allotted the plays to particular craft guilds, and the plays were performed on wagons, traversing the streets of the city and pausing at certain key sites to repeat each performance.[74] Other processions and images can also be found. A number of cities, including Rouen, Paris, Metz, Poitiers, Tarascon and Norwich, made late-medieval procession carrying the image of a dragon (often the one slain by St George) as their unifying symbol – the dragon depicting external threats to the city, which the city's power first neutralized and then co-opted to its own defence.[75] As they traversed the city, often carrying Christ's body in the form of the Host, medieval processions displayed the community to itself, in its geographical, institutional and symbolic space. The procession drew the image of the social body across the streets of the city. And the powerful symbolism of unity, embodiment and Christ's presence (plus, sometimes, other saintly benefactors) brought the people together, *made* the community through its ritual work.[76]

Or did it? When Italian chroniclers recorded communal penitential processions, such as the one begging for better weather at Bologna, they tended to present the people involved as one collective, undifferentiated group. Other records, however, reveal that such processions were hierarchically divided up by age and gender.[77] There is considerable evidence for such communal occasions prompting dispute, dissension and even violence rather than amity. Arguments between the different craft guilds in York over which had order of precedence in the processions were legion. The same was true of the different groups of clergy at Würzburg. Robert Grosseteste, bishop of Lincoln, told his clergy that they 'should not permit their parishioners to compete with each other over whose banners should go first in the annual visitation of the mother church, because brawls and even deaths result from this'. At Chester, on Corpus Christi day in 1399, the guild masters came armed with poleaxes and other weapons to confront their subordinate journeymen. Bishop Henry Despenser was, in April 1377, attacked by some of the inhabitants of Lynn during a civic procession after he arrogated to himself the ceremonial mace that would normally have been carried before the town's mayor. The Italian town of Anacapri won a court case to allow the laity to make a Palm Sunday procession to the shrine of San Costanzo, much to the annoyance of the clergy and townsmen of Capri; in 1338, the latter attacked the procession, shouting insults and throwing stones that broke the sacred images the Anacaprians were carrying.[78] One could continue to multiply the examples. Even when no overt violence or protest occurred, various writers have pointed out that such processions demonstrated social hierarchies and cultural divisions as much as they depicted unity and order.

Another area where community was clearly linked to social hierarchy is that of guilds or confraternities (there is no clear difference between these terms). A cursory glance gives the impression that guilds neatly divide up society in a similar way to the reciprocal divisions described in Brinton's picture of the body politic: trade guilds (tanners, tapsters, goldsmiths, for example) organized and regulated different areas of artisanal labour, while mercantile guilds ordered the merchant classes. Religious confraternities, meanwhile, gathered together people across social classes who were inspired by their devotions to a particular saint, or enthusiasm for a certain mode of piety. Upon closer examination, however, this neatness crumbles. The division between business guilds and religious confraternities was far from absolute, and in some places the two were indistinguishable. Every trade guild made some mention of religious faith as an element of its *raison d'être*, and in various cities it was the trade guilds who performed Corpus Christi plays. Confraternities would sometimes draw their membership from one social group rather than across the board and, as we will see, confraternity membership had financial as well as spiritual implications.

So what was a guild? The word 'gild' dates back to the early Middle Ages, and the first uses of it indicate a collective feast with some religious association to it. By the eleventh century the religious aspect, with greater church involvement, had been amplified. Guilds can thus be found from an early period, but they appear also to have expanded in number in the later Middle Ages. The foundation charter of a confraternity in Marseilles from 1212 sketches out the core purposes. Members were to swear to serve and protect the Church, to attempt to resolve peacefully any discord with another member, and to come when ordered to a counsel convoked by the bishop or ruler of the city. Each member was to give alms to the guild, which were then used in three ways: to pay for burials of guild members; to support members who had fallen into poverty; and to hold an annual feast. At this feast mass would be celebrated for living and dead members of the guild, and 'for all the faithful dead and for all priests in the city', and the poor who resided at the hospital of the Holy Spirit would be fed.[79] This range of activities provides a template that fits the vast majority of medieval guilds: sustaining peace and fraternity, providing charity, feasting and some involvement in local government. Susan Reynolds has provocatively suggested that the primary activity of guilds was drinking, with a bit of additional religious ceremony; 'if they called themselves a fraternity there might be more emphasis on religion and charity, and less on drinking, but that is by no means certain'.[80] This may be a little hard on some of the devout flagellant and *laudesi* (praise-singing) fraternities of later medieval Italy, but it does help to emphasize the social functions of guilds.

Guilds are the epitome of the link between religion and community in the medieval period, both in what they proclaim and what they conceal. The founding charters and statutes of guilds emphasize time and again the values of peace, amity and fraternity that the guild seeks to foster. An Italian penitent confraternity ordered in 1284 that 'to make peace between brothers and sisters, or indeed outsiders, in positions of discord . . . it is hereby ordered to employ, if the facility is available, the counsel of the diocesan bishop in this matter'. The English Guild of Holy Cross from Stratford-upon-Avon ordered that its annual Easter feast should be held 'in such a manner that fraternal love shall be enriched between them, and evil-speaking driven out, but peace always re-created between them,

and true amity upheld'.[81] Their almsgiving provided a social good, caring for
the wider community. The feast – both a religious ceremony and a secular celebration – was an essential communal ritual. Their works were done for the
betterment of the Christian faith. These things the records hammer home.
But, once again, recent work has shown that surface appearances belie more
complex realities.

To begin with, it is difficult to say quite how extensive the membership of guilds
was in the Middle Ages. Most historians understandably work on particular geographical areas, which further complicates matters. For example, one study of
confraternities in Geneva suggests that, by the fifteenth century, nearly everybody
belonged to one. Conversely, work on Bologna for the same period sees 10–20 per
cent of the adult population involved, and suggests that this is probably the case
across most of Europe.[82] It is clear that guilds were a familiar presence across
western Christendom, as most habitations, from city to village, had one, but also
that guild members formed a portion, not the totality, of the overall population.
The image that guild records provide of their members is of an enduring collective entity; calling for various good works and threatening expulsion from the guild
for serious breaches of conduct, they suggest an active, persistent membership.
Artworks commissioned by guilds similarly work to project a corporate image.[83]
But these appearances are deliberately deceptive. Guilds sought to present themselves as well-established structures that thus accrued for their members the
authority of tradition. But while some guilds did last a long time, many did not.
Some were brought together for specific tasks, such as the repair of particular
buildings or the resurrection of particular devotional practices.[84] Guilds formed
and reformed, in what André Vauchez has usefully described as a kind of
'Brownian motion'.[85] What sustained (or failed to sustain) guilds was a small core
group of officers and officials. In Italy, in imitation of patterns of civic government, these offices tended to circulate fairly quickly within the membership; but
in other areas – Normandy, for example – they were more permanent.[86] The
requirements of the bulk of the membership were to give alms – thus channelling
pious giving that would clearly have happened anyway, since non-guild members
also gave alms – and attending the annual feast. This is not to say that in some
places, in particular circumstances, guild members might not be much more
active. In the immediate aftermath of the Black Death in Venice, for example, the
Scuole Grandi helped to bury the many dead, and other guilds undertook similar
activities across Tuscany.[87] But it is to note that the guild records mislead us in
their picture of corporate identity. People opted into guild identity, but were not
subsumed within it. A man could, for example, belong to more than one guild:
the same person could join a flagellant confraternity, a praise-singing fraternity,
and a trade guild that put on a Corpus Christi play each year. These apparently
very different modes of piety were not mutually exclusive.[88]

Thus guild membership was not quite as clear-cut as it may first appear. While
certain guilds – particularly Italian flagellant and *laudesi* confraternities, but
also some similar foundations elsewhere in Europe – appear to have attracted
a fairly broad social spectrum of members, many guilds were divided up by class

and gender. To take the latter first, the picture shifts over time and place. There is some evidence of women belonging to pious guilds from the ninth century, and by the high and later Middle Ages strong evidence for female membership (often, but not always, as wives of other members) in trade guilds. By the mid-fifteenth century, however, due at least in part to worsening economic conditions, women were being forced out of these associations. In certain areas – Veneto for example – confraternities increased in female membership in the fourteenth and fifteenth centuries, but elsewhere – Bologna for instance – they declined during the same period.[89] There were a few guilds devoted entirely to women, such as one started in the fourteenth century attached to the church of Sant' Antonio in Perugia; and in late-medieval England some small guild-like associations in parishes, devoted to particular 'lights' (gaining alms to keep a candle alight in devotion to a particular saint), were all female.[90] Some guilds, such as the confraternity of Misericordia Maggiore in Bergamo, admitted women and allowed them to participate equally with men. But frequently women's devotions were restricted (they were not allowed to practise flagellation, for example) and they were not able to take on office-holding tasks.[91] Certain confraternities, such as the fourteenth-century flagellant groups in Assisi, specifically banned women and advised their brethren to 'avoid long conversations and gatherings of women like deadly plague, for they cause lust and dishonest living'.[92] While many guilds presented an image of their 'brethren and sistren' working equally together, the reality was more divisive, and particular local conditions could exacerbate gender differences.

In terms of class, the picture is also complicated. It is common to note that guilds involved people 'from all social classes', from the rich to – well, if not the poor, then at least the labourers.[93] This is true, of guild membership in aggregate, but can be misleading about how guilds actually linked to, and often reinforced, social strata. Craft and mercantile guilds, which could be very religiously involved, were necessarily divided along social lines: the tanner did not sit down with the cloth merchant. Certain groups, forming a large proportion of the population, were excluded from all guilds: the landless poor who could not afford even low entrance fees; the young; and in some areas, women. In Florence, membership of religious confraternities was limited to those who already belonged to a trade guild, effectively excluding (in that city) women and adult salaried workers.[94] At the same time, however, one study has emphasized how certain guilds in that city bridged social divides by bringing together noblemen and artisans in one brotherhood; and it has also been suggested that the *Scuole Grandi* – rich devotional confraternities – of Venice worked as a kind of mechanism for redistributing wealth (although this is not found elsewhere).[95] However, closer examination suggests that the nobility and upper classes in such confraternities were utterly disproportionate in number; thus, while they were 'fraternally' linked to *some* artisans, those artisans remained but a token few.[96] The guild presented not an accurate reflection of wider society, but an oligarchical collective who co-opted a symbolic portion of 'the poor' – honest artisans – to meet ideals of fraternity.

More normally, in other parts of Europe, guilds usually divided up along social strata. In northern Spain, during the thirteenth and fourteenth centuries, guilds seem to have been entirely the preserve of wealthier groups, and when more guilds appeared in the later fourteenth and fifteenth centuries, they focused individually around different social strata. Thus, although one could find poor labourers, middling artisans and rich nobles all participating in guilds, their institutions were usually separate, and often explicitly forbade membership to outside classes both up and down the social scale.[97] Nor was guild membership necessarily an individual act – in some areas, people joined as representatives of their family or kin or political faction.[98] It is true that guilds *could* form an arena that cut across other social lines, but in the main they preserved rather than challenged the structures and hierarchical order of community.[99]

In this light, two major activities of guilds – charitable giving and feasting – are thrown into an interesting perspective. To take charity first. An older historiography has seen guilds as providing the basis of what would later be called 'poor relief', easing the multiple burdens falling upon the sick and the penniless. One can certainly find provision of charity to the poor: for example, the confraternity of San Bartolomeo, in San Sepolcro, set out in its 1269 statutes that alms in the form of food and pennies, collected by the membership, would be distributed on Thursdays to the poor, to shrines and to prisoners. Clothes would be given out twice a year, of wool at All Saints (1 November) and of linen in the summer. The particular guild officials – 'rectors' as this guild named them – were also supposed to act as legal advocates for the poor in court, when occasion arose.[100] Here, as in thousands of other cases across Europe, the practice of charity was shaped by liturgical and biblical precedents. The seven works of mercy (see Chapter 2) were modelled on Christ's deeds in the New Testament. In these ways, it has been argued, guilds and their charity served an essential social function, contributing to what is seen as the stable, collective nature of the medieval community.

But more recent research has strongly questioned the overall drift of this analysis. For a start, what guilds promised to do in their statutes was not necessarily practised in reality: study of various guild expense accounts reveals much lower expenditure on charity than the ideal. The guild of Boston in Lincolnshire, for instance, was supposed to give 1000 loaves and 1000 herrings (in imitation of Christ's miracle) to the poor at its annual feast. The fifteenth-century accounts, however, reveal no trace of these purchases.[101] Where and when care for the poor was provided, it was often a symbolic act rather than a programme of social welfare, and the kinds of assistance rendered were often shaped by bourgeois ideas of what was 'suitable' for the poor.[102] Charity followed a script, allotting prescribed positions to both givers and receivers; by the late fifteenth century even giving comfort to prisoners had become a ritualized activity for Italian confraternities, with a manual of instruction on what precisely to say and what responses to expect.[103] A certain number of poor people might be fed from the leftovers after the confraternity feast or invited to the meal itself – for that one day of the year. For example, in late-fourteenth-century Gimel, in the diocese of Geneva, the local confraternity fed two paupers at their feast; in Begnins, in the fifteenth century, the confraternity of the Holy Spirit gave alms to those poor people who presented themselves at Pentecost.[104] I write here, following the language of the sources, 'the poor', but this easy label obscures two distinctions. The first is that the poor who benefited were those deemed the *deserving* poor – frequently understood to mean those with physical disabilities, or who had grown too old to work.[105] The able-bodied poor were less favoured. The second distinction is that 'the poor' homogenizes individual human beings into an amorphous mass. This tendency to think of impoverished people as an indistinct huddle aided their symbolic appropriation by other discourses: one could dispense patronage (and hence feel one had attained a certain status) to 'the poor', and simultaneously ignore the status of individual poor people as fellow human beings. Disparities of wealth, diet and opportunity were cast not as social effects but as natural and divinely ordained. 'God has ordered that there be rich and poor so that the rich may be served by the poor and the poor may be taken care of by the rich', explained the preacher Giordano da Pisa in 1304.[106]

Even this reciprocity was more notional than real. The majority of fraternal charity was limited to members of the guild; and giving any kind of charity was far more common in towns than in the countryside. In later medieval Cambridgeshire, for example, a little over 50 per cent of civic guilds provided charitable support for their members, whereas only 17 per cent of rural ones did likewise.[107] Even here, the picture is misleading: charity was limited to members who had experienced extraordinary and unexpected calamities, such as the loss of a limb or a fire destroying their possessions. The guilds proffering this service were frequently socially elevated and politically active, and one can read their aims here as preserving the social status of their brethren (and hence the collective honour of the guild) rather than providing any broader mutual aid.[108] They did not intend to support those who had become unemployed or the chronically poor. Provisions from the Guild of Holy Cross, Stratford-Upon-Avon, recorded in a royal survey of 1388 give a succinct flavour of these limitations: if any brother or sister is robbed or falls into poverty then '*so long as he bears himself well and honestly* toward the brethren and sistren, they shall find him food and clothing and other necessities' (my emphasis).[109] Practical support for the poor came much more sustainedly and usefully from those who were themselves lower down the social scale, from the support of families and neighbours. Judith Bennett has argued that 'help-ales' or 'scot-ales' were an important form of this local charity. Ale was brewed, and then sold at a higher than normal price at a social gathering, the profits going to repair bridges or for the upkeep of the parish church – or to assist an individual who had fallen into poverty. Help-ales were not absolutely inclusive, as vagrants and strangers were not welcome at or assisted by such events. But, nevertheless, this kind of charity was much more reciprocal and mutually supportive than the intermittent benevolence that the rich bestowed upon the poor.[110]

What then of guild feasts? These were often linked, in theory at least, to charitable giving as we have seen, with some token poor folk invited to the celebrations. But the primary focus of the feast was the fraternity itself and the feast was its central, cohesive ritual. Historians have viewed the reality or effectiveness of this cohesion in different ways. Some have seen the repeated emphases on 'peace' in the records setting out the conduct of feasts as a reflection of reality, or as providing an important arena for reconciling social tensions.[111] Others, reading the injunctions against quarrelling and fighting at feasts as betraying the real situation, have argued that such occasions were about division and dissension as much as community.[112] It is clear that feasts, like processions, were occasions when the guild attempted to produce a sense of community – but often a collective, communal identity that set the guild members apart from the rest of society. Nearly a fifth of urban guilds in the English late-medieval sources, for example, ordered their members to wear matching livery at the feast and in processions.[113]

If the express purposes of guilds – charity, fraternity, feasting – were not quite as straightforward as upon first view, what then was their function? It has been argued that, given a very large expansion in the number of guilds in the late fourteenth century, they provided a kind of alternative kin group to family in the wake of the demographic cataclysm of the Black Death; although others have emphasized that guilds could sit alongside family lines rather than replace them.[114] Providing kinship and social connections was undoubtedly a key role that guilds played. But the picture remains complex. One should note, first of all, that the collectivities discussed here as guilds could cover very varied forms of association. Rural guilds might be seen as little more than a particular way of organizing the alms- and tithe-giving of the parish, as their financial efforts were almost totally directed toward the upkeep of the local church and tending to particular altars. In contrast, many late-medieval civic guilds were strongly involved in town government, such that by the fifteenth century a certain guild – the Guild of Holy Trinity in Bishop's Lynn, or the Guild of St George in Norwich, to give just two East Anglian examples – could be seen as the town oligarchy at prayer.[115] In between these poles, we find a number of other confraternities providing 'a mode of access to social respectability' for their members. In The Hague, the militia guild of St George brought together the noble and non-noble elite of the city, providing a space within which their social divisions could be negotiated in the wider interests of oligarchical government.[116] Guilds provided a means by which the middling layers of society could act as patrons (by dispensing the collective alms of the brethren, or by commissioning artworks for the guild) thus gaining access to a role normally beyond their economic reach. This is the real function of charity, as practised by the guild – not a serious effort to alleviate endemic social problems, but a way of accessing the elevated status implied by *giving*. The production of 'social capital', as it has been described, was not merely a matter of personal pride; it had two real and important effects. One was access to political office; the other was access to economic credit.[117]

It may appear that we have travelled a long way from the pious concerns that apparently animated medieval corporate almsgiving and collective activity. In fact, this is not so. I am not arguing that guilds performed these social functions for their members instead of or in despite of more 'pious' motivations. It is, rather, that acts of charity – the foundation of medieval lay piety – were always caught up with concepts of communal governance and social hierarchy. In the secular realm, religious ideals *were* social concepts, and were played out within the web of power relations inherent in medieval society. This is made very clear when examining religious theatre, such as the Corpus Christi plays common in late-medieval Europe. Recent work on these productions has moved away from the idea of their operating primarily as a means of teaching theology to the laity, and has instead examined the ways in which they were implicated in their civic settings, both in terms of narrative content and physical staging. The impressive Corpus Christi cycles were produced by the guilds of cities such as York, and their overt message of Christian unity is complicated by that fact. As we have seen, there were squabbles within and between the guilds about the plays, and each guild produced a different play thus emphasizing division as much as unity.[118] Moreover, the neat divisions of crafts represented by the different guilds was more a fantasy of mercantile order than a true reflection of medieval economic activity. In truth, many people worked not only at their nominal guild trade but also at other jobs or selling other products. Heather Swanson has argued that the burden of putting on the Corpus Christi cycle, and other similar events, was 'instrumental in forcing a more rigid organization on the system of craft guilds'. The social 'wholeness' signalled by the plays was, under closer examination, a hierarchical and politically-ordered body – as, in fact, we would expect following the sermon of Thomas Brinton discussed above.[119] And in some Corpus Christi plays we see again the production of community through exclusion, as lurid tales of Jews desecrating the Host were performed for the audience.[120] Where drama did encourage feelings of unity and community, this was not a straightforward reflection of medieval society but something brought about by the cultural work that the play attempted to perform. The late twelfth-century *Jeu de Saint Nicolas*, written by Jean Bodel in the town of Arras, symbolically addresses divisions of elite and non-elite in society, coded in the play respectively as royal court and tavern. The miracles of St Nicholas within the drama are geared toward the sustenance of wealth (he restores and indeed increases lost treasure), and the play can be seen as easing possible tensions between the classes by emphasizing how everyone benefits from the pursuit of economic profit. Within the play, rich and poor never meet, and therefore their polarities of wealth are never confronted; they live in different worlds, but are joined together in their mutual pursuit of wealth, which, within the bourgeois setting of a medieval town, is not seen as incompatible with piety but rather a benefit springing from it. The *Jeu* therefore provides an ideological template for unity within a social hierarchy – though only by displacing beyond the dramatic space of the text any possible tensions that hierarchy might provoke.[121]

How then should we understand the apparent gap between the overt messages of unity that guild feasts and civic processions presented, and the more complex and fraught tensions they embodied? The question has wider implications for an understanding of communal ritual in general, and anthropological theory provides some tools here.[122] The functional anthropology of Victor Turner that we met in Chapter 1 could suggest that processions produce and sustain community through a collective engagement in liminal acts. The element of *communitas*, as Turner termed it, is built through collective symbolic action such as Corpus Christi processions, and the implications of wholeness and unity structurally encoded in the symbol of Christ's body and the circumnavigation of the city. Rituals work, in this model, to heal conflicts within the social body. A function-alist analysis thus tends to assume that, in the normal run of things, community is essentially stable, static and reciprocally sustained by all its members – in a word, that community *works*. Others, however, have demurred, arguing that social groups are always riven with conflict, hierarchy, divisions and exclusions. Corpus Christi processions could therefore be seen as occasions when a certain *part* of the community proclaims its hierarchical power over the rest of the social body – particularly the women, the poor and the Jews (forbidden by law from public spaces during such Eucharistic rituals) who were excluded from this image of 'wholeness'.[123] As Jacques Rossiaud has put it,

> the civic feast, by its liturgy and its symbolic proclamations, without doubt consti-tutes one of the best instruments of social control and of the regeneration of the civic community. By the deployment of ordained power, by the proclamation of instruct-ive sacred imagery, and by the recollection of their [past] triumphs, the ruling urban groups strove to maintain a coherent system of reverential comportment and visibly to impose their own definition of the city.[124]

The work of Clifford Geertz, however, presents some further analytical pos-sibilities, particularly the subtle idea that ritual and symbolic action are means by which communities can address (rather than salve) the tensions and fractures they contain. Claims to unity embedded in the rituals, although not a reflection of reality, could nonetheless be seen as providing a language for working out social disputes and a model to which one might aspire. The rituals do not instantly solve or erase social divisions, but provide a space wherein the social group, however fleetingly, can attempt to make itself into a community.[125] Thus community does not work automatically, but perhaps can be made to work through repeated symbolic action. Alternatively, one might argue that what ritual does is articulate – make manifest – social tensions. From this perspective, Corpus Christi processions provide a symbolic space for the community, with all its dissensions and divisions, to encounter itself. Hence occasions of dispute or even violence are not failures of community; they are an essential and inescapable part of it. A guild feast thus might bring about amity and peace, for a time; but equally might end in a fight. Its ritual work was open-ended, not dis-crete.[126] With some of these different analytical possibilities in mind, let us turn our attention finally to some key ritualized moments: birth, death and the mass.

Ritual moments

At Troyes, in northern France, in February 1447, something awful happened. Adeline Joufrin, a midwife, had attended at the labour of the wife of Guillaume

Fleury. The child was premature, and upon birth showed no signs of life. Adeline persisted nonetheless, and took the infant to the local church, where she sprinkled it with holy water and said the words of baptism over it. For six hours she tried thus to revive it. Eventually, defeat had to be admitted. The baby was buried by its grandfather and uncle in unconsecrated ground. The next day, however, Guillaume Fleury dug up his son. He washed the small body in hot water to warm its limbs, and brought the child back to Adeline. She took the corpse, at his insistence, and said, 'Infant, if you are not alive, I do not baptize you. But if you live, I baptize you in the name of the Father, the Son and the Holy Spirit.' The child, however, was clearly dead.[127]

Adeline was sentenced to a month in prison for her part in these traumatic events. For the bishop investigating the case, it was her impious action in falsely administering baptism to one already dead that was terrible. For us, other aspects may strike as more upsetting. But this case is not simply a demonstration that medieval people could feel deep and unhinging grief over lost children. The actions of both Adeline and Guillaume also tell us important things about ritual and community. First of all, baptism.[128] An unbaptized infant was marked by the stain of original sin: born human, it was already touched by the deeds of Adam and Eve in the Garden of Eden. Thus without baptism a child could not enter Purgatory and hope eventually to enter heaven. It was, from the thirteenth century onwards, believed instead to be confined to limbo (earlier commentators held that the child went straight to hell). Unbaptized, Guillaume Fleury's son was thus denied salvation. For this reason, the child had been buried outside the consecrated ground of the cemetery. Adeline was not at fault for attempting to baptize – the first attempt, at any rate – because the laity, and midwives in particular, were permitted the power to perform this rite in extreme circumstances. There were numerous cases of 'miraculous' saintly interventions at difficult births, allowing the child to live just long enough to be baptized, and sometimes just the insistence by one person present that they had seen the infant manage to move a limb or take a breath was sufficient to prompt a quick baptism before pronouncing death. Discerning the small flutterings of life in these circumstances was a communal act rather than a medical diagnosis. We know about the case from Troyes precisely because Guillaume Fleury had refused to accept the communal consensus on his bereavement. On the whole, however, one suspects that signs of life were interpreted with great latitude. People were unwilling to accept that infants could be denied entrance to heaven. Various groups labelled as heretical in the eleventh and twelfth centuries (a period when orthodox theology held that the unbaptized were destined for hell) strongly opposed the necessity for infant baptism. A group at Ivoy in the diocese of Trier held this position in the 1120s, and Henry of Le Mans, whom we met in Chapter 2, explicitly argued that children who died before the age of discretion gained salvation.[129] The Cathars voiced similar challenges, and Lollards in fifteenth-century Norfolk argued that 'the sacrament of baptism . . . is of little or no worth if the parents of the child are faithful'.[130] Different heretical groups had varying reasons for opposing this sacrament, from a claim to be the sole providers of salvation (as with the Cathars) to an insistence upon adult understanding and comprehension of faith (as with the Lollards). For many lay people in contact with these dissenters there may have been comfort in their rejection of orthodox theology, but not necessarily an acceptance of the heterodox alternative. Even supporters of the Cathars still had their children baptized; the ritual was, for them, about more than salvation. We will explore ideas about death, sin and salvation in the next chapter. Here, let us consider what else, beyond the theological, was at stake in Guillaume Fleury's sad little passion play of death and attempted resurrection.

Baptism was what linguistic philosophers call a 'performative speech act': the words of baptism performed the act, *were* the sacramental purification. The words were thus powerful. Given that this was one rite that lay people could perform, the Church was nervous about this fact, and many pastoral manuals and council statutes enjoined priests to teach their parishioners very carefully exactly what they were supposed to say if they had to baptize.[131] More normally, baptism was performed by a priest. In the early Middle Ages it had been the right of the bishop alone, but as parish priests gained sacramental power during the twelfth century it increasingly became their job. A change in timing accompanied this shift: except for England, where infant baptism was the norm from very early times, people were often not baptized until older, sometimes even in adulthood. Over the twelfth and thirteenth centuries European parishes shifted toward earlier baptism. And whereas the rite of confirmation (anointing with oil) had originally been congruent with baptism, now the two separated so that, by Adeline's time, all babies were baptized as soon as possible, but would only be confirmed after the 'age of discretion' – that is, the time when they were believed to be able to understand and willingly embrace the faith, often taken as 12 years for girls and 14 for boys.

Bringing baptism back to infanthood changed its wider ritual functions. The baptism of youths or adults was a moment of conversion, in theory at least, bringing the person into the faith. Given that in earlier periods baptism had often been administered collectively to a large group assembled at a cathedral, or gathered together on the occasion of an episcopal visit to their village, the rite would have had the flavour of a collective act – the group entering Christendom together. In contrast, the baptism of infants was potentially a more individual change: the individual entering the community. In fact, collective baptism even of infants still occurred on occasion throughout the period, and thus the sense of a collective transformation may have always been present. The rite had, moreover, several overlapping functions. It removed the stain of sin, in what could be seen as an act of exorcism: driving away those devils who might seek to harm the child. What was, strictly and theologically speaking, the absolution of an internal fault could thus be repositioned in practice as the removal of an external threat. There is good evidence that lay people tended toward the latter view. The idea of original sin, in particular, was not easily accepted particularly if (as in Guillaume Fleury's case) it meant the damnation of the child; in late-medieval England the laity were still being admonished 'without doubt, believe ye this / That it [an unbaptized infant] shall never come to bliss.'[132] Clearly, therefore, there was doubt on the subject. There is passing evidence for belief in other presences, potential threats from whom the child had to be protected, or who needed to be appeased. *Handlyng Synne* talks, condemningly, of belief in 'three sisters' who come to 'shape' the child's fate. Elsewhere in Europe, bracken was sometimes used to protect a newborn from evil. There is also some evidence for a medieval belief in 'changelings', demonic infants swapped for unbaptized babies in the first few hours after birth.[133] In line with these beliefs, baptism could be seen as a kind of protection spell. We can perhaps see a hint of this in Adeline's first attempt to baptize Guillaume's son: taking the child to church and attempting to revive it *through* the administration of the rite.

At the same time, baptism was also a ritual entry into the community, and the moment at which the child gained its own name. At an ideal level, the child was entering the vast notional family of Christendom (although one could argue that, having split confirmation away from baptism, the former more rightly played this role). At a more immediate level one may suspect that the community was seen as much more local than international: the village or parish. The child at baptism was to have three godparents (two of his or her own sex). They lifted the child from the font, and were supposed to take on the role of teaching the child about Christianity – the *Pater noster* and *Credo* at any rate, as we saw in Chapter 2. There was clearly another, more social aspect to this: the formation of kinship networks. Godparenthood could be a way of binding together individuals otherwise unrelated. The names given to children could be familial, or those of a saint, or taken from a godparent or other patron. Jean Rocas, a man questioned by inquisitors in 1321 for rather idiosyncratic beliefs about the nature of Christ, explained that although he did not believe in the salvific effects of baptism, he thought it was a very good thing because of the 'great friendship it contracts between men' – that is, the bonds of kinship it produced between the parents and godparents.[134] Once again, however, this community was hierarchical: a study of late fifteenth-century godparentage in the Swiss town of Porrentruy has shown that, although almost every social group was involved (and most people were godparents to more than one child), they were involved within rather than across their social strata. Merchants godparented the children of other merchants, artisans godparented those of artisans, the nobility other nobles. Thus the existing social lines were reinforced rather than dissolved by these kinship networks.[135]

No godparents would appear to have been present at Adeline's desperate attempt to bring the Fleury child to life, and no name for the child is given – emphasizing, from the perspective of the official record at least, that he never entered the community of the living. The second attempt at baptism tells us something else about community: how it extends into death. It seems fairly unlikely that Guillaume thought that rebaptizing his son could restore life to him, given that he had had to wash the gravedirt from his body before presenting it to the midwife. The efficacy of the rite lay elsewhere, perhaps with the salvation of the child's soul, but more certainly with his resting place. Guillaume's son had been buried outside the graveyard, as was the law for those who had died outside Christian communion. Outside the graveyard lay suicides, heretics, those who had died without final confession. Inside lay the community of the parish dead, who would be remembered in prayers at each mass. By having his deceased son baptized again, one suspects, Guillaume Fleury hoped not to bring him to life but to bring him back within the embrace of community, the literal bounds of the cemetery fence. Life, in this sense, definitely continued after death.

Consider the following account from an anonymous description of Pavia, written around 1330. The writer set out for posterity the habits and customs of the city, and included an explanation of what happened when someone died. A procession was held, led by crosses,

> followed by pairs of laity, often summoned there by a cryer, and then clerics and priests, who precede monks (if any have been called there). After this follows the deceased in a bed with a bolster and linen sheets and a covering under which they lay. If in truth the person is noble or a cleric in holy orders, on top of all this is placed the clothing of their status or order, so that it is visible to all. Finally there follow women, from amongst whom the kinsfolk of the deceased are supported hence by two men. And thereby they process to church with lights and ringing bells. In truth, after entering church, the laity leave, and only the clerics, priests and women remain with the dead person in church up until the burial. (Lately, I have heard that women are forbidden from this manner of procession.) For the person's soul, apart from that which is offered at the funeral and on the seventh day and on the anniversary of death and so forth, they make offerings at the parish church every Sunday for a year, and sometimes more, of bread and candles, which bread the priest blesses and distributes to the parishioners after mass on Sundays.[136]

A number of things are apparent here. One is simply the focus of the account itself. Although noting the commemorative actions of the relatives after burial – the formal commemorations on the seventh day and one year after death, and the more general offerings given throughout the year – the chronicler's perspective is that of the community at large. He talks most about what happened, very publicly, before interment. Everyone would suffer bereavement within their immediate family at some point; but more regularly they would participate in the kind of procession outlined above *not* as immediate kin but as part of the wider community. Here, as elsewhere, funerals and burial services were very public affairs, particularly for members of the elite.[137] Gender was also at play: women mourners at the back, then accompanying the body through its more intimate preparations for burial, as it was washed and anointed. In this particular account, one set of traditions (women's role in ritual grieving) collides with new sensibilities (the demand for 'suitable' public comportment). It was this tension that lay behind the ban against the presence of women in the procession, as the city authorities had deemed it unseemly for women to display such strong emotions in the streets.[138]

The funeral procession was another moment in the production of community, and again a hierarchical one. In contrast to some medieval images of death as the great 'leveller' – everyone, of whatever rank, reduced to much the same thing – we see here, and in many other places, a conspicuous adherence to status for the deceased, displaying their social level through clothing on the bier. Other funerary practices – burial and memorial masses – were similarly inflected. Most obviously, tombs were the preserve of the elite. Whether ostentatious or selfconsciously modest, they were a way of displaying a particular memorial image of the deceased.[139] But below the highest ranks, other nuances of status persisted. As already mentioned, people wanted to be buried within the bounds of the local graveyard. However, in the later Middle Ages it became increasingly desirable to be buried inside the parish church itself, a tendency that grew markedly stronger in the fifteenth century. It largely remained, though, a privilege for the wealthier citizens of the parish. And there were further hierarchical divisions of space within the church itself. People often desired burial closest to the site of the altar or, for the richest, in side chapels.[140] It was, indeed, the better-off who were most likely to specify a site of burial. Their choices were sometimes linked to their use of the church space while alive. The 1463 will of John Baret, a wealthy citizen of Bury St Edmunds, asked that he be laid to rest where 'my Lady Shardelowe was wont to sit' in church. Joan Mason, in 1511, asked to be placed between the font and the church door 'afore my stool [w]here I sit in the said church'.[141] Death and burial were tied up with matters of status and honour. One of the most important benefits that medieval guilds supplied to their members was provision for funeral services and burial in fitting style. The confraternity of San Cassiano d'Imola decreed in 1160 that if any brother became ill, others would visit him carrying candles to stand vigil, and that if he should die, all should hurry to the washing of the body and accompany the corpse to church and burial, and then sing mass for his soul four times a year. In the late fourteenth century, the Guild of Holy Cross in Stratford-upon-Avon, which we met above, describes similar arrangements: when a brother or sister died, the guild's main candle dedicated to the Holy Cross, along with eight smaller ones, would be carried from the church to the deceased's house and kept alight with the body until it was brought for burial. All brethren and sistren were to accompany the corpse. According to its statutes, the guild also provided a lesser burial, using just four candles, for any poor man or stranger who died in the area – an act of charity that also worked to signal the relative status of both recipient and donors.[142]

Burial was not the end of death's social aspects, as the dead were to be remembered in the parish's prayers. This brings us to the final topic I wish to deal with, the mass, when those prayers would be offered. The order of the full, sung mass was as follows. An introductory psalm admitted man's sinful state and made a general confession of sin and, on Sundays and feast days, the hymn *Gloria* then proclaimed the possibility of salvation. There followed readings from the Gospel and other declarations of faith. The priest then began to prepare the bread and wine for the sacrament, while the laity gave oblations in goods or cash (the 'offertory'). This done, the priest would lead the congregation in prayer. Then, partly obscured behind the rood screen, the priest performed the Eucharistic sacrament, transforming the material substances into the body and blood

of Christ. He would raise up the Host so that it was visible to all, an action her-
alded by the ringing of a bell (which summoned late-comers to at least witness
this central piece of magic). The priest would then make communion, and the
ritual would conclude by bestowing blessings upon the congregation, including
blessed bread, and the parishioners exchanging the kiss of peace (by the fifteenth
century, in England, rather than kissing each other, one kissed a board known
as the pax). A mass would be performed by the parish priest every day, but only
on Sundays were the laity expected to attend.

In practice, the details of the mass varied somewhat in different times and
places, and the full sense of liturgical theatre may only have been achieved in
more lavishly endowed situations rather than in every parish church throughout
the medieval period. Nevertheless, in whatever form, the mass can be seen as a
key ritual in the production of medieval community, as briefly discussed in
Chapter 1. This function was quite explicit: the theme of 'peace' was a central
refrain within the rite, and the kiss of peace a clear signal of amity. Using certain
anthropological models, John Bossy has argued further that the ritual drama of
the mass – particularly the consecration and subsequent division of the Host –
engendered community by re-enacting Christ's sacrifice: the violence of sacrifice
stood for the animosities and conflicts within the parish but, by being performed
symbolically rather than in actuality, worked to ease those tensions.[143]

It seems highly likely, given the collective participation of the laity within the
mass, and the explicit evocation of the theme of peace that it involved, that it
could indeed act in the ritual fashion that Bossy envisages. But this is not the
whole story. The narrative of sacrifice, and the cultural work it performs,
depends upon a certain audience viewpoint, with particular weight resting upon
particular liturgical moments, most importantly the central turning point of
Eucharistic consecration. But an ordinary lay parishioner's sense of what was
important during the ritual may not always have mapped exactly onto this
pattern.[144] There was little assumption on the part of the Church that the laity
would have a theological understanding of what the Eucharist embodied; and as
we shall see in Chapter 6, some people were doubtful that bread and wine could
be transformed bodily into Christ. Others had different doubts about the clergy's
role: one weaver from Varilhes said to neighbours, in about 1318, that everything the priests said and sang during mass was 'lies and foolishness', only done
in order to get oblations. This did not, however, prevent him from actually
attending mass, nor from performing acts of Christian charity; his sense of what
mattered, in this context, was perhaps therefore not a liturgical but a social one.
And in general, during the course of the mass, the laity were given their most
active roles during the prayers for the living and the dead, the offertory procession, and the final distribution of bread.[145] It may be that, for many, these were
the important points, involving collective action.

It is clear that mass was an important moment of communal interaction, but
its utility stretched beyond the liturgical framework outlined above. As discussed
in Chapter 2, the priest's sermon could perform a number of roles, one of which
was simply the announcement of recent news both local and national. Asked to

recall his presence at the baptism of a certain child for legal purposes, Robert de Eld told the king's court in 1379 that he had been present at the ceremony as he had attended mass in order to hear news from Ireland of the Earl of March. Other witnesses, similarly attesting, explained that they had gone to mass to buy corn from a certain parishioner, or to meet a friend, or before going on to conduct other business. Gender might also inflect these matters: the thirteenth-century Franciscan preacher Berthold of Regensburg said that while both men and women talk in church, men talk as if at a market about foreign news and such like, whereas women talk about problems with servants, troublesome husbands, a baby not putting on weight.[146] Some purposes for attendance, such as flirtation with the other sex, could be quite far from any pious thoughts. Alessandra Strozzi, an Italian woman of high standing, describes, in a letter of August 1465 to her son Filippo, her attempts at arranging a marriage partner for him:

> I must tell you how, during the *Ave Maria* at the first mass at Santa Liperata, having gone there several times on feast mornings to see the Adimari girl as she usually goes to that mass, I found the Tanagli girl there. Not knowing who she was, I sat on one side of her and had a good look at her . . .[147]

And, she reported triumphantly to Filippo, this new prospect was very pretty!

Moreover, the community that participated in the mass was not undifferentiated and equal. Parishioners listening to a sermon on Christian charity and fraternity were probably arranged according to various social divisions within the parish church. Pierre de Colmieu, archbishop of Rouen, ordered in the early 1240s that 'women, clergy and laity' should be separated in church. Frequently women sat on one side of the nave and men on the other (or else men in front and women behind) – according to the theologian William Durand (c.1237–96), this was to avoid the temptations of lust, and because women were impure.[148] Nor was gender the only divide. An early fifteenth-century Italian guide to appropriate behaviour in church indicates, disapprovingly, that people tended to look for 'all their tradesmen, neighbours, relatives and friends' when attending. Peter Quivel, bishop of Exeter, noted in 1287 that because people claimed certain stools in church as their own, fights over seating were breaking out. He therefore ordered that no one was allowed to claim a particular seat as 'theirs' – unless, of course, they were nobility or patrons of the church. Some of the liturgical elements themselves asserted social hierarchy, both past and present, as the names of important dead parishioners would be recorded in the breviary. The material ability of the wealthy to endow sacred objects and to contribute more lavishly to the offertory may have further signalled difference. And by the fifteenth century, the gentry and nobility tended to make use of private chapels in their own households, removing this upper strata from the arena entirely. Thus the local community at mass was divided up along lines of gender and social status.[149] Indeed, we could see the mass as providing a public stage upon which these divisions were asserted and even contested. An English sermon, for example, berates those who come to church dressed 'in noble attire' in order to show off to their neighbours.

When the pax board was introduced, it became customary to kiss it in sequential order of social hierarchy – something that unsurprisingly caused quarrels over disputed precedence. In 1455, parishioners from the village of Leigh-on-Mendip refused to bring the customary pax bread, for distribution at the end of mass as a sign of community, to the parish church at Mells, preferring instead to remain with their own local chapel. The local bishop ordered them to resume this practice, in an attempt to reassert community between the two locales.[150]

At the beginning of this chapter, I warned against seeing community as something obvious or natural. As we have seen, it was neither: division and dissension can be found at the heart of the apparently most communal of medieval practices, from processions to confraternities to the mass itself. One could argue, however, that the power of community is to make itself *appear* obvious and natural, performing this trick through precisely the mechanisms of order, exclusion and negotiation outlined above. A primary vehicle for effecting this cultural work is religious discourse and practice that not only explicitly enjoins peace and amity between Christians, but implicitly presents order, hierarchy and obedience as God-given. When the various rituals such as processions and the mass manage to produce community, they do so in this man-made shape. It is not, however, that first we have community and it is then forced into a social and gendered order. Medieval community *is* hierarchy, categorization and division. Or so it is, at least, from various dominant viewpoints. At certain points in time, other more egalitarian ideas, also drawing upon religious discourse, could be expressed, as we shall see in Chapter 6. The point, however, is that expecting rituals and ritualized behaviour to dissolve social enmity is unrealistic. There is no single mechanism, no button marked 'community' that, when pushed, causes all to fall dutifully into place. This is not to suggest that medieval society was hopelessly fraught with division and dissension. It is, instead, to note that processions, feasts, plays and so forth can work to ease (if not remove) social tensions, but can also work to express and provoke them. The activities surveyed above established a language and space within which tensions could be articulated, and renegotiations of social order could take place. The mass and processions provided a symbolic language for community: the kiss of peace, for example, an action also found in other, heretical, contexts (by the Cathars, among others) and in secular rituals of kinship. This could be a symbol of community; but, as Judas's betrayal of Christ reminds us, kisses can be put to many uses. Ritual does not turn its participants into puppets; it supplies them, rather, with possible roles that are invested with social meaning. One thing that these symbols proffer is the opportunity to refuse to kiss, refuse to deliver the pax bread, refuse to participate. During mass at Wisbech, for example, one John Freman called Margaret, the wife of John Dygby, 'stronge hoor' (whore) causing great uproar in church.[151] Delivering such an insult during the service not only made it as public as possible but also rejected the context of peace and charity – and John Freman must surely have known that. Such occasions are not, therefore, examples of the ritual going wrong, but one of the many possible outcomes ritual engenders.

5

Selfhood

Gendered Christian identities

Finding himself advanced in years and in possession of a young wife, the Goodman of Paris sat down to write. His bride would surely outlive him, and therefore need instruction and guidance after he had gone. Thus he produced a treatise, untitled, probably in the year 1393. It covered a variety of things, some very practical indeed: how to protect violets and marjoram against the cold during the winter months, how to remove the burnt taste from stew that has caught in the pot, how to catch fleas using a piece of bread smeared with glue and a candle at its centre. The initial chapters of the book, however, addressed what the Goodman called the 'chiefly necessary' duties of a good wife: 'the salvation of your soul and the comfort of your husband'.[1]

This spiritual and domestic conjunction is intriguing, and the roles of housewife and good Christian soul continue to intertwine in the following chapters. The Goodman sets out for his spouse instruction on daily prayers, attendance at mass, conduct in confession and guarding one's chastity. These lead seamlessly into more worldly matters: the need to love and obey one's husband, look after him bodily, and act as confidant and counsel to him as necessary. The latter duties are no less religiously inflected than the call to confession and prayers, as the Goodman supplies biblical examples and other *exempla* to demonstrate that the template for a wife's role is ordained by God. All of these demands are, the Goodman admits in conclusion, something of a burden, particularly given that, in contrast to household maintenance and other duties where a wife may have assistance from servants and other helpers, a woman must bear them by herself. It was for this reason that he wrote the 'doctrine' set down for his wife, as something that would aid her in performing her rightful role; 'for other women never had anything like it'.[2]

Like his young wife – only 15 years old when he married her and a little more 'gentle' in social status than he – we are going to use the Goodman's book to help guide us in this chapter. There are some potential problems here that should be noted at the outset and remembered throughout the journey. The Goodman came from an elevated and rather particular social background. He was not a noble-man, though he knew quite a few connected with the royal court; but he was rich, well-travelled, probably some kind of senior government official, and lived in the largest and most prosperous city in Europe. The very fact that he, while old, married a very young wife sets him apart from the vast mass of the laity. The normal pattern in northern Europe was for non-noble couples to marry in their twenties with little age gap between them. There may be a question mark, there-fore, over whether we can use everything that the Goodman says as evidence for the vast breadth of the social scale below his rank. One may be particularly wary, for example, of the fact that the Goodman was well educated and highly literate: few laymen could quote Livy, Augustine, Jerome, Peter Comestor and Petrarch, as he does at various points in the text. He was writing at the very end of the four-teenth century, and some of the theological and spiritual ideas reflected in the book may belong to that age more than to earlier ones. One may in fact wonder whether the framing premise of the text – old husband writing for young wife – was truly the case, or simply a literary device, not least because the manuscript survives in more than one copy and the book itself explicitly states that other people may later read and benefit from it. We do not even know his name. To call him 'the Goodman' is to follow a mistranslation of the title of the text that he wrote; but, for convenience, let us continue with this imposed nom de plume.

These caveats may, however, be overly suspicious. Various incidental domestic details in the book suggest that it tells truly of its origins. Most importantly, for our purposes, it is very clearly a book written by a layman, not an ecclesiastic. Although necessarily issuing from a fairly elite social position, it was not the only book of its kind; indeed, it marks the beginning of a period of textual production, particularly in France and England, of various guides to married life directed toward women.[3] We simply cannot tell how far down the social scale the influ-ence of such texts stretched, although we do know that by the late sixteenth century 'conduct books' (as the genre is now labelled) were quite widely dissem-inated. What we can say is that at least some of the ideas that the Goodman put into writing were part of a wider lay culture, and that the discourses regarding women and marriage upon which he drew for inspiration had, through their pres-ence in pastoral preaching for example, a much wider social reach than his manu-script.[4] The attraction of his book is therefore as one example of how a layperson might present ideas about the conduct of life in relation to religious ideals.

What it shows us, first of all, is that Christianity not only provided resources for communal action and production, as explored in the previous chapter; it was also a source of individual identity and selfhood. By 'selfhood', I mean the sense of the entity that we imagine inside us when we close our eyes; the inter-ior space of reflection, personal memory, inner feeling, secret hopes and fears and so forth. Some theorists – most notably the historian and philosopher Michel Foucault – have argued that this 'self' is not an innate core that exists and endures throughout life, but is better understood as something shaped and reshaped by the enticements and demands of the world around us. Exterior discourses – ways of talking, writing and acting that set the world into a particular shape – make claims upon individuals, and mould the particular 'selves' that they require. One could think here of monastic discipline. Monks lived under a Rule that governed their way of life, and that disciplined their body through fasting and other practices, in order to improve their inner soul. Moreover, the monk was not simply taught to obey these exterior injunctions as something imposed from above by the abbot: he was encouraged to *desire* to obey, because obedience itself was a virtue. Thus monasticism, in theory at least, presented a mechanism that sought to produce a particular kind of willingly obedient 'self'.[5] One could argue that something of this idea is shared by the Goodman: in presenting his wife with a set of ideas about how to conduct herself, how to pray, how to confess, he is attempting to provide her with a map for improving herself – or perhaps I should write, improving her 'self'. And he indicates that this is a heavy burden, but a rewarding one – she should *want* to improve herself along the lines he indicates. Medieval Christianity presented certain roles for people to fulfil, or at least to attempt to live up to. We met some of these in Chapter 2 when discussing *ad status* sermons: the division of the laity into groups such as maidens, widows, merchants, artisans, etc., each possessing particular nuances as to how to live a good Christian life and each having particular sins to which they were prone. From around 1150 or so, and developing in complexity and detail in the following centuries, these categories were presented to lay people as ideal roles upon which they should model their own behaviour. Thus what the Goodman does for his wife is, in part, to set out an ideal image of a good wife who conducts herself well, and then invite her to attempt to live up to the image.

One way of analysing these roles and images is to examine how they were gendered. Let us begin with women. There were two very famous polar opposites in religious discourse on women: the Blessed Virgin Mary and Eve. The former was the ultimate intercessor, mother of the Church and hence mother to all Christians, untouched by man, pure, but also the bodily link between God and this world. The other was the fount of all sin, the weakest part of human nature. Mary was literally inimitable. One could not hope to be like her, only aspire to follow her example as best one could. Eve, on the other hand, lurked within most women. It was her curiosity, lack of self-control, and willingness to give in to bodily desire that brought humanity to sin in the first place. The Goodman cites Mary as an example of obedience, bending to the will of the Angel Gabriel when he told her that she would conceive a child; and Eve as the contrasting example, 'by whose disobedience and pride she and all women were and shall be after her, were and have been accursed by the word of God'. Thus these two mothers hung over medieval women, one the unachievable ideal of perfection, the other a lurking reminder of their true nature.[6]

But they were not the only available images. Many other biblical models could be pressed into service, from the patient and enduring wives of Old Testament patriarchs, to the complex figure of Mary Magdalen, who, imagined as a prostitute saved by Christ, could be cited both as a reminder of women's lascivious nature and as an example of how even weak-willed and vain women could be redeemed, given the right circumstances. Medieval religious writings about women were often extremely misogynistic. This was particularly the case when monks were scaring each other about the hideous dangers that women posed to their own chastity: 'Physical beauty is only skin deep', explained Odo of Cluny (994–1049). 'If men could see beneath the skin, the sight of women would make them nauseous . . . Since we are loath to touch spittle or dung even with our fingertips, how can we desire to embrace such a sack of shit?'[7] Elements of this horror of women's bodies and desires leaked into wider cultural narratives about gender. But not *all* religious discourse was anti-women. Some elements of biblical teaching proposed the idea of gender equality, and some areas of religious enthusiasm – perhaps particularly those arising spontaneously among the laity – put this at least partly into practice, allowing women a more equal role in their faith.[8] More importantly, there were differences between how a monastic theologian might discuss women in the context of warning young monks against the company of women, and how a mendicant friar might present women in the context of model sermons on marriage designed to be delivered to a mixed lay audience. In sermons, as in the Goodman's book, we find both positive and negative images of femininity. Women were expected to model themselves to these idealizations, adopting the good and shunning the bad.

One overarching model was a tripartite division of the stages of life. Women could be seen as 'maiden, wife or widow', categories that had a veneer of 'naturalness' about them, but were in fact idealizations heavily imbued with moral meaning. Maidens were not simply young women but virgins. Sexually mature, but sexually unavailable, a maiden embodied the highest form of femininity in clerical eyes.[9] A wife was the husband's helpmeet, and under his authority, just as all men were under the authority of God. At the same time, she was bound to help him improve morally by exerting her influence in the domestic sphere.[10] A widow, freed from the demands of marriage, was expected to embody the Christian virtues of poverty and chastity. Precisely because of this prescription, medieval literature abounds with the opposite stereotype, depicting widows (such as Chaucer's Wife of Bath) as avaricious and libidinous.[11] A common trope attributed a 'hundredfold' reward in heaven to virgins for their chastity, with widows next in line, and wives trailing a poor third. For any individual woman, one of these three models would present itself at each stage of life. They described – and hence attempted to circumscribe – the entirety of the identities imaginable for women. Stepping outside of such conformities was difficult; one would likely end up either a saint or a whore.[12] While not the only ways in which women were described or understood, these clerical ideals therefore had effects in everyday life. Their categories informed, for example, legal rights and procedures, particularly with regard to women's autonomy in relation to men.[13] Agnes Wormes, a Dorset woman, left the home of her blind husband in 1391, having refused to have sex with him. When the local bishop discovered this, he cited

Agnes to appear at his court in order to bring her into line. Failing to fulfil essential wifely roles – paying the 'conjugal debt' and acting as carer – got one into trouble. A twelfth-century Castilian law code, drawing upon earlier statutes, ordained that a widow could possess her late husband's estate, so long as she lived 'honourably and chastely'; but if she had sex with someone 'and violates her husband's marriage bed', she lost the property to her sons.[14] Once again, transgressing one's role had material effects.

An essential element of feminine identity was obedience: submitting one's will to an authoritative male, whether he be father, husband, brother or spiritual adviser. Scripture commanded it so, as the Goodman quotes in his book: 'the man is the head of the woman, just as Christ is the head of the Church' (Ephesians 5:23).[15] Illustrating his point, he relates a number of different stories about female obedience, including the well-known and oft-repeated 'positive' example of Griselda, who patiently bore the tyrannical demands of her husband, and several cautionary tales about the misfortunes that befell women, their husbands and their households when wives were sly, proud, argumentative, rebellious or arrogant. Through these negative traits, here and in many other medieval texts and sermons, the positive corollaries were laid out for women. They should be honest, dutiful, humble, accepting and so on. Particularly important, for a bourgeois man like the Goodman, was the sense in which a woman's behaviour and honour were not just her own but those of her household too. When a woman brought shame through her sins, the shadow fell not only upon herself but also upon her family.

For this reason, women's activities outside the home were especially monitored. Thirteenth-century moralists enjoined women to walk to church with eyes cast down, attracting the gaze of no other; and to sit in church in silence, 'not like those vain females who discover the whole market, all their neighbours, friends and relations'. The fifteenth-century English poem *What the Goodwife taught her Daughter*, written by a cleric for a civic bourgeois audience, instructs the young women to whom it was directed not to walk too fast or talk too much, to avoid both the marketplace and the tavern, and to 'dwell at home' as much as possible.[16] To do otherwise is to diminish their 'worship', a term that encapsulates the link between religious ideals and secular ideas of honour. For both civic and religious authorities (often synonymous), the public presence of 'ungoverned' women – women out of the control of a male guardian – was a sign of social and political disorder.[17] Widows had, in theory at least, greater freedom than other women; but, the historian Carla Casagrande argues, it was for this very reason that 'widows – more than any other group of women – were obliged to observe strict religious practices, ranging from fasts and prayer to acts of charity'. These religious acts implied subordination to male spiritual directors: the widow's publicly devout actions tacitly announced her obedience to her priest and hence to a form of male authority.[18] Wives were governed, or 'covered' as the legal discourse would put it, by their husbands. In their public personae, they had a difficult line to tread: since at least the twelfth century, preachers had been decrying the sinful opulence of lay clothing, and by the late

Middle Ages women were particularly targeted. Extravagant clothes indicated both an attempt to elevate one's social status (the sin of pride) and a delight in bodily pleasures (the sin of *luxuria*, which can be translated as 'lust' but really covers a broader spectrum of worldly desire). At the same time, women should not dishonour their husbands by dressing *below* their social rank. Moreover, as the Dominican John of Freiburg explained in his late thirteenth-century pastoral manual, while showy female dress could engender lascivious behaviour, wives had a duty to dress sufficiently attractively to keep their husbands interested, lest the men tire of them and pursue adultery or even sodomy instead. As *Handlyng Synne* put it a century later, 'A wedded wife may attire herself / So that her husband loves no one but her / For his love she may do this / But for no other man do so.'[19] What women did in public reflected upon their men. The Goodman of Paris explains to his wife that she should dress 'honestly' without 'too much frippery, or too little'. Her hair and clothing should be neatly 'ordered'. Her controlled appearance thus reflects her controlled household.[20]

Women's need for male governance was explained by the belief that women were innately infirm, weak-willed, given to strong passions and confused behaviour. This weakness could have virtuous elements: it made a woman's love for her husband particularly devoted (and hence open to his governance). Some commentators from the thirteenth century and later also believed that women were particularly suited to perform acts of charity. Their soft-heartedness made them particularly empathetic in the presence of suffering, and they would rush to alleviate it through almsgiving and other works of spiritual mercy. Even this could be a problem, however, as women might give profligately from the household income; again, the guiding hand of a male was needed.[21] These feminine characteristics were rooted in their physical nature. Women's bodies were qualitatively different from male bodies, less strong, less ordered, less controlled. They were disruptive and unruly. They menstruated and they gave birth, which seemed to the male, clerical gaze a sign of weakness rather than strength. A number of terrors were associated with menstrual blood, including the idea that it could sour milk and cause mirrors to darken. And after childbirth, women had to undergo a purifying ritual – 'churching' – before being allowed back into the congregation.[22]

One is entitled to ask what degree of influence these sets of ideas, from the binary images of Mary and Eve to the fears of female corporeality, had upon lived experience. It is clear that women were *not*, in practice, confined to the home, but played roles in various areas of social and economic life. The very fact that poems such as *What the Goodwife Taught Her Daughter* warn against activities such as getting drunk, talking with young men, wandering through the town streets, telling jokes in church and such things, is surely evidence for their practice.[23] But equally, the existence of poems like *What the Goodwife*, along with countless pastoral manuals and sermons that similarly sought to regulate social behaviour, meant that when such activities were practised, they were at least liable to be understood within this moralized framework. One can see moments in the archival record informed by this morality: a 1392 apprenticeship indenture, for example, that bound Katherine Nougle (who was to be the servant of Avice Wodeford, a London silk worker) not 'to commit fornication or adultery in the house of her said mistress . . . nor play any unlawful or unseemly games whereby her said mistress may have any loss . . . She shall not customarily frequent a tavern.' Parishioners reported to an episcopal visitation in Cerisy in 1314 that 'Guillaume de Monteigneyo and his wife are diffamed that, because they keep a tavern, many foolish women diffamed of incontinence often go there.' Since the same record talks elsewhere in other contexts of 'prostitutes', this does not seem to be the implication for Monteigneyo's visitors – only that they were misbehaving women out on their own.[24] The most recurrent field of policing was women's sexual behaviour. A woman was warned of the multiple pitfalls of losing her reputation, dishonouring her father or husband, and tempting other men into sin. *Jacob's Well*, a fifteenth-century English text, explains that women can sin simply through attracting men's gaze, 'for they are the cause that the souls of many men are lost'. Various medieval commentators and writers believed that women possessed a much higher sexual drive than men, due to their disordered and unruly natures; for this reason, they were a danger to others as well as to themselves. Such a belief could interlink with class: Humbert de Romans was particularly concerned with the sexual conduct of lower status women, whereas he saw propertied housewives as better able to exercise self-control.[25] It was, in any case, most frequently the spectre of uncontrolled and shameful sex that hovered over women's public lives. In fifteenth-century Ferrara (and possibly much earlier also) races were held on the feast day of St George: first, the serious horse races, then comedic donkey races, and finally races of ribald men and prostitutes. By making these transgressors into a spectacle, they were arguably marginalized (in the sense discussed in the previous chapter). But they were also therefore presented very publicly to all women as negative examples, a warning of what might befall should one lose one's honour.[26] It is similarly notable that in defamation cases, which were policed by the church courts, those slanders against women frequently used sexual insults such as 'whore' or 'common woman'. Frequently those hurling the insult were themselves female, which may indicate the degree to which standards of honour and sexual behaviour had been internalized by women. 'Whore' was a label that could damage any woman, from homeless guttersnipe to king's mistress, although the status of the latter could allow her to elude it more frequently.[27]

What, then, of men? It depends, rather more than in the case of women, upon the kind of man envisaged. The noble classes, who are not a major focus for this book, had a particular body of texts aimed at them: works on chivalry. In both explicit manuals for chivalry (extant from the early thirteenth century onwards) and in fictional romance literature (surviving from the twelfth century and later), there is a clear melding of religious and secular discourses. Chivalry can be seen as a genre of texts written mostly by clerics about knights, that drew upon the heroic masculinity and idealized violence beloved of the warrior class, but attempted to reform it through Christian values. 'Reforming' did not imply the cessation of violence, but rather its redirection: in the service of the Church, against God's foes. The accoutrements of knighthood – sword, shield, buckler, saddle, horse and so forth – were invested with symbolic meaning, linking the knight to Christ. Quest narratives in chivalric fiction became, from the thirteenth century onwards, increasingly focused upon the attainment of spiritual grace. In the *Quest del Sant Graal*, for example, the Grail is presented as not so much a physical object as the purifying effects of true confession. The ideal knight, following at least some Arthurian romances, was to guard his honour (and indeed his chastity) in much the same fashion as a maiden was to guard hers – except that knights came better equipped to ward off others, and with a higher expectation that they were capable of exercising self-control. A good knight was, by his very nature, a good Christian; his ownership of violence in the service of the Church.[28]

Chivalric texts had, particularly by the fifteenth century, some readership beyond the nobility, but were essentially produced and consumed by elite culture. Nonetheless, certain themes that they presented were shared in other idealizations of male lay identity. One is simply that, given that the social strata or 'estates' of medieval society were ordained by God, fulfilling one's estate willingly and well was itself a Christian virtue. Where women were almost always covered by the 'virgins, wives, widows' triptych, men were allotted more roles: servant, sailor, artisan, labourer, merchant, among others. Being true to one's role was in itself morally virtuous. To be otherwise, either by attempting to aspire to a higher class or by protesting the inequalities of hierarchy, implied the sins of pride and envy. Another English poem, *What the Wise Man Taught His Son*, advises that a man should not seek office, should guard his tongue, and stay put lest neighbours think him 'unstable'.[29] The identities that religious discourse presented to ordinary laymen were largely socially quietist: fit in, do your job, don't kick against the pricks.

It was generally assumed that a layman, to qualify as a man rather than a youth, would be married.[30] Taking a wife implied becoming a master, having control of one's household even if otherwise socially disadvantaged. Jacobus de Voragine explained that, whereas a wife's love for her husband should be all-encompassing, almost blinding, so that she would willingly defer to him, a husband should love his wife moderately and wisely. His affection should not be excessive, lest he lose control and become irrational and passionate – 'effeminate', in fact, in a medieval sense. Control was very important, because the husband was responsible not only for his own actions, but also those of his spouse. He was duty-bound to provide for his wife, but enjoined by moralists to provide what she needed rather than what she wanted – to guard her against her own innate vanity. And he should 'correct' her, both verbally and physically, when it was necessary.[31] Physical chastisement (also directed against servants and apprentices) should not be 'excessive' – churchmen were very clear on that score – but it remained not simply a sanctioned option but a potential duty. At the same time, preaching *exempla* warned against the potentially disastrous consequences of a husband's uncontrolled anger.[32] Thus, as with knights, though sanctioning a less extreme level of conflict, religious discourse mapped out a 'proper place' for male violence – its corrective use within a social and gender hierarchy, under controlled circumstances.

Control is indeed the key word: control of others and control of oneself. In the early fourteenth century, Giardano da Pisa preached in Florence on how the laity should live, saying that people came to him and asked 'which is better, fasting and saying the Paternoster or collecting indulgences and going on pilgrimages? Or which is better: giving alms or serving the hospitals? Everyone asks questions of this kind.' The questions map a division between a contemplative inner piety and an active outer one – a polarity we shall explore further below. In any case, Giardano explained, there were many ways of living well. The active life included not only the works of mercy and such like, but also 'marriage, managing the family, governing it and teaching the commandments of God, ruling people, and also defending the faith against infidels'.[33] The progression from the household to the kingdom is informative: the implicit male identity sketched out and valorized here is founded upon the notion of governance. A good Christian man governs, at whatever level he finds himself. A king rules his country wisely, and defends the international church. An artisan rules his household wisely, and defends the faith of his family. Law cases further underline the structural similarities. In a late fourteenth-century English case before the church court, Thomas Nesfeld is said to have struck his wife Margery for staying out of the house without permission, an assault legitimated by Thomas and his counsel by presenting her actions as a 'rebellion'. Following canonical and moral ideals, Thomas is the sovereign lord, Margery the wayward and unchaste harlot.[34]

Implicit in male identity is its relation to female identity – what women were asserted as being, men were tacitly (or sometimes explicitly) asserted as not. If women were weak, unruly, and ill-disciplined, by implication men were strong and suited to governance. The Goodman of Paris says little specifically about male roles in his book, directed as it is towards his young wife. But a strong sense of male identity lurks behind the page, with the hand that holds the pen. To sit and write a set of instructions, a veritable map for living, was to fulfil the ideal of masculine identity: to provide governance for his wife even after death. However, male identities were more varied, within religious discourse, than those of women. In preaching *exempla* and other moralizing materials, for example, groups of men are prone to particular sins by virtue of their different social roles (merchant, artisan, baker, weaver, etc.). Women, in contrast, are liable to particular sins simply because they are women.[35] But there were some implicit elements to male identity shared across most classes. There were virtuous activities that men were better able to pursue, or that came ultimately under male governance: regular almsgiving, for example (as opposed, implicitly, to the impulsive and tender-hearted generosity of women), and other guild activities, as we have seen in the preceding chapter. Pilgrimage, while open to women, was most easily and most frequently undertaken by young men. When the formal position of churchwarden (a lay official who administered the parish church's finances) became prominent, it matched the pattern of other secular office-holding and was open only to men. Similarly, women were usually excluded from office-holding within guilds. Men gave material support for the church's fabric and did other 'good works'; these were simultaneously acts of charity, community and benefaction. And being a benefactor – one who does good (and therefore advertises the fact that they possess the necessary material resources to be *able* to do good) – was a key element in male, civic, bourgeois identity. In the towns and cities of medieval Europe, the oligarchy, and those who aspired to the oligarchy, called themselves 'goodmen' or 'worthy men' or 'honest men'; hence the name ascribed to our writer from Paris. Moral and financial worth slid silently together.[36]

This again raises the question of the relationship between image and reality. We should note that the religious discourses propagated in preaching and pastoral manuals were not the only ones to sketch out social identities, and that gender roles were not purely based upon what the Church had to say. Gender hierarchies depended upon a much broader set of cultural ideals, economic patterns and social practices than the Church's message alone. Nor did the Church always affirm existing social patterns: it attempted to redirect and control knightly violence, for example, and what the Church preached about marriage asserted cooperation and mutual support as much as hierarchy. But it is possible to argue that religious ideals, and particularly the demand for clerical celibacy in the twelfth century, had a profound influence upon gender roles; put crudely, that newly-celibate clerics found it useful to denigrate women's bodily natures as a means of reasserting their potentially challenged masculinity.[37] And it should be noted that religious discourse provided the strongest set of arguments for leaving social hierarchies unchallenged, by presenting them as God-given and hence immutable.

Were they seen that way? In Chapter 2 I emphasized that the laity did not simply imbibe clerical culture but interpreted it. We must surely be sensitive to elements of interpretation in this area, too. Certainly, looking at something like the conduct of marriage, there is evidence for mutuality and cooperation, just as there is for hierarchy and male domination – though mutuality was also an element in some clerical preaching about marriage.[38] In the final chapter, I will suggest some ways in which religious discourses could be used to express social dissent and challenges to hierarchies. But it is clear that these images of social roles and gender roles did have effects upon people's lives. One might posit a difference between what is stated in clear terms, and what glides silently beneath the surface of language. It is possible to imagine that many women, presented with an explicit denunciation of feminine lustfulness, could check the image against their personal experience and dismiss it with a derisive snort. Certainly one, rather unusual, woman, the professional author Christine de Pizan (*c.*1364–1430), was capable of demurring: 'why on earth was it', she wrote, 'that so many men, both clerks and others, have said . . . such awful, damning things about women and their ways?', and she authored several books in rebuttal.[39] Nevertheless, in listening to many *exempla* and other tales wherein women were presented as weak and men as strong, both sexes may have had certain ideas of gender affirmed. Perhaps most importantly, elements of these ideals clearly had material effects – as we have seen in some examples above and elsewhere in this book – because they informed legal practices.

Underlying all these different ideas about roles and identities was one essential element: sin. Women's weakness stemmed from Eve's original sin; women's weakness still mattered because it could lead to sin, both for women and for men. The roles that men played were demarcated by the different occasions that they offered for sin. Every day, echoes of the original encounter with the serpent in the Garden of Eden were played out, as people met with temptation and succeeded or failed in the struggle according to their natures. But to be clear: the Church largely expected them to fail. Its appointed role was to lead people away from sin, back towards God and salvation. The Church was needed because the laity (it taught) could not manage the journey by themselves. And it was this drama of sin and redemption that provided the motor for Christian selfhood. The 'self' that medieval Christianity, by the later Middle Ages, attempted to inculcate in all Christians was one that understood itself through the prism of sin, and attempted to change itself through the search for salvation, mediated by the clergy.

The branches of sin

A few pages into his book, having authorially awoken his wife, had her pray, and dressed her, the Goodman turns to a new topic:

> The third article [of this book] says that you should love God and keep yourself in His grace. Whereupon I counsel you that straightaway and laying aside all other tasks you refrain from drinking or eating at night or vespers, even a little bit, and you get away from all earthly and worldly thoughts, and whilst coming and going you put and hold yourself in a secret place, alone and far from people, and think of nothing but hearing your mass early the next morning, and after that giving account to your confessor of all your sins by a good, full and thoughtful confession.[40]

These words lead into one of the lengthiest chapters of the manual. The Goodman outlines attendance at mass (to which we shall return later), and then moves to lecture his wife on confession. The process must begin, he explains, with contrition, the 'sorrow of heart' that makes one repent sin and humbly seek forgiveness from God. Then comes confession, made to a priest, who is a kind of medic for one's soul. One should think long and deeply on all one's sins, so that one can 'recount them in order and describe their circumstances' to the confessor. Finally, the confessor will prescribe a penance, which will consist (so the Goodman thinks) of fasting or almsgiving or prayers. The Goodman then launches into the main bulk of the chapter: the nature and content of each of the seven deadly sins. Each sin is explained and glossed, subdivided into its different 'branches'. Thus the sin of pride, which is the root of all other sins, has the branches of disobedience, vainglory, hypocrisy, discord and aloofness. Each of these branches is discussed in full. Little images and examples pepper the explanations: 'hypocrites are like a foul and stinking dunghill covered with cloth of gold and silk, to have greater honour and glory'; 'God commands us to go to church and rise early, and the gluttonous woman will say "I must sleep. I was drunk yesterday. The church is not a hare, it will very well wait for me!"'.[41] Every sin concludes with an example of how one might begin to confess to it, before moving on to the next vice. Finally, in the last few pages of the chapter, the Goodman briefly sets out and glosses the seven virtues, 'whereby one may keep oneself from sin'. Thus humility, kindness, gentleness, diligence, generosity, temperance and chastity are briefly set to dance upon the page, but always handfast with the sins that they partner.

What should we make of all this, in the particular context of the Goodman writing for his wife? Were medieval people obsessed with sin, oppressed by its ever-present weight? Why did the Goodman think that explaining confession and sin to his young wife was so important? Does it suggest that lay people did indeed use it to structure the architecture of their internal worlds? This last question is a big one, and I shall return to it from different angles later in this chapter. For now, let us say something more about sin, first from the perspective of ecclesiastical writers, and then from that of the laity. There were seven of them, as we already know: pride, envy, wrath, sloth, avarice, gluttony, lust. These were mortal sins, those which took one away from God, and required explicit confession for the removal of their stain. Other faults, committed involuntarily in the usual course of life, were known as 'venial sins'. These could be atoned for during life by good works, and after death through purgatorial suffering and the prayers of others. To die without mortal sins confessed and absolved meant that one was almost certainly destined for hell and all its torments, from which there was no escape. In most other cases, certainly by the end of the twelfth century, one would end up in Purgatory, from which there was hope of release. A sin was a cut upon the body of Christ, a severing of oneself from the community of the faithful. To heal this wound, one must feel contrite; one must confess, placing the management of one's soul into the hands of the priest; and one must make 'satisfaction', through the performance of the penance imposed by the confessor. God would then through the power of the confessor, absolve the sin; the wound would heal seamlessly.

One could go on at substantially greater length about the theology of sin in the medieval period. Medieval theologians certainly did, having great intellectual fun further dividing and subdividing the 'tree' of sin and its many branches. I will say more below about one of the most important aspects, the doctrine of Purgatory. The finer theological subtleties were, however, of a demonstrably different order from the simpler message usually given to the laity in sermons and pastoral literature. Whereas some theologians had focused very strongly upon the interior workings of sin – Peter Abelard (*c.*1079–*c.*1142) famously argued that the *intention* to sin, rather than the deed, was the only thing that mattered – when coming to tell lay people about sin and the need for confession, clerics tended toward the external and the literal. Thomas of Cantimpré presents an *exemplum* of a man who slowly went from the good to the bad. As he sinned, he became ill; pale, thin, tired. Medicine did not help him. But nearing death he repented and confessed tearfully to a priest, who absolved him. At this, the man began to vomit. Out came seven little animals, black and dreadful, resembling toads. One by one, the animals fell rotten and dissipated. As they did – 'marvellous thing!' cries Thomas – the body and face of the penitent began to recover its former health. A sense of interior contrition is present in the story, subtly indicated by the tears that the man cries when confessing, but the more obvious facet of the tale is the representation of the seven sins as external creatures. The man expels them from inside him, but their independent exterior existence tends to encourage a sense of sin as less an innate human flaw and more an external threat under the direction of the Devil. Another *exemplum* tells of a demon leading a man to church on a chain. Having confessed, the man becomes invisible to the demon and hence is freed.[42] Again, the story encourages confession, but presents an outside foe as much as an inner fault.

The two are combined in the Goodman's text. Without contrition, or the intervention of the Virgin Mary, he explains to his wife, we would be 'chained to the gibbet of hell forever . . . unless the hot tears of our heart's contrition drive the enemy outside of us in our present life. But that may be done even as easily as hot water drives the dog from the kitchen.'[43] Sin is something interior here, but also a separate something – 'the enemy' (that is, Satan) – which one can expel. In all of these cases, one can see the *exempla* as presenting metaphors for sin thought suitable for a lay audience.[44] But it is not clear that such tales were understood (perhaps not even by their authors) as purely metaphorical. People did believe in demons, for example, as objective, external enemies. Demons could possess people, making them blaspheme or prophecy or cause mischief in the community. Usually, when accounts of exorcism were recorded, the demons were blamed and the possessed person seen as a victim rather than a perpetrator.[45] The sense of external threat may have been strengthened by the various late medieval depictions of hell. In San Gimignano, for example, a fresco by Taddeo di Bartolo from around 1390 presents particularly lurid scenes of the different punishments meted out to various sinners. Gleeful demons torture the souls in inventive and fitting ways: usurers eat coins shat from a demon, a false witness has his tongue ripped out, a sodomite is pierced from arse to mouth by a skewer. Other sinners are gouged, hung, flayed, throttled, stabbed, gutted – and eaten by the Devil himself, who has many hungry mouths.[46] Many other such artistic depictions can be found across Europe. Damnation, in these terms, was when the devils 'got you'. Evil could be seen, therefore, as the presence of these devils in this world. One can see something of the elision between the two in evidence given at the canonization inquiry for St Thomas Aquinas by Peter Francisci, a lay brother who had been a shoemaker before joining the order. He attested that Thomas's tomb had cured him of paralysis. This affliction had been brought on one day when he was resting from work and thinking of having a drink. A 'hairy man' suddenly appeared, gripped his feet and pressed them down on the bed, saying, 'Don't move, I will bring you some water'. Peter initially accepted the offer, but then realized that the man had turned into a dog with a human face, and had a horrible stench about him. 'Go away,' cried Peter, 'I will not drink!' The creature vanished, but Peter's body began to stiffen.[47] Peter was struggling with some sense of inner temptation here – his desire for a drink – but the devil doing the tempting was clearly external and physically threatening.

Another interesting element in the Goodman's homily quoted above is the domestic reference to getting dogs out of kitchens, which implicitly compares the management of sin to the management of the household. The English preacher John Mirk draws a similar image in one of his sermons, likening sin to a 'stinking thing' that one would not have in one's house.[48] In broader terms, sin was frequently presented as something social. Different groups were prone to different sins: 'Sins typical of men of the penitent's station must be inquired about', the *Summa Astesana* (1317) advised confessors. 'A knight must not be questioned about the sins of a monk or vice versa . . . Princes are to be questioned about justice, knights about plunder, merchants, officials, craftsmen and workers about perjury, fraud, lying, theft and so on . . . bourgeois and city dwellers generally about usury and chattel mortgage, peasants about covetousness and theft, especially in regard to tithes . . . '[49] Several things were operating here. The occasions that one's occupation presented for sinning slide towards a stereotype of social classes (the rapacious knight, the thieving peasant). Remembering the ideal of hierarchical reciprocity in medieval society, the sins themselves were ways in which each kind of person broke this social contract: the prince failing to dispense justice, the city merchant exploiting his wealth through usury. Much sin was, in this sense, a crime against one's neighbours. Moreover, as Jacques Le Goff has pointed out, the avoidance of these characteristic sins helped to form a sense of trade ethic and honour. Thus, around 1315, one finds the Dominican Guy de Toulouse taking extracts concerning commerce from John of Freiburg's *Summa confessorum*, translating them into the French vernacular and presenting them as a treatise on mercantile morals under the title 'Rule of Merchants'.[50] Another social prejudice in relation to sin was gendered. Women were frequently presented as a separate social class from the other trades, and in collections of *exempla* they tended toward a particular sin. Whereas the most frequent stories told of laymen concerned the sin of avarice, when moralists thought of women they thought of lust.[51] The message that women were prone primarily to sexual weakness or to prompting it, voluntarily or involuntarily, in men, was repeated in numerous confessors' manuals.[52]

Lust (*luxuria*) is an interesting sin, and worth considering further, not least because we can use it as a test case for how lay people responded to the Church's message. I do not want to give the impression that lust was all that concerned the Church. For much of the later medieval period the sin of avarice was more pressing, as the increase in mercantile activity and wealth, which began in the twelfth century, tended to make money matters a central concern.[53] But lust was, nonetheless, an important topic, and one to which most confessors' manuals and similar materials devoted particular attention. An initial look at medieval ecclesiastical writings can suggest a very negative view of sex: something very frightening, hugely sinful, full of body-horror and misogyny. But, as noted above, much of this is in texts directed at clergy as an aid to chastity. Sex for lay people was a different issue. Within the context of marriage, it could be seen not only as permissible but even, by a few writers, as something to be celebrated, a blessing. Thomas of Chobham for example wrote in a work of pastoral care, 'In contracting marriage, a man gives a woman his body, and she hers; apart from the soul, nothing under the sky is more precious.'[54] Almost all ecclesiastics, following biblical prescription, agreed that there was a mutual 'conjugal debt' – that both the man and the wife owed sexual congress to the other. Sex within marriage should also be for the purposes of reproduction: to attempt to avoid offspring, by whatever means, was sinful. And although twelfth-century theologians successfully argued, against older traditions, that sexual congress was not a necessary prerequisite for marriage, the canonical and pastoral assumption was nevertheless that most marriages would and should contain a sexual element.

One might be justified in going on to suggest that all other sexual conduct beyond the marriage bed was forbidden. However, it might be more accurate to say that all sexual conduct, including that within marriage, was subject to a system of constraint and monitoring. The Church did not assume that it could stop lay people from having sex – indeed, it signally failed to manage that even with its own clergy. What it sought instead was to regulate their sexual behaviour, punishing transgressions as a part of the wider system of penance and absolution discussed in this chapter. An early thirteenth-century Dominican confessors' manual sets out briefly and fairly clearly the main transgressions:

> Next is lust, which has many types, namely simple fornication, which is illicit love between an unmarried man and an unmarried woman; adultery, which is any violation of wedlock, as when a married woman comes to another man or vice versa; incest, which is illicit sex between blood relatives or kinfolk; debauchery, which is the illicit deflowering of a virgin.[55]

These transgressions are in a hierarchy; the kind of penance given for simple fornication would be lighter than for incest or debauchery. The manual goes on to discuss another four types of lust, which it rather unclearly describes as 'abuse, softness, shamefulness and sodomitical vice'. The first three may map in some way to masturbation, fantasizing and wet dreams; the fourth would appear to be unambiguous, but is in fact a more complex area than it first appears. 'Sodomy' could indicate sexual relations between two men, but in the medieval period it could also (depending upon the commentator) label a much wider range of sexual behaviour deemed 'unnatural'. Thus theologically sodomy might be sex between married people that was not 'normal': oral or anal sex, or even sex with the woman on top of the man.[56] These vices 'against nature' were the blackest end of the moral spectrum. As such, they were usually 'reserved sins': the parish priest would be unable to absolve a penitent who confessed them, but would have to pass the case on to the local bishop. The manual provides its confessors with a helpful verse to remember what is 'reserved' in this way:

> If they have committed incest, deflowered a virgin, or homicide,
> Sacrilege, patricide or sodomy,
> The bishop shall ask the Pope if they shall be spared the fire;
> And also murderers of clerics or those guilty of simony.[57]

While this scans better in the original Latin, it remains a rather ugly verse.

The most common focus, however, was upon lesser sexual sins. Husbands were admonished on how they might sin with their own wives, if for example they had sex on holy days or during fasting periods such as Lent. Some clerics thought that one might sin through 'excessive' desire for one's wife, presumably because of the loss of self-control this implied.[58] Jacques de Vitry warned that men who had sex with pregnant wives could accidentally cause the loss of the baby (a myth that sometimes persists to this day).[59] Thus sexual behaviour was something to be guided and questioned; not forbidden, but monitored. Our thirteenth-century manual sets out some further questions that the confessor should ask a man who has sinned sexually: whether the sin was hidden or manifest, because a public sin is greater as it can lead others astray; whether the sin occurred in a holy place, such as a churchyard; the nature and strength of his temptation to sin, whether it had come from eating hot food for example (believed to inflame lust); whether the woman was married or single, a virgin or a whore, or a non-Christian. Here, as in most such works, the confessor is cautioned to tread softly regarding details, so as not to put ideas into the penitent's head. The priest is advised to say something along the following lines: 'The natural mode, when a man clings together with a woman, is always with the man above and the woman laying beneath. Have you done otherwise? If you have, don't be ashamed to say.'[60] Apart from affirming ideas of what is 'natural' and 'unnatural' to the laity, these questions place intimate and domestic areas under the gaze of the Church. Or perhaps, we should say, the penitent is encouraged, with the help of the confessor, to place them under his own gaze. One's body, one's desires, one's eating habits and so forth become part of a moral regime.

How much of this matched the laity's beliefs and practices on sex? It is, of course, an impossibly broad question: which lay people, where, when, in what circumstances? There are, in fact, certain kinds of evidence that may suggest the outlines of an answer; not, perhaps, a single clear picture, but some sense of different possible responses and effects. We can note, first, that ideas of sexual chastity and the valuation of virginity had some attraction to the laity. At least some who entered convents and monasteries chose religion, and the vows of self-renunciation, because they believed in the value of this kind of life and particularly in the value of sexual abstinence. One can see similar enthusiasm among a few people who set up quasi-monastic lives for themselves, albeit without vows or a monastic Rule: the Beguine communities in southern France and Flanders, for example. Some others chose to live within chaste marriages, both husband

and wife mutually forswearing sex. Margery Kempe did this, as part of her programme for self-beatification; her account of her life shows the tensions that could result, however, as her husband was much less keen on the idea.[61] So the message of sexual renunciation, although not usually directed squarely at the laity, appealed to a few of them, at least in certain circumstances (Kempe already had a number of children). Female virginity also had a clear social resonance. Inasmuch as a daughter was the property of her father until marriage, her virginity constituted much of her 'value' to both parent and future husband, particularly among the higher social classes. Thus when a man took a woman's virginity, forcibly or otherwise, but did not marry her, financial compensation was often rendered, either through legal action or social expectation. In various other ways, too, virginity had a place within secular legal discourse, sometimes acting as a means of asserting the independent status of a single woman.[62] Lay valorization of female virginity did not operate within quite the same set of values as the Church's viewpoint, but it is probably fruitless to ask which informed the other. The point was that the Church's message sat comfortably with lay attitudes.

But other elements were, on occasion, clearly ignored. Various modes of what we would now call family planning were practised, from non-procreative sexual activities, to contraception, to abortion and possibly the occasional infanticide. The latter were not explicitly tolerated by secular authorities, but what constituted 'abortion', or how the death of an infant was recorded, were decided by the collective view of the community which might be relatively merciful in such matters.[63] The prosecution of sexual offences is, in fact, a rich area to consider for the broader question of how the laity thought about sex. Most offences fell, in theory at least, under the purview of ecclesiastical courts. In diocesan visitation, for example, crimes of adultery and fornication were frequently prosecuted, as we noted with the case of John Newland and Denise Penyes at the beginning of the previous chapter. But, to reiterate an earlier point, such prosecutions were not simply 'top-down' models of authority. A fornication case could only be brought to the bishop's attention by other lay people in the neighbourhood; it was their sense of morality that mattered as much as his. Study of such prosecutions suggests that the neighbourhood had its own gradations and sense of context for these sins. Fornication which resulted in pregnancy is common in the records, which may indicate not only that pregnancy or the birth of a child were rather public signs of an earlier misdemeanour, but also that the community was more concerned with the transgression when potentially fatherless children were at stake. Cases involving incest, or multiple partners, were also more likely to be brought to court. There is an overlap here with clerical morality, but not a perfect match: prosecutions of married men who committed adultery tend to be conspicuous by their relative absence, for instance.[64] Recent work on leyrwite – fines imposed upon unmarried women by the English manorial courts for fornication – gives a similar picture. In theory, leyrwite ran parallel to clerical condemnation of fornication, and its first appearance as an English word is in the poem *Hali Maidenhad* (1210x20) where it signifies devilish punishment for sexual sin. Within the practice of the manorial court, where local jurors controlled presentments, it would appear to have been applied selectively, falling hardest on never-married bondwomen during periods of high population when food was scarce. As Judith Bennett comments, 'medieval peasants seem to have been fairly tolerant of even women's sexual irregularity *except* when it was combined with poverty'.[65]

Guido Ruggiero's work on the prosecution of sex crime in late-medieval Venice permits further reflection upon the attitudes of lay authorities. The civic authorities who tried these cases often used a language to describe the transgressions that drew upon clerical rhetoric. Prosecuting one Giacomello Bono, who had had sex with Nicola, the niece of a master craftsman, the record says Giacomello's crime was 'not fearing God, law or justice, moved by the stimulation of sexual dissoluteness, in contempt of God and with dishonour for modesty, shame and clear contempt for Master Blasio her uncle'.[66] Other transgressors are described as 'not keeping God before [their] eyes' or 'moved by a diabolical will'. Women were usually depicted as passive in their sexual encounters, which mirrors the language of confessors' manuals; where they clearly had been the active partner in transgression, much stronger language, emphasizing feminine lustfulness, was used to describe them. This would seem to indicate a strong sense of shared values over sexuality between Venetian government and clerical moralists. But, once again, certain differences can be detected. While the rhetoric was thunderous, the policing was often gentle: most punishments for fornication were, at least until the fifteenth century, at the lightest end of the available scale. This was not necessarily a benign pattern. Somewhat in contrast to the Church's high valuation of virgins, the Venetian authorities tended to treat the rape of single women of marriageable age as a rather light and inevitable matter. 'Sacrilegious' sex crime, such as sleeping with nuns or non-Christians, or having sex in holy places, was strongly denounced as 'dishonouring' God – rather as Giacomello's seduction of Nicola dishonoured her uncle – and prosecuted. However, in cases concerning contact between Jews and Christians, it was perhaps only in the later fifteenth century that heavy fines and imprisonment were actually imposed. Where the Church and the Venetian state came together again, though, was in the vehement denunciation and fear of sodomy – meaning, in this instance, homosexuality. The penalty was death by burning. But even here one might suggest a certain space between lay and clerical attitudes (not to mention the fact that Venice clearly possessed a gay subculture despite the imprecations against this 'abominable vice'). Sodomy, within the world of Italian city states, tended to symbolize a certain loss of male control at the political level. The biblical image of the fallen city of Sodom was read as much for the idea of a city disastrously struck down as for the sinful deeds of man. And in some ways, the Venetian government's fear of sodomy outstripped even the Church's condemnations: city officials arrested four Franciscans who had walked naked through the city streets carrying crosses, followed by a large crowd. The Franciscans were, in imitation of their founder, demonstrating poverty. The policemen thought they were behaving unnaturally – though the authorities eventually let them go.[67] The conjunction of sexual imagery and politics occurs, too, in late-medieval Spain, but here the feared transgression was sex between Christians and non-Christians. Such contact, prohibited by the Church, had long been condemned. But in the early fifteenth century, under the charismatic preaching campaigns of the Dominican friar Vincent Ferrer, fear of Christian/Jewish or Christian/Muslim sex became charged with meanings of collective identity. Royal legislation reaffirmed the abomination of such 'crimes', re-segregated Christian from Jew and Arab, and inflicted the severest penalties. The sexual 'purity' of Spanish Christians came to constitute 'the central metaphor of a well-ordered Christian polity'.[68]

It would be terribly surprising – not just to us, but to medieval churchmen also, I suspect – if we were to find that the Church's condemnation of a broad spectrum of sexual behaviour was so successful that nobody sinned in these ways. What is more important is whether people, when engaged in these acts, or reflecting back upon them, understood themselves to be committing a sin. To know what someone who died more than 600 years ago thought is difficult – but there are very occasional moments when the evidence gives us at least a hint. One intriguing, and under-researched area, is the use of magic in regard to sex. This was long condemned by clerics, but the use of love potions or charms was clearly practised at various times and places. Specific evidence of women using menstrual blood, among other ingredients, to fashion a potion survives from England in the thirteenth century, southern France in the fourteenth century and Venice in the fifteenth century.[69] Two things are interesting here. One is the sense in which women's bodies, and particularly menstruation, are symbolically charged, just as in medical and ecclesiastical discourse, only here as a source of power rather than weakness or contamination. The other is that often the women did not see what they were doing as wrong. A southern French noblewoman, Beatrice de Lagleize, questioned by an inquisitor for her contact with heretics, was asked whether certain items she possessed were for doing *maleficium* (evil magic). No, she responded: no, they're just to make a love potion to use upon my daughter's beloved.[70]

On some occasions, we can see individuals who were strongly affected by the Church's message on sexual transgression. The rather extraordinary Margery Kempe was tormented by images of sexual sins and threatening men in her old age, presumably because she had heard such things strongly denounced throughout her active church-going life. It has been persuasively argued that some cases where women were possessed or tormented by *succubi* hinged upon the sufferer externalizing the guilt she felt about sexual desire, projecting it onto a demon. Men, too, could be afflicted with guilt: on his deathbed in 1401, Antoni Safàbrega confessed that he had committed adultery some years before with a married Muslim woman called Axa.[71] The fraught atmosphere of that time and place with regard to sex and race clearly made him feel that he could no longer conceal his earlier misdeed in the face of imminent demise. But other attitudes can also be found. A perhaps rather exceptional woman, Grazide Lizier, questioned by the same inquisitor as Beatrice de Lagleize, told the bishop that the sex she had had with a priest was not sinful 'so long as it was pleasing to her'. When she stopped liking it, it became sinful.[72] The numerous cases of fornication brought before church courts, and the many cases of marriage litigation that hinged upon the legal implications of earlier sexual contact, indicate that sex was, understandably, a source of pleasure to a lot of young medieval people – and therefore perhaps did not seem particularly bad to them, unless complications arose. Let us turn again to the Goodman of Paris. His moral advice on confession to his young wife contains a lengthy disquisition on lust, which has 'six branches' in his account: when a woman thinks of a man or a man of a woman; when someone consents to sin; when unmarried people have sex; when married people have sex; when relatives have sex; and 'a sin which is against nature, as one is corrupted by sodomy'. On this last matter, he says, it is not good to talk about it as it is so horrible.[73] This looks quite clerical; and in fact this is not surprising, because for all his discussion of sin the Goodman cribbed from the *Somme le Roy*, a very popular thirteenth-century vernacular text on confession. That he should want to include this work, should want to integrate a kind of confession manual into the instructions for his wife, is interesting in itself. But his particular slant on sexual matters elsewhere in the book gives a more complex picture than simply the adoption of clerical attitudes. Expounding upon the duty of discretion that wives owe to husbands and vice versa, the Goodman tells two intriguing tales. One was of a woman who had left her husband and fallen into prostitution. The man, caring still for his wife, arranged for her to return home, and through some complex chicanery made it appear that she had been away on pilgrimage. Thus she was received back into the neighbourhood with reverence rather than scorn. The other concerned a man known personally to the Goodman, who fathered an illegitimate child. Gossip sprang up about how the infant was kept by his mistress, so the man's wife arranged for the child to be better cared for and married off when older.[74] These are tales, for the Goodman, of exemplary behaviour. In both cases, what mattered to him, and what he was trying to communicate to his wife, was the importance of public appearances and honour. Whatever inner stain these sins may have left, what mattered was the brisk and thorough laundry of one's public vestments. Sin, in this sense, was a social matter.

This was a strong tendency in lay attitudes, and was not necessarily in opposition to clerical preaching on sin. Indeed, one can see the medieval sacrament of penance as something designed to reconcile social enmities. However, in at least some ecclesiastical writings, there is arguably a shift in the fifteenth century towards a much more interiorized and psychologized view of sin, possibly marked by an increased focus upon sexuality. The transition can be marked by the move from the seven deadly sins – the staple of most medieval morality texts – to the Ten Commandments. The latter became much more prevalent in the late Middle Ages and thereafter, and this, it is argued, marks a turn in morality away from 'horizontal' social negotiations, to a 'vertical' system of law and transgression.[75] This narrative of change may, however, paint too simple a picture of the earlier period. Both the Ten Commandments and an emphasis upon interior and sexual matters can be found in numerous ecclesiastical texts prior to the fifteenth century. And it may be the case that in practice, as the lofty ideals of moral reformers met with the varied geographies of lay implementation, the social tended to triumph over the spiritual in most times and places, even beyond the Reformation. Two things, at least, are clear. The system of sin had a universal reach and application in medieval Europe; but the precise understanding and implementation of that moral universe were altered by various circumstances, most frequently grounded in lay interpretation of what really mattered. The disjuncture between lay and clerical was not absolute, as the Goodman's use of *Somme le Roy* indicates. Indeed, it would be better to say that lay and clerical ideas overlapped to a great extent. But there was *some* disjuncture nonetheless, between theological ideals and parochial practice, as various reformist texts tell us. Robert Grosseteste, for example, noted that 'both clerics and laity are of the opinion that gluttony is not a mortal sin, because nothing bad comes from it'. An *exemplum* in a popular preaching manual depicts a reluctant church audience questioning the need to listen to moralizing sermons: 'Each man has five senses and knows when he has done what is right or wrong. Well enough does he know when he commits fornication or steals or gets drunk, that he is sinning.' And *Handlyng Synne*, in urging penitents to confess to masturbation and wet dreams, imagines the chief hurdle not to be shame or embarrassment (as other commentators tended to think) but lack of concern: you should confess all of this to your priest, warns the text, because 'it may be much, that you think is small'.[76] For some people, in some contexts, sin loomed large; and it was certainly always available as a way of viewing human crimes and foibles. But for others, it was not such a big thing: 'We acted just as all people do!' was apparently an excuse frequently proffered in confession.[77]

Purgatory and death

The unending torments of hell had been drummed into the laity for many centuries. By the thirteenth century, the more complicated ante-room of Purgatory – a place not unlike hell, in that one suffered there, but ameliorated by the promise of an eventual ticket into heaven – was understood to be the immediate destination for most people. Two things come together with Purgatory: the idea of a location, rather less distant than heaven, where the dead reside but can in some sense still be reached by the living; and the belief that penitential suffering – Purgatory as a state or process – could continue after death and hence help secure future salvation. Conjoining these elements produced not only Purgatory as a physical location, but the idea that the living could assist the dead in their search for salvation. By saying prayers and doing good works in memory of the dead, the living helped their souls on their way. Thus later medieval Christianity has been described as 'a cult of the living in the service of the dead'; or, as John Bossy reformulated the phrase, 'a cult of living friends in the service of dead ones', emphasizing the degree to which prayers were directed towards kinship and locality.[78] The doctrine of a specific place called Purgatory has been dated to the work of Parisian theologians in the 1170s, although it was only in 1254 that it received formal acceptance by the papacy, and the precise theology continued to be debated throughout the medieval period.[79] It has been argued, most forcefully by Aaron Gurevich, that the sense of an intermediary place that was neither heaven nor hell was an invention of the early medieval laity, not the clergy; that it rendered the harsh binary choice of salvation or damnation more negotiable for the ordinary person, thus restoring hope.[80] One can certainly find many earlier examples of a place where souls are tortured after death in a purgatorial fashion, usually recounted in vision literature (where someone recounts a dreamlike revelation) or in tales of ghostly visitations. These places of demonic punishment were counterbalanced, in the early Middle Ages, by holy places such as Cluniac monasteries; the former was a sort of dark mirror of the latter.[81]

But it is unclear how well defined these earlier ideas were. There was a spectrum of belief about the afterlife. For some of the laity the souls of the recently dead remained closely tied to the places where they had lived, at least for a while after death, and they sometimes returned as ghosts. (Something similar, of course, underlay the efficacy of holy relics and saintly burial places: the belief that these special dead had left part of themselves behind, accessible to the living.) Ghost tales usually involved people returning to their former habitations; they were often the victims of a 'bad death', like the vampire at the opening of this book, or had some other kind of unfinished business. Ghosts can be interpreted as a way in which the living attempt to sort out the emotional and social dislocations that their passing has caused. In the many ghost tales recorded in *exempla*, their unfinished business is usually represented as the quest for salvation, and thus they are turned into spokespeople for the developing doctrine of Purgatory. But other, more secular concerns can also be glimpsed: reparation of past debts, clarification about testamentary wishes, the legitimation of hereditary succession.[82] Ecclesiastical discourse could accommodate ghosts when they came as avatars of salvation, but in other areas lay ideas could be in tension with the clerical. Sometimes, for example, those poor wretches who were possessed were believed by their neighbours to be under the control, not of demons, but of the returning souls of the dead.[83] The feasts of All Saints and All Souls in early November provided a period when the boundaries thinned between this world and the next, through which conduit the dead might ease themselves back. The living lit bonfires, baked and distributed 'soul cakes' and rang church bells, perhaps to help the dead in Purgatory, perhaps to ward them off – or perhaps, as Peter Marshall persuasively argues, to do *both* at the same time. Historians have similarly suggested that the dances and other celebrations one can sometimes see happening in churchyards – condemned by ecclesiastical authorities – were attempts to propitiate the dead.[84]

It is clear that the precise theological concept of Purgatory, and perhaps more importantly the integration of the concept into a system of intercession by the living on behalf of the dead, was clearly down to the Church. It was the clergy – and particularly the mendicants – who promulgated and sustained the idea in sermons, art and liturgical practice, and they who administered and directed the forms of intercessionary behaviour. In this fully developed sense, it is uncertain just how quickly and universally Purgatory caught on.[85] Studies of wills, for example, tend to show specific mention of Purgatory only appearing in the later fourteenth century. Thereafter the frequency increases in some areas; but in others there continues to be silence. None of the 4000 or so fourteenth- and fifteenth-century wills surviving for the region around Lyons uses the word Purgatory, for example. Some studies have found city dwellers more likely to make reference to it; others, for different areas, have found the opposite, that it was in the countryside that the doctrine was best known.[86] It is difficult, though, to judge from this evidence alone, as wills survive infrequently from earlier centuries, and are shaped by the scribe or notary as much as the testator. One can see, particularly in the years after 1350, examples of spectacular investments by testators in their afterlife – which probably implies a knowledge of Purgatory and a belief in post-mortem intercession. Many made vague requests for prayers and masses to be said for their souls and those of their families. Richer testators set up private chapels and chantry foundations – endowments to priests whose primary function was to pray for the souls of the dead – and some attempt to make provision for literally thousands of memorial masses (though the expense of this limited its availability). Again, however, the practice varies markedly from place to place. A study of testamentary culture in southern France, for example, finds that 75 per cent of wills in the period 1300–1450 in the city of Toulouse requested one or more funeral masses for the salvation of the deceased's soul, but only 25 per cent in the nearby town of Lautrec. Similarly, in certain Italian cities nearly half of all testators requested perpetual masses for their souls, but in others less than 10 per cent did so. In some areas, practices changed markedly over time. In the French towns of Valréas and Cavaillon, for example, the proportion of testators requesting masses rose from less than a quarter at the start of the fifteenth-century to close to two-thirds by the 1470s. During the same period at nearby Avignon, however, the proportion stayed at around 30 per cent throughout.[87]

It is clear that this style of piety ebbed and flowed in complex ways. While one can say that anniversary masses and other intercessionary works were clearly an important feature of late-medieval lay religion, this should not be taken as a universal characteristic. As the various figures above indicate, even when the trend was particularly popular, a large minority of people did not call for these measures in their wills; and, we must remember, the lowest strata of society did not make wills – and may well not have had the resources to pay for even meagre intercessions. It has been argued that the great explosion of church rebuilding in fifteenth-century East Anglia, funded by the parishioners, is an implicit demonstration of the power of Purgatory to prompt pious acts.[88] This may be true, but one would also wish to factor into the phenomenon the fact that particular social groups did most of the giving, and the wider socio-economic contexts that facilitated their activities (in the specific case of Norfolk, its success in cloth production).[89] And it does not quite explain why a doctrine defined and promulgated in the thirteenth century only had this effect 150 years or so later on.

One response to this last point would be to refer to fourteenth-century mortality, and particularly the Black Death. A lot of Europeans died in the fourteenth century. A number were carried off by starvation following poor harvests in its second decade. Whether this matched the depredations of disease is a topic long debated; but it is clear that, regardless of earlier events, the plague that swept through Europe between 1348 and 1351 killed a substantial proportion of the population. It is important to note once again the fact of regional (and even local) variation: one village might be left largely untouched by the disease, while another was practically obliterated. It also seems likely that the emotional impact – and perhaps importantly not just of the 1348–51 outbreak, but the subsequent return of plague in the following decades – cannot simply be matched to statistical mortality rates. Even if similarly large numbers had died from famine earlier in the century, those had been slower deaths as part of a sadly familiar and relatively predictable process. The plague killed people swiftly, and in large numbers all at once. Quite what that did to people's attitudes is much debated. There is evidence from chronicles and other elite sources that some people, at least, thought the plague a herald of the coming Last Judgement. During the plague period, flagellant groups became active, particularly in Germany, attempting to expiate mankind's sins.[90] There may also have been longer-term effects. Several historians have found a difference in testamentary culture before and after the Black Death, some arguing that this illustrates a changed consciousness of death in the later fourteenth century. Here, for example, are the opening preambles to two wills, one from 1304, the other from 1393: 'In healthy mind, wishing to order my things for God and the salvation of my soul . . .' compared with, 'Given that all humanity is subject to death but once . . . it is fitting that each one of us should pay our tribute to it . . .'[91] Such qualitative evidence is difficult to evaluate, but Samuel Cohn's work on Italian cities makes a persuasive case for at least one effect of the plague (an effect linked, Cohn argues, to the return of the plague in the 1360s rather than its initial onslaught). His study of wills shows that, in earlier times, testators tended to divide up their bequests, 'liquidating, splintering and scattering' their belongings. This followed patterns of mendicant piety that encouraged the dissolution of material possessions. It perhaps also worked to spread one's bets quite widely, in terms of almsgiving and prayers for one's soul. After 1363, and the reappearance of plague, testators began to 'memorialize' themselves: concentrating their bequests on things like hospitals, fountains, perpetual masses and the like. The Italians had seen death become an annihilator, wiping out great swathes of people. Their testaments planned ways of being remembered; a desire for intercessionary prayers, but perhaps also simply a wish not to be obliterated by their passing.[92] Another, smaller study of wills from around Lausanne similarly finds a shift: wills from 1300 to 1330 in this locality rarely made any particular recommendations of the soul, but as the century progressed testators more frequently commended their soul to God, Mary and the saints. After 1370 – fitting perhaps with Cohn's hypothesis about further waves of plague – these commendations became more elaborate and specific, and began to mention the Last Judgement.[93]

All of this has led some historians to see late-medieval religion as obsessed with death and damnation, clutching desperately at promises of salvation.[94] The case can certainly be made for something along these lines, particularly in the fifteenth century, and it is clear that provision for the soul after death was an important factor for many people. However, I suspect that the presence of death can be overplayed – or at least needs further context.[95] Some possible problems with wills as sources were discussed in Chapter 1. Studies have found that most wills were made when the testator was approaching death, and hence had his or her imminent demise and hopes of salvation very much to the fore. Similarly, a correspondence can be demonstrated between periods when plague was rife and the drawing up of wills.[96] If events made people particularly aware of death, their thoughts clearly and unsurprisingly turned towards it, and towards their means of salvation. A man called Pierre Isarn was reported, in the late thirteenth century, to have been held excommunicate by the Church for 15 years. He fell gravely ill, and at that point sought to obey the mandates of the priest and was thus absolved. But having then recovered, and been cited by ecclesiastical officials to answer for his earlier misbehaviour, he refused to cooperate and was once again excommunicated.[97] The thought of death, and the periods of plague or other high mortality, were not constant and uninterrupted. Cohn's argument that it was the *return* of plague that affected testamentary patterns is important: it suggests that medieval people's reactions were more complex than historians have initially suspected. The physical fact of death was undoubtedly more present in the medieval period than it is in modern Europe; but this could make death much more familiar and less worrying. Lay people knew about Purgatory, in the sense that they had had the theology preached to them since at least the early thirteenth century, and lay people in the fifteenth century in particular set in motion post-mortem measures that were geared to that theology: memorial masses, obits, chantries, etc. But whether all lay people – including those investing in these means to salvation – felt that they would truly suffer the purgatorial fires after death, and hence were obsessed with freeing themselves from this punishment, is another matter.

Looking across the span of the later Middle Ages what comes across most clearly is the desire for a guarantee – or as close as could be obtained – of salvation. A written amulet from fifteenth-century England promises the bearer protection from various misfortunes: the snares of one's enemies, bearing children safely, dying without confession and not being falsely damned.[98] The desire for confession and salvation are highly orthodox; but the notion of an amulet assuring such things – written almost as a kind of deed or contract – is rather more mechanistic. The blessed Christopher of Cahors (d. 1272) enabled, it was said, a certain dying man to live long enough to confess his sins – which put to flight two demons who, appearing to be doctors, had gathered at his bedside. Such a story points both forwards and backwards: it emphasizes the need, and benefits, of confession, but it also speaks to an older tradition of the saint as protector during the dangerous passage to death.[99] The presence of the demons at the deathbed (common to many tales and artistic representations) suggests a belief that the person was being judged at the point of death, rather than waiting for the Last Judgement; and Christopher's banishment of the demons suggests that, in this instance at least, the deceased would continue to enjoy post-mortem protection. *Guaranteed* salvation is one of the prime factors mentioned when people turned to Cathar or Waldensian heretics: a witness would say that she 'believed in the heretics, such that if she died in their sect, she believed she would be saved'.[100]

People did not live their lives awaiting death at every moment. We are slightly misled here, I suspect, by the available sources. Death produces evidence in a way that life – for ordinary people – does not. Moreover, death is a particular theme (with all the interpretive complexities that artistic themes involve) of later medieval art and literature. Dying, and latterly macabre views of death, indeed figure prominently in these materials, and death, purgatory and damnation were undoubtedly present in many sermons.[101] I am not suggesting that people were ignorant of these things, or blasé about their implications. But the very fact that the Church invested substantial effort in *reminding* people about death and its price suggests that it was not an ever-present and universal concern. It was not something that 'went without saying': it was something said over and over. And in some of the sayings, one catches a glimpse of other attitudes. 'Some people', the fifteenth-century English moral tract *Jacob's Well* says, 'worry about their land, crops, cattle, household, family, tillage, milking, cheese- and butter-making' on their deathbeds, rather than repenting their dishonesty. Some, warns another poem, think warnings of Purgatory and damnation mere gossip, and imagine death to be a long way off.[102] These are presumably therefore fairly common attitudes, unless illness or other circumstances reminded individuals otherwise. Humbert de Romans similarly noted in the thirteenth century that 'some people, although they think occasionally of death, nevertheless envisage it as a long way away', and act accordingly.[103] A good sense of lay concerns is given in a letter written by Alessandra Strozzi, the elite Florentine woman we met matchmaking for her son in Chapter 4. She wrote on 6 September 1459 to her son Filippo about the recent death from illness of his brother Matteo. Having assured Filippo that Matteo had had doctors at his bedside, she continues:

> The other thing which has comforted me is that Our Lord gave him the opportunity while he was dying to free himself of sin, to ask for confession and communion and extreme unction; and all of this, I gather, he did with piety. We can hope from these signs that God has prepared a good place for him. And knowing we must all take this journey and not knowing how and not being sure of doing so in the way my beautiful son Matteo has . . . gives me peace, keeping in mind that God could have done far worse to me, because those who die suddenly, who are cut to pieces (and this happens to many of the dead), they lose their body and soul together. And if by His grace and mercy He leaves me both of you my sons, he won't give me any more suffering. Now my only thought is to hear that you've taken what has happened in the right way, because I know that you're grieving, but make sure it's not in a way which does you harm, so we don't throw the handle out after the axe blade.[104]

This displays a set of perfectly orthodox opinions – the need for confession and a good death – plus some interesting nuances. Alessandra has thought hard about her son's death, but she does not seem desperately worried that he might have ended up suffering the tortures of Purgatory. His good ending – and perhaps the sense that damnation is something that would only happen to other sorts of people – leaves his mother with a fairly strong sense that he is all right. And while Matteo's death is something for Alessandra and Filippo to reflect upon, this is to be in the right way: not harmfully, that is, we may assume, not obsessively or despairingly. Notably, the letter moves from death to life: 'Now my only thought' is of her living son. A similar balance pertains in the Goodman's book. He mentions death several times, most explicitly in the prayer he advises his wife to recite in her mornings, and, following his source text, in the introduction to his discussion of confession (though interestingly there is no mention of Purgatory, only the possibility of hell). The prayer reminds his wife of the future fact of death and calls for the Virgin Mary's intercession at that time; death and its provisions are part of life.[105] But not the only part. The author makes passing mention of his own future death several times, usually in the context of suggesting that his wife will then take another husband; but none of these moments occasion a great lamentation for his mortality or a desperate plea for prayers or masses for his soul. The Goodman was writing about all of life, not just its ending.

The practice of confession

From the inescapable starting point of sin – inescapable because to live was, for all but the most saintly, to sin – there followed a necessary sequence. The Goodman set it out for us above: sin, contrition, confession, penance. And finally, it was hoped, salvation. I have discussed sin and contrition above; what then of the next stage, confession? Our thirteenth-century confessors' manual can guide us once again. I should say a little more about this source. The author was an unknown Dominican, and he probably wrote the manual in the 1220s. It has no clear title, but is sometimes known by its opening words: *Cum ad sacerdotem* ('When [a sinner comes] to a priest . . . '). Modern authors have developed a typology of the confession texts that arose in the thirteenth century and stayed in use throughout the later Middle Ages. There were large, theological manuals concerning sin and confession – works such as Robert of Flamborough's *Liber poenitentialis* – which were directed toward priests and mendicant confessors, but which had the flavour of abstract academic discussion. Then there were short, more practical guides to conducting confession; given their brevity and focus, historians tend to see these as closer to parish practice.[106] This manual is of the latter group. It assumed that the confessor was a fellow mendicant, which meant that he might not know personally the penitents who confessed to him. (It also meant that at points the manual assumes the penitent is another monk, as *all* Christians made confession, not just the laity; indeed, monks were supposed to confess rather more frequently and thoroughly than lay people.) There are 29 medieval manuscripts of *Cum ad sacerdotem* still in existence, spread fairly widely across Europe. This is quite a high survival rate for what was not a valuable or high-status text. We may therefore suspect that there were originally many more, as the work was copied and recopied in different dioceses between the thirteenth and fifteenth centuries.[107] Thus the manual may show us something quite close to widespread practice.

The manual begins as follows: 'When a sinner comes to a priest to make confession of sins, he should say to the priest "Lord be with you". He [the priest] should respond to the sinner, "Amen".' After this little ritual opening, the confessor is advised to ascertain the status of the penitent: whether he is clerical or lay, in holy orders, a scholar, married or single, what his job is and so forth. Next, the confessor is to set the stage: he reminds the penitent that God forgives sin, and that he should therefore not hide any sins through shame or fear or honour. Indeed, the confessor says, I myself am a sinner, and 'often do – or at least hear – more [sins] than you'. The pair then arrange themselves. There was no wooden confessional box in the Middle Ages, as this was only invented in the sixteenth century. Instead, the two were to sit, usually in church, preferably with the penitent seated higher than the confessor, and in what we might call a 'visibly private' place; that is, somewhere apart from anyone else in the church, but where they could still be seen from a distance. The confessor was told to keep his head hidden within his cowl and was warned not to look at the face of the penitent, 'most of all and especially if it is a woman'. Then confession began. The penitent was not initially interrogated by the priest, but only prompted by him: 'Brother, say fearlessly whatever you wish.' Do not, the manual advises, do anything to put the penitent off his confession. Do not burst out laughing, for example, or cough or spit. Do not immediately rebuke them for some sin, and thus make them immediately ashamed. All sinners will blush with shame at some point; the confessor therefore does not have to jump upon them instantly. Be subtle, it suggests: 'it is better, with careful hand, to draw out the twisted serpent' (Job 26: 13).[108]

It could be that, given a proficient (or extremely innocent) penitent, the confession ends here. But *Cum ad sacerdotem* assumes that this may not be the case: 'After the sinner has made confession of all that he can draw from memory, if it seems to the priest to be imperfect and insufficiently told, he can make good the deficiency and inquire on the remainder.' What follows is familiar from the Goodman's treatise: an exposition of sin and its complexities. Suggested questions are provided by the manual, such as (concerning wrath) 'whether he has struck or threatened any cleric or neighbour' or (concerning gluttony) 'if the sinner has eaten to the point of nausea or drunk to inebriation'. Following the seven sins, the confessor is enjoined to inquire into the circumstances of the sin; but once again he is warned to be quiet if this may be more productive in getting the sinner to speak. Then – unusually for a text of this date – there are questions framed around the Ten Commandments. (These would probably be accommodated under various sins in other texts.) For example, swearing: 'ask whether they have . . . put down God, just as the French and other dreadful people do, who do not know how to put forward three words without cursing'. Next, as another framework for approaching sin, *Cum ad sacerdotem* sets out questions following the five bodily senses: 'Of taste, whether unnecessary salt has provoked lust . . . . Of touch, whether he has touched a woman shamefully.'[109] Certain questions and areas, as we saw above, are not suitable for confession to a priest or mendicant; sins such as murder and sacrilege are 'reserved' to the bishop, meaning that the penitent must head to the cathedral to confess these faults and receive punishment. Finally, after all these potential questions and modes of enquiry, 'one begins to censure, namely by showing the magnitude and enormity and badness of what they have confessed, and the goodness of God that should lead them to penance'. Ensuring that the sinner is sorry for what he has done, the priest then imposes a penance upon him, in negotiation with the sinner. The penance had to be finely balanced: severe enough to constitute satisfaction for the sin, but one that the sinner was 'willing and able to bear'. Fasting, prayers, bodily scourging, almsgiving and peace pacts could all be imposed; 'if it can be done', advises the manual, 'make the penance fit the crime'. For example, blasphemy or perjury would warrant prayers, whereas lust would be countered by scourging. And do not just give the same penance to every sin, 'as is done by wretched and greedy priests who impose masses for all sins'. The penance completed, the penitent's sins are absolved.

There are a number of interesting aspects to the view that *Cum ad sacerdotem* provides on confession: the emphasis on subtlety and restraint in drawing the sinner out, the fact that the first thing the text imagines entering the confessor's head upon hearing a sin would be laughter rather than shock, the thorough set of grids which the priest is enjoined to use to position and understand the kind of person that the sinner is. It would seem unlikely that every act of confession involved each mode of enquiry, due, if nothing else, to the time that this would take; and we should remember that the text proffers these questions only if the penitent appears unable to make a full confession unaided. Nevertheless, what *Cum ad sacerdotem* shows us is quite persuasively prosaic and practical. We may assume that it gives us a fair starting point for reconstructing medieval confession.

From the perspective of this book, the questions now prompted are about the lay experience of confession. How often did they confess, and in what circumstances? What did they understand themselves to be doing when confessing, and what was their lived experience of confession? When historically did confession become a part of lay religious practice? These are difficult areas to address, but let us begin with the last point. A crude response to the question of historical timing would be brief: in 1215. It was the Fourth Lateran Council of that year that first set out, as a part of Pope Innocent III's desire to reform and invigorate Christian society, the demand that everyone should confess at least once each year. This annual confession was a preparation for Easter communion, and hence theologically a form of purification and sociologically a form of social peacemaking.[110] One also made, or hoped to make, confession on the deathbed, in order to avoid hell and abbreviate one's stay in Purgatory.

However, while a few historians have maintained that the decisive turning point came in 1215, recent work has suggested a more complex set of changes over a much longer period. Let us first go back to the earlier Middle Ages, to the ninth and tenth centuries. In this period, at first glance, there would appear to be two forms of penance in use: public and private. Both implied some form of confession to prompt their imposition. Public penance was a ritual performance tied to Lent and Easter: at the beginning of the fasting period, the penitents, dressed in sackcloth, would be ritually excluded from church, possibly beaten, and certainly made to undergo other ascetic practices. On Maundy Thursday they would be publicly welcomed back into the church. Private penance, on the other hand, did not involve this element of ritual shaming. It would consist of fasts, fines and pilgrimages, and was imposed according to a list of tariffs set down in texts known as penitentials. Which kind of penance was used depended upon the circumstances of the sin: for public sins, public penance; for private sins, private penance. Given that the tariffs set out in the penitentials were both crudely formulaic and extremely strict – suggesting that they were rarely if ever used for the mass of ordinary people – past historians have drawn a distinction between early medieval and later medieval penance. The earlier form is seen as public, formulaic, collective and not particularly integrated into the religious life of the ordinary laity. Confession, in the sense set out by *Cum ad sacerdotem*, played little or no part in it – penance was something prompted by public statements of repentance, not by the complex interior narrative of later confession. The later, post-1215 practice is seen in contrast as private, individual, focused upon interior contrition, and an increasingly important part of lay religion.[111]

But, as recent work has shown, there are a number of problems with this contrast. In the first place, the neat divide between private and public penance in the earlier period was, in practice, much more blurred than the abstract treatises would suggest. 'Private' did not necessarily mean utterly secret, not least because activities such as fasting and pilgrimage are rather hard to perform without others noticing. It more likely meant 'not *directed* towards public display'. Moreover, public penance persisted well after the supposed shift to individualized private confession in the thirteenth century.[112] (We have indeed already seen several examples of later medieval public penances in this book, from Thomas Tailour to Denise Penyes; these were imposed in a legal setting, but remained penances nonetheless.) For another thing, one can find some examples of individual lay confession well before 1215. One view has seen this as a product of twelfth-century spiritual reform, with Lateran IV as the culmination of a high medieval process. Alexander Murray has persuasively argued that narrative sources, such as miracle collections and *exempla*, suggest that individual confession was pretty rare prior to the twelfth century. Whereas thirteenth-century *exempla* are full of tales that directly concern confession, or mention it in passing, the earlier narratives are almost entirely silent. Where this silence is broken in the tenth- and eleventh-century sources, Murray suggests, it is in a rare and particular context: somewhere near a monastery, where a theologically-trained and reformist abbot was in residence. The *idea* of individual confession and interior contrition certainly existed in the Carolingian period; but its practice, among the laity, was extremely rare.[113] However, other historians have argued that further examples of individual penance can be found in the earlier periods, and have demonstrated that liturgical texts which set out rituals of this kind were available not only to bishops but to some parish priests. Direct evidence of ordinary lay people confessing is still sparse prior to about 1200, but evidential silence does not necessarily mean that the practice did not exist – only that it was not much recorded. People in some areas of Europe were clearly being called to make Lenten confession from the ninth century at least. However, coming along all together to make 'individual' confession suggests that the act was in fact always – for both the early *and* later middle ages – quite collective and communal.[114] Indeed, as noted above, John Bossy suggested some years ago that the real change in the nature of confession and penance – a shift from an essentially communal act of peacemaking to an individual reflection upon the inner self – occurred only at the very end of the Middle Ages in the run-up to the Reformation.[115]

However one interprets the relative gloom of the earlier period, it is clear that from the late twelfth century onwards we have a better view of confession because of an increased number of varied sources. It may be that this increase does indicate a historical shift of some kind. By the thirteenth century, there was a clear link between preaching and confession: a key aim for preachers was to lead their listeners into confessing their sins and feeling contrition and repentance.[116] Examples of this conjunction can be found in earlier times, but with the founding of the mendicant orders, and Innocent III's efforts toward pastoral reform, it had gained programmatic status – and produced a lot of texts. A letter from Bishop Robert Grosseteste in the mid-thirteenth century describes the process as he applied it. He ordered the laity and clergy to assemble in each rural deanery and, accompanied by four mendicant friars, made a 'circuit' of his diocese, preaching, confirming, and having the mendicants hear confessions and impose penances. Moreover, the protests of 'certain people' – probably clergy – against these activities indicated that this was a *new* custom being instituted, in this area at least.[117] Certainly by the end of the thirteenth century every diocese, and perhaps every parish, in Europe knew that all laity should be confessing their sins individually at Easter, and knew that to assist them in this obligation, the parishioners should be getting regular sermons from their priest or from mendicant preachers. Snippets of evidence suggest that, at least in some parishes, the implementation of Lateran IV's programme was somewhat wobbly, and did mark a shift from an earlier, more symbolic and communal form of confession to something more individuated. The council of Bordeaux in 1234, for example, instructed priests that they should not hear batches of penitents – two or more confessing at the same time – but should do each one singly, in a publicly visible place.[118] An *exemplum* of a young priest in a new parish indicates a shift in what was said: an old parishioner confessed to adultery, theft, rape, perjury and homicide. Shocked, the priest asked if the elderly man had really committed all these crimes: 'Oh no,' he replied, 'none of them.' The penitent was simply repeating the list of sins that his previous priest had taught him to say. He proved unable to comprehend the idea of confessing his own particular misdeeds, and died without being shriven.[119] This kind of general confession was clearly a feature of twelfth-century practice. Alain de Lille distinguished 'general' from 'particular' confession, meaning by the latter individual confession at Easter. But he also suggested that confession should not be limited to particular sins, but should be 'all-encompassing' so that the penitent did not miss anything out. Gerald of Wales has a similar belt-and-braces approach: 'all mortal sins ought to be expressed explicitly in confession at least once, unless they are forgotten. But since no one knows all his faults, not having a memory of them, you ought at least to confess them in a general way, and thus you will not conceal any of your crimes.'[120]

Another possible shift presents itself, in that later medieval texts focused much more fully upon individual confession, and developed ever greater subtleties as to how it should be conducted. An early example comes from a thirteenth-century treatise:

> He who wishes to confess fully should subject the whole treasury of his memory to careful scrutiny, extracting from it his past acts, and passing them all in review before his mind's eye. The review should be thorough, orderly and conducted chronologically: that is, considering first what one did in the first year one can remember, then in the second, and so on.[121]

The somewhat impractical aspirations expressed here indicate that this is an idealized dream (and is possibly a representation of a final deathbed confession) rather than annual parochial practice. But the desire to prompt penitents into something approaching this reflective, autobiographical interrogation of the self developed in the following centuries. The need for inner contrition was repeatedly emphasized: 'to confess well, one has to go to the feet of the priest sorrowfully and repentant of every sin' preached Jacopo Passavanti (d. 1357). 'Contrition demands sorrow of heart in deep agony and repentance', the Goodman explains to his wife, and advises her, at the conclusion of mass, to spend some time with her eyes on the ground and her heart in heaven, 'think[ing] earnestly and sincerely with your whole heart of all your transgressions' as a preparation for confession.[122] Jean Gerson, in a treatise on confession written around 1406, remarks that 'until now I have discovered only a few persons who ever made complete and full confessions'. He was not primarily thinking of deliberate dissembling or omissions, but the way in which people failed to live up to the ideal of a complete outpouring of sin. His treatise, unlike *Cum ad sacerdotem* or other earlier manuals, takes the basics of sin and confession pretty much for granted. Instead, Gerson focuses upon technique: how to use a subtle mixture of gentleness and 'harsh goads' in drawing out the penitent, how to question and probe in a subtle manner in order to see whether a person has sinned without realizing it.[123] Gerson's idea of a 'full' confession is rather different from that of Gerald of Wales: whereas Gerald felt that all sin (in the abstract sense) should be confessed, Jean was interested in hearing every thought and deed.

Making a full and proper confession, for later ecclesiastical writers, was also a matter of telling one's sins in the right manner. 'Almost everybody confesses in a disorderly manner', Robert of Flamborough notes in his early thirteenth-century *Liber poenitentialis*. Much better, he thought, to confess according to the different species of sin, beginning with pride 'which is the root of all evil'. 'One must make an orderly confession', says the Goodman, 'and say your sins by the order and in the way that theology places them.'[124] To the extent that lay people followed this direction, it is a very interesting development. Confession involved looking back upon one's actions and admitting what was bad. Part of this – perhaps a large part, particularly before 1400 or a little earlier – could be done through the memory of other people's reactions: Jacques was displeased when I broke his fence, so that was a sin; our neighbours ostracized us after I got Agnes pregnant, so that was a sin; nobody likes being punched, so when I punched Pierre, that was doubtless also a sin, even if he did deserve it. However, as the complexity of confessional demands deepened, this review of one's self moved ever inwards. An increasingly detailed model of sin (remember all those 'branches' that the Goodman set out) governed what fell within its boundaries, and where exactly it lay. As Roberto Rusconi has put it, these developments were part of 'the subordination of the laity to the hegemony of clerical religious models'.[125] By the time of Jean Gerson's manual, one is dealing with a system of confession where the penitent does not so much report what he or she has done wrong, but proffers up their deeds and their thoughts for clerical inspection. Thus they *find out* whether or not they have done wrong – or how much wrong they have done.[126] Later medieval models of confession are notably based more upon a hierarchy between penitent and priest than the more equal relationship sketched out in *Cum ad sacerdotem*. In *Handlyng Synne* the potential penitent is made aware that in confessing to the priest he is submitting to God. The Goodman advises choosing a confessor who is 'a most wise and far-seeing coun-sellor . . . who can discriminate one sin from another and so cure them'.[127] Artistic depictions of confession, in contrast to *Cum ad sacerdotem*'s instruction for the confessor to sit a little lower than the penitent, tend to show the sinner kneeling before a seated priest or friar, clearly illustrating the hierarchy.[128]

Can we glean anything more about the laity's actual experience of confession? It is a hard task since the sacramental 'seal' of confession was not meant to be broken; if a priest told of what he had heard, he destroyed all trust. A German council, for example, decreed in 1243 that any priest who revealed secrets from confession would not only be deposed from office, but imprisoned in a monastery to do penance.[129] Nevertheless, there are a few moments when we can press our eye to a crack in the church door. This supplies a selection of indi-vidual images, stuttering and disjointed flashes of illumination rather than a smoothly unreeling film. Many come from preaching *exempla*, and therefore, particularly when depicting lay abuses or laxity, are inflected by a strongly cler-ical viewpoint. Some may be little more than a reformist stereotype trotted out on regular occasions. Other fragments, however, can be found in different sources, such as visitation records or inquisitorial interrogations. All are precious. What do they tell us?

A number of confraternities included the requirement to attend annual confession in their statutes, ordaining fines for those brethren who failed in their duty. Some in fact called for confession several times a year, a practice that increases in the fourteenth and fifteenth centuries. We know, therefore, that there was independent lay enthusiasm for confession (albeit backed up by a small fine for neglecting one's duty). But much of the evidence, by its nature, displays the less obedient. The urban, mercantile culture of confraternities could add a particular inflection to the penitent's approach to confession. Robert of Flamborough, writing *c.*1208, complained that people did not come to confess with the kind of solemn obedience that canonical texts imagined, but that instead the confessor had almost to barter with the penitent, dropping the amount of penance imposed in order to prompt a more full confession.[130] *Handlyng Synne* indicates several other ways in which people misbehaved. Some, says Robert Manning, 'in all their life will completely fail to be shriven', waiting instead until their deathbed to be cleansed of their sins. Some will confess one sin to one confessor, another to another – presumably in hope of gaining lighter penances. Others talk of other people's sins rather than their own, denouncing rather than confessing. A few make up sins to confess.[131] Although these may be seen as rather formulaic denunciations, each has some other supporting evidence for its practice. Many manuals warn against failing to confess, but not in identical terms – 'confess often, since you sin often, and don't, like a rustic person, put it off from year to year' advised Bishop Cadwgan of Bangor in about 1230.[132] The council of Apt noted, in 1365, that 'in many dioceses there are many people who call themselves Christians and yet who hardly ever bother to confess their sins or receive the body of Christ', and at Grenoble in the same period, an episcopal visitation recorded 'many in this parish who do not come to [the priest] to make confession . . . at Easter', a failure reported in other dioceses also. Caesarius of Heisterbach tells of a man who confessed his sins, and was enjoined by the priest to give them up and reform himself. 'He answered, "I can confess my sins, but I cannot pretend to give them up". Whereupon the priest refused to assign him any penance; and the man offered the usual fee and turned to go away.'[133] One can occasionally find people reported by their neighbours for non-attendance at church at Easter, which by implication meant that they had avoided annual confession. Guillaume Austatz of Ornolac, in 1320, and Nicholas Drye of Lynn, in 1430, were both denounced to their local bishops for, among other things, failing to make communion at Easter – though the bishops were actively searching for heretics, and both Guillaume and Nicholas may have had some involvement with such groups. But other cases from less complex contexts can be found. Parishioners from northern Spain denounced certain neighbours for similar laxity.[134] Thomas of Cantimpré included a number of tales in his collection of *exempla* of people who scorned to go to confession.[135] It is notable also that one of the three things that most bothered the Barcelonan parishioners about their priests' conduct of confession was when, out of laziness or other reasons, they failed to administer it at someone's deathbed.[136] This was the occasion when it really mattered – perhaps indicating that what *Handlyng Synne* warned against above was a fairly common working assumption.

Why would people not confess? Waiting to wipe clean the slate at the end of life would appear to be one reason. For some, according to various authorities, there was considerable doubt over whether hell and damnation actually existed, and hence whether one really needed to confess.[137] For others, it was doubtless embarrassing. Jean Gerson, in a letter to a bishop, noted that embarrassment over sexual sins in particular could stop people confessing, or confessing fully. 'We find boys and girls and very shy women and unlearned rustics from whom the confession of such sins can hardly be extracted.' Moreover, if these matters were left to be confessed to bishops or mendicants – specialists, in other words – the penitents were likely to 'take flight in terror'.[138] Another reason, linked to embarrassment, was fear of the priest breaking the confessional seal of silence. This was another bugbear in the Barcelonan visitation, alleged against several different clerics. The priest was very much part of the local community and revealing secrets to him could be difficult or even dangerous, as the wife of Berengar Catot found out when she confessed to adultery. Guilhem Bon, her confessor, told Berengar in front of several witnesses that he was being cuckolded; the husband threw his wife out of their house.[139] For this reason it is possible that some people much preferred making confession to mendicant friars (as in Grosseteste's account of the diocesan circuit). Dominican and Franciscan preachers were more separated from the quotidian grubbiness of local life. One could tell them shameful things, and they would take the knowledge *away* with them when they left.

The third of the Barcelonan complaints concerned sex: that priests were using the intimacy of confession to attempt to seduce female parishioners. This was a fear that all confession manuals had long held, warning women in particular to take care not to look at their confessor lest they tempt him (it was somehow the woman's fault, not the man's).[140] It is clear, from various pieces of evidence, that such things did happen on occasion. In fourteenth-century Montaillou, the extremely libidinous parish priest Pierre Clergue seduced Beatrice de Lagleize (whom we met earlier) when she came to make confession. Similarly, a gay man called Arnaud de Verniolles, although not an ordained priest, offered to act as confessor for several young men, in an attempt to seduce them in private. John Scarle, a parson in fifteenth-century London, tried to blackmail female parishioners into having sex with him by threatening to reveal what they had said in confession.[141] An investigation into the various misbehaviours of Bernard Guad, a priest in northern Spain, confirms similar activities. Elizabeth Benet, a parishioner, explained that two years ago, in Lent,

> she had gone to confess her sins to the said priest [Bernard] and when she was in church next to the altar, namely between the chancel and the two altars that are

there, she placed herself at the feet of the said priest and began to speak and to confess her secret sins to the priest, and when she had confessed the most part, not however all of it, the said priest said to the said woman 'there is no fairer woman in the parish than you . . .' with which words the said priest took her savagely and with force, and kissed her – which the said Elizabeth in no way had any wish for, and she wanted to go from him immediately. He took her hand and said 'if I cannot have anything else from you at least I will kiss your hand' and he kissed her hand; she however struggled and spoke against this, and thus without having made perfect confession left him. Asked if this was seen by anyone, she said no because the place is concealed thereby that they could not be seen by anyone who was in the said church similarly for reason of confession.[142]

One cannot treat this kind of record as a completely clear window onto events. Elizabeth is careful, for example, to frame the narrative in terms that emphasize her non-compliance and offended honour – the 'savagery' of Bernard, and her clear verbal and physical rejection of his advances – and she had to rebut a subsequent query about whether she had gone on to become Bernard's concubine. Her narrative is shaped by the legal context which produced it. Nevertheless, these caveats aside, some fascinating and precious details are revealed. Confession took place, as we would expect, in Lent. Other people might come along at the same period, and so confession was made in a slightly hidden, relatively private part of the church. It would appear, from how Elizabeth narrates events, that her confession was not delivered in response to clerical interrogation but was given in her own words, and that she knew just how much she wanted to say, since Bernard's assault had prevented her from making 'perfect' confession. She does not, interestingly, bemoan the fact that Bernard failed to absolve her – perhaps, given what we know of his behaviour, his parishioners felt that the good of confession came more from what they did than from what he supplied? It is to this theme – the laity's involvement in their own salvation – that we shall now turn.

Salvation and the body

He was German, and an evil man: sentenced to death for multiple rape and murder. We do not know his name, as Thomas of Cantimpré does not record it in the *exemplum* he made of the man's passing. The German, Thomas tells us, obtained a delay before his execution, and asked a young relative to fetch him an iron comb of the sort that women use for refining wool. Sharp-toothed and tough, in other words. This implement fetched, the man told his cousin, 'Strike me on the hands, the forearms, the upper arms, the feet, the legs, the thighs, the genitals, the ears, the nose, the lips, and finally on the head.' The young man, unwilling, did as he was bid; and the German, before the comb embedded itself in each part of his body, cried out 'Receive here your part of the punishment, vile members through which I accomplished my impious crimes.' The comb bit, the blood ran. And after these torments, Thomas tells us, the man was finally decapitated, but not before having tearfully regretted his crimes, and leaving alms for the poor and for prayers to be said for his soul.[143]

Although it may not seem it to modern eyes, this was a 'good death'. Dying well was a particular concern for medieval people, and towards the end of the Middle Ages manuals on how to achieve it circulated among the literate elite.[144] One element was social and familial: the desire to have sorted out one's estate, resolved enmities, provided for dependants, and attempted where possible to secure one's lineage. All this needed time, something that a quick death cruelly removed. But theologically, the concern was with salvation; and here too a degree of time was necessary. The German murderer and rapist died a good death because he was mercifully allowed time for penitential activity, and to do some final good works – almsgiving and money for prayers. I have discussed prayers above; let us here concentrate on that conjunction of iron comb and human flesh. Several things were at play. One, clearly, was the use of bodily chastisement as a form of penance, something we have previously encountered. The penance, in this case, simultaneously illustrates the contrition that the man felt for his evil deeds, and acts as a kind of satisfaction for the sin – paying back the bodily crimes that he had committed. It also, in its aspect as a kind of torture, prefigures the punishments awaiting all sinners in Purgatory. Another element is the idea of spontaneous penitential behaviour on the part of a lay person. Whether or not the German really existed, and truly did the things that Thomas describes, the *exemplum* provides a model to which the laity could aspire. Even great sins, the story suggests, can be atoned for by penance; and this penance can be something one takes upon oneself, rather than a punishment imposed by a priest or bishop. A further aspect is the focus upon the body, with an implicit division between the exterior body and the inner soul. The body is punished for its complicity in sin, and that punishment makes the cycle of sin, penance and redemption legible. It is literally written onto the body by the wounds the comb carved into the man's flesh.

These are all important aspects of penance and penitential behaviour, and their presence in a thirteenth-century *exemplum* reminds us that they were being widely preached – particularly by mendicant friars – to a lay audience. What is notable here, as elsewhere, is how penance points in two directions, inward and outward. Penitential practices such as fasting and scourging could control and eventually eradicate inner desires: great ascetics such as St Bernard of Clairvaux burned away any traces of lust within themselves by sitting in freezing cold water and rolling in nettles.[145] Jacques de Vitry tells of a very sinful woman who wouldn't accept various penances from her confessor because she couldn't bear the pain of scourging herself and couldn't stand fasting. Eventually her confessor asked her what she was willing to give up; 'pork', she said, since she hated it. Instantly she was afflicted by a strong desire for pork – and thus, through God's intervention in her desires, was brought to *true* penitence.[146] Penance thus had to get at a person's inner feelings and thoughts, work upon their interior. But at the same time, penance could often be directed outwards, as a lesson to others. As an inquisitorial manual puts it, speaking of the public penances given to heretical sinners, the aim was 'to correct the guilty life, or at least, to show who walks in darkness and who in light'.[147] The German's self-mutilation had the benefit, for Thomas, of illustrating both his sin and his repentance. Public penances clearly fulfilled the same function, telling the laity of the dangers of sin and the need for reparation. A late thirteenth-century manual for bishops talks of those being excluded from church at Lent as being sent out 'just as Adam was expelled from Paradise'. Thus the public theatre of their penance becomes a kind of sermon in itself. And in the rituals of exclusion and reincorporation that were particularly practised in northern France and Germany, the public penitent can be seen as standing in for all sinners.[148] Thus public penances implicated not only the one performing it, but also those watching.

There is some indication that the relationship between outer and inner aspects was not, in practice, quite what the theologians desired. It is clear, in the story of the pork-hating woman, that the idea of inner contrition was not easily absorbed by the laity. The hardship that she was willing to accept only became truly penitential with divine intervention. From her initial perspective, it would appear to be more of an external ritual, and a kind of quasi-financial transaction between sinner and confessor – where she clearly felt that she had got a bargain, until her sudden lust for pork arose. The language used by some of the sources strengthens this feeling. *Handlyng Synne* talks of how the grace given by God and Mary 'gives us profit', and that one should not confess partially or to more than one person, else 'God almighty is mis-paid'.[149] And, of course, the fact that the Church, in an increasing number of circumstances, would accept a cash alternative to certain forms of penance must have added to the transactional feeling. There are also hints that people's concerns were often more with their neighbours' opinions and the public shame of penance than with its interior and devotional aspects. Robert Grosseteste advised confessors to check that penances were done 'reverently' (*sancta*), 'that is, pained to have sinned because of God and not only because of the disparagement of sinners'. He further cautioned that, rather like the pork woman, penitents tended to obey the letter but not the spirit of the penance; for example, when enjoined to fast on bread and water, they added herbs to make a cordial, or made bread with spices or wine, and so forth. One can find a similar example of a man sentenced by inquisitors to wear yellow crosses on his clothing because of his previous contact with heretics. This he did – but tended to wear his clothes inside out, or with the sleeves rolled up, so that these badges of infamy were no longer visible. As the theologian Jacobus de Graytroede commented on the laity in general, 'There are many who feel no shame at sinning, but are ashamed to do penance.'[150]

So one possible lay reaction to penance was to try to get the best end of the deal, and to feel upset only by the public humiliation that it engendered rather than the breach with God that it was supposed to heal. Shame was important within the theology of penance – confessors' manuals emphasize that making the penitent feel ashamed in the sight of God was part of the job – but moralists did not intend simply social shame. Nevertheless, away from the dreams of theologians, that is frequently what they got. This public and social element raises the question of the *function* of sin, confession and penance. Was it purely about individual salvation? Or was it more truly a means of controlling society? This argument has been made by the American historian Thomas Tentler. In a study of post-Lateran IV treatises on confession, Tentler identified a number of features that link confessional practice with social control: the cataloguing of forbidden behaviour (ever increasing in its detail and complexity), the power of the confessor over the penitent, and the emphasis upon restitution prior to absolution, that in the case of a sin such as usury – where the profit made from lending money had to be returned to the borrower – clearly dealt with the social impact of the sin. Law and confession were not separate realms: in the highly influential penitential treatise written by Raymond de Peñafort in the 1240s, the canon law on matters such as marriage and tithing are included alongside theological discussions of sin. The system, Tentler argued, taught 'that sinners were accountable not only to God, but also to men [the clergy], who bound and loosed for Him'.[151]

The case for annual confession alone being an instrument of social control is problematic. For most people, as we have seen, it happened only once a year at most, which does not provide a very strong policing mechanism. Parish priests did have an elevated position, to a certain degree, within their local communities; but they were also part of that community, implicated in its moral and economic activities, and in general the control that they exercised was only effective if it corresponded with the will of the community. One Barcelonan parish, in fact, complained to the visiting bishop that their priest *failed* to tell off all the usurers, gamblers and fornicators in the locality. Power is clearly not the sole possession of the cleric here, but something spread more widely. However, this is not to reject Tentler's ideas completely. The system of confession and penance can be seen to be in a continuum with other elements of ecclesiastical power, most notably the church courts, but also more subtly a broad field of cultural attitudes and practices. As discussed in Chapter 4, ecclesiastical courts were often not so much a repressive authority held over the laity as an available resource within an ongoing quarrel, invoked by the community itself. However, in other areas, one can recognize a more 'top-down' element. A study of the regulation of sexual misbehaviour in late medieval Normandy, for instance, finds that people were quite strongly controlled by the courts.[152] The process of episcopal visitation may have been used by the locality to address its own particular disputes, but nonetheless prompted enquiry into areas of personal morality and both public and private behaviour under the auspices of a clear authority figure. And the kinds of public penance assigned for crimes such as fornication or adultery – being beaten around public places such as the church or marketplace – do not seem to have been either symbolic or easily shrugged off, if we can judge by the numbers of people who fled the ecclesiastical jurisdiction to avoid their punishment.[153]

To return to a theoretical discussion outlined in Chapter 1, if one is thinking in terms of force or repression the Church was clearly not that powerful. At no point was it capable of the kind of closely-focused control that a repressive modern state exercises. Medieval Europe was not like Communist East Germany during the second half of the twentieth century. Examining the detailed register of Oliver Sutton, the late thirteenth-century bishop of Lincoln, one finds quite a large number of excommunications – a principal weapon by which the Church attempted to govern its flock and protect its interests. Notably, however, many of these were blanket excommunications; that is, where the names of the malefactors was unknown.[154] This was not a strong form of policing, more a sign of relative impotence. Nor was it an independent mechanism of control: the Church needed secular support to implement such matters. Thus we find Sutton writing to the king, requesting the arrest of 'Henry of Hole, now living in Clee' who had long ignored the fact that he was excommunicate, and similarly regarding John of Risborough, to name just two obdurate laymen. Clearly, excommunication was sometimes a significant threat. On one occasion in 1292, a group of unknown laity assaulted William, the chaplain of Ecton, while he was pronouncing a general excommunication of malefactors, snatching his list of names from his hand and taking candles away from the assisting clerics.[155] In other contexts – notably when the Church was prosecuting heresy with the firm assistance of secular authorities – major excommunication could be a sentence of death. But the Church's ability to act on its own as an effective policing body was limited.

However, if one considers a more subtle sense of power, the Church's involvement in society may take on a different light. In all penitential literature, discussion of sin clearly outlined social norms as much as spiritual ones. Many of these sought to regulate the essential mechanisms of medieval society: don't make false oaths or break promises, don't defraud customers, don't exploit your office for personal gain, and so on.[156] That lay society, at a collective level, happily endorsed such elements does not mean that we are not observing power at work. In fact, quite the opposite. Power is most effective when those subject to its regulation are persuaded that it is in their own interests to fall into line. This does not imply that everyone is therefore completely obedient. It means, rather, that people by and large accept the system of behaviour and the moral code it presents to them, and hence see transgressions against that system in the same light as the Church – that is, as sin. In this sense, the range of activities and discourses set out by the Church that could broadly be labelled confessional – from the specific practice of Easter penance, to the church courts, to the moral values presented in conduct literature – clearly sustain social order. They do not *control* society, if by that we imagine powerful bonds of monitoring and policing; but they do *regulate* it, such that people who consistently transgress the given bounds are encouraged to see themselves as sinners and unchristian. At the same time, the mechanisms of confession and penance, including spontaneous penitential behaviour or other 'good works', made sin something manageable, part of a symbolic system of exchange – and, indeed, part of a cash economy. The mendicant friars in the burgeoning cities of Europe did not teach that the proto-capitalism of the mercantile classes was forbidden, but rather that the stain of sin it brought could be ameliorated by other expenditure, on pious offerings, prayers and indulgences. By the thirteenth century, much of Europe was used to the complexities of the marketplace, used to the idea of debt, negotiation and recompense. Sin became part of this system, an expense that might be unavoidably accrued during the normal course of life, but that could be paid off at a later date, the debt thus redeemed.[157]

One can see a movement through time, slowly developing across the twelfth and thirteenth centuries, whereby the kind of regulated life intrinsic to the monastery – literally living under a Rule, monitored from above, working off one's sins – slowly infiltrated all areas of Christian society. Various writers have, with different inflections, talked of the 'monasticization of the laity': a sense that lay people were being inculcated into a system of regulation that encouraged the monitoring of one's own self within a moral framework, and which used tools of penance as part of that self-making and remaking.[158] As Jacques de Vitry put it, 'Not only those who renounce the worldly life and cross over to the religious life do we judge as *regulares* [that is, living under a Rule], but also all Christ's faithful [that is, the laity], serving the Lord under the evangelical rule and living in an orderly manner under one highest and supreme abbot, we can call *regulares*.'[159] Thus annual confession, parochial visitation, and the kinds of self-regulation practised by guilds all bore witness to the extension of monastic mechanisms of discipline into lay society. That these were not necessarily 'top-down' mechanisms is not the issue. Power does not have come from above to be effective.

Nor does it have to be intentional. Various popes, Innocent III perhaps most of all, wanted to reform lay society, to engender greater levels of piety and moral life among all lay people. They never achieved quite what they set out to do; nor was the project of social reform and pastoral care a deliberate cover for some more nefarious plan. But the effects were not limited by intentions. The Church, bit by bit, partially and confusedly, taught lay people a particular way of viewing themselves and their actions. Penance and its surrounding accoutrements provided the laity with a kind of ritual language that could be adapted to various situations, whether or not under the direct control of ecclesiastical authorities. According to their 1237 statutes, the guild of Fullers at St-Trond in northern France adopted a system of fraternal correction for their members that looks extremely monastic: four brothers were to make regular inquiries into the 'conduct, life and honour' of the fullers, and any who fell short were warned three times and thereafter expelled. In the fifteenth century, particularly in Italy, boarding schools (for the children of the rich) and youths' confraternities (for those of the bourgeoisie) provided a controlled and semi-monastic framework which could contain and control youthful sexuality.[160] Penitential pilgrimages could be used as a part of secular peacemaking processes, and several books of customary law from fourteenth and fifteenth centuries Flanders list pilgrimages of different severities among their punishments for crimes of violence and other offences. Sometimes pilgrimage could be used as a commutation of other penalties: in 1290, a Flemish man called Jan Uttensacke, who had been brought to law by civic officials in a dispute over his actions as executor of a will, was initially sentenced to a large fine and imprisonment; but this was then commuted to making pilgrimage to Saint-Gilles in southern France and Canterbury in England. Pilgrimage could be, in these contexts, a kind of structured exile: the person was expelled from their town, and only allowed back once they had a letter from the shrine they were to visit.[161]

It is important to note that one can find some of the laity spontaneously and enthusiastically adopting penitential activities: the Church did not simply impose such things upon an unwilling populace. Indeed, in Italy, France and the Low Countries in the early thirteenth century, we find groups of lay people – particularly women – choosing spontaneously to adopt quasi-monastic lives modelled on penitential activities.[162] These Beguines (as they were often collectively called) clearly found spiritual benefit from it – although, as discussed earlier in this book, other social factors could also lie behind their mode of life.[163] The Italian phenomenon of flagellant confraternities presents a rather different model. Members did not live monastic lives, but undertook dramatic penitential activities – notably public processions where the men would beat themselves with chains or whips – at certain public festivals. It was, in this time and place, a very male form of piety, explicitly excluding women, and one adopted particularly by those seeking public office and political influence in the towns and cities. Flagellation at times of crisis – most famously during the Black Death, but in fact also at earlier and later points – was driven by the pressing need to appease God's wrath and atone for humanity's sins. But the more enduring flagellant confraternities were not born of millenarian fears or crisis: in San Sepolcro, for example, they start in the early fourteenth century during a period of economic growth. They were, in James Banker's words, 'the male laity, in full confidence of their abilities, grasping control over areas of their lives formerly regarded as outside their responsibility'.[164] Penance was important to these people, but not the only mode of piety. One might be a flagellant but also join a *laude* confraternity, give money to the local hospital or take part in collective feasts. Penitential piety was *part* of their lives, not their sole identity. And, once again, the fact of lay enthusiasm for penance does not mean that power was absent. The increased growth in lay penitential behaviour over the course of the Middle Ages is itself testament to ecclesiastical cultural hegemony. The Church provided a powerful way of viewing the world, human behaviour and the next world. At the same time, as the various examples here show, penitential models could be adapted and to some extent reinterpreted within different secular contexts. Ecclesiastical discourse provided the framework for meaningful action, but the particular enunciations of that action could subtly change within each particular context.

Selfhood

I want to take us back to the Goodman and his words to his wife, and back to the idea of the construction of selfhood mentioned briefly at the beginning of this chapter. We have seen that many of the Goodman's concerns were social ones, and that while he adapted an influential penitential manual written for the laity (*Somme le Roy*) in explaining confession, his illustrations of moral behaviour were often directed towards outward appearances more than inner states. But his book tackles things from a number of angles: he records not just one way to catch fleas, but six. Similarly, the patterns of religious behaviour outlined in the manual are multiple. Near the beginning, then, we find a rather different kind of idea of piety from the socially-directed morality of 'keeping up appearances'. After the Goodman's quite lengthy prayer to the Virgin Mary – to be said each morning, explicitly at the same time as monks ring Matins and say their own prayers – he talks of his wife's comportment at mass:

> When you have come to church, choose a secret and solitary place before a fair altar or image, and there remain and stay without moving hither and thither, nor going to and fro, and hold your head upright and keep your lips ever moving saying orisons and prayers. Moreover, keep your glance continually on your book or on the face of the image, without looking at man or woman . . . keep your thoughts always on heaven and pray with your whole heart . . .[165]

Further on he admonishes that when hearing the *Introit* that marks the beginning of mass, 'every man and every woman [must] restrain their thoughts and think of no worldly thing' but keep their heart only on God and prayers to God.

The picture of piety is an idealized one. We have seen in the previous chapter that people did many things at mass as well as pay attention. But it is an ideal to which higher-status men, and more particularly women, were encouraged to aspire in the later Middle Ages. A clear image of the self is present here, holding itself apart from the bustle of the world in a quiet inner space, and hoping there to find God. The injunction to 'restrain their thoughts' is explicit in its indication of self-control, self-*discipline*. A pale shadow of monasticism again hovers, evoking the quiet of the cloister, the inner reflection upon the deity, the endless project of controlling and reworking one's self to fit with a particular pattern of piety. One can find examples from earlier centuries of lay individuals who adopted similar attitudes towards faith. In the eleventh century, for example, a group condemned as heretics told a bishop that they had no need of the Church's ministry because they had a 'higher law' written *inside* themselves.[166] Various hermits, anchorites and anchoresses placed themselves apart from society (in theory at any rate) in the hope of finding themselves alone with God. But these were always very unusual individuals. What had changed by the Goodman's day was the compass of these aspirations. In the context of fifteenth-century, socially respectable, bourgeois piety we find something between an aspiration and a demand for reflective, interiorized religion. The Goodman's wife is to meditate upon an image, using prayer to focus her mind and heart, disciplining herself to take her 'self' outside secular life. The Goodman's text, and other texts like it, set out a model for piety; this model calls to people, attempts to co-opt them into its story. In this process of being hailed, greeted, *embraced*, the inner self adjusts to fit the place laid out for it. One should not see this as a harsh or bullying injunction. It is, rather, gentle, encouraging and caring. But equally, one should not mistake gentleness for the absence of power: through being cared for, encouraged to improve ourselves, we are shaped. We are made who we are – 'we' within a particular context, a particular story of ourselves, our souls, God and salvation. And for laywomen, interiorized religion was produced as much through a system of exclusions as encouragement. Their religious roles and activities were more limited than men's, and the 'inside' was the place left open to them. Less able to participate in certain kinds of public piety, women had further reason to explore their interior worlds.[167] It was not exclusively a female activity, however. One can see, in the late fourteenth century, that this kind of piety, mixed with the older tradition of Beguine communities, became semi-institutionalized. Groups calling themselves the 'New Devout' in the Low Countries lived together in lives of intense devotion. They were mainly made up of clerics but included some laymen, living in a sense like colonies of hermits, under no Rule but sharing ideas on how to 'break' their own will and give themselves over to God. The tools of their devotion were similar to those set out by the Goodman: a private room for each individual, intense prayer and the use of texts as an aid to meditation.[168]

Why, then, do we not find this until the fifteenth century (or just a little earlier)? One argument is that the early Middle Ages lacked a sense of human interiority and individuality; or, at least, did not place much value upon such things. Thus Alain de Lille, writing in the twelfth century on the sin of pride, explained that 'It is pride which makes a man stand out among the common herd, and makes him an oddity in the community, a solitary in public, a man apart in the monastery.'[169] It has been argued that it was the later twelfth century that 'discovered' the individual – discovered him (or very occasionally her) in various areas such as the emergent genre of autobiography, works on political citizenship, tomb portraiture, romance writing and courtly love. These were all fairly rarefied and elite 'discoveries'; but, it is argued, it was the spread of annual confession to the laity in the thirteenth century that encouraged these ideas to 'trickle down' to the wider populace. Confession provided a mechanism for individual interior examination, and hence made people aware of themselves *as* individuals. Confession, Colin Morris argues, was 'an attempt to introduce the idea of self-examination throughout society; at this point, at least, the pursuit of an interior religion did not remain the property of a small *élite* but entered every castle and every hovel in western Europe'.[170] Moreover, for some authors, it was this process that set the foundation stones for future western individuality and character: the paradigm of sin and interior reflection providing the roots of what Freud would much later hail as the psyche.[171]

One criticism of this argument has been that the twelfth (and indeed the thirteenth) century did not so much discover the individual – each person as a unique being, unlike any other – as it discovered a variety of *groups* within which selfhood could take different corporate shapes. Twelfth-century religious developed, discussed and argued over a variety of modes of life that would bring spiritual reform. Each person (individual in this sense) sought to reform themselves; but the process of reform was to adopt an existent template. Writers talked of 'putting on a new garment' or of the exemplary saints being imprinted upon the 'wax' of one's own self.[172] Another way of looking at this is to see individuality not as a trans-historical constant, but something produced and demanded in different ways in different situations.[173] For example, the encouragement to self-examination in confession, often directed as we have seen within the framework of one's trade or estate, does not inspire what a twenty-first-century psychologist might call 'self-realization'. 'Look inside yourself and discover what you really want to do with your life' says a modern guide to well-being. 'Look inside yourself to discover if you are properly living up to your God-given social role' admonishes the medieval confessor. The option of changing that role is not, for the most part, on the menu. And the kind of 'self' ideally sought by medieval confessional practices was not individual in the sense of quirky, idiosyncratic or unique: it was a self that was journeying as close to God as it could possibly get. God was the ultimate goal of the interior quest, not one's innate humanity or 'inner child' or psychological well-being.[174]

This is not, however, to reject completely the idea of a growing medieval apprehension of individual selfhood; or perhaps we should say, a growing number of ways in which individual selves were pulled into focus and smoothed into shape. Confessional discourses were undoubtedly powerful here. One mark of thirteenth-century confession manuals, particularly those written by churchmen such as Robert Grosseteste seized by enthusiasm for lay reform, was the way in which they envisaged confession as a pedagogic process. Grosseteste's treatise *Deus est*, for example, suggests discussing the six works of mercy with a penitent, asking whether they had performed any of these good works. Failure to do so was not a sin, but confession provided an opportunity (in this bishop's mind at least) to spread good Christian practice. From about the same period, Guiard de Laon, bishop of Cambrai, less ambitiously (and perhaps closer to parochial practice), ordered that priests should enjoin their parishioners in confession to learn how to say the *Pater noster*, the Creed and the *Ave Maria*.[175] As manuals grew in complexity, so this pedagogy grew to include the job of working upon one's self to reform it morally and spiritually. *Handlyng Synne*, as its title suggests, presents dealing with sin as a task. 'Handling' one's sins is a skill that the manual sets out to teach; but it is not a straightforward job, to be done and then completed. It is, rather, a self-discipline, a form of vigilance, that has no absolute end point. 'We handle sin every day, in word and deed, all that we do' warns the manual. 'There's no beginning or end to sin, and anywhere you open this book, you'll find a beginning; and however much you read you won't have total understanding.'[176] *Jacob's Well*, a later (c.1440) and lengthier vernacular text on confession, uses another labouring metaphor for the work upon the self that it sets out. The body, it explains, is like a hole – the 'pit of lust'. It is polluted by the five senses, which allow temptation and sin to flow into the body. The bottom of the pit is filled with the ooze of sin. This must be dug out with the spade of cleanness ('cleanness' meaning all manner of good moral action and conscience) in order that one can find grace.[177]

Medieval ideas about selfhood and spirituality were often entwined with ideas about the body. The Goodman, following his source text on confession, figures the soul as a damsel, the daughter of the powerful lord (God), seated within the castle of the body, which must be protected from exterior enemies (the Devil).[178] But the castle can be breached, because the body is not seamlessly sealed but permeable. Through our eyes, ears and other senses, the temptation to sin can seep inward. Medieval culture offered several partial solutions. One was virginity, a state that, particularly for women, might keep the body sealed up and protected. Another was solitude, absenting oneself from others and their temptations. A third was bodily mortification, trying to beat the flesh into submission. But the body itself could also be a trap. Jacques de Vitry tells of a virgin at the mirror who smiles at her reflection. Instantly, she is lost: she begins to preen and bare her skin to see if it makes her more beautiful. 'Her body is still home, but in God's eyes she is already in a brothel, trussed up like a whore preparing to ensnare the souls of men.'[179] The later Middle Ages, however, also began to develop a different kind of response that tried to work less harshly upon the body in order to achieve inner sanctity. As in the Goodman's text, the necessary tasks and movements of the lay body in its civic and domestic duties could, with effort, be directed toward God. Other books give greater detail than the Goodman: the *Decor puellarum* ('The Beauty of Young Women') written by John the Carthusian (d. 1483) of Venice instructs how everyday tasks can be redirected toward the spiritual. His description of what to do at dinner suggests that the task might be quite demanding:

> When you sit down at table, meditate on the Nativity; say the *Benedicite* and make the sign of the cross on the table; while eating the first course, think of the Circumcision; while eating the second, of the Adoration of the Magi; and when you have had enough to eat, meditate on the Massacre of the Innocents and the Flight into Egypt.[180]

This may represent the extreme aspiration for this kind of spiritual programme, but less burdensome encouragements were also available. The texts proffering this guidance were directed to the nobility and upper bourgeoisie, but permeated some way further down the social hierarchy in the fifteenth century as literacy increased and books became more affordable.

Someone who might be imagined to have been influenced by this kind of discourse is the English mystic Margery Kempe whom we have met at several points in this book. Kempe illustrates another late medieval conjunction of body and spirit: what is known as 'affective piety', where the great devotion and inner meditation upon Christ and God of the penitent produces outward bodily affects. In Kempe's case, these were crying, wailing and shouting – all clearly extremely dramatic, particularly when visited upon her while at mass in church with her neighbours, or at a pilgrimage shrine with other travellers. It is also clear from her example, however, that this was a pretty rare kind of piety. The neighbours were frequently annoyed by her carryings on, the pilgrims wouldn't sit with her, and when travelling outside her locality she several times found herself suspected of heresy because of her unconventional behaviour.[181] Indeed, if our focus is upon the ordinary laity, it seems clear that there was something of a conflict over the relationship between outer behaviour and inner piety, in terms of ecclesiastical and social norms. We met it near the beginning of this chapter, when noting the bind in which bourgeois women found themselves, trying to negotiate the dual demands of looking presentable for their husbands' honour and delectation, while looking humble and unostentatious for the needs of charity and piety. It was not just women, however; ecclesiastical writers could be pessimistic about any layperson's ability to pursue pious activity as they ought. Preaching about pilgrimage, for example, Giardano da Pisa suggested that such journeys were more an opportunity for sin than a means to redemption. 'There is more danger than benefit', he explains. 'People go here and there mistaking their feet for God . . . Pulling yourself together, contemplating the creator, weeping about your sins, and the misery of your neighbour, is better than any trip you could ever make.' So here contemplation is the safer route. But elsewhere we find the opposite: a fifteenth-century English devotional text warns that lay people of all social estates 'rarely achieve' the spiritual heights that true contemplation demands, and therefore should not attempt it lest they err.[182]

Some historians have seen a general move, in the later fourteenth and fifteenth centuries, from collective to individual piety, from a rather formulaic set of religious practices to a more meaningful, 'private' and personal piety. It is certainly true that there are more examples of the laity in the later Middle Ages practising something like the latter. This should not be seen, however, as the development of a more unfettered, 'individual' mode of belief, but as the adoption of different models of how to be pious. Kempe can be seen, and was seen by her neighbours, as idiosyncratic; but in fact she clearly had models of religious comportment that provided her with inspiration for imitation. Imitation (*imitatio*) was the key mechanism by which late medieval devotional discourse imagined refashioning the self.[183] In any case, the kind of highly interiorized devotion discussed here was never the province of all the laity. It became available as a model to more of them by the end of the Middle Ages, but other collective forms of behaviour always stayed predominant. We should not, moreover, see these models as necessarily in tension with or distinct from other, more communal, pieties. One could belong to a guild and attend processions and feasts while also owning and meditating upon devotional books. Individualism and interiority were complemented by communalism and collective activity, and perhaps we should see the former as only making sense for the laity in the context of the latter. It was because doing belief usually meant doing things publicly with one's neighbours that doing something privately and 'inside' felt special and particularly devout.[184]

For medieval culture, the question of how the 'inner' and the 'outer' related was an abiding concern. Within religious discourse it had a particular urgency. How could one tell from outer appearances what the inner heart truly felt? How did one know if people really believed – and believed correctly? Confession, as a bringing forth of what was inside, went some way towards allaying that concern. A frequently recorded *exemplum* tells of a priest who was granted the ability to discern the state of men's souls by their faces. As his parishioners came up to receive the Host, he could see the nature of their sin: lechers had blackened faces, those with red faces were full of ire, those in charity shone brightly like the sun.[185] The point of telling such a story in a sermon was presumably to inculcate a degree of beneficial nervousness among one's real parishioners – what were they giving away? What, then, had they better do about it? But the story tells us something else as well: that priests, not normally given such gifts by God, could *not* discern the inner hearts of their flock. Bodies were fantasized as legible, but all too often remained opaque. And what might lurk there, unknown by those with the care of souls, unseen by authority? In the next chapter, we will try to see.

6

Dissent

Heresy

Historical sources are sometimes inaccurate and often misleading. Given that they are the creation of fallible human beings, one would be surprised were it otherwise. Occasionally, however, a record is deliberately untruthful. One such instance comes in Guibert de Nogent's *Monodiae*, his 'solitary songs' of memoirs. Guibert was a Benedictine monk, born around 1055 in Clermont, and became abbot of Nogent in 1104. The *Monodiae* was written around 1115, about eight years before his death, and concerns his own life and events in his locality. Towards the end of the book Guibert tell us that there were certain heretics in the village of Bucy, near Soissons, led by two peasant brothers called Clement and Evrard. They did not believe in Christ's Incarnation, and they rejected baptism of children before the age of reason ('whoever the godparents may be,' Guibert comments). They abhorred the Eucharist, and did not distinguish between sacred cemeteries and profane ground for burials. And they and their male and female followers condemned marriage and procreation, but slept together indiscriminately. And they murdered any resulting offspring. And they thought heterosexual intercourse to be a crime, and so had homosexual sex instead. And they held meetings in hidden cellars, having sex with a young girl who lay naked before them. And:

> soon the candles are extinguished, they shout 'Chaos!' from all sides and everyone has intercourse with the first person who happens to be at hand. If a woman becomes pregnant in the process, they come back to the same spot after she has given birth. A large fire is lit, and those sitting around toss the baby from one hand to another through the flames until the child is dead. When the child's body has been reduced to ashes they make bread with these ashes and a part is distributed to everyone as a kind of sacrament, and once it is taken no one ever recovers from that heresy.[1]

All of this, Guibert goes on to note, makes it possible to identify them as Manichaeans, since these beliefs and activities are very like Augustine of Hippo's account of those heretics.

Why do I think Guibert is lying in this account – or, at least, not adhering to modern standards of verity? There are several reasons. The most straightforward is his reference to Augustine. Much of Guibert's 'knowledge' of the heretics came not from the world outside his door – north-eastern France in the early twelfth century – but from his library. Since Augustine of Hippo wrote about heretics on a different continent some six centuries earlier, we may have our doubts about this method. It is clear, also, that Guibert's desire to defame outstrips his sense of logic or coherence: these people simultaneously condemn sex, have gay sex and have straight orgies. In fact, very similar stories had long been, and would long be, told of minority religious groups. Romans talked of how early Christians got up to the same kinds of activities, and religious 'Ranters' in seventeenth-century England would be similarly accused.[2] Given, finally, that the broader context of Guibert's account is his condemnation of Jean, Count of Soissons, who among other apparent crimes had favoured this sect, one can fairly dismiss what he says as propaganda.

Except that if we dismiss it completely, we discard the only extant piece of evidence concerning these religious dissenters. And in this chapter, these are precisely the kind of people I want to discuss: those who did not follow the Church's path in their interpretation of Christianity, or who even relinquished much of the faith altogether. Here is the rub. Almost all of the material concerning heresy, at least up until the late fourteenth century, is the product of those persecuting it. Often – particularly in the eleventh and twelfth centuries – the orthodox writers could see little more than the shadows of their own hate. Guibert's account is far from useless. It provides a good sense of what a monastic author like himself feared and, in his fear, fantasized. The threat, to his eyes, is hidden and is potentially widespread. The central mysteries of Catholicism, particularly in this period the growing importance of Christ's physical presence in the Host, are under attack. Sexual perversions are rife, a dark twin to the increased emphasis upon celibacy among the clergy. And the spread of the heresy lies not in any intellectual or emotional or salvational benefit that it proffers to potential converts, but in its poisonous, magical ability to warp souls. All of this is helpful in understanding the cultural contours of monastic writers confronted by a religious threat. The challenge remains, however, whether one can say anything about the threat itself, free from the lurid projections of a hostile author.[3]

I will attempt to meet this challenge, for these and other heretics, a little further on. First, however, we must be clear about all of the problems that lie in our path. The sources – Guibert's and others – are not only prejudiced and tend simply towards stereotyped depictions. They work hard, at a profound level beyond the conscious intention of their authors, to shape the phenomenon they depict. Let me illustrate this with another extract from the *Monodiae*. The local bishop, Lisiard, had summoned Clement and Evrard to account for themselves, since they were known to have held meetings outside the church and were famed as heretics.

> To which Clement replied, 'My lord, have you not read in the Gospel where it says "Blessed are the heretics" [*beati eritis*[4]]?' Since he was illiterate he thought the word *eritis* meant 'heretics', and moreover he thought 'heretics' was to be understood in the sense of 'heirs', though not of God to be sure.[5]

Guibert's intentions here are fairly clear: to ridicule Clement. The phrase from the Gospel passage means 'Blessed are you if/when . . .' Only an illiterate (in the sense of non-Latin reading) idiot could think *eritis* meant 'heretics'. Ha-ha-ha, we are encouraged to chortle; stupid heretics. But concealed by laughter, this joke also carries with it another, more serious idea: that 'heretic' is not a label applied to Clement by Guibert or Lisiard, but is a term Clement himself has accepted. I am a heretic, he appears to be saying, and I am blessed.

This is the bigger lie, and all the more dangerous for the fact that, unlike orgies and infanticide and demonic bread, it is less obvious. It is a lie that Guibert, I suspect, did not himself know that he was telling. He expected there to be heretics, expected heretics to have an independent, external existence; for did it not say in the Bible 'There must be heresies, that they which are proved be manifest among you' (I Cor. 11:19)? Heresy was out there, lurking in the darkness. Heretics were, at some level, all connected, part of a bigger threat. Ultimately, they answered to Satan, not God. Thus when people like Clement and Evrard were revealed, they brought the label 'heretic' with them. Only this is not in fact the case. Heresy is always, in every circumstance, in the eye of the beholder. 'Heretic' is always, in every case, a name flung at someone else. As the historian R. I. Moore has put it, 'heresy exists only in so far as authority chooses to declare its existence'.[6] This is a point made many times by those who study heresy; but it is also a point that tends repeatedly to slip from one's grasp. The sources encourage this: they divide the world, so neatly and persuasively, into half. On one side, orthodoxy, on the other, heresy. But heresy, for modern historians, should always be understood as 'heresy' (in what literary critics call scare quotes); or, more cumbersomely, 'those-phenomena-that-some-authority-has-labelled-heresy'. Heretics do not *choose* to become heretics – they are made heretics by others. They may choose to behave differently, interpret differently, believe differently from others. They may indeed choose to criticize others, decry other religious practices, even denounce the Church and all its works. But 'heresy' is a label that these two sides thus fight over, rather than something that innately sticks to one side rather than the other.

We have already met a number of heretics (people-given-the-label-heretic-by-someone-else) in this book. As I argued in Chapter 1, looking at people involved in heresy can tell us a lot about lay belief and practice, orthodox as well as heretical. But in this chapter, I wish to focus upon those who illustrate the limits of ecclesiastical hegemony and control. The first place to look is therefore at those who rejected orthodoxy, or who slipped outside it, or who discovered themselves to have diverged from it. While hanging on to the caveats outlined above, let me give a brief overview of medieval heresy, initially in chronological terms, to provide some points of reference – remembering, all the while, that this is an overview that fits into the perspective of someone like Guibert more than someone like Clement.[7]

Given that my focus is upon groups beyond the world of intellectual theologians, our narrative begins in the very last years of the tenth century. A scattering of evidence from different chronicle accounts shows certain people in the period 970–1050 who were labelled heretics. A peasant in Châlons called Leutard, for example, apparently sent away his wife as if 'by command of the Gospel', broke the image of the cross in the local church, and preached to his neighbours that there was no need to pay tithes. Revealed to be a heretic by the local bishop, he allegedly threw himself to his death in a well. In about 1018 'Manichaeans' appeared in Aquitaine, living lives of chaste austerity, denying the need for baptism or for worshipping the cross. A few years later a small group of canons at Orleans, connected to the royal court, denied Christ's human Incarnation and presence in the Host, and rejected the power of saints. They, too, were accused of orgies and using the ashes from infanticide as a viaticum. Upon discovery, they were burned to death. There are a few further examples, but no very clear pattern, other than the hostile representations of the sources that emphasize the hidden and secretive nature of the groups, and frequently describe them as 'Manichaeans' – probably because those heretics from the early centuries of the Church were known to the chronicle authors via St Augustine's works.[8]

In the second half of the eleventh century, these kinds of heresies are difficult to discern, as the Investiture Controversy and its accompanying reforms cast a strong light that obliterates all tonal variation within the sources. 'Heresy' continues to be thrown about as a term, but as a tactical insult deployed by all sides in an explicit struggle over the Church's future direction.[9] Other groups might well have continued to exist in this period – but we cannot see them. Only in the early twelfth century do heretics come once more into view. In Utrecht, around 1113, a man called Tanchelm preached that churches were to be shunned, that immoral priests could not perform sacraments, and that the laity should withhold tithes. Hostile sources allege that he 'married' a statue of the Virgin Mary. We have already met Clement and Evrard, denying infant baptism and the Incarnation of Christ at Soissons. And we have also met, back in Chapter 2, perhaps the most representative figure of early twelfth-century heresy: Henry of Le Mans. Henry, and his sometime collaborator Peter de Bruys, were wandering preachers, spreading the reformist word. Their heresy lay essentially in not bowing to episcopal authority, but some reports also impute doctrinal errors to the pair: that children do not need baptism, for if they die they go straight to heaven; that immoral priests could not produce Christ's body in the Host; that confession and penance were not commanded in the Gospels, and so forth. There is little sense of a larger movement surrounding these figures, but their impact would appear to be greater than those from the preceding century, since

Bernard of Clairvaux – perhaps the most important churchman of the age – embroiled himself in the dispute.

It is later in the twelfth century that a different kind of heresy appears: the large, well-organized sect. The two most famous are the Cathars and the Waldensians, although one could also point to other groups such as the Patarenes and, a little later and mostly staying on the right side of orthodoxy, the Humiliati and the Beguines. Of these, the Waldensians present the most straightforward beginning point, and I have mentioned their origins already in previous chapters: in 1173 a merchant called Waldes (in some later sources, Peter Waldes), upon hearing a minstrel in the streets of Lyons tell the story of an early saint, experienced an epiphanic conversion. He promptly gave away his property, commissioned a vernacular translation of the Gospels, and began to preach in public. Within a few years he had attracted followers who, an early source tells us, 'became devotees of voluntary poverty. Little by little, both publicly and privately, they began to declaim against their own sins and those of others.'[10] Their heresy was not originally doctrinal but purely about obedience: they preached, and persisted in preaching, without episcopal permission. Early in the thirteenth century, one faction within the group rejoined the Catholic church, becoming the 'Poor Catholics' and recruiting in Italy. The remaining Waldensians – themselves sometimes known as 'the Poor of Lyons' – continued to prosper, finding a receptive audience in France, Italy and Germany. Poverty and preaching remained at their core, but, for some of their number at least, other doctrinal facets began to appear. Prompted by a desire to reform the lives of the laity, in the light of the inadequacies of parish priests and the threat of other heresies, the Waldensians took upon themselves the sacramental offices of confession and mass. The most long-lived of medieval heresies – they survived up to, and in changed form after, the Reformation – further divergent beliefs appeared over the years. By the fourteenth century, Waldensians rejected the swearing of oaths; denied the existence of Purgatory; argued that immoral priests were unable to work sacramental miracles; took the injunction 'thou shalt not kill' to apply in all situations; disparaged the power of the Church, and thought it pointless to worship saints.[11]

Identifying a beginning point for Catharism – and indeed agreeing upon what 'Catharism' actually constituted – is a rather harder task. 'Cathar' was never a word used by the heretics themselves, nor was it ever applied to them in southern France where they most famously resided. The label comes from a German source of the 1160s, referring to heretics in that area; the names that the Cathars themselves used most frequently were Good Men (or Women), or Friends of God.[12] Modern historians have used the label 'Cathar' to refer to those heretics, found particularly in Languedoc and in Italy, who were dualists: that is, they believed in two gods. One deity was good, and created the spirit; the other was bad, and created all physical matter, including the human body. (One form – 'mitigated dualism' – believed that the good god created the bad god; 'absolute dualists' believed that both gods were equal in power.) From this viewpoint – theologically radically different from Catholicism but in certain ways not a million miles from the belief in God and the Devil – sprang all the rest of their faith. A 'perfected' Cathar had to undergo a ceremony called the *consolamentum* that purified his or her corrupt body. This ritual ensured that upon death, their soul would rejoin the good god; without it, one would end up reborn, either as another person or an animal. Having become a Perfect, one renounced sexual activity and even the physical touch of the opposite sex, one gave up eating meat, and one embraced poverty and preaching. Everything about the Catholic Church was anathema: it had all gone terribly wrong back in the fourth century when the Church embraced material wealth and by implication the corporeal world. The sacraments were worthless, Purgatory was a joke, confession and penance were just ways of extorting money.[13]

It is difficult to identify when and where all this started. Many historians see the influence of earlier heretics from Bulgaria and Byzantium known as Bogomils, who had some similar beliefs and practices. There is the possibility of missionary work from this direction, either in the eleventh or the twelfth century. Some accounts of heresies in the early twelfth century may indicate the first appearance of dualist Perfects, but it is difficult to be certain. What is clear, however, is that by the 1160s dualist groups were in existence, and that, particularly in southern France, they became well organized and well established in the following decades. Southern French Cathars gained support from the nobility of the region, and they formed something that at least pretended to the title of a 'Church', appointing diocesan bishops, with deacons and lesser officials beneath them. This structure crumbled, however, in the thirteenth century, as first crusade and then inquisition attacked the heresy and its supporters. Although some links were sustained between groups in Italy, northern Spain and southern France, by the third decade of the fourteenth century, all the Perfects were dead and gone and, despite the best efforts of later thriller writers and conspiracy theorists, the heresy was no more.[14]

No new group arose for most of the fourteenth century, but shadows cast by fear and hatred did appear. The Beguines fell under suspicion of heresy in certain places, as did the Franciscan third orders (laity who had allied themselves to the friars). The inquisitor Bernard Gui, referring to the latter group who had fallen out with the Church over how literally and absolutely to take their vows of poverty, ironically described them as 'led astray by their own imagination', a phrase more accurately applied to the inquisitors themselves.[15] Lurid fears, reminiscent of Guibert de Nogent's fantasies, can be found. Particularly in Germany, people confessed to some extraordinary acts, sometimes under torture, always under the possibility of torture. Believing themselves (it was alleged) to be devoutly free in spirit, witnesses claimed that they could undertake any apparent sin without shame or consequence. John Hartmann for example, confessing in Erfurt in 1367, explained that a free spirit could have sex with his own mother or sister on the very altar of a church, and would still be without sin.[16] This is largely the projection of inquisitorial fantasy, and part of a growing concern over how mysticism should be policed by the Church. A more objective phenomenon did appear, however, in the late fourteenth century, and this time in England. The

Oxford theologian John Wyclif (d. 1384) developed a circle of followers who emphasized the absolute authority of Scripture over other claims to religious authority. This led to an enthusiasm for vernacular translations of the Bible, and to a split with Catholic orthodoxy. By the end of the century, popular groups apparently influenced by Wyclif's theology known as Lollards began to be prosecuted. They rejected the power of saints, the utility of pilgrimage, and did not believe in the presence of Christ in the Eucharist.[17] The Lollards – who also survived in some fashion up to the Reformation – had explicit links with another group, the Hussites. These Bohemian rebels, initially led by Jan Hus, were partly inspired by Wyclif, whose works were read at the University of Prague. Pithy condensations of Wycliffite ideas gained a wider dissemination outside academe: 'It is contrary to Scripture that churchmen should have possessions', 'Temporal lords can at will take away temporal goods from the Church'. These radical manifestos fed into two wider contexts, the Great Schism (rival popes in Rome and Avignon denouncing each other), and a nascent spirit of Czech nationalism that resented German influence and control in Bohemia. A variety of heretical ideas, some looking very much like Waldensianism, some like strands of Lollardy, came into play in the febrile field of Bohemian politics in the early fifteenth century. The main emphasis, however, was upon independence: the desire for Czech religious practices to be freed from papal control. Here, in contrast to Lollardy or Waldensianism, the sacrament of the altar became something strongly embraced rather than rejected. Hussite reformers, seizing control of various parishes, took the symbol of the chalice containing Christ's blood, and the right of the laity to take frequent communion from it, as a key element in their struggle. The Hussite revolution continued to evolve in the fifteenth century, fighting off successfully a crusade called against it, and surviving in certain forms up to the Reformation.[18] It was, much more than any other heresy, tied up with political and social revolt – and for those reasons I will return to it in a different section later in this chapter.

Let us remind ourselves once again: heresy is in the eye of the beholder. And the essence of heresy is not doctrinal, for all kinds of different theological positions could be held, debated and revised throughout orthodox Christendom without being labelled 'heretic' – including, for example, such a central feature as the manner in which Christ was present in the Eucharist.[19] The essence of heresy is not doctrinal divergence but disobedience. A 'heretic' is made not when someone posits an unusual point of belief – that churchmen should live in poverty, or that the Eucharist is merely commemorative of Christ's sacrifice – but when, having been challenged on this point by authority, someone persists in so believing. A key implication follows: that there be an 'authority' able, willing and capable of making this claim for obedience.[20] Moreover, each claim is itself a bid for authority. The essence of authority is the ability to make claims of this sort successfully. If the bid fails, authority does not in fact exist. The other side of the story, therefore, is what is commonly called the Church's 'reaction' to heresy, but which might more properly be seen as the Church's claims to authority and obedience that produce and sustain heresy as *heresy* (rather than as debate, reform, doubt or variation) – and, just as importantly, produce and sustain the Church as the Church. Orthodoxy creates heresy (heresy is in the eye of the orthodox beholder), and in so doing, also creates orthodoxy (the beholder knows himself to be *authoritative*).

Going back to the eleventh century, the first denunciations and bids for authority are in the hands of the local bishop. Frequently we know of 'heresy' in this period through accounts written about episcopal activities, such as the *Deeds of the bishops of Liège*. Their ways of dealing with heretics varied, from persuasion to executions by the local secular authority. In the twelfth century more complex sources are extant, as bishops and leading monks began to coordinate and discuss their methods for asserting authority. Figures such as Bernard of Clairvaux wrote letters and sermons denouncing heresy, and preaching campaigns against heretics were launched, particularly in southern France. Other writers produced polemical treatises criticizing heretical theology, and denouncing heretics, most frequently as 'wolves in sheep's clothing' or similar terms – a way of re-presenting their apparent piety as devilish deception. The surviving sources are therefore not simply reflections of what was happening during the period, but essential elements themselves in the struggle for control of orthodoxy. Sermons and treatises sought to persuade, sought agreement that certain positions be labelled 'heretical' – and thus others, by implication, orthodox. Increasingly the favoured means of persuasion was demonization: the circulation of stories not dissimilar to Guibert's orgiastic tale, and the assertion that the only real solution to heresy was to destroy it.[21] The culmination of these measures was the Albigensian Crusade (1209–29) that, at the behest of Pope Innocent III – one of the greatest asserters of ecclesiastical authority – waged a messy war in southern France in an attempt to eradicate the Cathars.[22] It led, eventually, to political control of Languedoc by the French crown, and dealt a fatal blow to the organized structure of the Cathar Church. But it did not remove the heretical faith itself; how could it, with such crude and violent tools?

What followed was a more subtle weapon: inquisition. It is important to note that there was no central, institutional outfit called 'The Inquisition' in the Middle Ages. Nor was it much of a feature in Spain. Both the permanent papal Inquisition and the Spanish Inquisition were creations of the later fifteenth century. We are dealing instead with a legal technique – inquisition (*inquisitio*) – that from the early 1230s was directed by the papacy against the laity in the search for heretical 'depravity' (*inquisitio heretice pravitatis*). Inquisitors were not permanent appointments, but frequently Dominican friars given the task of investigating a particular area for a specific period of time.[23] Some, such as Bernard Gui, became expert at the task and wrote manuals on how to pursue it; but Gui still illustrates the point that the job was not permanent, as he spent as much time writing histories of his order as he did chasing heretics. Inquisition worked by asking questions and writing down the answers. The questions could, after 1252, be accompanied by torture or the threat of torture (although how much this actually occurred before the fourteenth century is unclear). The answers were only successful if they rendered useful information to the inquisitors, such as the names of other people involved with the Perfects.[24] Thus a very much larger number of people – at least 7000 and perhaps many more in mid-thirteenth-century Languedoc – found themselves faced with authority proffering the label 'heretic' at them.[25] Mostly, they fell into line and were obedient. All would receive a penance, usually a pilgrimage, a fine and a demand to wear yellow badges identifying their crime for a set period. This was because inquisition was, among other things, an act of pastoral care. Inquisitors aimed to bring people back from their heretical sin and to warn others away from these faults. If, however, one remained obstinate, or 'relapsed' into former activities after having promised not to, one became a heretic. The punishment was death, by burning, at the stake. We do not have evidence of the outcomes of all enquiries, but what does survive shows that penance was much more common than execution.[26] Those who lived knew, however, that the threat of death hung over them, as the ultimate assertion of orthodox authority. After its success in France, inquisition continued to be the Church's favourite tool in dealing with heresy, and was used in Italy, Germany and Spain in the following centuries.[27] Papally-appointed inquisitors were only briefly active in England (in the early fourteenth century, prosecuting the recently-condemned Knights Templar) but the legal procedure of inquisition was employed by bishops against Lollardy in the fifteenth century.[28]

The activities of ecclesiastical authority produced almost all the evidence we have extant for those they labelled heretics. Apart from a couple of theological tracts written by Waldensians and by Cathars, we are reliant upon hostile treatises, sermons and inquisitors' records. (The Lollards and Hussites are more of an exception, as Wycliffites produced quite a body of sermons and other works; linking these to the wider phenomenon of Lollardy is not a straightforward task, however.) Inquisitorial registers are by far the richest material for study, though they present more subtle methodological problems for historians than the more obvious biases of something like Guibert de Nogent's *Monodiae*.[29] It is possible, nevertheless, to use all these sources to present a rather different picture of those phenomena labelled heresy. Returning to our overview, one can pick out several causative strands that thread through the different groups. Enthusiasm, particularly linked to images of apostolic revival, is a powerful theme. This would seem to be the motivating factor behind a group of Italians discovered proselytizing in Arras in 1025. They told the investigating bishop that they had been taught about the Gospel and the apostles, and 'accepted no scripture other than this but to this they held in word and act'.[30] The beginnings of the Waldensians depict a similar sense of excitement about apostolic Scripture, leading to the desire to enact and preach its message – even to the exclusion of other models of religiosity and holiness. All heretics were, at heart, religious enthusiasts; they drew attention precisely because they did things like preach or live in ostentatious piety. Another strand, fuelling the enthusiasm of some, was revelation: the belief that they (and only they) had had some secret truth revealed to them about the path to salvation. This we see with the Orleans group of 1022, who seem to have claimed access to the Holy Spirit, through the laying on of hands, which permitted them to understand 'the profundity and divine excellence of all the Scriptures'.[31] One can see the Cathars in rather a similar light, both laying on hands and claiming a particular revelatory knowledge: that the God who created the physical world did not have people's best interests at heart. To the extent that some of those poor unfortunates prosecuted as 'Free Spirits' did claim a special insight into sin and purity, another link can be drawn. Finally, in some instances, there is the desire to reform both Church and society. Henry of Le Mans clearly falls into this camp, as does his erstwhile comrade Peter de Bruys. Perhaps the earlier peasant Leutard, breaking crosses and denouncing tithes, could be placed in their company. Certainly Wyclif and his later followers can be seen as reformers, impelled to criticize the Church because they wished to remake it.

Of course, these three lines of enthusiasm, revelation and reform are not separate but interwoven. Lollards had a similar attitude towards Scripture as the Orleans group; Waldensians did not seek conflict with the Church but rather, in the first instance, to reform its ideas about preaching; the mysticism of those prosecuted as Free Spirits sprang from an enthusiastic immersion in certain ideas about the *imitatio Christi*. And groups changed, under the pressure of persecution. Those early Waldensians who rejoined Catholicism did not have to alter much of their beliefs other than over the matter of obedience. Later Waldensians were necessarily further from orthodox embrace, and probably had a much stronger sense of themselves as possessing the true revelation of how to follow apostolic tenets. What is most important to note in every case, however, is that these lines of inspiration were not peculiar to heresy. They were very much present in the developments of orthodoxy, too. The 'heretics' of the eleventh and early twelfth centuries were part of a wider phenomenon of wandering preachers who denounced clerical abuses and preached the virtues of apostolic piety. Some, such as Robert of Arbrissel and Norbert of Xanten, ended up founding monastic houses.[32] Mysticism, driven by a sense of revelation, was an important aspect of late-medieval spirituality. Intense Christocentric religiosity, feeding certain strands of Lollardy, was a wider aspect of late-medieval English orthodoxy.[33] Reform was a constant concern and watchword for many parts of the Church, propounded by such pre-eminent figures as Peter the Venerable of Cluny and Pope Innocent III. Even the dualism of the Cathars, theologically perhaps the most divergent position from orthodoxy, had clear links with some strands of Catholicism in its emphasis upon the impurity of the body and the desirability of freeing one's spirit. Even it was a *Christian* heresy, not a different faith altogether.

If we can hold ourselves apart from the rhetoric of hostile sources that portray heretics as poisonous, deceptive, maddened outsiders, another possibility comes into view: looking at the ordinary people involved with these groups, as part of a continuum with other kinds of lay piety. With the earliest groups and sources, this is difficult. Chroniclers and other writers in the eleventh and early twelfth centuries were not much concerned with the behaviour of the laity in general. The flock was prone to stray – led into error by heresiarchs – but in theory this was easily corrected by removing the heretical leader, or demonstrating the error of his ways. Any sense of the laity as actively involved is rare; or rather, if active, they are depicted as 'heretics' rather than ordinary people. Small clues are occasionally present, however. In the case of the wandering preacher Tanchelm, active in Utrecht and Antwerp around 1112–15, who taught that unworthy priests could not perform the sacraments and that the laity should therefore not receive communion and should withhold tithes, the hostile source tells us that 'he easily persuaded those who were already willing, for he preached only those things which he knew would please, either by their novelty or by the predisposition of the people'.[34] So some of the laity, whether 'predisposed' or otherwise, would seem to have responded positively to denunciations of clerics and their sacramental powers, and been pleased to be let off clerical taxation. Henry of Le Mans, whose preaching ability was discussed in Chapter 2, would seem to have had success on similar grounds, one chronicler noting that where he had spread his errors 'Christians hardly visit the churches; rather they condemn the holy service. They refuse offerings to priests, first fruits, tithes, visitation of the sick, and the usual reverences.'[35]

Perhaps, following Tanchelm's denouncers, there were then two negative factors that pushed some lay people toward heretics: seeing the clergy disparaged, and being freed from their exactions. But were there also more positive elements of attraction? One thing that many of the early sources seem to acknowledge, however grudgingly, about heretics was their personal charisma. Tanchelm, Henry, Peter de Bruys and others shone brightly, and drew people to their light. One may posit an innate element here – some people just are more charismatic than others – but that is not the whole story. The heretics knew which buttons to push, not just doctrinally but in their self-presentation. The apostolic strand identified above in a number of heretical groups played well to a wider audience. People liked the idea that men similar to the original apostles were there in their village, talking to them, even touching them. Again, one must emphasize that this is not *against* orthodoxy, but in line with it. The laity knew about the apostles and their worth because of what they had been taught, heard preached and seen painted.

With the later heresies, the Cathars, Waldensians and Lollards, we have a more detailed picture of lay involvement because of the richer sources that inquisition produced. The image is still not clear, however. Inquisitorial records illuminate certain areas but are silent about others, and what they do illuminate is shaped by deep currents of ideology not immediate apparent on the surface. For example, in the very extensive trials against Perfects and their supporters in mid-thirteenth-century Languedoc, almost nothing is asked or recorded about beliefs. The questions are all 'who, where, what, when?' An obedient witness was one who confessed practical information. By the early fourteenth century, this had changed. A witness had to confess about not only what they did but also what they thought, felt and believed.[36] Furthermore, the way in which inquisitors understood what was confessed could be subtly different from the laity. Varied ways of greeting and blessing, for example, were tidied up by inquisitors into a heretical rite of 'adoration', taken as a key sign of allegiance to the Perfects' sect.[37] The registers do not easily record complexity in lay relations with heretics: difference is flattened out into categories of guilt. The heretics themselves are presented as distant, rather corporate figures. In fact the Perfects were very much part of the communities within which they lived, playing active roles in practical as well as spiritual terms. And most lay people knew about ten Perfects or less, on most occasions dealing with just one or two of them, suggesting the possibility of a more personal set of relationships with the faith than the image of a collective heretical 'Church' might suggest.[38]

What else does the evidence reveal? Locality and family are clear factors, which is unsurprising given their importance within orthodox faith. Families permeate French Catharism. A witness called Barsalona of Brugairolles explained to an inquisitor in 1243 how, 40 years before, she had seen a Cathar at her father's house. The heretic was in fact her uncle Franc, and also present were her father, his wife and her own brother. Her sister Veziada was also a Perfect, as was her godmother.[39] Among a group of Lollards from the Chiltern Hills, prosecuted in the 1460s, a study has found that about half of the men and three-quarters of the women involved were related to another person connected with the sect. Small family groups could spread faith through marriage and upbringing. In the early fifteenth century, Lollards at Coventry included a brother and two sisters whose mother had taught them the heresy, and who in turn taught their spouses.[40] An inquisitorial way of looking may lurk here, however: they sometimes asked witnesses whether someone came from 'heretical kin'. This should not make us jump in the opposite direction, but it should alert us to the fact that a certain weight of interpretation was placed upon some kinds of contact. Families did not automatically follow heretical paths together, and could in fact fall out over such things. Thomas Colins, for example, tried to teach his son John various Lollard doctrines, but John was 'so much discontented . . . that he said he would disclose his father's errors, and make him to be burned; but his mother entreated him not so to do'.[41] It is important not to assume that family bonds negated the possibility of individual reflection and judgement upon heretical beliefs or ways of life. Family and neighbourhood were important factors, and something like 'peer pressure' could certainly play a role. But belief and disbelief were also involved.

In the case of both Catharism and Waldensianism, lay involvement changed as the sects warped under the pressure of persecution. In the second half of the twelfth century, certainly in southern France and perhaps elsewhere too, one did not have to make a clear choice between Perfects and others. Catholic clergy and Cathar Perfects held public theological debates for the nobility, each side claiming victory. One would be able to hear a mixture of dualist, orthodox reformist and traditionalist preaching in the streets of Toulouse. Inquisitorial evidence makes it clear that people mixed their allegiances: a large number of people, for example, had contact with both Waldensian and Cathar heretics, despite the fact that the former abhorred the latter just as much as the Catholic Church did. A woman called Peironne let the Waldensian preacher Pierre de Valle stay in her house, fed him and listened to his words; but also went to hear the preaching of the Cathars, and sent them bread and wine and nuts. Bernard Remon explained that he saw Waldensians preach and believed they were good men, and then went to see Cathars, wanting to see 'who were better'. Many other examples can be found.[42] By the later thirteenth century, the surviving Perfects were living largely clandestine lives. Lay supporters had become just that – essential support for the sect, and hence more active, more implicated and smaller in number. They led the Perfects around from place to place, kept them fed, and tried to protect them from the inquisitors and their spies. By the early fourteenth century, when a small group of Perfects launched a revival of Catharism in the Pyrenean mountains, there is a clearer sense of belonging or not belonging to the larger group surrounding the heretics. People talked of the benefits of marrying someone who had similar knowledge of 'the Good', as they termed it.[43]

A heavily persecuted faith requires a higher level of commitment from its supporters. In the case of the Waldensians, it was the process of persecution itself that turned the phenomenon into a sect. The supporters of the Waldensian preachers became morally and legally implicated in the heresy under inquisitorial investigation, and a more tight-knit and secretive faith was thus formed. A Cathar supporter from the early fourteenth century similarly explained to an inquisitorial spy that people tended to want to see the Perfects only in groups of two or three, so that if anyone betrayed the others, the numbers of witnesses were limited and could be more easily discredited. The context of interaction for these believers had clearly upped the stakes of their support. Similarly, in Coventry in the late fifteenth and early sixteenth centuries, after more than a century of intermittent prosecutions of Lollards, one can find evidence of a group using secret passwords to gain admittance to their meetings, to protect themselves from outsiders.[44] However, for every heretical group, there was a blurring around the edges. The core of the Waldensians, Cathars, Lollards and others was formed from a group of inspired, dedicated and often literate people who saw themselves as the 'elect', passing on knowledge of their faith. Around them were a larger group of supporters, essential for the survival of the heresy, but not themselves as fully implicated (in the case of the Cathars, for example, the supporters only expected to receive the purifying ritual of the *consolamentum* upon their deathbeds). But while this larger group must surely have included some who were extremely committed and devout, it always also had those who were less strenuous in their faith. Moreover – and not necessarily mapping purely onto this latter section of the group – many who embraced a heretical faith did not entirely relinquish their Catholicism. For example, in late fourteenth-century Germany it was the practice for all lay people to have one of the apostles as a kind of patron saint. Waldensian believers can be found who continued to practise devotion to their individual saint, despite the blanket rejection of saints by their sect. Others similarly continued to see some benefit or power inherent in holy water, again despite their faith's rejection of priestly sacramental power.[45] Supporting a sect did not necessarily mean accepting all that it preached without question. A Waldensian supporter called Katherina Huter did not accept their rejection of Purgatory, because she did not think that 'those who were not fully good' could come into heaven. Arnaud Pons of Vernaux believed that the Cathar Perfects were good men, but did not believe what they said about the Eucharist or against marriage.[46]

The attraction of heretics to the laity was not purely the intellectual content of their faith, nor was their doctrine accepted unquestioningly. Other factors played an important role. An older historiography argued that class and gender were key determinants: that heresy, in diverging from the norms of medieval faith, also allowed a protest against or escape from the repressive currents of medieval society.[47] Recent work has rejected both claims, pointing to the socially-heterogeneous support that heresies received, and demonstrating that women were less active and less predominant in number in the sects.[48] Peter Biller has argued that the Cathars – often seen as particularly pro-women – had a notably misogynist theology that may well have repelled women from their faith, though this is not obviously the case with other heresies.[49] The case against a strong or disproportionate pull to either women or plebeian groups is extremely persuasive, and does a good job in trying to strip away some of the flowery romance that has grown up around heresy in popular literature. At the same time, however, one might still explore the possibility that heresy allowed the space for certain ideas and practices that were less acceptable elsewhere, and that this could add to heresy's appeal for some people. Thus while one cannot, in all conscience, argue that the salvational theologies of medieval heresies constitute an ideology of socio-economic critique, one can point to the pleasure and sense of justice that an aggrieved peasant might feel when hearing Cathars or Lollards denouncing tithes. Similarly, while neither Cathars nor Waldensians nor Lollards presented a proto-feminist utopia or anything like gender equality, the degree of activity available to women within their groups was probably greater than that offered by most orthodox channels.[50] This was insufficient to attract disproportionate numbers into their sects, but it may have been a factor for those women who *did* adhere to the heresies.[51]

The clearest factor in lay support, however, links these later heresies back to the twelfth-century charismatic preachers: that the heretics were particularly holy and lived apostolic lives. This could take an extreme form. Some supporters of Waldensians believed that the preachers had visited heaven and hell, thus gaining their spiritual authority directly from the afterlife. The Perfects could similarly be seen as angels given flesh. The Lollards were less prone to this kind of gloss, but at least a few of their supporters talked of how certain preachers had become saints after death.[52] More common was simply a recognition that what the heretics sought to do was live by apostolic principles – and a contrast between this behaviour and that of orthodox clergy. 'Their sect is the best,' said Jean Juvenal of Mentoulles of the Waldensians in 1487, 'because they live as apostles and follow the life of Christ and of poverty, and they have the full power to accord or withhold absolution.' Around 1300, the shepherd Pierre Maury was told by his brother Guillaume that Perfects had come to the locality, 'who held the way that the blessed Peter and Paul and the other apostles had held, who followed the Lord, who did not lie nor do wrong'. John Skylan of Bergh

Apton, confessing to Lollardy in 1430, admitted saying that 'the cursed Caiaphases, bishops and their proud priests every year make new laws and new ordinances to kill and burn all Christ's true people who would teach or preach the true law of Christ'.[53] In each case, the combination of message and mode of life was what impressed the laity. They did not necessarily aspire to emulate these heretical apostles, but could be pleased to have them – and their promise of salvation – available. Asked by the bishop of Toulouse in the late twelfth century why the nobility and others did not get rid of the Cathars, Pons Adhémar of Roudeille famously replied 'we cannot: we were brought up with them, there are many of our relatives amongst them, and we can see that their way of life is a virtuous one'.[54] What is not always noted is that immediately prior to this statement Pons had admitted that the Catholic clergy had the better theological arguments. The combination of family, kinship and exemplary lives was powerful *despite* the specific beliefs.

None of this should suggest that every medieval layperson was always pleased to see alternatives to the orthodox Church and fervently embraced any anticlerical or apostolic heretics who appeared in their area. At certain times and places, lay support was very strong, most notably perhaps in southern France in the late twelfth century, where many from the nobility to the peasantry were pleased to have the dualist Perfects in residence. At other times – in fifteenth-century England, for instance, in the wake of concerted anti-Lollard propaganda from the Lancastrian throne – town officials and others could be quick to pounce on any they thought might be heretical. Early sources sometimes present lay people as acting more precipitously and violently against heretics than the clergy: Guibert de Nogent alleges that Clement and Evrard, having been condemned by the bishop and failed a trial by ordeal, were seized by a lynch mob and burnt, while the ecclesiastics were still debating what their fate should be.[55] But in such circumstances it is never quite clear what the chronicler means by 'the people' (all the townspeople? or royal officials? or the local nobility and their men?). Nor can one be certain whether or not the author is trying to present events in a way that minimizes any clerical fault, should the meaning of 'heresy' be revised at some future point of time. It could be awkward if one burnt a group of preachers, only to discover later that they had archiepiscopal or papal blessing. In other words, gauging lay attitudes to heresy (to what the clergy labelled as heresy) is tricky. The sources tend either to present a weak-willed and credulous flock who follow any new charlatan, or a reassuringly devout mob who wreak righteous havoc on the Church's enemies. Inquisitorial sources mainly tell us about lay people who supported heretics. When other positions appear denouncing heresy, one cannot be certain to what extent the witness is saying what they think the inquisitor wants to hear. It is notable that on at least some occasions when civic authorities took it upon themselves to prosecute heresy independent of inquisitorial tribunals, as was the case in fourteenth-century Germany, they were considerably more merciful than the clergy, happy simply to banish the offending Waldensians or Beguines from the town, sometimes only for a set period.[56] But generalizing is basically impossible.

Lay attitudes varied dependent upon the time and place – and, most essentially, upon the degree of persuasive demonization propounded by the ecclesiastical authorities.

What, finally, does all this tell us about the medieval Church and power? As I have argued above, heresy is first and foremost an illustration of power – the power to label and condemn. Heresy is not the irruption of deviance within an otherwise stable arena. It is the sign, rather, that authority is attempting to police that arena, place labels on what it rejects, and thus attempt to shape belief and action to a desired orthodoxy. This is not to claim that religious divergence was invented. The dualist Perfects and the evangelical Waldensians would have existed whether or not Catholicism sought to suppress them. But they existed as *heresy* because of orthodox authority. And perhaps more importantly, the sense in which we apprehend Cathars, Waldensians and Lollards as recognizable sects with followers and supporters is largely due to inquisitorial evidence. That evidence is itself the product of a shift in ecclesiastical power, as the Church, over the course of the thirteenth century, began to see individual lay people as a site to be policed rather than as an undifferentiated flock to be shepherded. Inquisition was far from universal; inquisitors did not lurk in every dark corner and, outside southern France, the numbers of people they tried were only a small proportion of any area's population. The direct power that they wielded was limited. But they mark the sharp end of a shift in emphasis, as the role of the individual lay Christian became more detailed in its requisites.

Thus one can see heresy as being not so much about the limits of power but about its extent and dominion. The phenomena labelled 'heresy' demonstrate that Christianity was (as it still is) multi-stranded in its faith. The Church, particularly from the thirteenth century onwards, placed increased effort into shaping those strands and snipping off what it saw as stray. It was never successful in this and, as I emphasized in the previous chapter, never approached the levels of social control wielded by repressive modern police states. But it did take the first faltering steps in that direction. It had a number of tools: preaching that demonized certain groups as outsiders, poisonous and devilish; political power that removed the socio-economic support for divergent groups; inquisitorial systems that policed communities and individuals. Most important of these was the attempt to make an inquisitorial way of thinking natural to all Christians: to have everyone recognize that they were either 'in' or 'out', either with the Church and obedient, or against the Church and outside it. Certainly one could move from the outer realm and be accepted back into the 'bosom of the Church', as various texts put it. But in so doing, one had to recognize that one had crossed over an essential line, dividing 'them' from 'us'.

It is therefore interesting to note occasions when lay people seem to have thought in a rather different, less binary shape. Na Flors del Mas told inquisitors in the 1240s that 'she did not firmly believe the heretics to be good men, but sometimes believed them to be good and sometimes disbelieved' – an equivocation echoed by a surprising number of other witnesses across the ages. Hans Rudaw, confessing in Stettin in 1393, explained that he did not support the Waldensians but his wife did. He had not forbidden her to receive their preachers or to confess to them, as he saw no wrong in her doing so, and 'he had not wanted to forbid his wife but let her maintain paternal rites'. Custom and family honour permitted plurality, in other words.[57] Frequently the salvation and good example that those labelled heretics proffer are understood by lay people as one available option among several, not the only path to righteousness. Their faith could admit multiplicity. Thus Guillemette Arzelier, in conversation with some Cathars who were trying to convert her, said that if they could truly save her soul, better than the priests, then she would support them. Better than, not instead of. Arnaud de Ravat, who thought the Cathars were good men and friends of God, makes the matter more explicit: 'he heard the heretics say that there was no salvation except in the heretical faith, but the witness did not believe in that error'.[58]

These moments, it seems to me, are better illustrations of the limits of power, and a more interesting kind of dissent, than the pious enthusiasms of dualist or Wycliffite preachers. Some lay people, confronted with difference, could accept it. Their view of the moral universe was not split only into two. Even when confronted with explicit ecclesiastical condemnations of heresy, they could demur. Pierre Espeyre-en-Dieu, a weaver from Narbonne, attended the public execution of two Beguines in the fourteenth century. A friar preached about their crimes and their stubbornness, and hyperbolically proclaimed 'these men wish to be burned for barley and for the colour brown; these men . . . are very badly informed'. Pierre thought this most unjust, and left the scene very troubled. In Bologna, in 1299, inquisitors were similarly engaged, reading out the crimes of those they were sentencing to death. A nobleman, Paolo Trintinelli, shouted out from the audience that 'this was an evil deed, that the inquisitor could have whatever he wanted written, and that he, Paolo, would not give a single bean for those writings. He considered the inquisitor a greater heretic than the condemned man.'[59]

Social dissent

> People were hurrying to Niklashausen as if they were frantic and fleeing from an attacking enemy during a war. They said simply that no-one could stop them, and that they were compelled to hurry along. Wives left their husbands, children quit their homes, and farmers abandoned their fields. Frequently as many as 8000 people came to Niklashausen during one day . . .
>
> Thus the Youth, that is the aforementioned *rusticus*, began to preach, asserting that his authority was from God, and that he was able to lead souls from hell. He spoke openly against the pope and the authority of the Church, not fearing excommunication, and he even said with impunity that the priests ought to be killed. To which unique voice the hearts of all the laity rejoiced, and joked and so forth.
>
> It is possible to describe to you the articles that were prepared by certain public notaries [spying on the sermons], but all tended toward this: that all goods of the entire world ought to be held in common and divided equally among all, and that all

authority of superiors is worthless. From these ideas the pilgrims composed a song
which they sang when returning to their homes carrying their banners before them:

O God in heaven on you we call
Help us seize our priests and kill them all.[60]

This was the report of a cleric, name unknown, writing in some alarm to his
superior on 21 July 1476. The illiterate peasant 'Youth' whom he describes
preaching was a shepherd and drummer-boy called Hans Behem, who lived in
Niklashausen, a village in southern Germany near Würzburg. Hans had been
visited by the Virgin Mary in a vision. She had told him that God and Christ
were angry with mankind, and ready to destroy them all – indeed they had been
chastising those in Hans's area with exceptionally bad weather in the early
spring of 1476. The cause of God's anger was mankind's vanity. Thus (as one
contemporary source reports) at the end of Lent, Mary told Hans 'if you wish
to do my will, then you will soon burn your drum, and preach to all the folk,
and tell them that they should make a pilgrimage to Niklashausen; and they
should take off their false braids and their pointed shoes and their neckerchiefs –
these are vain things'.[61] This was not a unique message. The call, often associated with the Virgin Mary, to build bonfires of vanities had been a feature of
Bernardino da Siena's preaching in Italy, and had similar dramatic effect when
practised by Savonarola in Florence. But to have such an exhortation from the
mouth of a peasant was something different – not least when the Virgin apparently started to prompt rather more radical proclamations. According to the
spies mentioned above, Behem preached that the emperor and the pope were
crooks, that ordinary people were oppressed by spiritual and secular taxation
and duties, that the greedy clergy had too high an income, that if the wealth of
the powerful were redistributed in common there would be enough for all, that
princes and lords should have to work for their livelihood, and that excommunication was worthless.[62]

We could, if we wish, label Hans Behem a heretic, and see events in
Niklashausen as more suitably located in the previous section of this chapter.
Certainly some at the time called him 'heretic', and, arrested by the bishop of
Würzburg, Behem suffered a heretic's fate, being burnt at the stake later that
summer. But as with various examples above, heretic was a contested term: 'And
the priests say I was a heretic', preached Behem, 'and they want to burn me.
If they knew what a heretic was, they would realise that they were heretics, not
I.' Perhaps more importantly, there was no 'sect' associated with the Drummer,
no new re-creation of priesthood and laity, no alternative sacraments or novel
rituals. The call to cleansing poverty in atonement for sin was very traditional.
But the context was important, and points us toward rather different phenomena than those popular heresies discussed above. The study of dissent raises
questions about direction: dissent *from* what, *towards* where? For most heresies,
the matter at stake was salvation, and the dissent was over the means of obtain-
ing it and the nature it would take. Where one was headed remained largely
coterminous with orthodox views: the next life, hopefully in heaven. But one can

have other kinds of dissent than this. In Niklashausen, following several years of appalling harvests, and in the context of weighty clerical exactions on the laity, both as spiritual directors and feudal landlords, the dissent clearly involved social, political and economic matters as much as the soul. As we have seen, Behem preached the common ownership of land by all, the abolition of tithes and taxes, an end to all clerical and secular privilege, and the freedom of all peasants from servitude. The reaction was extraordinary: from all across the region people came, the vast majority from the same lower orders as Hans. They flocked to hear the Drummer and his songs, and their actions clearly present a form of social revolt with a religious character. Their cry 'kill all priests' – threatened but not practised – was not a rejection of all religion. But it identified the clergy, in that time and place, as both oppressive masters over the labouring poor and as proponents of an ideology of passivity that helped to keep the peasantry in their place.

The Drummer of Niklashausen is sometimes presented as an utterly extraordinary phenomenon, either a curious and rather baroque anomaly or the earliest dumb stirrings of the Reformation. But Behem, and the crowds who came to listen, were not in fact historically unique. To see him thus covers up an interesting and important strand of medieval dissent. In 1525 some of the threats uttered at Niklashausen were put into practice, as protracted plebeian violence broke out in Germany. Attempts have been made to link this Peasants' War with Reformation ideals. Luther famously, however, rejected the peasants' cause, and the early reformers had as hierarchically-static views about society as any medieval prince. The ideological calls from 1525 in contrast look rather like earlier statements of equality and justice: 'it has until now been the custom for the lords to own us as their property. This is deplorable, for Christ redeemed us and bought us all with his precious blood, the lowliest shepherd as well as the greatest lord.' Thus asserted the *Twelve Articles of the Peasants of Swabia* (a revolutionary manifesto of the time), and they were not alone. Peasants at Attenweiler told the abbey of Weingarten that they wished to be free and 'to have no other lord but Almighty God alone who has created us. For we believe Holy Scripture, which is not to be obscured, that no lord should possess others, for God is the true Lord.' [63] In 1522, according to hostile sources, the peasants of Bavaria were saying that they wanted to kill all the clergy – a familiar call. [64] Moreover, 1476 points not only forward to 1525 (and various intervening insurrections) but also backwards, to a number of other occasions when religious images and ideals informed popular risings. For example, in 1315 at Sens, following a very poor harvest and famine, 'many of the people joined together . . . because of the countless vexations and extortions they owed . . . chiefly to the court of the Archbishop of Sens, . . . [through which] they were wretchedly oppressed and from day to day endured injustice'. They rejected the ecclesiastical hierarchy, and began to force priests, under threat of death, to produce the sacraments for them – a reminder, once again, that it was the hierarchy of Church and society that was rejected, not religion itself. [65] Uprisings in Flanders soon after saw similar sentiments expressed. The 'commune' formed by the rebels rejected arbitrary taxation by the nobility, and similarly resisted tithes. By 1325 the area was in outright civil war, and placed under interdict. In the following year, under the leadership of Jacques Peyt, the rebels executed the nobles who refused to join them, and harassed the local clergy, whom they accused of 'loving the lords more than the commune'. Peyt himself 'was such an unbeliever he would not enter church', and was alleged to have declared that there should be only one priest in the world, who should then be hanged.[66]

In making sense of these kinds of events, one might point first to the ways in which religious ideas and imagery provided a language for political dispute. This is surely unsurprising, since it was exactly what princes and monarchs had long been doing themselves. The later Capetian kings of France, for example, made various propagandistic uses of Louis IX and his sanctity, and attempted to add further royal saints to join him. The language of kingship was sacramental, and the ownership of that power was something intermittently disputed at the highest levels as well as the lowest: on 25 July 1332 the king of Castile had himself knighted at the cathedral of Compostella by an automated statue of the kingdom's patron saint – a novel example of sacralizing royal power while pointedly avoiding the involvement of the local episcopacy.[67] If we are prepared to make the leap to admitting the existence of political culture within the ranks of ordinary society (still surprisingly hard for some historians to do), at certain moments Christianity provided a lexicon for social dissent. A common form was the use of religious foci for the formation of collective bonds. Thus in 1198, struggles in Milan between the nobility and the craftsmen led to the latter forming a guild dedicated to Saint Ambrogio in order to pursue their aims. One could find similar examples from many other times and places.[68] Mary and Christ, the most powerful intercessors, were frequently depicted as the protectors of rebels. We have seen this already at Niklashausen. It was similarly the case in Speyer in 1502, where the rebellious peasant associations known as *Bundschuh* required all 'those who joined their associations [to first] say five *Paternosters* with the *Ave Maria*', and painted the Virgin Mary on their banners.[69] Another common factor was timing. At Florence, the citizens rose up against the rule of Walter of Brienne on St Anne's Day in 1343, and Anne subsequently became a symbol of republicanism for that city.[70] The large-scale popular uprising in France known as the Jacquerie first began on Monday 28 May 1358 when the men of Biauvoisin, Saint-Leu-d'Essérent and Nointel joined together to attack the local nobility; 'each day they grew in number, and killed all gentlemen and gentlewomen that they found', as a fearful chronicler recorded.[71] That year, 28 May was the Monday before Corpus Christi. In 1381, when England similarly saw a large plebeian revolt, matters took place in early June, with two of the most dramatic events – the burning of Lambeth Palace and the destruction of the Savoy – happening on 12 and 13 June. That year, 13 June was Corpus Christi Day.[72] We might recall that this feast was, by the later fourteenth century, one of the most important festivals of the year, and one particularly related to the display of hierarchy and community. It was thus a period both when people were often preparing for public collective action – in peaceable times, a procession and feast – and also a moment when a certain kind of Christian social ideology (hierarchical, static, ordered) was being articulated, and hence available to be countered.[73]

We also find abstract principles of equality and justice articulated through a version of Christianity. Most famous was the refrain 'When Adam delved and Eve span / Who then was the gentleman?' The chronicler Thomas Walsingham put this into the mouth of the rebellious priest John Ball, who, in his sermon at Blackheath on 12 June 1381, called for social equality and the common owner-ship of land.[74] Ball, however, did not coin the phrase: it can be found in Latin sermons written by the highly orthodox Thomas Brinton, bishop of Rochester in 1374 and 1377. There its meaning is rather different, a sharp warning against noble pride rather than a call for social equality.[75] This, it would appear, was the initial context of the proverb, and a reminder in itself of how innately hierarch-ical Christian society was, once it had left the Garden of Eden. But in 1381 the meaning of the phrase was reworked, whether solely by John Ball or more widely as a common call to arms. And it had a long afterlife in this more radical sense, repeated and circulated in the vernacular in fifteenth-century Germany and Sweden.[76] Another idea, found in several late medieval and early modern contexts, was the assertion of equality through Christ's sacrifice: that all were redeemed *and made equal* through the shedding of 'his precious blood'. We saw this above in the German Peasants' War of 1525. It can be found also in England, in the Norfolk rising of 1549, and the wider concept is clearly present in the Hussite rebellion (which prized the chalice containing Christ's blood as its symbol) and several earlier episodes of popular violence.[77]

The Hussite risings indicate another set of ideas and images: the valuation of poverty. It seems clear that several different streams came together in fifteenth-century Bohemia to form the raging torrent that eventually swept through the country. One was the university-based ideas of Wyclif and Hus, mentioned above. But popular preachers were also extremely important, particularly to the radical Taborite wing of the movement. The most famous of these was the cleric Jan Zelivsky, but numbers of laymen and laywomen also preached to their com-rades. Czech nationalism, struggling to be born, played a large role, and was bound up also with class conflict against lords who were not only oppressive but foreign. The context of schism in the Church fed into the theology of the Hussite intellectuals, and a fervent devotion to Christ and Christ's sacrifice into its more popular appeal – perhaps precisely because of the link made, here and elsewhere, between Christ's sacrifice and freedom from servitude. Servitude, as many cler-ical commentators were fond of reminding their audiences, was the result of sin. It was the expulsion of Adam and Eve from the Garden of Eden that led to the need for work, and thus to the divinely-ordained hierarchical society of medieval Europe. The great Taborite enthusiasm for communion of both bread and wafer (a practice known as *utraquism*) and the prominence given to the chalice were perhaps a rejoinder to this. For why had Christ shed his blood? To free us from sin. And hence also, it appeared to the Czech masses, to free them from servi-tude. Zelivsky described himself as 'the preacher of the poor, deprived and oppressed people' and it was the simultaneous holiness and injustice of poverty that fuelled the more radical end of Hussitism. This came to a head in July 1419, when a crowd listened to Zelivsky preach at Prague, followed him as he led them out of the church carrying the Host before him, and stormed the town hall, throwing the city's councillors out of the upper-floor windows. In the years that followed, under constant attack by the Church and by the Bohemian king, the Taborites formed a kind of communist group. Proclaiming unity in Christ, in 1420 they issued a public manifesto to their nascent nation:

> Henceforth at Hradiste and Tabor there is nothing which is mine or thine. Rather, all things in the community shall be held in common for all time and no-one is permitted to hold private property . . . No longer shall there be a reigning king or ruling lord; for there shall be servitude no longer. All taxes and exactions shall cease and no-one shall compel another to subjection. All shall be equal as brothers and sisters.[78]

Part of this radicalism was linked to millenarian beliefs: an expectation of the coming apocalypse, particularly in light of the crusading attacks that besieged the rebels in their new communities.[79] As with Niklashausen, later that century, the coming Last Judgement could be used as a spur to equality. But equally, as the later conflicts in Germany demonstrate, not everyone involved in popular uprisings was thinking purely about salvation. Calls for equality and freedom had their own force and benefit.

Thus Christianity could provide ideological images for political action and social reform. It is important to note 'could' rather than 'did'. For the most part, the Christian faith was quietist rather than rebellious, preached acceptance of social hierarchies rather than their overthrow, and saw 'reform' as moral and spiritual rather than socio-economic and political. The Church was directly implicated in the socio-economic frameworks of society through its landholding and tithing structure, and in the politics of all kingdoms through the increasingly close alignment in the later Middle Ages of higher clergy with state bureaucracy. For preachers with the care of souls, a stable and hierarchically differentiated society was not simply a given fact, but often thought a necessary arena of struggle within which individuals could pursue their efforts at personal salvation.[80] But as I have argued throughout this book, the laity were capable of reinterpreting the messages with which they were presented. Christianity as a set of beliefs (rather than as an organized religion) contained more radical potentials. It is important to note – as many historians have done – the presence of lower clergy, and unbeneficed priests in particular, in certain social movements: the famous John Ball, the radical Hussite priests who preached revolution and others. But it is also important not to assume that all the ideology, religious or otherwise, of popular uprising automatically sprang from these characters. For a start, one can see other leading figures who were not clergy – Wat Tyler in 1381, for instance – and occasions when no clergy seem to have been involved, as would appear to be the case at Sens in 1315. More importantly, it is clear that both medieval sources and (some) modern historians have shared a prejudice that only the educated clergy were capable of re-interpreting Christianity into a radical message. Various hostile commentators on Niklashausen, for instance, writing decades after the event, suggested that a mysterious Franciscan or Beghard preacher had been lurking behind Hans Behem, feeding him his lines. But there is no contemporary evidence to support this: the spies sent to report on Behem's sermons, for example, do not mention any other person. Behem was perfectly capable of conceiving his message by himself. The occasional presence of clergymen in revolts does not substantially alter their composition or their ideology; it does not, for example, lessen the presence of anticlericalism, directed largely against clerical lords but also more widely applied, in various risings.[81] Assuming always a radical clerical presence in popular politics is mistaken in very much the same way, and for very much the same reasons, as assuming that the religion and beliefs of the laity were simply those given to them by the clergy. As we have seen throughout this book, the laity were more complex, active and heterogeneous than that. The links between religious imagery and popular revolts are part of that heterogeneity.

One might, of course, object that such events are, by their nature, extraordinary. People did not spend their lives in revolt, and their use of and reactions to religion and Church in those periods should perhaps be seen as anomalous. If this is so, one can nonetheless insist on including moments of rebellion as one of the many and varied contexts within which lived religion is conducted. But one can also make a further point: it is not only in the most famous (and violent) events that the connections outlined above can be seen. Smaller rumblings in the medieval body politic can also be detected, and linked to religious imagery and practice. The connection between guilds and civic politics has already been mentioned, and is perennial. Questions of timing also pertain: as noted in Chapter 4, at Chester, Corpus Christi day in 1399 was marked by the mastercraftsmen of the weavers making assault and affray on William of Wynbunbore, Thomas del Dame and their servants and journeymen.[82] The reasons are unknown, but the ritual context familiar. Peasants at Darnhall in Cheshire, frustrated in their attempts in 1336 to gain respite from their servitude to the local abbot, 'sent some of their number on behalf of them all on a pilgrimage to St Thomas of Hereford; and these men, contrary to their oath, came to the King in the northern parts, and for many days were begging his favour'.[83] The use of pilgrimage is not, it seems to me, purely incidental. While it allowed the men the means to approach the king, it was perhaps also part of the mode of public dissent. Less focused examples can also be found. Apprentices and youths in Orvieto spent the night before Good Friday in 1295 assaulting those on their way to church, stealing the holy water sprinklers and blessed bread, tearing down neighbourhood signs, and electing 'lords' and even a mock 'Christ' amongst their number.[84] This was not a serious revolt, if by 'serious' we mean one aiming at substantial social change. But such moments could be seen as moments when what James Scott calls 'the hidden transcript' – grumbling discontent with dominant power that lies beneath the surface of public deference – breaks momentarily into view. Such occasions are important, Scott argues, as rehearsals for those more dramatic periods of revolt. Thus one could argue that without the little events of 1295, 1336 and 1399 there would have been no spectacular risings in 1358, 1381 or 1525.[85]

And some of the ideas and feelings of those later rebellions are found earlier too. At Anvers, in the thirteenth century, a cleric called Guillaume Cornelius preached the purity and power of poverty, arguing that 'as rust is consumed by fire, so all sin is destroyed by poverty and is annulled in the eyes of God', that social hierarchies were therefore to be inverted and that all *religiosi* were damned. Raymond de Laburat, whom we met in Chapter 2, incensed by the tithing demands of the local bishop, argued that all clergy bar one (necessary to consecrate the Host) should go overseas to fight the Saracens, or better still should work in the fields instead of the poor peasants. It is impossible to tell what motivated the persons unknown who assaulted Henry of Donington and another cleric in 1292, 'forcing one cleric to kiss the posterior of a certain horse', but we can note the ridicule – and also the fact that, during the last nine and a half years of Bishop Oliver Sutton's episcopate, 62 assaults on clergy are recorded in his visitation records, about one every other month on average.[86] Anticlericalism is treated by some historians as if it were something like the common cold: a perennial, involuntary and rather meaningless complaint. It could in fact have varied causes and manifestations, but at certain points involved serious resentment of real economic effects and the power that the clergy wielded over personal lives.[87] We should not assume that all medieval lay people were constantly itching to punch the nose of the local priest, still less that they dreamt every night of social revolution. But the presence of anticlerical actions and attitudes was recurrent and widespread: the Drummer of Niklashausen was popular not because he preached novelties in his denunciation of clerical privilege, but because it spoke to a deep-seated and long-present resentment among the laity. Since antiquity, Thomas of Cantimpré noted, there have been five enmities between different animals: between man and snake, wolf and sheep and so forth. 'And,' he concludes, 'I will add a sixth: between perverse lay man and priest.'[88] Anticlericalism was always present in Christianity, and was one part of lay religion.

Another view on these moments of popular revolt again echoes the patronizing prejudices of medieval sources: that the general populace were an easily-led bunch of sheep, swayed into tumultuous action by a few troublemaking ringleaders. When not disturbed by such people, it is imagined, the natural position of the laity was at rest, happily attending mass, paying tithes and observing the deferential hierarchies of their era. This, it seems to me, will not do. One should not leap to the other extreme, imagining a constant war of oppression and rebellion bubbling under the surface of medieval Europe until the long-awaited eruptions of the Reformation. But equally one has to realize that occasions of mass movement, protest and revolt are not caused solely by one honey-tongued preacher. Hans Behem may well have been a fine orator, but what drew people to him from across southern Germany – people who in any case, until they arrived at Niklashausen, could not possibly have heard him speak – was not simply a gilded tongue. Behem represented something to them, they invested him with a certain power, and in that sense he was a creation of theirs, rather than the other way around. A mass of people gathers, often making a kind of pilgrimage under some symbol or slogan; this pattern we have seen above. Sometimes, but not always, a single figure is identified as a leader or spokesman. Sometimes, but not always, a programme of action and revolt is outlined. At other points imagining a way forward is too difficult, and protest against the current situation is all that the group can provide. In all of these cases, some wider concern or desire, beyond the visions of an individual shepherd, are at stake.

And in this sense, the mode of dissent that I am attempting to describe here stretches out beyond even the events discussed above. Often the context is some kind of crisis – bad storms, a failed harvest, political violence, the kingdom under threat. At Puy, following atrocious weather and the loss of crops in 1183, a movement known as the Capuciati arose. A simple carpenter called Durand had a vision of the Virgin Mary, which led him to preach the need for peace, as the lords and rulers did not provide it themselves. He gained followers, and 'under the cover of mutual charity, they joined themselves together by oaths, that to one in need his companion would render counsel and aid against all'. They wore white linen or wool, carrying an image of the Virgin on their breast and the script 'Lamb of God, who bears the sins of the world, give us peace'. They had 'no fear, no reverence' of their superiors, 'but tried to assert the liberty of all, which they said was drawn to the initial condition of all creatures from the first peasants'.[89] This all looks startlingly familiar, yet nearly three centuries separate the Capuciati from Niklashausen. On the news that Louis IX had been captured on crusade in 1251, a rising of shepherds marched to Paris, also under the sign of the lamb, ostensibly to seek to give aid to their absent king, but also with clear anticlerical and levelling aims. They preached against the mendicant friars, calling them 'vagabonds and hypocrites', and attacked clergy at Paris and Orleans. They aimed, one rather panicky commentator wrote, 'first to extirpate the clergy from the land, second to erase the *religiosi*, then to destroy the knights and nobles'.[90] This, he thought, was because they wanted to let Islam conquer the West – a rather unlikely motive. More probable is the call for freedom and equality found elsewhere. Another rising occurred in 1320, following the famines of the preceding decade: shepherds, inspired by a vision, marched to Paris and demanded leadership by the king against the enemies of Christendom. Their ire was clearly not solely directed at 'Saracens', however, as (according to Bernard Gui who chronicled the event) they robbed churches, attacked Jews and 'struck terror and dread of their name in the communities of the towns and the castles, and in the rectors and leaders of them, and among the princes and the prelates and rich persons'.[91]

Does dissent necessarily have to involve violence? There is a certain pattern to mass movements that may stretch even wider. One thinks here, for example, of the famous Children's Crusade of 1212. These events (in fact two risings, one in France and one in Germany) took a similar structural form to the preceding phenomena: in France, a child had a vision, which spurred a large, local pilgrimage.

The same occurred in Germany, except that the group did manage to head East, where they succumbed to various unpleasant fates.[92] The crusade is under-researched, and it is impossible to say much more about its motives and meanings, but the similarities are suggestive. This is also the case with the Alleluia movement in Italy. Here, the tendency to focus upon a charismatic individual is very strong, as the person apparently at the centre – John of Vicenza – was a Dominican preacher who arrived in Bologna in 1233 to be hailed as a great prophet and mediator. Many followed him as he travelled the region, attempting to heal political divisions and bring peace. He worked various miracles before falling from popularity and being imprisoned. The context would appear to be the highly fraught politics of the city and the region, which both created the need for a figure like John and ultimately destroyed him. But beyond his charismatic message, we see again people using religious practices and language to attempt to change their social and political world.[93] Flagellant processions and peace movements occurring in 1260 are partly linked to the crusades, but again have some of these protest characteristics.[94] The massed desire for peace reoccurs in Italy in 1399, once more following a period of severe weather: a peasant was visited by the Virgin Mary who warned him that God and Christ were furious with the world and wished to destroy humanity – a familiar message. To avert this, he had to preach the need for penitent dress and behaviour, crying 'mercy, mercy, mercy, peace, peace, peace'. Travelling first to Genoa, a grand band of pilgrims made peace accords between political factions. Further groups then developed, travelling to different parts of northern Italy. Hints of some anti-hierarchical feeling can be detected: many apparently said 'I believe in God, but not in the pope or anti-pope' (the context being the Great Schism).[95] Thus, as these examples show, the desire for protest and change can take the form of enthusiasm as well as denunciation, discipline as well as violence. All of these phenomena, it seems to me, are forms of dissent.

Unbelief

The image that adorns the cover of this book is a curious one. It comes from a Book of Hours owned by Johann Siebenhirter, created around 1470. The Hours themselves are unremarkable, containing the usual collection of prayers and texts that one would expect. There is no gloss to the picture, and hence its meaning is open to interpretation. What it shows is, in one sense, quite clear. A bishop oversees three priests who are administering communion to three lay people. One Host has a tiny boy standing on it – a familiar figure of Christ's presence in the Eucharist, and an echo of anti-Semitic Host-desecration narratives of the kind mentioned in Chapter 4. At the opposite end of the short line, another Host has a toad upon it. In the middle, the Host is just a piece of bread.

What does this represent? One suggestion is 'the progression from orthodoxy to heresy': that the good believer experiences the Host as containing Christ, but if his faith slips, the Host becomes, or is experienced as, merely bread, and slipping further, turns to some evil (the toad).[96] This is possible, though it seems to me equally likely that seeing the Host as just bread could be the heresy, and the toad-Host represents magical misuse of the sacrament. But given that the manuscript provides no authoritative explanation, let us feel free to interpret it in a third way – in a way that at least some observers in the fifteenth century might, perhaps, have seen it. What if the three figures present not a progression from one state to another, but a range of beliefs? The child-Host is clearly orthodox devotion, seeing and experiencing Christ's body in communion. Whether heresy or magic (the two in any case becoming conflated in the fifteenth century), the toad-Host is equally clearly an evil belief – just look at the swarthy man who is receiving it. Could, then, the middle position – the Host as nothing more nor less than a piece of bread – be neither heresy nor orthodoxy, but unbelief? That is, neither fervent acceptance nor fervent rejection, but scepticism? Disbelief? Atheism?

An immediate objection that many medievalists would raise is that such thoughts (as noted in Chapter 1) are not supposed to be possible in the Middle Ages. Doubt, in the sense of wavering or confusion, can be seen, but simply needed the application of good parochial preaching to be allayed. Uncertainty about the mechanisms of certain elements of faith – the Resurrection, or transubstantiation, for example – was intermittently present, but not any serious disbelief in the existence of the soul or the presence (in whatever fashion) of Christ in the Eucharist.[97] In this last section, however, and in concert with a few other historians, I want to present the contrary case: that disbelief, in several different forms, did exist.[98] Medieval theologians writing abstract treatises on faith may not have been able (or willing) to conceptualize unbelief – but it can nonetheless be found, in sources that take us closer to the lived religion of the parish.[99] Certain examples have arisen throughout this book, as I have pointed to the wide spectrum of lay attitudes. In this final section I will suggest that quite a bit of disbelief existed, in different forms and degrees; and that its existence tells us important things about the overall shape of lay religion.

We have in one sense already met disbelief earlier this chapter: all those Cathars, Waldensians, Lollards and others who rejected certain orthodox tenets. However, as Susan Reynolds astutely points out, many of these apparent disbelievers are really believers.[100] Cathar Perfects, Waldensian preachers, Wycliffite readers had a fervent faith of their own, and their rejection of something like Christ's presence in the Eucharist was part of a system of belief that placed other positive, and similarly transformative, ideas in its place. We might not look too quickly away from those labelled 'heretics', however. While the proselytizing elite of each sect undoubtedly fell outside the realm of unbelief, it is interesting to note how recurrent certain (dis)beliefs are across time and space, occurring in theologically distant heresies. Many heretics rejected the idea that Christ was bodily present in the Eucharist. It is similarly the case with the power of the saints, Purgatory and the sacramental abilities of priests. Ideas differed over why each of these things was so, and what, if anything, took their place. But that these disbeliefs found support among the wider body of people who were at least partially persuaded by the heretics' proselytizing is interesting. From the perspective of the sources that show us these lay people they are, of course, nothing more than the followers of heresies. But we may wonder at the motivation of each person who found a Cathar preacher persuasive. Here was a good man, living a good life, saying that certain fundamentally difficult concepts were in fact untrue. Did the audience's approval rest upon the entirety of the message (there being two gods, salvation only through their sect, and so on) – or did it, for some, simply chime with their own scepticism?

It is hard to pursue this line further, as whatever strands of disbelief might have existed tend to be swamped by the programmatic depiction of 'heresy' in the available sources. Let us then turn our eyes elsewhere. And let us begin with the softest end of unbelief, the general lack of engagement or enthusiasm that can be found quite frequently. Ask whether 'when hearing masses', the confession manual *Cum ad sacerdotem* advises, '[the penitent] has quickly been brought to boredom'.[101] A not uncommon and fairly innocent reaction, one might suspect. Might this kind of inattention and indifference lie behind those occasions when people missed mass altogether, or did not participate as they should? Most episcopal visitations turn up something of this nature. In Hereford in 1397, at Burghill parish, 11 women were said not to come to church on Sundays and feast days; at Dormington 'Margaret Northyn chatters in church, disrupting the divine service'; at Westburg, 'the parishioners say that for the last three years John Alayn has not received the Body of Christ at Easter as every parishioner is bound to do'. The bishop of Montauban bewailed the fact, in 1337, that many men did not come to mass on Sunday. Visitations from Cérisy around that time turn up many specific examples to back up his complaint. At Barcelona in 1303, 'they said that Pedro de Insula did not come to church nor had they seen [him do this] for 10 years, nor his mother nor his wife . . . except at times of solemn festivals', and elsewhere, 'they said that nearly all the parishioners are bad church-goers such that when mass is celebrated they play in the streets and blaspheme God'. In 1409, Juliana Farman and Margery Coterell were excommunicated and imprisoned in Sherborne castle for having failed to attend church or take communion for five years.[102] Nor was Sunday worship the only area where one finds lay people failing to heed the Church's injunctions. Some examples can be found of rejecting clerical involvement in marriage: three cases from the Barcelonan visitations, where in one instance the couple 'strongly reject solemnizing it in the eyes of the church'.[103] Bishop Eudes of Rouen, visiting parishes in the mid-thirteenth century, found people working on feast days, eating meat on fasting days. A harvester on the estates of the bishop of Winchester was threatened with excommunication in about 1310 for summoning tenants to work on holy days by blowing a large horn. He 'retorted that he was going to cart hay whether the rector liked it or not'. A study of tradesmen and shop-keepers in fourteenth-century Prato has found that the restrictions (emphasized by local guilds as well as the priests) against working on feast days and Sundays were almost completely ignored.[104]

This ragbag of examples would probably be labelled 'laxity' or simply laziness by many modern historians, and more than a few medieval bishops. But it is worth thinking a bit further about what that laxity means. Clearly belief was not universally fervent. Even within the relatively limited roles assigned to the ordinary laity, some people could not be bothered or did not want to participate. This presumably means that whatever belief they had in certain key tenets of Christianity – Christ's sacrifice, the need for salvation, the sacramental powers of the priest – this belief was not very strong. It did not motivate them. One may argue that in certain cases – failing to have a marriage blessed, for example – other motives or factors intruded: in this case, the possibility that one or both of the couple wanted later to annul the marriage. This is most probably so; but once again, religious belief is being placed relative to other ideas and desires. The couple's consideration of wedlock clearly allowed them to think outside the bounds of religion, a practice that various historians have deemed impossible for credulous medieval people. Certainly some medieval commentators thought that the failure to abide by the demands of the Church implied a lack of faith. Robert Grosseteste, writing for confessors, explained that:

> There can be said to be many [kinds] of unbelief [*infidelis*]. He is indeed unfaithful who does not believe the articles of faith; and who acts or speaks against the faith, such as idolaters or excommunicates or sorcerers; and who does not faithfully carry out the articles of faith; or who does not serve the faith when they can or instruct the unfaithful.[105]

For Grosseteste, of course, all these slightly different attitudes were sinful, and hence, God and penitent willing, redeemable. In like fashion, describing lay disengagement from religion as laxity implies the cure: a more reform-minded bishop, better educated clergy, charismatic mendicant preaching, and this kind of thing would quickly disappear. Perhaps so. But two things then remain. First, that some (quite wide) level of disbelief born from boredom, uninterest, distraction, or the weighing of other factors, still pertains, prior to the 'cure'. Secondly, that a portion of this disbelief might still prove resistant to the cure, grounded in a stronger rejection of religious doctrine and practice. By the nature of the evidence, we cannot tell; evidence of people failing to come to church, failing to confess, to take communion and such like tells us by itself nothing more than that. But to interpret it always in the first way – as a minor infraction by weak-willed believers – is to interpret it from a particular viewpoint: that of a reasonably complacent medieval episcopacy.

Are there, then, any grounds beyond the wide oceans of supposition for interpreting it – some of it – in the second light? I think so. As a next step, let us note that one can see people disobeying ecclesiastical injunctions and beliefs more proactively, and sometimes from particular motives, outside the context of organized heretical sects. People who are, in other words, dissenting, even if only briefly, within particular situations and in regard to particular beliefs. The Dominican Jean de Vienne preached at Bologna, noting sadly how all the men of the city wore roses (perhaps as part of a Maying festivity) whereas disciples of Christ had been crowned with thorns, and for this reason he rather theatrically excommunicated the roses. A few days later, so the *exemplum* tells us, 'an arrogant and vain youth' saw a young boy carrying a crown of roses, snatched it from him and put it on his head. According to the moralizing story, the flowers burst into flames, burning off all the youth's hair.[106] Whether or not we are persuaded by this detail, the tale relates one kind of rebellious disbelief that could presumably have been rather common. In the late thirteenth century, a man called Pons de Mont quarrelled with the clergy over their decision not to bury his granddaughter, who had presumably not been baptized, with candles. He declared himself an enemy of the church, and subsequently ridiculed the blessing of a cemetery.[107] His unbelief was situational and specific; not a rejection of God, souls, salvation and so forth, but a rejection of the sacramental power of the Church, fuelled by anger. But it is unbelief nonetheless.

One has to wonder in similar vein how to interpret the widespread evidence for blasphemy in the Middle Ages. Anger could fuel what we might call insults against God, which are clearly not evidence of unbelief in the atheistic sense, but anger and despair against a deity who has let one down. During a period of famine, for example, a chronicler records Florentines 'lamenting strongly against God', crying out 'Ah God! Why don't you kill us rather than letting us starve? You always want us dead!'[108] One can see legislation against this kind of blasphemy from the thirteenth century onwards. Punishments were initially light, but by the fifteenth century theologians and civic authorities were more concerned and acted more harshly.[109] Theological discussion and legislation recognized that blasphemy could be the result of 'passion', and hence the words of insult against God, Mary or the saints might not be intentional. 'Blasphemy sometimes bursts out indeliberately . . . breaking out into words welling up in the imagination without heed to their meaning', noted Thomas Aquinas. With a slightly different emphasis, a thirteenth-century Castilian law code explains that blasphemy is not the same as the speech of heretics, Jews or Moslems: 'We desire here to speak of others who, actuated by passion, attempt to insult [God] and his saints.'[110] Insulting a deity is not the same as disbelieving in him; in fact, quite the opposite. One can read some of these instances as evidence of a fierce belief in God and a close sense of connection to him. But this was not the only sense in which blasphemy existed, nor the only viewpoint that authorities held upon it. In the fourteenth century, some confessors' manuals saw such speech as a mortal sin and deliberate act. By the fifteenth and sixteenth centuries, secular authorities in both Italy and Spain were taking blasphemy as a much more serious crime. In the late fourteenth century, the influential inquisitor Nicholas Eymerich argued that there were two kinds of blasphemy. The first did not oppose the articles of faith, but spoke insultingly of God. This, he said, was not the business of inquisition. But the second kind was: this was where someone directly attacked the articles of faith. They might say, for example, that God cannot make the weather good or make it rain, or they dishonoured the Virgin Mary, calling her a whore. Those who utter such blasphemies, Eymerich explained, are not simple blasphemers but should be considered as heretics or suspects of heresy by the inquisitor. The suspicion of heresy should be more or less strong depending upon whether the person blasphemes in any circumstance, or only on certain occasions such as when gambling. But the inquisitor should make sure he studied this matter very closely. The blasphemers, Eymerich noted, often say that they are good Catholics in their heart.[111]

But, as we have seen at several stages in this book, a layperson's sense of what made him or her 'a good Catholic' may not necessarily have a theological focus but a more social basis. And intention is a complex issue. One might intend words to shock those in earshot without thinking much about their theological import (perhaps the most likely case); but one may nonetheless be formulating a shocking statement that *has* theological import. The ability to do the latter is then of interest in our current argument. When, in 1526, a servant boy called Angelo was reported in Toledo for saying 'I deny God and Our Fucking Lady, the whore of the cuckolded arsehole', he probably (as he protested) had no intention of propounding a complex theology based upon the non-existence of God and the sexual activity of Mary.[112] But he was capable, nonetheless, of thinking it up as something to say; as, apparently, were many others from his home city of Naples. Moreover, as Maureen Flynn interestingly argues, given that the most common occasion for blasphemy seemed to be when people were gambling, it is possible that in the context of a game ruled by fate, they were rejecting 'if only at a subconscious level' the presence of God in the events of life. However, she goes on to suggest, the presence of insult leads one back towards an affirmation of belief rather than anything like modern atheism.[113] Nevertheless, I would suggest, blasphemy opens up a space of possibility for sceptical thought. The places of the gaming tables, the market square and the tavern were often the location for 'loose speech', a 'lax tongue against God'.[114] Richard Lyllyngston of Castle Combe admitted, when questioned by his bishop in the fifteenth century, that 'whan so ever was eny prechyng or techyng of the word of god in the pulpyte, I wold contrary hit atte alehouse'.[115] There was surely a potential continuum, in these kinds of contexts, between insulting God, mocking God's abilities, and questioning God's power. You were still a good Catholic – because were you not sitting in the tavern with all your neighbours, having accompanied them to mass?

The cases discussed above are but a fraction of the surviving evidence, and the evidence itself surely but a fraction of actual practice, since it seems unlikely that every instance of blasphemy, laxity or passing scorn was diligently recorded in some ecclesiastical archive. If these cases open up a space within which unbelief *could* exist, I should point now to occasions where it clearly *was* expressed. There are in fact a number of examples of people questioning, doubting, ridiculing or simply rejecting various elements of Catholic belief.

Let us begin with the saints. Medieval people were perfectly capable of disbelieving in certain specifics about sanctity. For example, the friend of a butcher who was paying reverence to relics of Mary Magdalen told him that 'he had not kissed her shin bone but the arm of some ass or pack animal which the clerics show to simple folk for the purpose of enriching themselves'.[116] This kind of scepticism was particular rather than general. Not believing that a bone belonged to

Mary Magdalen did not mean that one did not believe in Mary Magdalen herself – although it could, of course, mean that, lacking true material remains, one did not believe she was an available intercessor. But other disbelief is also attested. The poet Gautier de Coinci, writing about the miracles of the Virgin Mary, noted that some men would not believe in her powers. As the corpse of St Vincent Martyr passed through a southern French town, a woman was enjoined to put down her work to honour the body. 'She jeeringly said that it was more likely to be the body of some heathen Moor or Spaniard than a martyr.' A man called Mandrian Battiloro, from the city of Lucca, admitted in the fourteenth century of having long derided the supposed powers of St Zita, a local servant woman who had died in the previous century. Every time her corpse farted, he said, she laid an egg. Whenever he saw an infirm person being carried to the shrine, he told the bearers to throw them to the ground. And whenever he heard of a miracle 'or the ringing of the bells that rang [to announce] the miracles of the aforesaid body, he always expressed derision'. The very miracle collections and canonization records that detail the sanctity of saints are littered with examples of this kind, because of the denouement to the stories: the disrespectful person is punished (in Mandrian's case by loss of speech) and then cured by the very saint they had doubted.[117] But surely not every person who ridiculed, doubted or rejected the authenticity or power of a saint was similarly converted? And while some instances of scepticism were clearly limited to the particular saint, others appear more general in their disbelief. As the relics of St Aldhelm were carried past him, an unnamed man lowered his breeches and farted at them.[118] One can trace the use of such a ribald gesture into much later popular politics, where farting or defecating in the direction of gentry and nobility indicated deep-seated contempt and an utter rejection of their authority.[119] Such hostility may have been rare (although its very existence and formulation are important). Perhaps more common was a quieter sort of disbelief, rooted in spoilt expectations. A traveller called Gerard described how St Thomas Becket cured his fistula, but that having then gone to Flanders, the complaint reappeared. 'Thomas, you worthless man,' Gerard said, 'silly old fool, you weren't martyred but strangled, why have you rendered void my labours? My pilgrimage was stupid!' His blasphemy was in words only and not in his soul, and thus Thomas favoured him with another cure. It is only, however, because of the second cure that we know of Gerard's doubts. Similarly, a brother took his crippled sister to St Aldhelm's shine every year in hope of a cure. On the third year, the brother, 'wearied and unbelieving', left her – at which point she was, of course, cured.[120] How many others would have left wearied and unbelieving, or experienced a recurrence of their complaint – and because there was no subsequent cure, stayed in that state? And, for the same reason, are left unrecorded?

As the picture from Siebenhirter's Hours makes clear, the Eucharist – arguably the most central mystery and symbol to medieval Catholicism – is another area where we see unbelief. Medieval preachers recognized that the presence of Christ's body in the Eucharist was a difficult concept: 'It is a big thing to think of', Remigio de Girolami said in a sermon, 'that the bread and wine become

Christ's true body and blood . . . It is a big thing to think of, that it should be in so many places, on all the altars, in heaven and on earth, in over 100 000 places . . . But God is there to help our faith, so that a man must not say: "What is this that I am supposed to believe?".' Presumably, therefore, some men did say exactly that, despite the Dominican preacher's best efforts. Humbert de Romans advises preachers to tell stories that will demonstrate to 'simple people' that the Eucharist is not merely a 'figure' of Christ's body, but its real presence. In the early fourteenth-century *Handlyng Synne*, lay communicants are assured that 'if you feel no taste / But only wine and bread of flour', not to worry: this is how God has ordained it, because if it actually tasted like a body, people would not want to eat it. Again, then, the material experience of communion presumably did raise doubts for some. Another English model sermon cuts through the problem in a blunt fashion: 'Do not believe that this does not take place, do not doubt whether it takes place, do not inquire how it takes place.'[121]

But people did doubt and inquire. Theologians doubted (most famously Berengar of Tours (d. 1088)) and lay people doubted. Ribald rejections of what was, from one viewpoint, a rather strange form of food, can be found at various times and places. In Cambrai in the eleventh century, a man encouraged his neighbours to shun communion on the grounds that he would rather drink beer. A young scholar heard two tramps talking in the hospital at Laurac, at some point prior to 1245, about the mass. One said that 'as long as you have a good faith, it is just as good to communicate with the leaves of a tree or even with the turd of an ass as with the sanctified Host'.[122] Ridiculing the idea of Christ's presence in the Host is frequently found in the inquisitorial trials of both Cathar and Lollard heretics. Some of this was undoubtedly due to their divergent theologies. In the case of the Cathars, the rejection of all corporeal matter (and hence a refusal to believe that Christ ever took on bodily form); with the Lollards, it followed the Wycliffite rejection of what could not be demonstrated by Scripture, and hence saw the Eucharist as commemorative rather than transformative. But in many of the instances where lay supporters of these sects recount the rejection of the Host, they do so in less abstract and more sceptical terms, most commonly saying that if Christ's body was really present, even if it was as big as a mountain it would have been eaten up by now given the number of times priests said mass. This belief can be found elsewhere too, including late fourteenth-century Austria – rather far from any Cathar or Wycliffite influence. It has been linked back to Berengar of Tours, but it seems to me just as likely that he was adopting a phrase already in circulation in the eleventh century as that he provided the image for all later heretics.[123] A frequent context seems to have been the materiality of the ingredients for making the bread that would be consecrated. A peasant from Montauban, Bernard de Soulhac, had said many times that the Host was nothing but dough, nothing but the bread that one ate every day, and that 'if the body of Christ is that corn which he has in his storehouse, he could make many more bodies of Christ'.[124] Bernard had several unorthodox ideas (we will meet a few more of them below) – but he did not appear to have had any particular contact with Cathars. Philip Browne of Hinton, under suspicion of Lollardy in later fifteenth-century England, admitted that while reaping corn he had said to the people present:

> 'I could show you the way in to Heaven' and declared the Ten Commandments, and after that said these words: 'what makes these false priests say that they can make the Body of Christ, which is not in their power?' saying that it is as good and as profitable to eat rye bread at Easter as that which is ministered to the poor people and consecrated by priests.[125]

Browne may have heard Wycliffite preaching (though there is only the slightest evidence for this) just as Bernard may have heard Cathar sermons. But in both cases it is interesting that the physical fact of corn prompted and shaped their expressions of doubt. Browne in fact states that he had earlier been brought back to orthodox belief on the Host by hearing the local bishop preach, but had then returned to his doubts after further reflection. Other people questioned by the same bishop who prosecuted Browne gave their own thoughts on the matter. Isabel Dorte thought that it was impossible that the wheat in the fields today could become the body of Christ tomorrow, 'because if it were indeed God, a mouse or rat would not have the power to eat it'. Harry Benet of Spene, clearly having thought about it hard, said that 'if there were three hosts in one pyx, one of them consecrated and the others not consecrated, a mouse would as well eat the consecrated host as the other two unconsecrated', and the mouse would not do this if Christ's body was truly present. This approaches the level of a scientific investigation – a thought experiment, if not a practical one.[126] Again, one must emphasize that there is not necessarily any Wycliffite or Lollard context to these words, beyond the fact that they had led to Benet, Dorte and Browne falling under suspicion. It is important to note that at much the same time one can find similar doubts in France, an area completely free from any Wycliffite or other sectarian influence. An episcopal visitation of Troyes turned up Jean Foisel who said that the Eucharist was without value, a view shared by several of his neighbours.[127] People in late-medieval England fell under suspicion for doubts about the Eucharist because of Lollardy, but their doubts did not necessarily make them Lollard. Thomas Broughton of Hungerford explained to the local bishop that

> I have every year received the said holy sacrament not because I had any steadfast belief in it, but that I should not be noted and known of the people. And being in the Church or elsewhere when the said holy sacrament was present, I feigned with my hands to honour it as Christian men are accustomed to do, but my mind and intent was nothing thereto, but to God almighty above in Heaven thinking that he was not there present in the blessed sacrament.[128]

This he had done for the past 25 years. Was Thomas – as he surely felt himself to be – quite alone? Or were his doubts and dissembling perhaps tacitly shared by others?

With both saints and the Eucharist, one could clearly express doubts about a facet of religion without it implying that one rejected everything. Broughton, for instance, explicitly says that he believes in God while not believing in the Host. But yet deeper scepticism can also be found. Across the five centuries that this book has surveyed, occasional evidence can be found for people who did not believe that the soul had eternal life, and hence that heaven and hell, Purgatory and the Resurrection were all myths. Like a modern-day atheist, for some of them at least, death was simply the end. Alpert of Metz, in the early eleventh century, tells of a tavern conversation wherein a man claimed that 'the soul of man is nothing, and in his last breath it is utterly dispersed on the breeze'. Thomas of Cantimpré, some two centuries later, relates a similar scene. Two men, drinking wine, talk of the afterlife. One says 'we are shamelessly fooled by the bad clerics who say that the soul can live separately after the destruction of the body', and his companions laugh in agreement. Italian mendicant preachers bewail a similar lack of belief among their audiences. Giordano da Pisa (d. 1311) queried: 'Tell me now, how many unbelievers exist? Who nowadays believes in the good things unseen, the good things of paradise?' And moreover: 'There are many people today who do not believe there is another life, or that things could be better than in this one.'[129] Humbert de Romans reported 'unbelievers' (*infideles*) who 'are very unhappy when their loved ones die. This is because they do not believe that they will live after this life.'[130]

Are these just stories made up by preachers to shock their audiences into a more active faith? This may be their intent, but in doing so they relate a kind of unbelief that is clearly both recognizable and a matter of concern. Moreover, one can find more direct evidence of people espousing such doubts. We met a late example, from fifteenth-century England, at the very beginning of this book: Thomas Tailour, who believed that, like the blowing out of a candle, the soul is destroyed upon the death of the body. He was not alone. At the end of that century, a German called Hermann of Ryswick was condemned for teaching, among other things, that the soul died when the body died. In late medieval Spain, inquisitors investigating *conversos* (Jews who had been forced to convert to Christianity) found some beliefs that were neither Jewish nor Christian. A cleric called Diego Mexias was reported in 1485 to have said that 'there is nothing except being born and dying and having a nice girl-friend and plenty to eat'; Pedro Gomez el Chamorro (d. 1500) warming himself by the fire, fed up with the cold weather, exclaimed 'I vow to God, there is no soul'; Diego de Barrionuevo, 'I swear to God that this hell and paradise is nothing more than a way of frightening us, like people saying to children "the bogeyman will get you".'[131] Various people caught up in the search for Cathar heretics in southern France in the early fourteenth century had similar beliefs. A woman called Guillemette Benet of Ornolac told her neighbours on several occasions that the soul was nothing but blood, or wind. Both thoughts came from experience, the first upon having banged her nose accidentally and observing the subsequent nosebleed; the second, in something like a spirit of scientific enquiry, by closely observing the dying child of a friend to see if anything left the infant's mouth upon the moment of death. Seeing only the exhalation of breath, she came to believe that this was all the soul was, and that there was no heaven or hell or other life. Another man called Raymond de l'Aire from the same area – but with no apparent connection to Guillemette – held similar beliefs. His arose from something that an old man had told him, that a donkey had a soul just as a man had a soul. From this starting point, Raymond 'had by himself deduced' that since an animal dies when all its blood is drained, and a man similarly, the soul was nothing but blood. And as with Guillemette, he was confirmed in this belief because he saw nothing leave a person's mouth when they died.[132]

One can further find just a little evidence of complete unbelief, a scepticism that encompasses all of creation, extending even to God himself. Around 1200, a prior of Holy Trinity, Aldgate wrote that 'there are many people who do not believe that God exists. They consider that the universe has always been as it is now and is ruled by chance rather than by Providence. Many people consider only what they can see and do not believe in good or bad angels, nor do they think that the human soul lives on after the death of the body.' Later that century, the Dominican preacher Remigio de' Girolami preached to Florentines that 'the fool, taking leave of his senses, oblivious of the name of God, says in his heart "there is no God"' (Pss. 14:1, 53:1). Other of his compatriots agreed that this was a problem with the laity of the city (though they may have been interpreting the implications of Florentine citizens' actions rather than reporting explicit unbeliefs).[133] Arnaud de Savinhan, a stonemason from the Pyrenees in the early fourteenth century, appears to have believed in God but at certain points to have thought that the world had always existed and would always exist, independent of its deity. This was similarly the case in 1500 with a *converso* called Francisco, who said to a friend 'what makes you think that the world must end? Don't think that the world must end, or believe it. The world must end for anyone who dies, but you shouldn't believe anything like its ending: don't believe that when you die you'll go to the other world.'[134] A rather odd man called Gausbert d'Aula, questioned by an inquisitor in the late thirteenth century, admitted that he had often urinated in the local cemetery – but only because of a weak bladder, he said. He also admitted that he had been asking people if they believed in the God who made the wind and the rain, and when they concurred, had told them that this meant they believed God had an anus and a vagina. Quite what he intended by this image is unclear, but he had also once said that God did not provide him with the material goods of life, but that they came from his own labour. At the end of his deposition he piously asserted that he had great devotion for God and the Blessed Virgin Mary and all the saints. Perhaps this was true. Perhaps it became true in the presence of an inquisitor. At any rate, his belief that material goods came from labour rather than supernatural power was shared by others. Guillaume Orseti was accused of saying that 'God never made anything that flowered or germinated, nor made any of the terrestrial world, but [they were made by] rotten earth and men digging and working the land.'[135] This statement can be found elsewhere in the records.

How did people arrive at unbelief? One wonders whether people like Guillemette Benet and Raymond de l'Aire were experiencing a disjuncture between the images provided by sermon stories and religious art that explained death and the afterlife, and their observation of material reality. The soul was often depicted in art as a miniature figure, sometimes being emitted from the mouth. The failure of anything resembling this to turn up in reality may have furthered their scepticism. In the case of beliefs concerning the mortality of the soul or the eternity of the world, one might argue that some kind of Aristotelian thought was an influence, given that elements of Aristotelian philosophy have been demonstrated to be present in certain late medieval sermons.[136] However, this does not seem to me to explain all of the evidence discussed so far. It is not at all clear just how broadly such university-derived sermons spread, once one leaves the confines of north Italian cities and other highly literate and highly populous areas. Another, more obvious, objection is that some of the beliefs of this nature seem to appear before Aristotle became firmly embedded in university curricula; and that, in any case, some of the people espousing these beliefs explicitly point to physical experience and their own thoughts as the cause. To look for a 'learned' background to these ideas rather mirrors the assumptions of the medieval inquisitors recording them, seeking out some mysterious heresiarch behind the individual, misled by the assumption that critical ideas originate only with the intelligentsia.

What seems most often present is the role of reflection upon material experience in these people's unbelief, a trait shared by Guillemette, Raymond, Guillaume Orseti and others. A village official called Guillaume Austatz – perhaps also influenced by Cathar beliefs that he had heard from his mother – was in extreme doubt as to whether the body would ever be resurrected. Whatever heterodox theology he had been exposed to, it was experience that prompted real doubt. He and a group of onlookers were watching a new grave being dug in the churchyard at Ornolac, various old bones being brought to the surface as the gravediggers worked. Seeing them, Guillaume wondered to his companions, 'It is said that the souls of the dead return in the same flesh and bones as those in which they once were in . . . And how is it possible that the souls that were formerly in these bones can return there?' Further interrogated by the inquisitor investigating him in 1320, he gives a flavour of how complex doubt could be:

Asked if he had ever believed that human bodies could not be resurrected, he said yes, for almost all that day, because of the aforesaid words he had said [on seeing the bones dug up], but, as he said, he did not believe this at other times, as to its possibility, but, as he said, for about two years, after he had heard from his mother, amongst other things, what the said heretic Pierre Autier [a Cathar] had said to her, that human bodies would not be resurrected, he was in doubt and doubted if the bodies of dead men would be resurrected or not, and sometimes his conscience was drawn to one part and at other times to the other, and, as he said, at some times he believed that there would be no Resurrection . . . although he never totally believed this, sometimes staying in the contrary belief, because he had heard this preached in church, and moreover because Guillaume de Alzinhac, priest of Carbona, who had

sometimes stayed in the house of his mother at Lordat, had said to him that there
would be a future resurrection of dead men and women, which he taught to him
when he was a young boy and lived with his mother at Lordat.[137]

Several things collide in Guillaume's statement: the words and beliefs of authority figures (his mother, his old priest), abstract orthodox and heterodox theology,
and his own thoughts and experiences. For how many others would similar dis-
sonances occur?

This is a key question, but clearly unanswerable. We only know about people
who got into trouble, which in all cases means people who voiced their doubts
or scepticism, rather than keeping quiet about it. In most cases, it additionally
means that we see only those who voiced scepticism in places and at times when
bishops and other ecclesiastics were proactively searching out heretical groups –
and hence also swept up these people. It may be argued that it was precisely the
presence of heresy – in the sense of a competing theology and challenge to ecclesiastical power – that prompted individuals like Guillaume Austatz to come up
with their own view on things. By implication, therefore, most other Christians,
listening to a reasonably univocal Christian message, would never be troubled by
such doubts. But I find this an unsatisfying argument. Cases like Austatz (and all
those cited above) demonstrate that at least some lay people had the capacity to
reflect internally upon the mysteries of religion, and to come to their own conclusions, divergent from what they had been taught by either priest or heretic.
Part of what prompted that reflection was lived experience, not dogma. It seems
likely to me, therefore, that both the lived experiences and the mental capacities
could be found elsewhere, far from any heterodox sect, far from the investiga-
tory web of inquisition – and hence, for the most part, far from the view of the
modern historian.

It is clear that for some people, scepticism in one area could, like a small stone
knocked carelessly down a hillside, cause a larger cascade, collapsing the entire
edifice of faith. One such was Durand de Rufiac, brought before inquisitors in
France in 1273. He said that the soul was nothing but blood, having come to
this belief after watching how animals died. He also said (although he then
denied believing it) that even if the body of Christ was as big as a mountain, it
would have been eaten by now in the Host. He thought paying money for the
remission of sins was stupid, and that St Lawrence and the other martyrs had
not chosen martyrdom but been forced into it. He said something similar to
Guillaume Orseti's belief that it was the wetness and putrefaction of the earth
that caused things to grow, and he was reported to have said that 'when he was
a young man he frequently made the sign of the cross, and no good came of it,
but when he grew older he omitted to cross himself and much good came of
it'.[138] Another was Raymond de l'Aire, who not only disbelieved in the soul, but,
prompted by another man called Pierre Rauzi, thought that God and the Virgin
Mary were nothing but the material world around him, that God had never
made the world but that it had always existed, that there was no reason to obey
the Church's rules against consanguinial sex, that the consecrated Host was

nothing but bread, that there was no Resurrection, that Mary and Joseph had had sex and that Christ was made 'through fucking and shitting out' just like any other person, and that Christ was not crucified for our sins nor ascended to heaven. Moreover – it hardly needs adding – he didn't think there was any value to what the priests did during mass or in other holy offices. Interestingly, none of this meant that Raymond did not conform to some degree. He gave alms, he said, but not because he believed it would do his soul any good, but 'only so that he would have a good reputation amongst his neighbours, and they would repute him to be a good man'.[139]

This is not to suggest that legions of radical sceptics lurked in the parishes of Europe, silently awaiting the dawn of some future Enlightenment. I suspect that, in the breadth of their unbelief, Raymond and Durand were not unique but fairly unusual. While they held to an entire programme of scepticism, many of the cases cited above were more limited and specific. This, it seems to me, is the more likely case to project – carefully and hesitantly – into the silences of the surviving archives. The most common case is likely to be not 'atheism' in a modern sense – a complete rejection of God and the supernatural – but rather a sense in which, while God probably exists, he is clearly a long way off and little concerned in the practicalities of human affairs. We need not imagine fervent atheists lurking. But we should admit the possibility that many people periodically experienced doubt, scepticism and unbelief, and that these experiences could lead them to question and reject ecclesiastical authority.

The most common form of scepticism, it seems to me, was doubt over whether all (or even much of) the Church's message was true, or was indeed the only way of looking at things. The ability of heretical sects to thrive at different times and places arose most frequently not from a strong lay antipathy toward Catholicism but a rejection of its claim to *sole* authority. In a similar sense, the use of what we rather awkwardly label 'magic' by the laity – the mixture of healing, charms and soothsaying discussed in Chapter 3 – was not part of a conscious opposition to the Church, but was nonetheless pursued in the face of ecclesiastical censure when such arose. In other words, if what I have been describing in this last section can be called 'dissent', it is a very different kind of dissent from self-conscious schismatic opposition to the Church. It is, in fact, a much more interesting kind of dissent – a dissent of plurality, doubt and relativism. Its most radical expression is not the shocking statements about sex, bodies and God mentioned above, but the explicit recognition of what we might call comparative religion. Bernard de Soulhac, the peasant mentioned above decrying the Eucharist, also apparently declared that the Jews and Saracens had a better faith than Christians. A pursemaker in thirteenth-century Bologna was reported for saying that, just as there were 72 different languages, so there were 72 different faiths – an argument that nicely foreshadowed later anthropological theory. In the context of emphasizing the necessity of baptism for salvation, the English text *Handlyng Synne* notes that 'often we hear unlettered men say' that they do not know whether the Jews are saved or not. A peasant woman called Juana Pérez was reported in 1488 for saying that 'the good Jew would be saved, and the good Moor, in his law, and why else had God made them?' She was not a *conversa* but a Christian, and she was not alone in her opinion.[140]

Conclusion

Medieval lay piety was many things: excitable, lazy, repressive, accepting, gendered, hierarchical, socially levelling, deeply devout and deeply sceptical – which is to say, there was no *one* medieval lay faith but a spectrum of faith, belief and unbelief. And this was perhaps apparent to medieval people themselves and perhaps for a few a spur to the kind of ecumenical views described above. Histories of European religion often describe a broad move toward toleration over *la longue durée*. The medieval period is usually positioned as the dark and repressive past from which more enlightened souls escaped in the sixteenth, seventeenth and eighteenth centuries. In works of political philosophy and theology, there is of course something to this. But one could make a case for arguing that in the much wider world of lived religion, some of that shift was in precisely the other direction. One of the things that changed with the Reformation and Counter-Reformation was the arrival of a much stronger sense of having to position oneself securely within a precise doctrinal framework. Acceptance of difference became concomitantly harder. The roots of this, as much else, lay in the preceding medieval centuries, and one might even describe both the Protestant and Catholic Reformations as the eventual outcome of a process of definition, sharpened categorizations, and increased demands from the structures of faith that began in the thirteenth century if not before. There is little point in medievalists and others, tacitly or explicitly, either celebrating or mourning the coming of the Reformation. More important is to note that what changed was not only the doctrinal content of belief, but the practice and compass of faith. In the thirteenth century, if describing oneself as a good and dutiful Christian, one would likely talk of how one paid tithes, gave alms, went on (or talked about going on) pilgrimage and attended mass with one's neighbours. In the sixteenth or early seventeenth century, in a Protestant country, being a good and dutiful Christian differed not only in doctrine but perhaps more importantly in practice. One would point to regular attendance at sermons, abstinence from quite a broad range of improper activities, participation in well-structured acts of charity, of how one read the Bible at home with one's family and contemplated one's faith. In a Counter-Reformation Catholic state, similar emphases upon practices of familial and personal devotion could also be attested, despite the fact that the two faiths differed in other respects. The shape of religion, the claims that it laid upon the laity, changed. And because, post-Reformation, religion became much more deeply imbricated with the structures of the secular state, the mechanisms for monitoring and prompting personal religious conformity were that much stronger than in most medieval times and places.[141]

I do not wish to end by leaving any romantic and quixotic suggestion that the Middle Ages were, instead of an age of faith, an age of toleration and mutual respect. Those people slaughtered by crusaders, burnt as heretics, made to wear distinguishing badges, or forcibly converted to Christianity, would all have some sharp things to say about such a view. But I would like to suggest that power – that recurrent issue which I have raised throughout this book – was, in relation to religion, of a different order before and after the Reformation. What the sixteenth and seventeenth centuries brought, it seems to me, was a tightening up of definition and control, and a closing down of a certain fuzziness and room for manoeuvre. Medieval lay religion was, above all else, a religion of activity, and medieval beliefs were beliefs of practice more than reflection. One might argue that belief was performative, in the linguistic as much as the theatrical sense: that the words and deeds involved in faith were not signs 'of' belief that resided elsewhere, but were the very citation and production of belief itself. What is then important here is that practice could encompass more than religion. The activities that people perform in their lives – those means by which they order their communities, sustain and challenge hierarchies, form connections and create enmities, produce identities and construct Others – are not only religious activities. Other labour and other recreation also come into play. And here, at certain moments, other possibilities are born. Pierre Lafont of Vaychis, at some point around the turn of the fourteenth century, was told by a tinker while on his way to Lombardy – and then thought it worthy to repeat to his neighbours – that 'one should not do ill to heretics or Jews or Saracens, no more than to a person who worked well. It was a sin to do ill to heretics, Jews and Saracens if they worked well and earned their living.'[142] This speaks not only of tolerance, but of priorities. A man lives well, works hard, plays his communal role – what then matter his beliefs?

Notes

Abbreviations

AASS	*Acta sanctorum*, ed. J. Bollandus *et al.* (1643–1883)
AHR	*American Historical Review*
CdF	Cahiers de Fanjeaux
Doat	Bibliothèque Nationale, Paris, collection Doat
EETS e.s.	Early English Text Society extra series
EETS o.s.	Early English Text Society original series
Fournier	J. Duvernoy, ed. *Le Registre d'inquisition de Jacques Fournier évêque de Pamiers (1318–1325)*, 3 vols (Toulouse: Privat, 1965)
JEH	*Journal of Ecclesiastical History*
JMH	*Journal of Medieval History*
Mansi	G. D. Mansi, *Sacrorum Conciliorum Nova et Amplissima Collectio*, 53 vols (1759–98. Repr. Graz: Akademische Druck- und Verlagsanstalt, 1961)
P&P	*Past and Present*
Reg. Langton	D. P. Wright, ed., *The Register of Thomas Langton, Bishop of Salisbury 1485–93*, Cantenbury and York Society 74 (1985)
Reg. Sutton	R. M. T. Hill, ed., *The Rolls and Register of Bishop Oliver Sutton, 1280–1299*, Lincoln Record Society 76, 8 vols (Woodbridge: Boydell, 1948–86)
SCH	Studies in Church History
TRHS	*Transactions of the Royal Historical Society*

1 Belief

1 William of Newburgh, *Historia rerum anglicarum*, V, xxiv, in R. Howlett, ed., *Chronicles of the Reigns of Stephen, Henry II and Richard I*, RS 82, 2 vols (London: Longman, 1885), II, pp. 479–82. English translation (slightly amended

here) in J. Stevenson, ed., *The Church Historians of England* (London: Seeleys, 1866), IV, ii, pp. 660–1. Brief discussion in J.-C. Schmitt, *Ghosts in the Middle Ages: The Living and the Dead in Medieval Society*, trans. T. L. Fagan (1994. Chicago: Chicago University Press, 1998), pp. 82–3.

2 *Reg. Langton*, pp. 70–1.

3 See M. Hunter, 'The Problem of "Atheism" in Early Modern England', *TRHS*, 5th ser., 35 (1985): 135–57; D. Wootton, 'Lucien Febvre and the Problem of Unbelief in the Early Modern Period', *Journal of Modern History* 60 (1988): 695–730. On medieval unbelief, A. Murray, 'Piety and Impiety in Thirteenth-Century Italy', SCH 8 (1972): 83–106; S. Reynolds, 'Social Mentalities and the Case of Medieval Scepticism', *TRHS*, 6th ser., 1 (1991): 21–41; and other works cited in Chapter 6.

4 On Protestant (mis)appropriation of medieval heresy, see A. Friesen, 'Medieval Heretics or Forerunners of the Reformation: the Protestant Rewriting of the History of Medieval Heresy', in A. Ferreiro, ed., *The Devil, Heresy and Witchcraft in the Middle Ages* (Leiden: Brill, 1998), pp. 165–89.

5 See comments by Keith Thomas in his review of Eamon Duffy's *The Voices of Morebath*, in the *New York Review of Books* vol. xlix, no. 17 (7 November 2002): 56.

6 J. van Engen, 'The Christian Middle Ages as an Historiographical Problem', *AHR* 91 (1986): 519–52. For a varied discussion of the issues, J. Delumeau, ed., *L'Historien et la foi* (Paris: Fayard, 1996).

7 F. Engels, *The Peasant War in Germany* (1850. Repr., Moscow: Progress, 1956), pp. 42–52. For a later Marxist example, see M. Erbstösser, *Heretics in the Middle Ages*, trans. J. Fraser (Leipzig: Edition Leipzig, 1984). On the Marxist tradition, R. Manselli, 'Les Approches matérialistes de l'histoire du catharisme', CdF 14 (1979): 229–48.

8 M. Innes, *State and Society in the Early Middle Ages: The Middle Rhine Valley 400–1000* (Cambridge: Cambridge University Press, 2000), pp. 17–18.

9 E. P. Thompson, *The Making of the English Working Class* (Harmondsworth: Penguin, 1968), p. 13.

10 N. Z. Davis, 'Some Tasks and Themes in the Study of Popular Religion', in C. Trinkaus and H. A. Oberman, eds, *The Pursuit of Holiness in Late Medieval and Renaissance Religion* (Leiden: Brill, 1974), p. 308.

11 This brief analysis is informed by Van Engen, 'Christian Middle Ages'; P. Biller, 'Popular Religion in the Central and Later Middle Ages', in M. Bentley, ed., *Companion to Historiography* (London: Routledge, 1997), pp. 221–46; D. Julia, 'Religion', in J. Le Goff, R. Chartier and J. Revel, eds, *La Nouvelle Histoire* (Paris: CEPL, 1978), pp. 488–94; A. Dupont, 'La Religion – anthropologie religieuse', in J. Le Goff and P. Nora, eds, *Faire de l'histoire: Nouvelle approches* (Paris: Gallimard, 1974), II, pp. 105–36.

12 G. Macy, 'Was there a "the Church" in the Middle Ages?', SCH 52 (1996): 107–16; idem, 'The Dogma of Transubstantiation in the Middle Ages', *JEH* 45 (1994): 32–40; idem, 'Nicolas Eymeric and the Condemnation of Orthodoxy', in Ferreiro, ed., *Devil, Heresy and Witchcraft*, pp. 369–81. Macy's modern

theological agenda is made explicit in the conclusion to the third of these articles.

13 J. Le Goff, *Time, Work and Culture in the Middle Ages*, trans. A. Goldhammer (Chicago: University of Chicago Press, 1980); A. Vauchez, 'Présentation', in *Faire croire: Modalités de la diffusion et de la réception des messages religieux du XIIe au XVe siècle* (Rome: Ecole Française de Rome, 1981), pp. 7–16.

14 J.-C. Schmitt, ' "Religion Populaires" et culture folklorique', *Annales: Economie, Sociétés, Civilisations* 31 (1976): 941–53; idem, *The Holy Greyhound: Guinefort, Healer of Children since the Thirteenth Century*, trans. M. Thom (1979. Cambridge: Cambridge University Press, 1983).

15 A. J. Gurevich, *Categories of Medieval Culture*, trans. G. L. Campbell (1972. London: Routledge, 1985); idem, *Medieval Popular Culture: Problems of Belief and Practice*, trans. J. M. Bak and P. A. Hollingsworth (Cambridge: Cambridge University Press, 1988).

16 R. I. Moore, *The Formation of a Persecuting Society: Power and Deviance in Western Europe, 950–1250* (Oxford: Blackwell, 1987); B. Stock, *The Implications of Literacy: Written Language and Models of Interpretation in the Eleventh and Twelfth Centuries* (Princeton, NJ: Princeton University Press, 1983).

17 See further M. T. Clanchy, *From Memory to Written Record: England, 1066–1307*, 2nd edn (Oxford: Blackwell, 1993).

18 S. Justice, 'Inquisition, Speech, and Writing: A Case from Late-Medieval Norwich', *Representations* 48 (1994): 1–29.

19 E. Duffy, *The Stripping of the Altars: Traditional Religion in England 1400–1580* (New Haven, CT: Yale University Press, 1992).

20 For example (and very influentially) van Engen, 'Christian Middle Ages'; L. E. Boyle, 'Popular Piety in the Middle Ages: What is Popular?', *Florilegium* 4 (1982): 184–93.

21 T. Tentler, 'Seventeen Authors in Search of Two Religious Cultures', *Catholic Historical Review* 71 (1985): 254. The collection under review was *Faire croire*, cited above, n. 13.

22 On the influence of national intellectual traditions, see H. Teunis, 'Negotiating Secular and Ecclesiastical Power in the Central Middle Ages: A Historiographical Introduction', in H. Teunis *et al.*, eds, *Negotiating Secular and Ecclesiastical Power* (Turnhout: Brepols, 1999), pp. 1–16.

23 A point made emphatically in J.-C. Schmitt, 'Religion, Folklore and Society in the Medieval West', in B. Rosenwein and L. K. Little, eds, *Debating the Middle Ages* (Oxford: Blackwell, 1998), pp. 376–87. For a good recent example of a balanced view, taking strength from both sides of the debate, see K. L. Jolly, *Popular Religion in Late Saxon England: Elf-Charms in Context* (Chapel Hill, NC: University of North Carolina Press, 1996), pp. 6–34.

24 D. Iogna-Prat, *Order and Exclusion: Cluny and Christendom Face Heresy, Judaism, and Islam (1000–1150)*, trans. G. R. Edwards (Ithaca, NY: Cornell University Press, 2002), p. 31.

25 See S. Menarche, *The Vox Dei: Communication in the Middle Ages* (Oxford: Oxford University Press, 1990), pp. 41–50 and *passim*.

26 On recent English historiography, see the sensitive and thoughtful comments in A. D. Brown, *Popular Piety in Late Medieval England: The Dioceses of Salisbury, c.1250-c.1550* (Oxford: Oxford University Press, 1995), p. 3.

27 For example, D. Hebdige, 'From Culture to Hegemony', in Hebdige, *Subculture: The Meaning of Style* (London: Routledge, 1979), pp. 5–19; a more critical analysis in J. C. Scott, *Domination and the Arts of Resistance: Hidden Transcripts* (New Haven, CT: Yale University Press, 1990), pp. 70–107; a productive use of Gramsci in J. B. Given, *Inquisition and Medieval Society: Power, Discipline and Resistance in Medieval Languedoc* (Ithaca, NY: Cornell University Press, 1997).

28 See P. Bourdieu, *Outline of a Theory of Practice*, trans. R. W. Nice (Cambridge: Cambridge University Press, 1977).

29 See M. Foucault, *Power/Knowledge: Selected Interviews and Other Writings, 1972–1977*, ed. C. Gordon (London: Harvester Wheatsheaf, 1980); applied to religion in T. Asad, *Genealogies of Religion: Discipline and Reasons of Power in Christianity and Islam* (Baltimore, MD: Johns Hopkins University Press, 1993).

30 For example, D. Weinstein and R. M. Bell, *Saints and Society: The Two Worlds of Latin Christendom, 1000–1700* (Chicago: University of Chicago Press, 1987); M. C. Marandat, *Le souci de l'au-delà: La pratique testamentaire dans la région Toulousaine (1300–1450)*, 2 vols (Perpignan: Presses Universitaires du Perpignan, 1998).

31 For an overview of these and other influences, see P. Burke, *History and Social Theory* (Cambridge: Polity, 1992).

32 V. Turner, *The Ritual Process: Structure and Anti-Structure* (London: Routledge, 1969).

33 C. W. Bynum, 'Women's Stories, Women's Symbols: A Critique of Victor Turner's Theory of Liminality', in eadem, *Fragmentation and Redemption* (New York: Zone, 1992), p. 32. For analyses strongly influenced by Turner, see M. James, 'Ritual, Drama and Social Body in the Late Medieval English Town', *P&P* 98 (1983): 3–29, and further discussion in Chapter 4, pp. 139–42.

34 C. Geertz, 'Religion as a Cultural System', in idem, *The Interpretation of Cultures* (London: Fontana, 1993), p. 119.

35 C. Geertz, 'Thick Description: Toward an Interpretive Theory of Culture', in idem, *Interpretation of Cultures*, pp. 3–30 (first published 1973).

36 T. Asad, 'Anthropological Conceptions of Religions: Reflections on Geertz', *Man* 18 (1983): 237–59; J. Clifford and G. E. Marcus, eds, *Writing Culture: The Poetics and Politics of Ethnography* (Berkeley, CA: University of California Press, 1986).

37 For a medieval interpretation along precisely these lines, see the case of Jean Rocas in J. H. Arnold, *Inquisition and Power: Catharism and the Confessing Subject in Medieval Languedoc* (Philadelphia, PA: University of Pennsylvania Press, 2001), pp. 173–80.

38 Davis, 'Some Tasks and Themes', p. 309.

39 Schmitt, *Ghosts*, p. 7.

40 R. Needham, *Belief, Language and Experience* (Oxford: Blackwell, 1972), pp. 1–24.

41 L.E. Boyle, 'The Fourth Lateran Council and Manuals of Popular Theology', in T. Heffernan, ed., *The Popular Literature of Medieval England* (Knoxville, TN: University of Tennessee Press, 1985), pp. 30–43.

42 S.J. Kahrl, 'Secular Life and Popular Piety in Medieval English Drama', in Heffernan, ed., *Popular Literature*, p. 86.

43 Arnold, *Inquisition and Power*; J. H. Arnold, 'The Historian as Inquisitor', *Rethinking History* 2 (1998): 379–86.

44 S. McSheffrey, 'Heresy, Orthodoxy and English Vernacular Religion, 1480–1525', *P&P* (forthcoming).

45 For further source criticism, see C. Burgess, 'Late Medieval Wills and Pious Convention: Testamentary Evidence Reconsidered', in M. Hicks, ed., *Profit, Piety and the Professions in Later Medieval England* (Gloucester: Sutton, 1990), pp. 14–33.

46 Doat 25 fo. 253v; P. Binski, *Medieval Death: Ritual and Representation* (London: British Museum Press), p. 52.

47 J. H. Arnold and K. J. Lewis, eds, *A Companion to the Book of Margery Kempe* (Cambridge: Brewer, 2004); R. Evans, 'The Book of Margery Kempe', in P. Brown, ed., *A Companion to Medieval Literature and Culture* (Oxford: Blackwell, 2004).

2 Acculturation

1 Fournier II, pp. 318–19. See E. Le Roy Ladurie, *Montaillou: Cathars and Catholics in a French Village 1294–1324*, trans. B. Bray (Harmondsworth: Penguin, 1980), pp. 261–2; Arnold, *Inquisition and Power*, pp. 180–90.

2 R. Fletcher, *The Conversion of Europe: From Paganism to Christianity 371–1386 AD* (London: Fontana, 1998).

3 See B. Hamilton, *Religion in the Medieval West* (London: Edward Arnold, 1986), pp. 58–67, and appendix pp. 200–1 for contents of the Vulgate Old Testament.

4 C. Douais, ed., *Documents sur l'ancienne province de Languedoc* (Toulouse: Privat, 1901–4), II, pp. 3–44.

5 I Cor. 5:6–11; E. Vodola, *Excommunication in the Middle Ages* (Berkeley, CA: University of California Press, 1986), pp. 3–7.

6 R. L. Benson and G. Constable, eds, *Renaissance and Renewal in the Twelfth Century* (Cambridge, MA: Harvard University Press, 1982).

7 J. W. Baldwin, *Masters, Princes and Merchants: The Social Views of Peter the Chanter and His Circle* (Princeton, NJ: Princeton University Press, 1970).

8 J. A. Brundage, *Medieval Canon Law* (Harlow: Longman, 1995).

9 Jacobus de Voragine, *The Golden Legend*, trans. W. G. Ryan (Princeton, NJ: Princeton University Press, 1993), I, pp. 129, 324–5, 369.

10 Caesarius Heisterbacensis, *Dialogus miraculorum*, ed. J. Strange (Cologne: Heberle, 1851), I, pp. 255–6 (X, 56); Thomas de Cantimpré, *Bonum universale de apibus*, ed. G. Colvenere (Douais, 1627) II, 57, 20; T. F. Crane, ed., *The* Exempla, *or Illustrative Tales from the* Sermons vulgares *of Jacques de Vitry* (London: Folklore Society, 1890), p. 7 (no. 20).

11 K. L. Jansen, *The Making of the Magdalen: Preaching and Popular Devotion in the Later Middle Ages* (Princeton, NJ: Princeton University Press, 2000), p. 29.

12 P. Brown, *The Body and Society: Men, Women and Sexual Renunciation in Early Christianity* (London: Faber & Faber, 1989).

13 Schmitt, *Ghosts*, p. 20.

14 P. Biller, *The Measure of Multitude: Population in Medieval Thought* (Oxford: Oxford University Press, 2000).

15 J. Le Goff, *The Birth of Purgatory,* trans. A. Goldhammer (London: Scolar Press, 1984); M. Rubin, *Corpus Christi: The Eucharist in Late Medieval Culture* (Cambridge: Cambridge University Press, 1991). See Chapters 4 and 5 (pp. 125–6 and 163–5 respectively).

16 C. J. Hefele, *Histoire des conciles*, trans. H. Leclerq (Paris: Letouzy et Ané, 1914), V.ii, p. 1708.

17 E. Male, *Religious Art in France in the Thirteenth Century*, 3rd edn, trans. D. Nussey (London: Dent, 1913), p. 30.

18 See M.-D. Chenu, 'The Symbolist Mentality', in idem, *Nature, Man and Society in the Twelfth Century*, ed. and trans. J. Taylor and L. K. Little (1957. Toronto: University of Toronto Press, 1997), pp. 99–145; D. d'Avray, 'Symbolism and Medieval Religious Thought', in P. Linehan and J. Nelson, eds, *The Medieval World* (London: Routledge, 2001), pp. 267–78.

19 Mansi 22, cols. 131–6, canons I, II, III, VI and VII.

20 S. Wenzel, ed., 'Robert Grosseteste's Treatise on Confession, *Deus est*', *Franciscan Studies* 30 (1970): 253 – in confession, the priest is to ask whether, if a child is baptized, he was taught the *Pater noster* and the *Credo*. J. Bossy, 'Blood and Baptism: Kinship, Community and Christianity in Western Europe from the Fourteenth to the Seventeenth Centuries', SCH 10 (1973): 129–43; idem, *Christianity in the West 1400–1700* (Oxford: Oxford University Press, 1985), pp. 118–21.

21 F. M. Powicke and C. R. Cheney, eds, *Councils and Synods, 1205–1313* (Oxford: Clarendon Press, 1964), II, p. 900; trans. in J. Shinners and W. Dohar, eds, *Pastors and the Care of Souls in Medieval England* (Notre Dame, IN: University of Notre Dame Press, 1998), pp. 127–8.

22 W. Ullmann, 'Public Welfare and Social Legislation in the Early Medieval Councils', SCH 7 (1971): 1–39.

23 The full text of Lateran IV is translated in H. Rothwell, ed., *English Historical Documents: Volume III 1189–1327* (London: Eyre & Spottiswoode, 1975), pp. 643–76; on the statement of faith, see also R. N. Swanson, *Religion and Devotion in Europe, c.1215–c.1515* (Cambridge: Cambridge University Press, 1995), pp. 21–3.

24 J. W. Baldwin, 'From the Ordeal to Confession: In Search of Lay Religion in Early Thirteenth-century France', in P. Biller and A. J. Minnis, eds, *Handling Sin: Confession in the Middle Ages* (York: York Medieval Press, 1998), p. 200.

25 M. Gibbs and J. Lang, *Bishops and Reform 1215–1272* (Oxford: Oxford University Press, 1934); R. Brentano, *Two Churches: England and Italy in the Thirteenth Century*, 2nd edn (Berkeley, CA: University of California Press, 1988), pp. 106–7.

26 A. Vauchez, *The Laity in the Middle Ages: Religious Beliefs and Devotional Practices*, trans. M. J. Schneider (1987. Notre Dame, IN: University of Notre Dame Press, 1993), p. 99.

27 For example, statutes of Lincoln 1239 (Powicke and Cheney, *Councils and Synods*, I, p. 269); statutes of Winchester 1262x65 (ibid., pp. 713–14); statutes of Albi 1254 (Mansi 23, cols 829–53); Synod of Breslau 1248 (Hefele, *Histoire des conciles*, V.ii, p. 1709).

28 Wenzel, ed., '*Deus est*', p. 287.

29 Baldwin, 'Ordeal to Confession', p. 199; but the possibility that this was in Latin is my interpretation.

30 Boyle, 'Fourth Lateran Council', p. 35.

31 John Mirk, *Festial: A Collection of Homilies*, ed. T. Erbe, EETS e.s. 96 (London: Kegan Paul, 1905), p. 282.

32 Brown, *Popular Piety*, p. 18.

33 L. Bolzoni, *The Web of Images: Vernacular Preaching from its Origins to St Bernardino da Siena*, trans. C. Preston and L. Chien (Aldershot: Ashgate, 2004), p. 159.

34 Bernard Gui, *Practica inquisitionis heretice pravitatis*, ed. C. Douais (Paris: Alphonse Picard, 1886), pp. 44–5, 84.

35 J. H. Arnold, 'The Labour of Continence: Masculinity and Clerical Virginity', in A. Bernau, R. Evans and S. Salih, eds, *Medieval Virginities* (Cardiff: University of Wales Press, 2003), pp. 102–18. See further Chapter 5, p. 145 and *passim*.

36 *Actus pontificum Cenomannis in urbe degentium*, translated in W. L. Wakefield and A. P. Evans, eds, *Heresies of the High Middle Ages* (New York: Columbia University Press, 1991), pp. 107–14.

37 H. Grundmann, *Religious Movements in the Middle Ages*, trans. S. Rowan (1935. Notre Dame, IN: University of Notre Dame Press, 1995).

38 Hefele, *Histoire des conciles*, VI.i, p. 290, c. 22.

39 See Wakefield and Evans, *Heresies*, pp. 111–12, 116–1.

40 Jocelin of Brakelond, *Chronicle of the Abbey of Bury St Edmunds*, trans. D. Greenway and J. Sayers (Oxford: Oxford University Press, 1989), p. 37. For other evidence, see G. R. Owst, *Preaching in Medieval England* (Cambridge: Cambridge University Press, 1926), pp. 156–7; T. N. Hall, 'The Early Medieval Sermon', in B. M. Kienzle, ed., *The Sermon* (Turnhout: Brepols, 2000), pp. 228–33.

41 Arguing strongly for prior establishment, see D. W. Robertson Jr., 'Frequency of Preaching in Thirteenth-Century England', *Speculum* 24 (1949): 376–88. Owst thought it less likely, except during Lent: *Preaching*, pp. 145–6.

42 On timing and contexts of preaching, see H. Leith Spencer, *English Preaching in the Late Middle Ages* (Oxford: Clarendon Press, 1993), pp. 20–33; N. Bériou, 'Les Sermons latins après 1200', in Kienzle, ed., *Sermon*, pp. 416–20; C. Delcorno, 'Medieval Preaching in Italy (1200–1500)', ibid., pp. 458–69; L. Taylor, 'French Sermons 1215–1535', ibid., pp. 721–6.

43 Schmitt, *Ghosts*, p. 123; Owst, *Preaching*, p. 196 n. 2.

44 Humbert de Romans, 'Treatise on the Formation of Preachers', in S. Tugwell, ed. and trans., *Early Dominicans: Selected Writings* (New York: Paulist Press, 1982), p. 336.

45 John H. Arnold, 'The Preaching of the Cathars', in C. Muessig, ed., *Medieval Monastic Preaching* (Leiden: Brill, 1998), p. 195. The indoor sermons were not, of course, in church but in the houses of Cathar supporters.

46 Tugwell, ed., *Early Dominicans*, p. 318.

47 Jansen, *Magdalen*, p. 146 n. 2; Owst, *Preaching*, p. 225.

48 C. H. Lawrence, *The Friars: The Impact of the Early Mendicant Movement on Western Society* (Harlow: Longman, 1994), pp. 120–1; Spencer, *English Preaching*, p. 22.

49 M. Zink, 'Les destinaires des recueils de sermons en langue vulgaire au XIIe et XIII siècles. Prédication effective et prédication dans un fauteuil', in *La Piété populaire au Moyen Âge* (Paris: Bibliothèque Nationale, 1977), p. 62.

50 K. Rivers, 'Memory and Medieval Preaching: Mnemonic Advice in the *Ars praedicandi* of Francesc Eiximenis (ca 1327–1409)', *Viator* 30 (1999): 267 and n. 77; K. J. Lewis, *The Cult of St Katherine of Alexandria in Late Medieval England* (Woodbridge: Boydell, 2000), pp. 150–1; Spencer, *English Preaching*, p. 202.

51 Owst, *Preaching*, pp. 202 (and n. 3), 14.

52 *The Book of Margery Kempe*, ed. S. B. Leech, EETS o.s. 212 (London: Oxford University Press, 1940), p. 152; Arnold, 'Preaching of the Cathars', p. 201.

53 Owst, *Preaching*, p. 56.

54 Alan of Lille, *The Art of Preaching*, trans. G. R. Evans (Kalamazoo, MI: Cistercian Studies, 1981).

55 See Chapter 5 for further discussion.

56 Jacques de Vitry, *Exempla*, p. 76 (no. clxxix).

57 Quoted in, respectively, A. Casenave, 'Langage catholique et discours cathare: Les Ecoles du Montpellier', in A. Casenave and J.-F. Lyotard, eds, *L'Art des confins: Mélanges offerts à Maurice de Gandillac* (Paris: Presses Universitaires de France, 1985), p. 140; A. Murray, 'Confession as an Historical Source in the Thirteenth Century', in R. H. C. Davis and J. M. Wallace-Hadrill, eds, *The Writing of History in the Middle Ages: Essays Presented to R. W. Southern* (Oxford: Clarendon Press, 1981), p. 298; Bolzoni, *Web of Images*, p. 19.

58 D. L. d'Avray, *The Preaching of the Friars: Sermons Diffused from Paris before 1300* (Oxford: Clarendon Press, 1985), p. 231; Humbert de Romans, collection of *exempla*, in Tugwell, ed., *Early Dominicans*, p. 373.

59 Owst, *Preaching*, p. 64.

60 Rivers, 'Memory and Medieval Preaching'. See similarly Alan of Lille, *Art of Preaching*, p. 20: 'But let the sermon be brief, less prolixity should cause boredom.'

61 Tugwell, ed., *Early Dominicans*, p. 376; Alan of Lille, *Art of Preaching*, p. 18; Owst, *Preaching*, p. 87; J. Sweet, 'Some Thirteenth-Century Sermons and Their Authors', *JEH* 4 (1953): 28.

62 Alan of Lille, *Art of Preaching*, p. 22.

63 C. W. Bynum, *Metamorphosis and Identity* (New York: Zone, 2001), p. 58.

64 R. Schnell, 'The Discourse on Marriage in the Middle Ages', *Speculum* 73 (1998): 772.

65　H. Martin, *Les Ordres mendiants en Bretagne, vers 1230–vers 1530* (Paris: CNRS, 1975), p. 317ff.; Owst, *Preaching*, p. 143 n.3; *Book of Margery Kempe*, p. 29; Fournier III, p. 231; A. Vauchez, *Sainthood in the Later Middle Ages*, trans. J. Birrell (1988. Cambridge: Cambridge University Press, 1997), p. 314.

66　A. Brandeis, ed., *Jacob's Well*, EETS o.s. 115 (London: Kegan Paul, 1900), pp. 114–15 (see further L. Carruthers, ' "Know Thyself": Criticism, Reform and the Audience of *Jacob's Well*', in J. Hamesse *et al.*, eds, *Medieval Sermons and Society: Cloister, City, University* (Louvain-La-Neuve: Fédération Internationale des Instituts d'Etudes Médiévales, 1998), pp. 219–40); Owst, *Preaching*, p. 176; P. B. Roberts, 'Preaching in/and the Medieval City', in Hamesse *et al.*, eds, *Medieval Sermons*, p. 159.

67　Arnold, *Inquisition and Power*, p. 170; Owst, *Preaching*, p. 181. See also N. Bériou, *L'Avènement des maîtres de la parole: La prédication à Paris au XIIIe siècle* (Paris: Institut d'Etudes Augustiniennes, 1998), I, pp. 248–55.

68　*The Chronicle of William of Puylaurens: The Albigensian Crusade and its Aftermath*, ed. and trans. W. A. Sibly and M. D. Sibly (Woodbridge: Boydell, 2003), p. 10; R. Muchembled, 'Witchcraft, Popular Culture, and Christianity in the Sixteenth Century, with Emphasis upon Flanders and Artois', in R. Foster and O. Ranum, eds, *Ritual, Religion and the Sacred: Selections from the Annales ESC* 7 (Baltimore, MD: Johns Hopkins University Press, 1982), p. 215.

69　Arnold, 'Preaching of the Cathars', p. 204; Owst, *Preaching*, p. 56; Roberts, 'Preaching in/and the Medieval City', p. 158; Bériou, *L'Avènement des maîtres*, I, p. 252.

70　Most recently and forcefully D. L. d'Avray, *Medieval Marriage Sermons: Mass Communication in a Culture Without Print* (Oxford: Oxford University Press, 2001), but see also Jansen, *Magdalen*, p. 6; Owst, *Preaching*, p. 42. For a nuanced picture of medieval 'media', see Menarche, *Vox Dei*.

71　Jansen, *Magdalen*, p. 8.

72　H. Edgren, ' "Primitive" Paintings: The Visual World of *Populus rusticus*', in A. Bolvig and P. Lindley, eds, *History and Images: Towards a New Iconology* (Turnhout: Brepols, 2003), pp. 301–22.

73　B. Williamson, 'Liturgical Image or Devotional Image? The London *Madonna of the Firescreen*', in C. Hourihan, ed., *Objects, Images and the Word: Art in the Service of the Liturgy* (Princeton, NJ: Princeton University Press, 2003), pp. 298–318; eadem, 'Altarpieces, Liturgy and Devotion', *Speculum* 79 (2004): 341–406.

74　L. G. Duggan, 'Was Art Really the "Book of the Illiterate"?', *Word and Image* 5: 3 (1989): 231; M. Camille, 'Seeing and Reading: Some Visual Implications of Medieval Literacy and Illiteracy', *Art History* 8: 1 (1985): 26; Jean Gerson, *Early Works*, trans. B. P. McGuire (New York: Paulist Press, 1998), p. 224, letter 18 (*c.*1404).

75　Duggan, 'Book of the Illiterate'; Celia M. Chazelle, 'Pictures, Books and the Illiterate: Pope Gregory I's Letters to Serenus of Marseille', *Word and Image* 6:2 (1990): 138–53.

76　Lewis, *Cult of St Katherine*, p. 29.

77 Mirk, *Festial*, p. 171. See Camille, 'Seeing and Reading'; M. Carruthers, *The Book of Memory: A Study of Memory in Medieval Culture* (Cambridge: Cambridge University Press, 1990), pp. 221–9.

78 Mirk, *Festial*, p. 171; see T. A. Heslop, 'Attitudes to the Visual Arts: The Evidence from Written Sources', in J. Alexander and P. Binski, eds, *Age of Chivalry: Art in Plantagenet England 1200–1400* (London: RCA, 1987), p. 29.

79 Bolzoni, *Web of Images, passim*.

80 Amy G. Remensnyder, 'The Colonization of Sacred Architecture: The Virgin Mary, Mosques, and Temples in Medieval Spain and Early Sixteenth-Century Mexico', in S. Farmer and B. H. Rosenwein, eds, *Monks and Nuns, Saints and Outcasts: Religion in Medieval Society* (Ithaca, NY: Cornell University Press, 2000), pp. 189–219.

81 V. Sekules, *Medieval Art* (Oxford: Oxford University Press, 2001), p. 76; E. Welch, *Art and Society in Italy, 1350–1500* (Oxford: Oxford University Press, 1997), pp. 140–2.

82 Sekules, *Medieval Art*, p. 94.

83 Welch, *Art and Society*, pp. 277–80.

84 A. Nilsén, 'Man and Picture: On the Function of Wall Paintings in Medieval Churches', in Bolvig and Lindley, eds, *History and Images*, pp. 336–40.

85 C. Platt, *The Parish Churches of Medieval England* (London: Secker & Warburg, 1981), p. 46.

86 Sekules, *Medieval Art*, p. 83; C. Lansing, *Power and Purity: Cathar Heresy in Medieval Italy* (Oxford: Oxford University Press, 1998), pp. 168–77.

87 C. Caldwell, 'Doctors of Souls: Inquisition and the Dominican Order, 1231–1331', unpublished PhD thesis (University of Notre Dame, IN, 2002), p. 311.

88 R. Fulton, *From Judgement to Passion: Devotion to Christ and the Virgin Mary, 800–1200* (New York: Columbia University Press, 2002).

89 Nilsén, 'Man and Picture', p. 326.

90 M. Kupfer, *Romanesque Wall Painting in Central France: The Politics of Narrative* (New Haven, CT: Yale University Press, 1993).

91 M. Camille, *Gothic Art: Visions and Revelations of the Medieval World* (London: Weidenfeld & Nicolson, 1996), p. 12.

92 M. Camille, *Image on the Edge: The Margins of Medieval Art* (London: Reaktion, 1992), p. 77; B. Abou-El Haj, 'The Urban Setting for Late Medieval Church Building: Reims and its Cathedral between 1210 and 1240', *Art History* 11 (1988): 17–41; R. Branner, 'Historical Aspects of the Reconstruction of Reims Cathedral, 1210–1241', *Speculum* 36 (1961): 34–5; N. Tanner, 'The Cathedral and the City', in I. Atherton *et al.*, eds, *Norwich Cathedral: Church, City and Diocese, 1096–1996* (London: Hambledon, 1996), pp. 259–61. See also M. Camille, 'At the Sign of the "Spinning Sow": The "Other" Chartres and Images of Everyday Life of the Medieval Street', in Bolvig and Lindley, eds, *History and Images*, pp. 249–76.

93 D. Alexandre-Bidou, 'Une foi en deux ou trois dimensions? Images et objets du faire croire à l'usage des laïcs', *Annales: Histoire, Sciences Sociales* 53:6 (1998): 1155–90.

94 K. Kamerick, *Popular Piety and Art in the Later Middle Ages: Image Worship and Idolatry in England 1350–1500* (Houndmills: Palgrave, 2002), pp. 75–105.

95 F. J. Furnivall and W. G. Store, eds, *The Tale of Beryn*, EETS e.s. 105 (1887), p. 6 (Prologue, lines 147–56). See also Heslop, 'Attitudes', p. 30.

96 P. Binski, 'The Crucifixion and the Censorship of Art around 1300', in Linehan and Nelson, eds, *Medieval World*, pp. 342–60.

97 Doat 25, fo. 56v; Welch, *Art and Society*, p. 207.

98 A. Hudson, ed., *Selections from English Wycliffite Writings* (Toronto: University of Toronto Press, 1997), p. 87.

99 *Golden Legend*, I, pp. 25–6; also Mirk, *Festial*, pp. 14–15.

100 *Reg. Langton*, p. 78.

101 Wakefield and Evans, *Heresies*, p. 72; *Reg. Langton*, p. 78.

102 Welch, *Art and Society*, p. 103.

103 S. V. Cohn, *The Cult of Remembrance and the Black Death: Six Renaissance Cities in Central Italy* (Baltimore, MD: Johns Hopkins University Press, 1992), p. 245.

104 W. Kemp, *The Narratives of Stained Glass Windows* (Cambridge: Cambridge University Press, 1997), pp. 71–2; Doat 25 fos 15v–16r.

105 M. B. Parkes, 'The Literacy of the Laity', in Parkes, *Scribes, Scripts and Readers: Studies in the Communication, Presentation and Dissemination of Medieval Texts* (London: Hambledon, 1991), pp. 275–97; Clanchy, *Written Record*; Ralph V. Turner, 'The *Miles Literatus* in Twelfth- and Thirteenth-Century England: How Rare a Phenomenon?', *AHR* 83 (1978): 928–45.

106 J. K. Hyde, 'Some Uses of Literacy in Venice and Florence in the Thirteenth and Fourteenth Centuries', in Hyde, *Literacy and Its Uses: Studies on Late Medieval Italy*, ed. Daniel Waley (Manchester: Manchester University Press, 1993), pp. 112–35; d'Avray, *Preaching*, p. 36.

107 J. Jenkins, 'Reading and *The Book of Margery Kempe*', in Arnold and Lewis, eds, *Companion*, pp. 113–28; M. Aston, 'Lollardy and Literacy', in eadem, *Lollards and Reformers: Images and Literacy in Late Medieval Religion* (London: Hambledon, 1984), p. 199.

108 L. E. Boyle, 'Innocent III and Vernacular Versions of Scripture', in K. Walsh and D. Wood, eds, *The Bible in the Medieval World: Essays in Memory of Beryl Smalley*, SCH subsidia 4 (Oxford: Basil Blackwell, 1985), p. 98.

109 P. Biller, 'The Cathars of Languedoc and Written Materials', in P. Biller and A. Hudson, eds, *Heresy and Literacy, 1000–1530* (Cambridge: Cambridge University Press, 1994), pp. 61–82.

110 M. Richter, 'Latina lingua – sacra seu vulgaris?', in W. Lourdaux and D. Verhelst, eds, *The Bible and Medieval Culture* (Leuven: Leuven University Press, 1979), pp. 16–34; C. R. Sneddon, 'The "Bible du XIIIe siècle": Its Medieval Public in the Light of its Manuscript Tradition', in ibid., pp. 127–40.

111 B. Millett, 'Women in No Man's Land: English Recluses and the Development of Vernacular Literature in the Twelfth and Thirteenth Centuries', in C. M. Meale, ed., *Women and Literature in Britain 1150–1500* (Cambridge: Cambridge University Press, 1993), pp. 86–103; E. Robertson, *Early English Devotional Prose and the Female Audience* (Knoxville, TN: University of Tennessee Press, 1990).

112 Jansen, *Magdalen*, p. 8; Spencer, *English Preaching*, p. 36; Owst, *Preaching*, pp. 53, 279.

113 J. Shaw, 'The Influence of Canonical and Episcopal Reform on Popular Books of Instruction', in Heffernan, ed., *Popular Literature*, pp. 44–60.

114 M. Milway, 'Forgotten Best-Sellers from the Dawn of the Reformation', in R. J. Bast and A. C. Gow, eds, *Continuity and Change: The Harvest of Late Medieval and Reformation History* (Leiden: Brill, 2000), pp. 113–42.

115 Baldwin, 'Ordeal to Confession', p. 200; Richard Kieckhefer, *Magic in the Middle Ages* (Cambridge: Cambridge University Press, 1989), p. 108.

116 A. C. Bartlett, *Male Authors, Female Readers: Representation and Subjectivity in Middle English Devotional Reading* (Ithaca, NY: Cornell University Press, 1995), p. 18; J. M. Gellrich, *The Idea of the Book in the Middle Ages: Language Theory, Mythology and Fiction* (Ithaca, NY: Cornell University Press, 1985); Carruthers, *Book of Memory*, p. 71.

117 J. Coleman, *Public Reading and the Reading Public in Late Medieval England and France* (Cambridge: Cambridge University Press, 1996).

118 See Spencer, *English Preaching*, p. 197.

119 Jordan of Saxony, *On the Beginnings of the Order of Preachers*, trans. S. Tugwell (Chicago: Parable, 1982), p. 7.

120 Council of Toulouse 1229, c. 14 (Mansi 23, cols 191–204); Council of Tarragona 1234, c. 2 (ibid., cols 329–32); N. Watson, 'Censorship and Cultural Change in Late-Medieval England: Vernacular Theology, the Oxford Translation Debate, and Arundel's Constitutions of 1409', *Speculum* 70 (1990): 821–64.

121 A. Hudson, *The Premature Reformation: Wycliffite Texts and Lollard History* (Oxford: Clarendon Press, 1988), p. 231; McSheffrey, 'Heresy, Orthodoxy and English Vernacular Religion'.

122 Stock, *Implications of Literacy*, pp. 88–151.

123 F. Riddy, ' "Women Talking About the Things of God": A Late Medieval Subculture', in Meale, ed., *Women and Literature*, p. 110; Coleman, *Public Reading*, p. 29.

124 H. Harrod, 'Extracts from Early Wills in the Norwich Registries', *Norfolk Archaeology* 55 (1855): 335; Spencer, *English Preaching*, p. 161; J. R. H. Weaver and A. Beardwood, eds, *Some Oxfordshire Wills, Proved in the Prerogative Court of Canterbury, 1393–1550*, Oxfordshire Record Society 39 (1958), pp. 42–3; Bartlett, *Male Authors, Female Readers*, p. 13.

125 Bartlett, *Male Authors, Female Readers*, pp. 22–3.

126 J. K. Hyde, 'Italian Pilgrim Literature in the Late Middle Ages', in idem, *Literacy and Its Uses*, pp. 136–61.

127 M. Populer, 'La culture religieuse des laïcs à la fin du Moyen Âge: le carnet des notes d'un bourgeois de Francfort (ca. 1470–1482)', *Moyen Âge* 102 (1996): 479–527; 'A Fifteenth-Century English Yeoman's Commonplace Book', in J. Shinners, ed. and trans., *Medieval Popular Religion 1000–1500: A Reader* (Peterborough, ON: Broadview Press, 1997), pp. 335–76.

128 Shinners, ed., *Medieval Popular Religion*, p. 357.

129 R. N. Swanson, 'Medieval Liturgy and Theatre: The Props', in SCH 28 (1992), pp. 239–54; D. Bevington, ed., *Medieval Drama* (Boston: Houghton Mifflin, 1975), pp. 3–8, 21–4. For further problems defining 'drama', see C. Symes, 'The Appearance of Early Vernacular Plays: Forms, Functions, and the Future of Medieval Theater', *Speculum* 77 (2002): 778–831.

130 M. Twycross, 'Some Approaches to Dramatic Festivity, Especially Processions', in M. Twycross, ed., *Festive Drama* (Cambridge: Brewer, 1996), p. 5.

131 B. Bolton, 'Message, Celebration, Offering: The Place of Twelfth- and early Thirteenth-Century Liturgical Drama as "Missionary Theatre"', in SCH 35 (1999), p. 97.

132 C. Sponsler, 'Drama and Piety: Margery Kempe', in Arnold and Lewis, eds, *Companion*, pp. 142–3.

133 Symes, 'Appearance of Early Vernacular Plays', p. 781.

134 Cadwgan, *De modo confitendi*, in J. Goering and H. Pryce, 'The *De modo confitendi* of Cadwgan, bishop of Bangor', *Mediaeval Studies* 62 (2000): 22 (l. 175ff); E. C. Rodgers, *Discussions of Holidays in the Later Middle Ages* (New York: Columbia University Press, 1940), p. 33; N. Orme, 'Children and the Church in Medieval England', *JEH* 45 (1994): 565; A. MacKay, 'The Hispanic-*Converso* Predicament', *TRHS*, 5th ser., 35 (1985): 175 n. 75.

135 Clanchy, *Written Record*, p. 111–12; idem, 'Images of Ladies with Prayer Books: What Do They Mean?', SCH 38 (2004): 106–22; L. R. Poos, 'Social History and the Book of Hours', in R. S. Wieck, ed, *The Book of Hours in Medieval Art and Life* (London: Sotheby's, 1988), pp. 33–8; P. Cullum and P. J. P. Goldberg, 'How Margaret Blackburn Taught Her Daughters: Reading Devotional Instruction in a Book of Hours', in J. Wogan-Browne *et al.*, eds, *Medieval Women: Texts and Contexts in Late Medieval Britain* (Turnhout: Brepols, 2000), pp. 217–36.

3 Intercession

1 Miracles of Armanno Punzilupo, in G. Zanella, *Itinerari ereticali: Patari e catari tra Rimini e Verona* (Rome: Nella Sede dell'Istituto, 1986), appendix I, p. 78. See also Lansing, *Power and Purity*, pp. 92–6.

2 Zanella, *Itinerari ereticali*, pp. 74, 82–3. For other examples of saints curing possession, see M. Goodich, 'Battling the Devil in Rural Europe: Late Medieval Miracle Collections', in J.-P. Massaut and M.-E. Henneau, eds, *La Christianisation des campagnes* (Brussels: Institut Historique Belge de Rome, 1996), pp. 139–52.

3 P. Brown, 'The Rise and Function of the Holy Man in Late Antiquity', in idem, *Society and the Holy in Late Antiquity* (Berkeley, CA: University of California Press, 1982), pp. 103–52; P. Brown, 'Arbiters of the Holy: The Christian Holy Man in Late Antiquity', in idem, *Authority and the Sacred: Aspects of the Christianization of the Roman World* (Cambridge: Cambridge University Press, 1995), pp. 55–78.

4 Vauchez, *Laity*, pp. 6–7, *Sainthood*, p. 17.

5 R. Finucane, *Miracles and Pilgrims: Popular Beliefs in Medieval England* (1977. London: Macmillan, 1995), p. 28.

6 Innes, *State and Society*, p. 30.

7 Zanella, *Itinerari ereticali*, pp. 87, 72.

8 Vauchez, *Laity*, p. 172; Weinstein and Bell, *Saints and Society*; but see A. Kleinberg, *Prophets in Their Own Country: Living Saints and the Making of Sainthood in the Later Middle Ages* (Chicago: University of Chicago Press, 1992), pp. 10–11.

9 A. Vauchez, 'Lay People's Sanctity in Western Europe: Evolution of a Pattern (Twelfth and Thirteenth Centuries)', in R. Blumenfeld-Kosinski and T. Szell, eds, *Images of Sainthood in Medieval Europe* (Ithaca, NY: Cornell University Press, 1991), p. 31.

10 E. Durkheim, *The Elementary Forms of the Religious Life*, trans. J. W. Swain (London: George Allen & Unwin, 1915), pp. 316–17; see Lansing, *Power and Purity*, p. 11.

11 M. Goodich, 'The Politics of Canonization in the Thirteenth Century: Lay and Mendicant Saints', *Church History* 44 (1975): 294–307.

12 Vauchez, *Sainthood*, pp. 158–217.

13 Vauchez, *Sainthood*, p. 117.

14 For context, see L. Bitel, *Isle of the Saints: Monastic Settlement and Christian Community in Early Ireland* (Ithaca, NY: Cornell University Press, 1990).

15 H. Leyser, *Hermits and the New Monasticism: A Study of Religious Communities in Western Europe, 1000–1150* (London: Macmillan, 1984).

16 Jansen, *Magdalen*, p. 289.

17 L. Georgianna, *The Solitary Self: Individuality in the* Ancrene Wisse (Cambridge, MA: Harvard University Press, 1981), p. 57.

18 Iogna-Prat, *Order and Exclusion*, p. 69.

19 Jacques de Vitry, *Exempla*, p. 21 (no. 53).

20 L. Pellegrini, 'Female Religious Experience and Society in Thirteenth-Century Italy', in Farmer and Rosenwein, eds, *Monks and Nuns, Saints and Outcasts*, pp. 97–122.

21 M.D. Lambert, *Medieval Heresy: Popular Movements from the Gregorian Reform to the Reformation*, 3rd edn (Oxford: Blackwell, 2002), pp. 202–3; R.E. Lerner, *The Heresy of the Free Spirit in the Later Middle Ages* (Notre Dame, IN: University of Notre Dame Press, 1972), pp. 68–78.

22 Jean Gerson, *Early Works*, pp. 334–64; D. Elliott, 'Seeing Double: John Gerson, the Discernment of Spirits, and Joan of Arc', *AHR* 107 (2002): 26–54.

23 For a contentiously iconoclastic view, see L. J. R. Milis, *Angelic Monks and Earthly Men: Monasticism and its Meaning to Medieval Society* (Woodbridge: Boydell, 1992).

24 J. G. Sperling, *Convents and the Body Politic in Late Renaissance Venice* (Chicago: University of Chicago Press, 1999).

25 Jansen, *Magdalen*, pp. 136–7.

26 W. Simons, *Cities of Ladies: Beguine Communities in the Medieval Low Countries, 1200–1565* (Philadelphia, PA: University of Pennsylvania Press, 2001), p. 116.

27 B. Cazelles, 'Introduction', in Blumenfeld-Kozinski and Szell, eds, *Images*, pp. 2–3.

28 Bartlett, *Male Authors, Female Readers*, p. 118; Vauchez, *Sainthood*, pp. 532–3.

29 In Margery's case, the models clearly included St Bridget of Sweden, St Katherine of Alexandria and St Margaret of Antioch. See K. J. Lewis, 'Margery Kempe and Saint-Making in Later Medieval England', in Arnold and Lewis, eds, *Companion*, pp. 195–215.

30 *AASS*, March I, pp. 502–32.

31 *AASS*, March III, pp. 398–439.

32 C. W. Bynum, 'Jesus as Mother and Abbot as Mother: Some Themes in Twelfth-Century Cistercian Writing', in eadem, *Jesus as Mother: Studies in the Spirituality of the High Middle Ages* (Berkeley, CA: University of California Press, 1982), pp. 110–69.

33 G. Dickson, 'The Flagellants of 1260 and the Crusades', *JMH* 15 (1989): 227–67.

34 G. Klaniczay, 'Fashionable Beards and Heretics' Rags', in idem *The Uses of Supernatural Power: The Transformation of Popular Religion in Medieval and Early Modern Europe*, trans. S. Singerman (Princeton, NJ: Princeton University Press, 1990), pp. 51–78.

35 Humbert de Romans, 'Treatise on the Formation of the Preachers', in Tugwell, ed., *Early Dominicans*, p. 286; Jordan of Saxony, *On the Beginnings of the Order of Preachers*, trans. Tugwell, p. 6.

36 Account by Jordan of Giano, 1262; extracted in G. G. Coulton, ed. and trans., *Social Life in Britain from the Conquest to the Reformation* (Cambridge: Cambridge University Press, 1956), pp. 239–46.

37 Arnold, *Inquisition and Power*, pp. 144, 160–1; Martin, *Ordres mendiants*, p. 173.

38 J. Duvernoy, 'Les Albigeois dans la vie sociale et économique de leur temps', *Annales de l'Institut d'Etudes Occitanes* (1962–63): 64–73; A. Roach, 'The Cathar Economy', *Reading Medieval Studies* 12 (1986): 51–71.

39 Zanella, *Itinerari ereticali*, p. 66.

40 Zanella, *Itinerari ereticali*, pp. 64, 50, 56, 49.

41 Vanchez, *Sainthood*, pp. 405–6; Kleinberg, *Prophets*, pp. 31–6.

42 M. Bull, ed. and trans., *The Miracles of Our Lady of Rocamadour: Analysis and Translation* (Woodbridge: Boydell, 1999), p. 13; M. Carrasco, 'Sanctity and Experience in Pictorial Hagiography: Two Illustrated Lives of Saints from Romanesque France', in Blumenfeld-Kosinski and Szell, eds, *Images*, pp. 33–66.

43 A. Vauchez, 'Saints admirables et saints imitables: Les functions de l'hagiographie ont-elles changé aux derniers siècles du moyen âge?', in *Les Fonctions des saints dans le monde occidental (IIIe–XIIe siècle)* (Palas Farnèse: Ecole Française de Rome, 1991), pp. 161–72.

44 *Life of Saint Paula* ll. 1222–8, in B. Cazelles, ed. and trans., *The Lady as Saint: A Collection of French Hagiographic Romances of the Thirteenth Century* (Philadelphia, PA: University of Pennsylvania Press, 1991), p. 288.

45 Jansen, *Magdalen*, p. 147.

46 Lewis, *Cult of St Katherine*, p. 154; K. J. Lewis, 'Model Girls? Virgin-Martyrs and the Training of Young Women in Late Medieval England', in K. J. Lewis *et al.*, eds, *Young Medieval Women* (Stroud: Sutton, 1999), pp. 25–46; K. J. Lewis,

'Pilgrimage and the Cult of St Katherine of Alexandria in the later middle ages', in
J. Stopford, ed., *Medieval Pilgrimage* (York: York Medieval Press, 1999),
pp. 145–60.

47 Vauchez, *Sainthood*, p. 406.

48 A. Vauchez, 'La religion populaire dans la France méridionale au XIVe siècle,
d'après les procès de canonisation', *CdF* 11 (1976), p. 100; Finucane, *Miracles
and Pilgrims*, pp. 54–5; Gurevich, *Medieval Popular Culture*, pp. 39–77.

49 Vauchez, *Sainthood*, pp. 148–51, 425.

50 William of Newburgh, *Historia*, p. 655; Finucane, *Miracles and Pilgrims*,
pp. 131–5; J. M. Theilmann, 'Political Canonization and Political Symbolism in
Medieval England', *Journal of British Studies* 29 (1990): 241–66. On Longbeard,
see J. Gillingham, 'The Historian as Judge: William of Newburgh and Hubert
Walter', *English Historical Review* 119 (2004): 1275–87.

51 G. I. Langmuir, 'Thomas of Monmouth: Detector of Ritual Murder', *Speculum* 59
(1984): 820–46; but see also J. M. McCulloh, 'Jewish Ritual Murder: William of
Norwich, Thomas of Monmouth, and the Early Dissemination of the Myth',
Speculum 72 (1997): 698–740. Further discussion in Chapter 4, pp. 118–22.

52 Vauchez, *Sainthood*, p. 131 n. 10.

53 K. Foster, ed. and trans., *The Life of St Thomas Aquinas: Biographical
Documents* (London: Longmans, Green & Co, 1959), p. 84.

54 Jean de Joinville, 'Life of Saint Louis', in *Chronicles of the Crusades*, trans.
M. R. B. Shaw (Harmondsworth: Penguin, 1963), p. 314.

55 Swanson, *Religion and Devotion*, p. 163; P. Geary, 'Humiliation of Saints', in
S. Wilson, ed., *Saints and Their Cults: Studies in Religious Sociology, Folklore and
History* (Cambridge: Cambridge University Press, 1983), pp. 123–40.

56 Vauchez, *Sainthood*, p. 446. But see also, for evidence of less focus upon relics in
Brittany and Wales, J. M. H. Smith, 'Oral and Written: Saints, Miracles, and
Relics in Brittany, c. 850–1250', *Speculum* 65 (1990): 309–43.

57 Vauchez, *Sainthood*, p. 134 n. 18.

58 J. Paul, 'Miracles et mentalité religieuse populaire à Marseille au début du XIVe
siècle', *CdF* 11 (1976), 69–70.

59 Vauchez, *Sainthood*, p. 453.

60 Finucane, *Miracles and Pilgrims*, p. 93; *AASS*, March III, p. 437.

61 Vauchez, *Sainthood*, p. 461; Mirk, *Festial*, pp. 241–2.

62 V. Reinburg, 'Praying to Saints in the Late Middle Ages', in S. Sticca, ed., *Saints:
Studies in Hagiography* (Binghamton, NY: Medieval and Renaissance Texts and
Studies, 1996), pp. 269–82; Duffy, *Stripping of the Altars*, p. 161.

63 Finucane, *Miracles and Pilgrims*, p. 142.

64 P. A. Sigal, 'Un aspect du culte des saints: le châtiment divin aux XIe et XIIe
siècles d'après la littérature hagiographique du Midi de la France', *CdF* 11 (1976),
pp. 39–59.

65 Marandat, *Le souci de l'au-delà*, II, p. 553.

66 Brentano, *Two Churches*, p. 153; D. Herlihy, 'Tuscan Names, 1200–1530', in
idem, *Women, Family and Society in Medieval Europe* (Providence, RI: Berghahn,
1995), pp. 346–51.

67 Finucane, *Miracles and Pilgrims*, p. 154; Coulton, *Social Life in Britain*, pp. 221–6 (the compiler – Peter, prior of Holy Trinity, London – was relating a family story about his own grandfather).

68 Vauchez, *Sainthood*, p. 139.

69 V. R. Bainbridge, *Gilds in the Medieval Countryside: Social and Religious Change in Cambridgeshire c.1350–1558* (Woodbridge: Boydell, 1996), pp. 61–2.

70 Vauchez, *Sainthood*, p. 451.

71 Arnold, *Inquisition and Power*, pp. 127–8; Robert Mannyng of Brunne, *Handlyng Synne*, ed. I. Sullens (Binghamton, NY: Medieval and Renaissance Texts and Studies, 1983), p. 280, ll. 11275–8.

72 Brentano, *Two Churches*, p. 195; *Golden Legend*, I, p. 38.

73 Duffy, *Stripping of the Altars*, p. 326; B. Hamilton, 'The Cathars and Christian Perfection', in P. Biller and B. Dobson, eds, *The Medieval Church: Universities, Heresy, and the Religious Life. Essays in Honour of Gordon Leff*, SCH subsidia 11 (Woodbridge: Boydell & Brewer, 1999), p. 21; *Book of Margery Kempe*, p. 253.

74 M. Roquebert, 'Le Catharisme comme tradition dans la "familia" languedo-cienne', *CdF* 20 (1985), p. 226ff; M. Lambert, *The Cathars* (Oxford: Blackwell, 1998), p. 152. See also Chapter 6.

75 M. Bull, *Knightly Piety and the Lay Response to the First Crusade: The Limousin and Gascony, c.970–c.1130* (Oxford: Clarendon Press, 1993), particularly pp. 166–71.

76 D. Webb, ed., *Pilgrims and Pilgrimage in the Medieval West* (London: I.B. Tauris, 2001), pp. 117, 157, 159. See further Chapter 6, pp. 215–16.

77 Jacques de Vitry, *Exempla*, p. 47 (no. 102).

78 Finucane, *Miracles and Pilgrims*, p. 59.

79 L. Smoller, 'Defining the Boundaries of the Natural in Fifteenth-Century Brittany: The Inquest into the Miracles of Saint Vincent Ferrer', *Viator* 28 (1997): 333–59.

80 D. Webb, *Medieval European Pilgrimage* (Houndmills: Palgrave, 2002), p. 65; S. Farmer, *Surviving Poverty in Medieval Paris: Gender, Ideology, and the Daily Lives of the Poor* (Ithaca, NY: Cornell University Press, 2002), p. 52.

81 Doat 25 fo. 249r–v; see Arnold, *Inquisition and Power*, p. 135.

82 See similarly for a later period, D. Gentilcore, *Healers and Healing in Early Modern Italy* (Manchester: Manchester University Press, 1998).

83 Doat 25 fo. 56r.

84 Webb, *Medieval European Pilgrimage*, p. 52.

85 See S. Reynolds, *Kingdoms and Communities in Western Europe 900–1300* (Oxford: Clarendon Press, 1984), pp. 101–54.

86 *Handlyng Synne*, pp. 24–6, l. 877ff.; Webb, *Medieval European Pilgrimage*, p. 34; Vauchez, *Sainthood*, p. 462.

87 D. Webb, *Patrons and Defenders: The Saints in the Italian City States* (London: I.B. Tauris, 1996), p. 17.

88 For example, Doat 23 fo. 91r; Doat 25 fos 5r, 210v; A. Pales-Gobilliard, ed., *Le Livre des sentences de l'inquisiteur Bernard Gui 1308–1323* (Paris: CNRS, 2002), I, p. 778; Fournier I, p. 204.

89 Fournier III, p. 307

90 Le Roy Ladurie, *Montaillou*, pp. 31–3.

91 Schmitt, *The Holy Greyhound*; *Reg. Sutton*, III, p. 37; K. L. French, *The People of the Parish: Community Life in a Late Medieval English Diocese* (Philadelphia, PA: University of Pennsylvania Press, 2001), p. 176; Kieckhefer, *Magic*, p. 181; D. Webb, *Pilgrimage in Medieval England* (London: Hambledon and London, 2000), pp. 141–79. For earlier examples that do not appear to have attracted censure, see Smith, 'Oral and Written'.

92 Arnold, *Inquisition and Power*, p. 203; Council of Bordeaux 1234, c. 49, in O. Pontal, ed., *Les Statuts synodaux français du XIIIe siècle* (Paris: Bibliothèque Nationale, 1983), II, p. 68.

93 Doat 25, fos 122v–123r; Doat 26, fo. 25r.

94 D. Watt, *Secretaries of God: Women Prophets in Late Medieval and Early Modern England* (Cambridge: Boydell, 1997).

95 S. Wilson, *The Magical Universe: Everyday Ritual and Magic in Pre-Modern Europe* (London: Hambledon and London, 2000), p. 68. See also Gurevich, *Medieval Popular Culture*, p. 82.

96 J. Goering and P.J. Payer, eds, 'The *Summa Penitentie Fratrum Predicatorum*: A Thirteenth-Century Confessional Formulary', *Mediaeval Studies* 55 (1993): 35, ll. 169–73; John of God, *Liber penitentiarius*, ed. P. J. Payer, 'The Origins and Development of the Later Canones Penitentiales', *Mediaeval Studies* 61 (1999): 104; Cadwgan, '*De modo confitiendi*': 21–2; Synodal book of Sisteron 1225x35, c. 40 (Pontal, ed., *Statuts synodaux*, II, p. 202).

97 J. H. Mundy, 'Village, Town, and City in the Region of Toulouse', in J. A. Raftis, ed., *Pathways to Medieval Peasants* (Toronto: Pontifical Institute of Medieval Studies, 1981), pp. 161–2; *Register of Bishop Philip Repingdon, 1405–1419*, ed. M. Archer, Lincoln Record Society 74 (1982), III, p. 195; Kieckhefer, *Magic*, pp. 59–60.

98 Jolly, *Popular Religion*, pp. 6–8 (also Kieckhefer, *Magic*, p. 58); J. Goering, 'The *Summa de Penitentia* of Magister Serlo', *Mediaeval Studies* 38 (1976): 26.

99 Kieckhefer, *Magic*, pp. 4–5. See also pp. 79–80: 'misuse' of holy objects was more likely to be seen as 'superstition' than magic.

100 Kieckhefer, *Magic*, p. 56. See further K. Thomas, *Religion and the Decline of Magic* (London: Penguin, 1973); Wilson, *Magical Universe*; R. Kieckhefer, 'The Holy and the Unholy: Sainthood, Witchcraft, and Magic in Late Medieval Europe', in S. L. Waugh and P. D. Diehl, eds, *Christendom and its Discontents: Exclusion, Persecution, and Rebellion, 1000–1500* (Cambridge: Cambridge University Press, 1996), pp. 310–37.

101 V.I.J. Flint, *The Rise of Magic in Early Medieval Europe* (Oxford: Clarendon Press, 1991).

102 G. R. Owst, '*Sortilegium* in English Homiletic Literature of the Fourteenth Century', in J. Conway Davies, ed., *Studies Presented to Sir Hilary Jenkinson* (London: Oxford University Press, 1957), pp. 273–4.

103 M. Derwich, 'Les Bénédictins et la christianisation des campagnes en Pologne', in Massaut and Henneau, eds, *Christianisation*, p. 113.

104 Kieckhefer, *Magic*, pp. 69–75.

105 N. Cohn, *Europe's Inner Demons: An Inquiry Inspired by the Great Witch Hunt* (St Albans: Paladin, 1976); W. Stephens, *Demon Lovers: Witchcraft, Sex, and the Crisis of Belief* (Chicago: University of Chicago Press, 2002); M. D. Bailey, *Battling Demons: Witchcraft, Heresy, and Reform in the Late Middle Ages* (University Park, PA: Pennsylvania State University Press, 2003).

106 J. M. Marti i Bonet, ed., 'Els processos de les Visites Pastorals del primer any de pontificat de Ponç de Gualba (a. 1303)', in J. M. Marti i Bonet *et al.*, eds, *Processos de l'Arxiu Diocesa de Barcelona* (Barcelona: n.p., 1984), pp. 64, 109–11.

107 Webb, *Medieval European Pilgrimage*, pp. 32–3.

108 Webb, ed., *Pilgrims and Pilgrimage*, p. 117.

109 Hugh of Poitiers, *The Vézelay Chronicle of Hugh of Poitiers*, ed. and trans. J. Scott et al. (Binghamton, NY: SUNY Press, 1988), pp. 181, 319–31; B. Abou-el-Haj, 'The Audiences for the Medieval Cult of Saints', *Gesta* 30 (1991): 7.

110 Webb, *Pilgrimage in Medieval England*, p. 189.

111 Webb, *Medieval European Pilgrimage*, pp. 51, 155.

112 *Register of John de Grandisson, Bishop of Exeter (1327–1369)*, ed. F. C. Hingeston-Randolph (London: G. Bell, 1899), III, p. 1232; see Webb, *Pilgrimage in Medieval England*, p. 154.

113 Webb, ed., *Pilgrims and Pilgrimage*, p. 132

114 J. H. Arnold, '"A Man Takes an Ox by the Horn and a Peasant by the Tongue": Literacy, Orality and Inquisition in Medieval Languedoc', in S. Rees-Jones, ed., *Learning and Literacy in Medieval England and Abroad* (Turnhout: Brepols, 2003), pp. 42–3.

115 Brown, 'Rise and Function'; Brown, 'Arbiters of the Holy'.

116 P. Biller, 'Cathar Peace-Making', in S. Ditchfield, ed., *Christianity and Community in the West: Essays for John Bossy* (Aldershot: Ashgate, 2001), pp. 1–23; P. Biller, '*Multum ieiunantes et se castigantes*: medieval Waldensian Asceticism', in idem, *The Waldenses, 1170–1530*, Variorum reprints (Aldershot: Ashgate, 2001), p. 77; S. J. Ridyard, 'Functions of a Twelfth-Century Recluse Revisited: The Case of Godric of Finchale', in R. Gameson and H. Leyser, eds, *Belief and Culture in the Middle Ages: Studies Presented to Henry Mayr-Harting* (Oxford: Oxford University Press, 2001), pp. 236–50.

117 V. I. J. Flint, 'The Saint and the Operation of the Law: Reflections Upon the Miracles of St Thomas Cantilupe', in Gameson and Leyser, eds, *Belief and Culture*, pp. 342–57.

118 N.B. Warren, *Spiritual Economies: Female Monasticism in Later Medieval England* (Philadelphia, PA: University of Pennsylvania Press, 2001), pp. 111–33.

119 Vauchez, *Sainthood*, p. 182.

120 G. M. Gibson, 'Saint Anne and the Religion of Childbed: Some East Anglian Texts and Talismans', in K. Ashley and P. Sheingorn, eds, *Interpreting Cultural Symbols: Saint Anne in Late Medieval Society* (Athens, GA: University of Georgia Press, 1990), pp. 100–1.

121 Abou-el-Haj, 'Audiences', pp. 7–9.

122 P. A. Haywood, 'Demystifying the Role of Sanctity', in J. Howard-Johnston and P.A. Haywood, eds, *The Cult of Saints in Late Antiquity and the Middle Ages* (Oxford: Oxford University Press, 1999), p. 130.

123 Vauchez, *Laity*, pp. 141–52.

4 Community

1 N. Terpstra, *Lay Confraternities and Civic Religion in Renaissance Bologna* (Cambridge: Cambridge University Press, 1995), pp. 26–7.

2 S. L. Parker and L. R. Poos, eds, 'A Consistory Court from the Diocese of Rochester, 1363–4', *English Historical Review* 106 (1991): 658–9.

3 M. Rubin, 'Small Groups: Identity and Solidarity in the Late Middle Ages', in J. Kermode, ed., *Enterprise and Individuals in Fifteenth-Century England* (Gloucester: Sutton, 1991), p. 134.

4 For example, Reynolds, *Kingdoms and Communities*; D. G. Shaw, *The Creation of a Community: The City of Wells in the Middle Ages* (Oxford: Clarendon Press, 1993), particularly pp. 2–8; French, *People of the Parish*.

5 Terpstra, *Lay Confraternities*, pp. 24–7.

6 Vauchez, *Laity*, p. 9; Reynolds, *Kingdoms and Communities*, pp. 81–90; G. Rosser, 'The Cure of Souls in English Towns before 1000', in J. Blair and R. Sharpe, eds, *Pastoral Care Before the Parish* (Leicester: Leicester University Press, 1992), pp. 267–84.

7 Innes, *State and Society*, pp. 42–3; Fletcher, *Conversion*, p. 468ff.

8 J. Kloczowski, 'Les Paroisses en Bohème, en Hongrie et en Pologne (X–XIII siècles)', in *Le Istituzioni ecclesiastiche della 'societàs christiana' dei secoli XI–XII: Diocesi, pievi, parrochie*, Miscellanea del Centro di Studi Medievali, VIII (Milan: Università Catholica del Sacro Cuore, 1977), pp. 187–98.

9 Reynolds, *Kingdoms and Communities*, pp. 93–4.

10 For example, Customs of the diocese of Salisbury, 1228x56; Canterbury decree 1295 (Powicke and Cheney, eds, *Councils and Synods*, I, pp. 510–51; II, pp. 1385–6; trans. Shinners and Dohar, *Pastors*, pp. 222–6, 219–20); Synod of Arras 1280x90, cc. 69, 70 (J. Avril, ed., *Les Statuts synodaux français du XIIIe siècle, t. IV: Les statuts synodaux de l'ancienne province de Reims* (Paris: CTHS, 1995), p. 199).

11 C. Dyer, *Standards of Living in the Later Middle Ages: Social Change in England c.1200–1520* (Cambridge: Cambridge University Press, 1989), pp. 109–87.

12 *Handlyng Synne*, p. 233, l. 9325.

13 *Reg. Sutton*, III, pp. 39, 153, 110; IV, pp. 21–2.

14 Arnold, *Inquisition and Power*, pp. 184–5.

15 A. Teulet, ed., *Layettes du Trésor des Chartes* (Paris: Plon, 1866), II, pp. 306–9, at p. 308 (no. 2428), here dated as 1235 but see J. H. Mundy, 'The Parishes of Toulouse from 1150 to 1250', *Traditio* 46 (1991): 186.

16 See generally G. Constable, 'Resistance to Tithes in the Middle Ages', *JEH* 13 (1962): 172–85.

17 On indulgences, see Swanson, *Religion and Devotion*, pp. 217–25.

18 A. K. McHardy, 'Careers and Disappointments in the Late-Medieval Church: Some English Evidence', SCH 26 (1989), pp. 111–30.

19 Fletcher, *Conversion*, p. 441.

20 Mansi 24, col. 510, c. 24; Powicke and Cheney, eds, *Councils and Synods* II, p. 601; *Oculis sacerdotis*, in Shinners, ed. and trans., *Medieval Popular Religion*, p. 20.

21 R. Fossier, ed., *Chartes de coutume en Picardie (XI–XIIIe siècle)* (Paris: Bibliothèque Nationale, 1974), pp. 483–4.

22 See further D. Dymond, 'God's Disputed Acre', *JEH* 50 (1999): 464–97; E. Duffy, *The Voices of Morebath: Reformation and Rebellion in an English Village* (New Haven, CT: Yale University Press, 2001), pp. 6, 57 and *passim*.

23 *Handlyng Synne*, p. 225, ll. 8991–8.

24 T. Wright, ed., *The Book of the Knight of La Tour Landry*, EETS o.s. 33 (London: Trübner, 1868), pp. 51–2 (Ch. 35); see further D. Elliott, 'Sex in Holy Places: An Exploration of a Medieval Fantasy', in eadem, *Fallen Bodies: Pollution, Sexuality and Demonology in the Middle Ages* (Philadelphia, PA: University of Pennsylvania Press, 1999), pp. 61–80.

25 A. Murray, 'Medieval Christmas', *History Today* 36: 12 (December 1986): 35.

26 S. Shahar, 'The Boy Bishop's Feast: A Case-Study in Church Attitudes towards Children in the High and Late Middle Ages', SCH 31 (1994), pp. 243–60; P. H. Greenfield, 'Festive Drama at Christmas in Aristocratic Households', in Twycross, ed., *Festive Drama*, pp. 34–40.

27 *Dives and Pauper*, ed. P. H. Barum, EETS o.s. 275, 280 (Oxford: Oxford University Press, 1976–1980), I, p. 157.

28 For all of the above, see R. Hutton, *The Rise and Fall of Merry England: The Ritual Year 1400–1700* (Oxford: Oxford University Press, 1994); C. Phythian-Adams, 'Ceremony and the Citizen: The Communal Year at Coventry, 1450–1550', in P. Clark and P. Slack, eds, *Crisis and Order in English Towns, 1500–1700* (London: Routledge, 1972), pp. 57–85; R. W. Scribner, 'Ritual and Popular Religion in Catholic Germany at the Time of the Reformation', *JEH* 35 (1984): 47–77. Interesting and evocative, though with some inaccuracies, is G. C. Homans, *English Villagers of the Thirteenth Century* (Cambridge, MA: Harvard University Press, 1942), pp. 353–81.

29 S. Crane, *The Performance of Self: Ritual, Clothing and Identity During the Hundred Years War* (Philadelphia, PA: University of Pennsylvania Press, 2002), pp. 39–72.

30 Vauchez, *Laity*, p. 156.

31 A. W. Lewis, 'Forest Rights and the Celebration of May: Two Documents from the French Vexin, 1311–1318', *Mediaeval Studies* 53 (1991): 259–77; C. Humphrey, *The Politics of Carnival: Festive Misrule in Medieval England* (Manchester: Manchester University Press, 2001), p. 85.

32 S. Billington, *Midsummer: A Cultural Sub-Text from Chrétien de Troyes to Jean Michel* (Turnhout: Brepols, 2000), pp. 117–18.

33 H. R. Luard, ed., *Roberti Grosseteste Epistolae*, Rolls Series 25 (London: Longman, 1861), p. 317. On scot-ales, see p. 131 below. For similar prohibitions

directed particularly at the clergy, see council of Avignon 1209, c. 17; Paris 1212, c. 16; Rouen 1231, c. 14 (Mansi 22, cols 791–2, 842; 23, col. 216).

34 J.-C. Schmitt, '"Jeunes" et danse des chevaux de bois', in idem, *Le corps, les rites, les rêves, le temps: Essais d'anthropologies médiévales* (Paris: Gallimard, 2001), p. 157 (Reprint of 1976 article).

35 *Handlyng Synne*, pp. 225–31, ll. 9011–239. See also p. 118, ll. 4695–8: men would rather hear of dances and entertainments than of God and heaven.

36 Reynolds, *Kingdoms and Communities*, p. 151.

37 French, *People of the Parish*, p. 27.

38 Jacques de Vitry, *Exempla*, p. 77 (no. 183).

39 Mirk, *Festial*, pp. 149–50.

40 Owst, *Preaching*, p. 215.

41 Brown, *Popular Piety*, p. 120.

42 Mundy, 'Village, Town and City', p. 148; Bainbridge, *Gilds*, p. 60.

43 Bonet, ed., 'Els processos', pp. 58–60.

44 *Les Miracles de Nostre Dame par Gautier de Coinci*, ed. V. F. Koenig (Geneva: Droz, 1955–1961), II, ll. 209–11. See M. Boulton, 'Anti-Jewish Attitudes in Twelfth-Century French Literature', in M. A. Signer and J. Van Engen, eds, *Jews and Christians in Twelfth-Century Europe* (Notre Dame, IN: University of Notre Dame Press, 2001), pp. 234–54.

45 Lateran IV, canons 68 and 69.

46 Council of Pont-Audemer 1257, Synod of Breslau 1266, and Council of Anse 1299 (J. F. O'Sullivan, ed., *The Register of Eudes of Rouen* (New York: Columbia University Press, 1964), p. 325; S. Grayzel, ed., *The Church and the Jews in the Thirteenth Century, Volume II: 1254–1314* (Detroit, MI: Wayne State University Press, 1989), pp. 245, 262.)

47 For recent arguments, see J. Cohen, 'A 1096 Complex? Constructing the First Crusade in Jewish Historical Memory, Medieval and Modern', in Signer and Van Engen, eds, *Jews and Christians*, pp. 9–26; R. Chazan, 'From the First Crusade to the Second: Evolving Perceptions of the Christian-Jewish Conflict', ibid., pp. 46–62; also M. Frassetto, 'Heretics and Jews in the Writings of Adémar of Chabannes and the Origins of Medieval Anti-Semitism', *Church History* 71 (2002): 1–15.

48 G. Langmuir, *Toward a Definition of Antisemitism* (Berkeley, CA: University of California Press, 1990), pp. 209–36.

49 M. Rubin, *Gentile Tales: The Narrative Assault on Late Medieval Jews* (New Haven, CT: Yale University Press, 1999).

50 J. Muldoon, *Popes, Lawyers and Infidels: The Church and the Non-Christian World 1250–1550* (Liverpool: Liverpool University Press, 1979), pp. 30–1.

51 Rubin, *Gentile Tales*, pp. 48–57, 116–19.

52 D. H. Strickland, *Saracens, Demons, and Jews: Making Monsters in Medieval Art* (Princeton, NJ: Princeton University Press, 2003).

53 J. Shatzmiller, *Shylock Reconsidered: Jews, Moneylending and Medieval Society* (Berkeley, CA: University of California Press, 1990). On England, see R. C. Stacey, 'Jews and Christians in Twelfth-Century England: Some Dynamics of a Changing Relationship', in Signer and Van Engen, eds, *Jews and Christians*,

pp. 340–54; V. D. Lipman, *The Jews of Medieval Norwich* (London: Jewish Historical Society of England, 1967).

54 Rubin, *Gentile Tales*, p. 194.

55 J. Cohen, *The Friars and the Jews: The Evolution of Medieval anti-Judaism* (London: Cornell University Press, 1982).

56 R. C. Stacey, 'Anti-Semitism and the Medieval English State', in J. R. Maddicott and D. M. Palliser, eds, *The Medieval State* (London: Hambledon, 2000), pp. 163–77.

57 D. Nirenberg, *Communities of Violence: Persecution of Minorities in the Middle Ages* (Princeton, NJ: Princeton University Press, 1996), pp. 43–68, 124.

58 Bonet, ed., 'Els processos', p. 59.

59 See also D. Nirenberg, 'Religious and Sexual Boundaries in the Medieval Crown of Aragon', in M. D. Meyerson and E. D. English, eds, *Christians, Muslims, and Jews in Medieval and Early Modern Spain: Interaction and Cultural Change* (Notre Dame, IN: University of Notre Dame Press, 2000), pp. 141–60.

60 Rubin, *Gentile Tales*, p. 5.

61 L. L. Otis, *Prostitution in Medieval Society: The History of an Urban Institution in Languedoc* (Chicago: University of Chicago Press, 1985); R. M. Karras, *Common Women: Prostitution and Sexuality in Medieval England* (Oxford: Oxford University Press, 1996).

62 P. Richards, *The Medieval Leper and His Northern Heirs* (Cambridge: Brewer, 1977), pp. 48–61.

63 R. Helmholz, ed., *Select Cases of Defamation to 1600*, Seldon Society 101 (London: Seldon Society, 1985), pp. 5–6. Various examples can be seen in fourteenth-century visitations from northern France: G. Dupont, ed., *Registre de l'officialité de Cerisy 1314–57*, Memoires de la Société des Antiquaries de Normandie, 3rd ser., 10 (Caen: Le Blanc-Hardel, 1880).

64 Similarly for heresy accusations, see J. B. Given, 'Factional Politics in a Medieval Society: A Case from Fourteenth-Century Foix', *JMH* 14 (1988): 233–50.

65 Moore, *Formation of a Persecuting Society*.

66 F. Pederson, *Marriage Disputes in Medieval England* (London: Hambledon, 2000), pp. 59–84.

67 See many cases of contumacy in F. S. Pearson, ed., 'Records of a Ruridecanal Court of 1300', in *Collectanea*, Worcestershire Record Society 29 (1912), pp. 69–80; and general excommunications in *Reg. Sutton, passim*.

68 Brentano, *Two Churches*, p. 234.

69 Fournier II, p. 77.

70 D. Nirenberg, 'Mass Conversion and Genealogical Mentalities: Jews and Christians in Fifteenth-Century Spain', *P&P* 174 (2002): 3–41.

71 A. J. Fletcher, *Preaching, Politics and Poetry in Late Medieval England* (Dublin: Four Courts Press, 1998), p. 148.

72 M. Douglas, *Natural Symbols* (London: Barrie & Rockliff, 1970); M. Rubin and S. Kay, eds, *Framing Medieval Bodies* (Manchester: Manchester University Press, 1994).

73 C. Zika, 'Hosts, Processions and Pilgrimages: Controlling the Sacred in Fifteenth-Century Germany', *P&P* 118 (1988), pp. 38–9.

74 Rubin, *Corpus Christi*, pp. 243–87.

75 Vauchez, *Laity*, p. 136; Le Goff, *Time, Work and Culture*, pp. 159–88.

76 Phythian-Adams, 'Ceremony and the Citizen'.

77 R. C. Trexler, 'Ritual in Florence: Adolescence and Salvation in the Renaissance', in C. Trinkaus and H. A. Oberman, eds, *The Pursuit of Holiness in Late Medieval and Renaissance Religion* (Leiden: Brill, 1974), pp. 221–2 n. 6.

78 *Roberti Grosseteste Epistolae*, p. 75; Rubin, *Corpus Christi*, p. 263; Zika, 'Hosts, Processions and Pilgrimages', p. 40; French, *People of the Parish*, p. 33; L. M. Clopper, ed., *Records of Early English Drama: Chester* (Toronto: University of Toronto Press, 1979), pp. 15–16; K. Parker, 'Lynn and the Making of a Mystic', in Arnold and Lewis, eds, *Companion*, pp. 61–3; Brentano, *Two Churches*, pp. 132–3.

79 G. G. Meersseman, *Ordo Fraternitas: confraternite e pietà dei laici nel medioevo* (Rome: Herder, 1977), I, pp. 202–4.

80 Reynolds, *Kingdoms and Communities*, p. 73.

81 Meersseman, *Ordo Fraternitas*, I, p. 397; T. Smith, *et al.*, eds, *English Gilds*, EETS o.s. 40 (London: Trübner, 1870), pp. 216–17.

82 L. Binz, 'Les confréries dans le diocese de Genève à la fin du moyen âge', in *Le Mouvement confraternel au moyen âge: France, Italie, Suisse* (Rome: Ecole Française de Rome, 1987), pp. 233–61; Terpstra, *Lay Confraternities*, p. 83.

83 E. Schiferl, 'Italian Confraternity Art Contracts: Group Consciousness and Corporate Patronage, 1400–1525', in K. Eisenbichler, *Crossing the Boundaries: Christian Piety and the Arts in Italian Medieval and Renaissance Confraternities* (Kalamazoo, MI: Medieval Institute Publications, 1991), pp. 121–40.

84 Bainbridge, *Gilds*, p. 37.

85 A. Vauchez, 'Conclusion', in *Le mouvement confraternal*, p. 400.

86 C. Vincent, *Des Charités biens ordonnées: Les confréries Normandes de la fin du XIIIe siècle au début du XIVe siècle* (Paris: Ecole Normale Supérieure, 1988), p. 234.

87 J. Henderson, *Piety and Charity in Late Medieval Florence* (Oxford: Clarendon Press, 1994), p. 299.

88 N. Terpstra, 'Death and Dying in Renaissance Confraternities', in Eisenbichler, ed., *Crossing the Boundaries*, pp. 179–200. For similar points on how the records mislead regarding trade guilds, see G. Rosser, 'Crafts, Guilds and the Negotiation of Work in the Medieval Town', *P&P* 154 (1997): 3–31.

89 For an overview, see G. Casagrande, 'Women in Confraternities between the Middle Ages and the Modern Age', *Confraternitas* 5 (1994): 3–13; G. Casagrande, 'Confraternities and Lay Female Religiosity in Late Medieval and Renaissance Umbria', in N. Terpstra, ed., *The Politics of Ritual Kingship: Confraternities and Social Order in Early Modern Italy* (Cambridge: Cambridge University Press, 2000), pp. 48–66.

90 Casagrande, 'Women in Confraternities': 10; K. L. French, 'Maidens' Lights and Wives' Stores: Women's Parish Guilds in Late Medieval England', *Sixteenth Century Journal* 29 (1998): 399–425.

91 M. T. Brolis, 'A Thousand and More Women: The Register of Women for the Confraternity of Misericordia Maggiore in Bergamo, 1265–1339', *Catholic Historical Review* 88 (2002): 231–46.

92 Casagrande, 'Women in Confraternities', p. 10.

93 For example, R. F. E. Weissman, 'Cults and Contexts: In Search of the Renaissance Confraternity', in Eisenbichler, ed., *Crossing the Boundaries*, p. 209.

94 Vincent, *Des Charités biens ordonnées*, p. 222; R. C. Trexler, *Public Life in Renaissance Florence* (New York: Academic Press, 1980), p. 15ff; J. Henderson, 'Confraternities and the Church in Late Medieval Florence', SCH 23 (1986), p. 71.

95 R. F. E. Weissman, *Ritual Brotherhood in Renaissance Florence* (New York: Academic Press, 1982); B. Pullan, *Rich and Poor in Renaissance Venice: The Social Institutions of a Catholic State* (Oxford: Blackwell, 1971), but see also R. MacKenney, 'Devotional Confraternities in Renaissance Venice', SCH 23 (1986), pp. 85–96.

96 See figures presented (but not analysed in this way) in Weissman, *Ritual Brotherhood*, p. 68.

97 M. Flynn, *Sacred Charity: Confraternities and Social Welfare in Spain 1400–1700* (Houndmills: Macmillan, 1989), pp. 15–6, 20, 24.

98 Brolis, 'A Thousand and More Women', p. 244.

99 Rubin, 'Small Groups', pp. 140–1.

100 J. R. Banker, *Death in the Community: Memorialization and Confraternities in an Italian Commune in the Late Middle Ages* (Athens, GA: University of Georgia Press, 1988), Appendix I, pp. 189–90.

101 Reynolds, *Kingdoms and Communities*, p. 69; S. Lindenbaum, 'Rituals of Exclusion: Feasts and Plays of the English Religious Fraternities', in Twycross, ed., *Festive Drama*, p. 58.

102 Bainbridge, *Gilds*, p. 105; Farmer, *Surviving Poverty*, pp. 80–90 and *passim*.

103 K. Falvey, 'Early Italian Dramatic Traditions and Comforting Rituals: Some Initial Considerations', in Eisenbichler, ed., *Crossing the Boundaries*, pp. 33–55.

104 R. L. A. Clark, 'Community versus Subject in Late Medieval French Confraternity Drama and Ritual', in A. Hindley, ed., *Drama and Community: People and Plays in Medieval Europe* (Turnhout: Brepols, 1999), pp. 36–7; Binz, 'Confréries dans le diocèse de Genève', p. 235.

105 M. Rubin, *Charity and Community in Medieval Cambridge* (Cambridge: Cambridge University Press, 1987), p. 254 and *passim*; Farmer, *Surviving Poverty*, p. 3 and *passim*; B. R. McRee, 'Charity and Gild Solidarity in Late Medieval England', *Journal of British Studies* 32 (1993): 203–5.

106 Swanson, *Religion and Devotion*, p. 211.

107 Rubin, *Charity and Community*, p. 254.

108 McRee, 'Charity and Gild Solidarity'.

109 Smith *et al.*, eds, *English Gilds*, pp. 218–19.

110 Farmer, *Surviving Poverty*, pp. 90–104; J. M. Bennett, 'Conviviality and Charity in Medieval and Early Modern England', *P&P* 134 (1992): 19–41. See also Dyer, *Standards of Living*, pp. 234–57.

111 C. Vincent, *Les Confréries médiévales dans le royaume de France XIIIe–XVe siècle* (Paris: Albin Michel, 1994), pp. 130–5; Weissman, *Ritual Brotherhood*; Brown, *Popular Piety*, pp. 179–80.

112 Lindenbaum, 'Rituals of Exclusion'.

113 B. R. McRee, 'Unity or Division? The Social Meaning of Guild Ceremony in Urban Communities', in B. Hanawalt and K. Reyerson, eds, *City and Spectacle in Medieval Europe* (Minneapolis, MN: University of Minnesota Press, 1994), pp. 189–207.

114 J. Chiffoleau, *La Comptabilité de l'au delà: Les hommes, la mort et la religion dans la région d'Avignon à la fin du moyen-âge* (Rome: Ecole Française de Rome, 1980); Vincent, *Des Charités biens ordonnées*, p. 223.

115 Parker, 'Lynn'; B. R. McRee, 'Religious Gilds and Civic Order: The Case of Norwich in the Late Middle Ages', *Speculum* 67 (1992): 69–97.

116 Vauchez, 'Conclusion', in *Le mouvement confraternal*, p. 399; F. J. W. van Kan, 'Around St George: Integration and Precedence during the Meetings of the Civic Militia of The Hague', in W. Blockman and A. Janse, eds, *Showing Status: Representations of Social Positions in the Late Middle Ages* (Turnhout: Brepols, 1999), pp. 177–95.

117 Weissman, *Ritual Brotherhood*, p. 24; McRee, 'Charity and Gild Solidarity'; Trexler, *Public Life*, p. 15; Rosser, 'Crafts, Gilds and the Negotiation of Work', pp. 9, 27–31.

118 For many social aspects of the plays, see Rubin, *Corpus Christi*, pp. 271–87.

119 H. Swanson, *Medieval Artisans: An Urban Class in Late Medieval England* (Oxford: Blackwell, 1989), p. 120; S. Beckwith, *Signifying God: Social Relation and Symbolic Act in the York Corpus Christi Plays* (Chicago: University of Chicago Press, 2001), pp. 42–55.

120 Rubin, *Corpus Christi*, p. 287.

121 C. Sponsler, 'Festive Profit and Ideological Production: *Le Jeu de Saint Nicolas*', in Twycross, *Festive Drama*, pp. 66–79.

122 For a helpful overview, see G. Koziol, 'The Dangers of Polemic: Is Ritual Still an Interesting Topic of Historical Study?', *Early Medieval Europe* 11 (2002): 367–88.

123 Mary Erler, 'Palm Sunday Prophets and Procession, and Eucharistic Controversy', *Renaissance Quarterly* 48 (1995): 58–81.

124 J. Rossiaud, 'Les Rituels de la fête civique à Lyon, XIIe–XVIe siècles', in J. Chiffoleau, L. Martines and A. P. Bagliani, eds, *Riti e Rituali: nelle Società Medievali* (Spoleto: Centro Italiano di Studi Sull'Alto Medioevo, 1994), p. 285.

125 James, 'Ritual, Drama and Social Body, pp. 3–29.

126 G. Rosser, 'Going to the Fraternity Feast: Commensality and Social Relations in Late Medieval England', *Journal of British Studies* 33 (1994): 430–46; Clark, 'Community versus Subject'; Humphrey, *Politics of Carnival*.

127 C. Walravens, 'Insultes, blasphèmes ou hérésie? Un procès à l'officialité épiscopale de Troyes en 1445', *Bibliothèques de l'Ecole des Chartres* 154 (1996), pp. 491–2.

128 For what follows, see J. D. C. Fisher, *Christian Initiation: Baptism in the Medieval West* (London: SPCK, 1965); M. Rubellin, 'Entrée dans la vie, entrée dans la chrétienté, entrée dans la société: Autour du baptême à l'époque carolingienne',

Annales de l'Est, 5th ser., 34 (1982): 31–51; S. Shahar, *Childhood in the Middle Ages*, trans. C. Galai (London: Routledge, 1990), pp. 45–52; Orme, 'Children'.

129 Wakefield and Evans, *Heresies*, pp. 105, 116.

130 N. Tanner, ed., *Norwich Heresy Trials 1428–31*, Camden Society 4th ser., 20 (London: Royal Historical Society, 1977), p. 60.

131 For example, council of Albi 1230, c. 31 (Pontal, ed., *Statuts synodaux*, II, p. 18).

132 *Handlyng Synne*, p. 239, ll. 9569–70.

133 *Handlyng Synne*, p. 17, l. 572 and p. 241, l. 9663; V. Charon, 'The Knowledge of Herbs', in L. Milis, ed., *The Pagan Middle Ages* (Woodbridge: Boydell, 1998), p. 124; Schmitt, *Holy Greyhound*, pp. 74–80.

134 Bossy, 'Blood and Baptism', pp. 133–5; Arnold, *Inquisition and Power*, p. 174.

135 P. Pegeot, 'Un exemple de parenté baptismale à la fin du Moyen Age: Porrentruy 1482–1500', *Annales de l'Est*, 5th ser., 34 (1982): 53–70.

136 Anonymous Ticiensis, *Liber de laudibus civitatis Ticiensis*, ed. R. Maiocchi and F. Quintavalle, Rerum Italicarum Scriptores, new edn 11, i (Citta di Castello, 1903), pp. 19–20.

137 Brown, *Popular Piety*, pp. 101–4.

138 D. O. Hughes, 'Mourning Rites, Memory, and Civilization in Premodern Italy', in Chiffoleau *et al.*, eds, *Riti e Rituali*, pp. 23–38.

139 Binski, *Medieval Death*, pp. 71–115.

140 Brown, *Popular Piety*, p. 93 n. 5; J.-P. Deregnaucourt, 'L'élection de sépulture d'après les testaments douaisiens (1295–1500)', *Revue du Nord* 65 (1983): 345–7.

141 S. K. Cohn, 'The Place of the Dead in Flanders and Tuscany: Towards a Comparative History of the Black Death', in B. Gordon and P. Marshall, eds, *The Place of the Dead: Death and Remembrance in Late Medieval and Early Modern Europe* (Cambridge: Cambridge University Press, 2000), pp. 26–7; R. Dinn, '"Monuments Answerable to Men's Worth": Burial Patterns, Social Status and Gender in Late Medieval Bury St Edmunds', *JEH* 46 (1995): 241, 248.

142 Meersseman, *Ordo Fraternitas*, I, p. 66; Smith *et al.*, eds, *English Gilds*, pp. 214–15.

143 J. Bossy, 'The Mass as a Social Institution 1200–1700', *P&P* 100(1983): 50–3.

144 M. Rubin, 'What Did the Eucharist mean to Thirteenth-Century Villagers?', in P. R. Coss and S. D. Lloyd, eds, *Thirteenth-Century England* IV (Woodbridge: Boydell, 1992), pp. 47–55.

145 Arnold, 'A Man Takes An Ox . . .', pp. 41–7; V. Reinburg, 'Liturgy and the Laity in Late Medieval and Reformation France', *Sixteenth-Century Journal* 23 (1992): 529–32.

146 French, *People of the Parish*, p. 1; P. Biller, 'The Common Woman in the Western Church in the Thirteenth and Early Fourteenth Centuries', SCH 27 (1990), p. 140.

147 H. Gregory, ed. and trans., *Selected Letters of Alessandra Strozzi* (Berkeley, CA: University of California Press, 1997), p. 155.

148 Additions to the Synod of the West 1238x44 (Pontal, ed., *Statuts synodaux*, II, p. 132, c. 8); M. Aston, 'Segregation in Church', SCH 27 (1990), pp. 237–94.

149 Welch, *Art and Society*, p. 185; Statutes of Exeter 1287, c. 12, Powicke and

Cheney, eds, *Councils and Synods* II, pp. 1007–8; Brown, *Popular Piety*, p. 92; French, *People of the Parish*, p. 92. See also C. P. Graves, 'Social Space in the English Medieval Parish Church', *Economy and Society* 18 (1989): 297–322.

150 Owst, *Preaching*, p. 170; Bossy, 'Mass', p. 56 and n. 74; French, *People of the Parish*, pp. 25–6.

151 L. R. Poos, 'Sex, Lies and the Church Courts of Pre-Reformation England', *Journal of Interdisciplinary History* 25 (1995): 601.

5   Selfhood

1 G. E. Brereton and J. M. Ferrier, eds, *Le Menagier de Paris* (Oxford: Clarendon Press, 1981), p. 3. The book was translated, with a few omissions and bowdlerizations, by Eileen Power: *The Goodman of Paris: A Treatise on Moral and Domestic Economy by a Citizen of Paris c. 1393* (London: Routledge, 1928).

2 *Menagier*, p. 112.

3 C. P. Collette, 'Chaucer and the French Tradition Revisited: Philippe de Mézières and the Good Wife', in Wogan-Browne *et al.*, eds, *Medieval Women*, pp. 151–68.

4 On conduct literature in general, see most recently K. Ashley and R. L. A. Clark, eds, *Medieval Conduct* (Minneapolis, MN: University of Minnesota Press, 2001).

5 T. Asad, 'On Ritual and Discipline in Medieval Christian Monasticism', *Economy and Society* 16 (1987): 187.

6 *Menagier*, p. 75; P. S. Gold, *The Lady and the Virgin: Image, Attitude and Experience in Twelfth-Century France* (Chicago: University of Chicago Press, 1985), particularly pp. 43–75; J. Dalarun, 'The Clerical Gaze', in C. Klapisch-Zuber, ed., *A History of Women in the West II: Silences of the Middle Ages* (Cambridge, MA: Harvard University Press, 1992), pp. 15–42; J. M. Bennett, 'England: Women and Gender', in S. H. Rigby, ed., *A Companion to Britain in the Later Middle Ages* (Oxford: Blackwell, 2003), pp. 87–106.

7 Odo of Cluny, *Collationem Libri Tres*, II, ix, PL 133 col. 556: quoted in Dalarun, 'Clerical Gaze', p. 20.

8 Discussed further in Chapter 6, p. 204.

9 K. M. Phillips, 'Maidenhood as the Perfect Age of Woman's Life', in K. J. Lewis *et al.*, eds, *Young Medieval Women* (Stroud: Sutton, 1999), pp. 1–24; K. M. Phillips, *Medieval Maidens: Young Women and Gender in England, 1270–1540* (Manchester: Manchester University Press, 2003).

10 D. Elliott, 'Marriage', in C. Dinshaw and D. Wallace, eds, *The Cambridge Companion to Medieval Women's Writing* (Cambridge: Cambridge University Press, 2003), pp. 40–57; S. Farmer, 'Persuasive Voices: Clerical Images of Medieval Wives', *Speculum* 61 (1986): 517–43.

11 H. Leyser, *Medieval Women: A Social History of Women in England 450–1500* (London: Weidenfeld & Nicolson, 1995), pp. 168–86.

12 Karras, *Common Women*, particularly pp. 102–30.

13 C. Beattie, 'The Problem of Women's Work Identities in Post Black Death England', in J. Bothwell, P. J. P. Goldberg and W. M. Ormrod, eds, *The Problem of Labour in Fourteenth-Century England* (York: York Medieval Press, 2000), pp. 1–19.

14 *Register of John Waltham, Bishop of Salisbury 1388–1395*, ed. T. C. B. Timmins (Canterbury & York Society, 1994), p. 117 (no. 929); D. J. Kagay, trans., *The Usatges of Barcelona* (Philadelphia, PA: University of Pennsylvania Press, 1994), p. 101 (C4).

15 *Menagier*, p. 70.

16 Jerome of Siena, quoted in C. Casagrande, 'The Protected Woman', in Klapisch-Zuber, ed., *History of Women*, p. 95; T. F. Mustanoja, ed., *The Good Wife Taught Her Daughter* (Helsinki: Annales Academae Scientiarum Fennicae, 1948), pp. 160–1.

17 P. J. P. Goldberg, 'The Public and the Private: Women in the Pre-Plague Economy', in P. R. Coss and S. D. Lloyd, eds, *Thirteenth-Century England III* (Woodbridge: Boydell, 1991), p. 85; B. A. Hanawalt, 'At the Margins of Women's Space in Medieval Europe', in eadem, *Of Good and Ill Repute: Gender and Social Control in Medieval England* (Oxford: Oxford University Press, 1998), pp. 70–87.

18 Casagrande, 'Protected Woman', p. 91.

19 D. Elliott, 'Dress as Mediator between Inner and Outer Self: The Pious Matron of the High and Later Middle Ages', *Mediaeval Studies* 53 (1991): 288; *Handlyng Synne*, p. 85, ll. 3337–40.

20 *Menagier*, pp. 9–10. See R. L. Kruger, '"Nouvelles choses": Social Instability and the Problem of Fashion in the *Livre du Chevalier de la Tour Landry*, the *Menagier de Paris*, and Christine de Pisan's *Livre des Trois Vertus*', in Ashley and Clark, eds, *Medieval Conduct*, pp. 62–3.

21 Casagrande, 'Protected Woman', p. 97.

22 G. M. Gibson, 'Blessing from Sun and Moon: Churching as Women's Theater', in B. A. Hanawalt and D. Wallace, eds, *Bodies and Disciplines: Intersections of Literature and History in Fifteenth-Century England* (Minneapolis, MN: University of Minnesota Press, 1999), pp. 139–54.

23 F. Riddy, 'Mother Knows Best: Reading Social Change in a Courtesy Text', *Speculum* 71 (1996): 86.

24 Riddy, 'Mother Knows Best': 78; Dupont, ed., *Registre de l'officialite de Cerisy*, p. 293.

25 *Jacob's Well*, p. 159; Farmer, *Surviving Poverty*, p. 108.

26 D. Shemek, 'Circular Definitions: Configuring Gender in Italian Renaissance Festival', *Renaissance Quarterly* 48 (1995): 1–40.

27 Poos, 'Sex, Lies, and the Church Courts'; R. M. Karras, '"Because the Other is a Poor Woman She Shall Be Called His Wench": Gender, Sexuality and Social Status in Late Medieval England', in S. Farmer and C. B. Pasternack, eds, *Gender and Difference in the Middle Ages* (Minneapolis, MN: University of Minnesota Press, 2003), pp. 210–29.

28 M. Keen, *Chivalry* (New Haven, CT: Yale University Press, 1984); H. Chickering and T. H. Seiler, eds, *The Study of Chivalry: Resources and Approaches* (Kalamazoo, MI: Medieval Institute Publications, 1988); R. Kaeuper, *Chivalry and Violence in Medieval Europe* (Oxford: Oxford University Press, 1999).

29 F. J. Furnivall, ed. *The Babees Book*, EETS o.s. 32 (London: Trübner, 1868), pp. 48–52.

30 R. M. Karras, *From Boys to Men: Formations of Masculinity in Late Medieval Europe* (Philadelphia, PA: University of Pennsylvania Press, 2002), p. 16.

31 S. Vecchio, 'The Good Wife', in Klapisch-Zuber, ed., *History of Women*, pp. 105–35.

32 B. Hanawalt, 'Violence in the Domestic Milieu of Late Medieval England', in R. Kaeuper, ed., *Violence in Medieval Society* (Woodbridge: Boydell Press, 2000), pp. 197–214.

33 Jansen, *Magdalen*, p. 109.

34 P. J. P. Goldberg, 'Masters and Men in Later Medieval England', in D. M. Hadley, ed., *Masculinity in Medieval Europe* (London: Longman, 1999), pp. 62–3.

35 R. M. Karras, 'Gendered Sin and Misogyny in John of Bromyard's *Summa Predicantium*', *Traditio* 47 (1992): 237.

36 R. H. Hilton, *English and French Towns in Feudal Society: A Comparative Study* (Cambridge: Cambridge University Press, 1992), pp. 115–16.

37 J. A. McNamara, 'The *Herrenfrage*: The Restructuring of the Gender System, 1050–1150', in C. A. Lees, ed., *Medieval Masculinities: Regarding Men in the Middle Ages* (Minneapolis, MN: University of Minnesota Press, 1994), pp. 3–29.

38 S. Chojnacki, 'The Power of Love: Wives and Husbands in Late Medieval Venice', in M. Erler and M. Kowaleski, eds, *Women and Power in the Middle Ages* (Athens, GA: University of Georgia Press, 1988), pp. 126–48; Schnell, 'Discourse on Marriage'.

39 Christine de Pizan, *The Book of the City of Ladies*, trans. R. Brown-Grant (London: Penguin, 1999), pp. 5–6.

40 *Menagier*, p. 12.

41 *Menagier*, pp. 20–2, 35.

42 Thomas de Cantimpré, *Bonum universale*, II, 50, 2; *Handlyng Synne*, pp. 303–4, ll. 12189–220.

43 *Menagier*, p. 16.

44 Shaw, 'Influence of Canonical and Episcopal Reform', p. 57.

45 B. Newman, 'Possessed by the Spirit: Devout Women, Demoniacs, and the Apostolic Life in the Thirteenth Century', *Speculum* 73 (1998): 737. But see also N. Caciola, *Discerning Spirits: Divine and Demonic Possession in the Middle Ages* (Ithaca, NY: Cornell University Press, 2003), p. 50.

46 Binski, *Medieval Death* p. 179.

47 Foster, ed. and trans., *Life of St Thomas Aquinas*, pp. 89–90.

48 Mirk, *Festial*, p. 130.

49 J. Le Goff, 'Trades and Professions as Represented in Medieval Confessors' Manuals', in idem, *Time, Work and Culture*, p. 119.

50 N. Bériou, 'Autour de Latran IV (1215): La naissance de la confession moderne et sa diffusion', in Groupe de la Bussière, *Pratiques de la confession: Des pères du désert à Vatican II* (Paris: CERF, 1983), p. 83.

51 Karras, 'Gendered Sin', pp. 241–2.

52 J. Murray, 'Gendered Souls in Sexed Bodies: The Male Construction of Female Sexuality in Some Medieval Confessors' Manuals', in Biller and Minnis, eds, *Handling Sin*, pp. 79–93; J. Murray, 'The Absent Penitent: The Cure of Women's

Souls and Confessor's Manuals in Thirteenth-Century England', in L. Smith and
J. H. M. Taylor, eds, *Women, the Book and the Godly* (Cambridge: Brewer,
1995), pp. 13–25.

53 L. K. Little, *Religious Poverty and the Profit Economy in Medieval Europe*
(Ithaca, NY: Cornell University Press, 1978).

54 P. Biller, 'Marriage Patterns and Women's Lives: A Sketch of a Pastoral
Geography', in P. J. P. Goldberg, ed., *Woman is a Worthy Wight: Women in
Medieval English Society c.1200–1500* (Stroud: Sutton, 1992), p. 70.

55 Goering and Payer, '*Summa*', p. 31, ll. 99–103.

56 H. J. Kuster and R. J. Cormier, 'Old Views and New Trends: Observations on the
Problem of Homosexuality in the Middle Ages', *Studi Medievali* 25 (1984):
587–610; M. D. Jordan, *The Invention of Sodomy in Christian Theology*
(Chicago: University of Chicago Press, 1998).

57 Goering and Payer, '*Summa*', p. 41, ll. 272–5.

58 On sex and marriage, see T. N. Tentler, *Sin and Confession on the Eve of the
Reformation* (Princeton, NJ: Princeton University Press, 1977), pp. 162–232.

59 Jacques de Vitry, *Exempla*, p. 95 (no. ccxxix).

60 Goering and Payer, '*Summa*', pp. 33–4, ll. 136–58.

61 A. Goodman, *Margery Kempe and Her World* (London: Longman, 2002),
pp. 68–9; D. Elliott, *Spiritual Marriage: Sexual Abstinence in Medieval Wedlock*
(Princeton, NJ: Princeton University Press, 1993).

62 K. M. Phillips, 'Four Virgins' Tales: Sex and Power in Medieval Law', in Bernau
et al., eds, *Medieval Virginities*, pp. 80–101.

63 P. Biller, 'Birth-control in the West in the Thirteenth and Early Fourteenth
Centuries', *P&P* 94 (1982): 3–26.

64 A. Finch, 'The Disciplining of the Laity in Late Medieval Normandy', *French
History* 10 (1996): 169–70.

65 J. M. Bennett, 'Writing Fornication: Medieval Leyrwite and its Historians', *TRHS*
6th ser., 13 (2003): 154.

66 G. Ruggiero, *The Boundaries of Eros: Sex Crime and Sexuality in Renaissance
Venice* (Oxford: Oxford University Press, 1985), p. 17.

67 Ruggiero, *Boundaries of Eros*, pp. 23, 47–9, 20, 96, 70–88, 110, 141.

68 D. Nirenberg, 'Conversion, Sex, and Segregation: Jews and Christians in Medieval
Spain', *AHR* 107 (2002): 1081.

69 Goering, ed., 'Magister Serlo', p. 26; Fournier I, p. 248; Ruggiero, *Boundaries of
Eros*, pp. 33–4.

70 Arnold, *Inquisition and Power*, pp. 203, 277 n. 158.

71 Newman, 'Possessed by the Spirit', p. 744; Nirenberg, 'Conversion, Sex and
Segregation', p. 1091. See also Biller, 'Common Woman', p. 136.

72 Fournier I, pp. 302–6; see P. Dronke, *Women Writers of the Middle Ages*
(Cambridge: Cambridge University Press, 1984), pp. 204–9.

73 *Menagier*, pp. 37–9. Power's translation omits this section.

74 *Menagier*, pp. 109–11.

75 J. Bossy, 'The Social History of Confession in the Age of the Reformation', *TRHS*,
5th ser., 25 (1975): 21–38; J. Bossy, 'Moral Arithmetic: Seven Sins into Ten

Commandements', in E. Leites, ed., *Conscience and Casuistry in Early Modern Europe* (Cambridge: Cambridge University Press, 1988), pp. 214–34.

76 Wenzel, ed., *'Deus est'*, p. 280; Owst, *Preaching*, p. 178; *Handlyng Synne*, p. 192, l. 7610.

77 U. Schemmann, *Confessional Literature and Lay Education: The* Manuel de Pechez *as a Book of Good Conduct and Guide to Personal Religion* (Düsseldorf: Droste, 2000), p. 65.

78 Bossy, 'Mass', p. 42.

79 Le Goff, *Birth of Purgatory*.

80 A. Gurevich, 'Popular and Scholarly Medieval Cultural Traditions: Notes in the Margin of Jacques Le Goff's Book', *JMH* 9 (1983): 71–90. See also A. Bernstein, 'Theology between Heresy and Folklore: William of Auvergne on Punishment after Death', *Studies in Medieval and Renaissance History* 5 (1982): 1–44; G. Edwards, 'Purgatory: Birth or Evolution ?', *JEH* 36 (1985): 634–46; B. McGuire, 'Purgatory, the Communion of Saints, and Medieval Change', *Viator* 20 (1989): 61–84; C. Watkins, 'Sin, Penance and Purgatory in the Anglo-Norman Realm: The Evidence of Visions and Ghost Stories', *P&P* 175 (2002): 3–33.

81 Iogna-Prat, *Order and Exclusion*, p. 251.

82 Schmitt, *Ghosts*, particularly pp. 172, 178–81; Le Roy Ladurie, *Montaillou*, pp. 345–51.

83 N. Caciola, 'Spirits Seeking Bodies: Death, Possession and Communal Memory in the Middle Ages', in Gordon and Marshall, eds, *Place of the Dead*, p. 75.

84 P. Marshall, *Beliefs and the Dead in Reformation England* (Oxford: Oxford University Press, 2002), pp. 14–15; Schmitt, *Ghosts*, p. 183; N. Caciola, 'Wraiths, Revenants and Rituals in Medieval Culture', *P&P* 152 (1996): 3–45.

85 On the thirteenth century, see Watkins, 'Sin, Penance and Purgatory'.

86 Chiffoleau, *La comptabilité de l'au-delà*, pp. 408–24; Banker, *Death in the Community*, p. 177; Marandat, *Le souci de l'au-delà*, I, pp. 263–89; M.-T. Lorcin, 'Les clauses religieuses dans les testaments du plat pays lyonnais aux XIVe et XVe siècles', *Moyen Age* 78 (1972): 318; M. Bastard-Fournié, 'Le purgatoire dans la région Toulousaine au XIVe et au début du XVe siècles', *Annales du Midi* 92 (1980): p. 17.

87 Marandat, *Le souci de l'au-delà*, II, p. 506; Cohn, *Cult of Remembrance*, pp. 206–9; Chiffoleau, *La comptabilité de l'au-delà*, pp. 335–8.

88 C. Burgess, '"A Fond Thing Vainly Invented": An Essay on Purgatory and Pious Motive in Later Medieval England', in S. J. Wright, ed., *Parish, Church and People: Local Studies in Lay Religion 1350–1750* (London: Hutchinson, 1988), pp. 56–84.

89 Graves, 'Social Space', pp. 312–14; Kamerick, *Popular Piety*, pp. 70–2.

90 R. E. Lerner, 'The Black Death and European Eschatological Mentalities', *AHR* 86 (1981): 533–52.

91 Martin, *Les Ordres mendiants*, p. 350.

92 Cohn, *Cult of Remembrance*, pp. 17–18; Cohn, 'Place of the Dead'.

93 V. Pasche, *'Pour le salut de mon âme': Les Lausannois face à la mort (XIVe siècle)* (Lausanne: Université de Lausanne, 1989), p. 35. But see also M. Lauwers, *La*

mémoire des ancêtres, le souci des morts: Morts, rites et société au moyen âge (Diocèse de Liège, Xie–XIIIe siècles) (Paris: Beauchesne, 1997) for claims regarding earlier attitudes.

94 For example, J. Huizinga, *The Waning of the Middle Ages* (1924. Harmondsworth: Penguin, 1955), pp. 140–52; and, with greater nuance, M. Aston, 'Death', in R. Horrox, ed., *Fifteenth-Century Attitudes: Perceptions of Society in Late Medieval England* (Cambridge: Cambridge University Press, 1994), pp. 202–28.

95 For a balanced and persuasive view, see Marshall, *Beliefs and the Dead*, ch. 1.

96 L. Lavanchy, *Ecrire sa mort, décrire sa vie: Testaments de laïcs lausannois (1400–1450)* (Lausanne: Université de Lausanne, 2003), p. 80; Pasche, *'Pour le salut'*, p. 30.

97 Doat 25, fos 61v–62r.

98 Shaw, *Creation of a Community*, pp. 282–3.

99 H. Dedieu, 'Quelques traces de religion populaire autour des Frères Mineurs de la province d'Aquitaine', CdF 11 (1976), p. 231; Schmitt, *Ghosts*, p. 29.

100 For example, deposition of Hélis de Mazerolles (1244), Doat 23 fo. 179v.

101 For an overview, see Binksi, *Medieval Death*.

102 *Jacob's Well*, p. 305; *The Debate of Body and Soul*, in J. Gardner, ed., *The Alliterative Morte Arthure, The Owl and the Nightingale, and Five Other Middle English Poems* (Carbondale, IL: Southern Illinois University Press, 1971), pp. 161–73.

103 A. Murray, 'Religion among the Poor in Thirteenth-Century France: The Testimony of Humbert de Romans', *Traditio* 30 (1974): 321.

104 Gregory, ed. and trans., *Selected Letters*, pp. 79–81.

105 *Menagier*, pp. 6–9.

106 J. Delumeau, *Sin and Fear: The Emergence of a Western Guilt Culture, 13th–18th Centuries,* trans. E. Nicholson (1983. New York: St Martin's Press, 1990), pp. 199–208.

107 Goering and Payer, 'Summa', pp. 1–15.

108 Goering and Payer, 'Summa', pp. 25–8, ll. 1–57.

109 Goering and Payer, 'Summa', pp. 28–38, ll. 58–238.

110 Bossy, 'Moral Arithmetic'.

111 For a summary and critique of this past historiography, see S. Hamilton, *The Practice of Penance 900–1050* (Woodbridge: Royal Historical Society, 2001), pp. 2–23.

112 M. de Jong, 'What was *Public* About Public Penance? *Paenitentia Publica* and Justice in the Carolingian World', in *La Giustizia nell'alto medioevo (secoli IX–XI),* Settimane di Studio 44 (Spoleto: Presso Sede del Centro, 1997), II: 863–902; M. C. Mansfield, *The Humiliation of Sinners: Public Penance in Thirteenth-Century France* (Ithaca, NY: Cornell University Press, 1995). On the wider shift from earlier to later penitential systems, see P. J. Payer, 'The Origins and Development of the Later *Canones penitentiales*', *Mediaeval Studies* 61 (1999): 81–105.

113 A. Murray, 'Confession Before 1215', *TRHS*, 6th ser., (1993): 51–81.

114 Hamilton, *Practice of Penance*; S. Hamilton, 'The Unique Favour of Penance: The Church and the People c.800-c.1100', in Linehan and Nelson, eds, *Medieval World*, pp. 229–45; R. Meens, 'The Frequency and Nature of Early Medieval Penance', in Biller and Minnis, eds, *Handling Sin*, pp. 35–62.

115 Bossy, 'Social History'; Bossy, 'Moral Arithmetic'. For an overview of discussion, see P. Biller, 'Confession in the Middle Ages: Introduction', in Biller and Minnis, eds, *Handling Sin*, pp. 1–33.

116 R. Rusconi, 'De la prédication à la confession: Transmission et contrôle de modèles de comportement au XIIIe siècle', in *Faire croire*, pp. 67–85.

117 Powicke and Cheney, *Councils and Synods*, I, p. 265.

118 Bordeaux 1234, c. 8 (Pontal, ed., *Statuts synodaux*, II, p. 48).

119 Caesarius Heisterbacensis, *Dialogus miraculorum*, I, p. 164 (III, 45).

120 Alan of Lille, *Art of Preaching*, pp. 124–5; Gerald of Wales, *Gemma Ecclesiastica*, in Geraldus Cambrensis, *Opera*, RS 21 (London: Longman, 1862), II, p. 111.

121 Murray, 'Confession as an Historical Source', pp. 277–8.

122 Jansen, *Magdalen*, p. 213; *Menagier*, p. 15.

123 Jean Gerson, 'On the Art of Hearing Confessions', in Gerson, *Early Works*, pp. 365–77.

124 Robert of Flamborough, *Liber poenitentialis*, ed. J. J. F. Firth (Toronto: PIMS, 1971), p. 62; *Menagier*, p. 19.

125 R. Rusconi, '*Ordinate confiteri*: La confessione dei peccati nelle *summae de casibus* e nei manuali per i confessori (metà XII – inizi XIV secolo)', in *L'Aveu: Antiquité et moyen-âge* (Rome: Ecole Française de Rome, 1986), p. 313.

126 H. Martin, 'Confession et contrôle social à la fin du moyen âge', in Groupe de la Bussière, eds, *Pratiques de la confession*, pp. 122–3; K. Lochrie, *Covert Operations: The Medieval Uses of Secrecy* (Philadelphia, PA: University of Pennsylvania Press, 1999), pp. 12–42.

127 *Handlyng Synne*, p. 282, ll. 11353–6; *Menagier*, p. 17.

128 For example, plates 1–3, 7–10, 12–25 (various manuscript illuminations, frescoes and other sources, 13th–early 16th centuries, mostly Italian) in R. Rusconi, *L'ordine dei peccati: La confessione tra Medioevo ed età moderna* (Bologna: Il Mulino, 2002).

129 Council of Fritzlar, 1243, c. 4 (Hefele, *Histoire des conciles*, V.ii, p. 1626).

130 L. K. Little, 'Les techniques de la confession et la confession comme technique', in *Faire croire*, pp. 90, 98.

131 *Handlyng Synne*, p. 121, ll. 4793–7; pp. 289–92, ll. 11619–764; p. 294, ll. 11831–40.

132 Goering and Pryce, eds, '*De modo confitiendi*', p. 17.

133 P. Adam, *La vie paroissiale en France au XIVe siècle* (Paris: Sirey, 1964), pp. 269–70; Caesarius Heisterbacensis, *Dialogus miraculorum*, I, p. 156 (III, 35). For other examples, see Murray, 'Piety and Impiety', pp. 93–4.

134 Fournier I, pp. 191–9; Tanner, ed., *Norwich Heresy Trials*, pp. 173–4; Bonet, ed., 'Els processos', p. 52.

135 Murray, 'Confession as an Historical Source', p. 296 and n. 1.

136 Bonet, ed., 'Els processos', pp. 70, 90, 94, 103, 114.

137 A. Murray, 'Counselling in Medieval Confession', in Biller and Minnis, eds, *Handling Sin*, p. 74.

138 Gerson, *Early Works*, pp. 240–1.

139 Bonet, ed., 'Els processos', pp. 111–12.

140 D. Elliott, 'Women and Confession: From Empowerment to Pathology', in M. C. Erler and M. Kowaleski, eds, *Gendering the Master Narrative: Women and Power in the Middle Ages* (Ithaca, NY: Cornell University Press, 2003), pp. 31–51.

141 Arnold, *Inquisition and Power*, pp. 198, 214–25; S. Bardsley, 'Sin, Speech and Scolding in Late Medieval England', in T. Fenster and D. L. Smail, eds, *Fama: The Politics of Talk and Reputation in Medieval Europe* (Ithaca, NY: Cornell University Press, 2003), p. 151.

142 Bonet, ed., 'Els processos', p. 115.

143 Thomas de Cantimpré, *Bonum universale*, II, 51, 5.

144 Binski, *Medieval Death*, pp. 33–47.

145 J. Murray, '"The Law of Sin That is in My Members": The Problem of Male Embodiment', in S. J. E. Riches and S. Salih, eds, *Gender and Holiness: Men, Women and Saints in Late Medieval Europe* (London: Routledge, 2002), pp. 9–22.

146 Jacques de Vitry, *Exempla*, pp. 119–20 (no. cclxxxiv).

147 Gui, *Practica*, p. 175.

148 Mansfield, *Humiliation*, pp. 227 (plate 5, pontifical of Beauvais), 179.

149 *Handlyng Synne*, pp. 6, 294, ll. 145–6, 11835–6.

150 Wenzel, ed., '*Deus est*', p. 255; Fournier II, pp. 434–8; Tentler, *Sin and Confession*, p. 129.

151 T. N. Tentler, 'The Summa for Confessors as an Instrument of Social Control', in Trinkaus and Oberman, eds, *Pursuit of Holiness*, p. 123. See also the subsequent argument between Tentler, Leonard Boyle and William Bouwsma, pp. 126–37.

152 Finch, 'Disciplining of the Laity'.

153 See numerous cases of contumacy in Pearson, ed., 'Records of a Ruridecanal Court', pp. 69–80 and similarly in Parker and Poos, eds, 'Consistory Court . . . Rochester'.

154 For example *Reg. Sutton* IV, pp. 4, 8–9, 15–6, and *passim*.

155 27 December 1292, *Reg. Sutton* IV, p. 54; 1 April 1293, *Reg. Sutton* IV, p. 75; *Reg. Sutton*, IV, pp. 35–6.

156 M. Haren, ed., 'The Interrogatories for Officials, Lawyers and Secular Estates of the *Memoriale presbiterorum*', in Biller and Minnis, eds, *Handling Sin*, pp. 123–63.

157 See, similarly, Michel Lauwers's discussion of the 'economy' of death and salvation: Lauwers, *La mémoire des ancêtres*, pp. 474–91.

158 For example Vauchez, *Laity*, p. 72 (and quoting earlier work); Caldwell, 'Doctors of Souls'; Delumeau, *Sin and Fear*. See also P. von Moos, '*Occulta cordis*: Contrôle de soi et confession au moyen âge', *Médiévales* 29 (1995): 131–40; 30 (1996): 117–37.

159 C. Muessig, 'Audience and Sources in Jacques de Vitry's *Sermones feriales et communes*', in Hamesse et al., eds, *Medieval Sermons and Society*, p. 201.

160 Mansfield, *Humiliation*, p. 263; Trexler, 'Ritual in Florence', pp. 240–5.

161 F. L. Ganshof, 'Pèlerinages expiatoires flamands à Saint-Gilles pendant le XIVe siècle', *Annales du Midi* 78 (1966): 391–407.

162 See Vauchez, *Laity*, pp. 119–27.

163 Chapter 3, p. 78.

164 Banker, *Death in the Community*, p. 182.

165 *Menagier*, p. 38

166 G. Duby, 'Solitude', in G. Duby, ed., *A History of Private Life, II: Revelations of the Medieval World*, trans. A. Goldhammer (Cambridge, MA: Belknap Press, 1988), p. 528.

167 Casagrande, 'Protected Woman', p. 91; Elliott, 'Dress as Mediator', pp. 304–6.

168 J. Van Engen, 'The Sayings of the Fathers: An Inside Look at the New Devout in Deventer', in Bast and Gow, eds, *Continuity and Change*, pp. 279–320.

169 Alan of Lille, *Art of Preaching*, p. 54.

170 C. Morris, *The Discovery of the Individual: 1050–1200* (New York: SPCK, 1973), p. 73.

171 Le Goff, 'Trades and Professions', p. 114; Delumeau, *Sin and Fear*.

172 C. W. Bynum, 'Did the Twelfth Century Discover the Individual?', in eadem, *Jesus as Mother: Studies in Twelfth Century Spirituality* (Berkeley, CA: University of California Press, 1982), pp. 82–109.

173 J. Tambling, *Confession: Sin, Sexuality, the Subject* (Manchester: Manchester University Press, 1995), p. 58.

174 J. F. Benton, 'Consciousness of Self and Perceptions of Individuality', in Benson and Constable, eds, *Renaissance and Renewal*, p. 285; R. D. Logan, 'A Conception of the Self in the Later Middle Ages', *JMH* 12 (1986): 253–68.

175 Wenzel, ed., 'Deus est', pp. 258–9; Statutes of Guiard de Laon, 1238x48, c. 149 (Avril, ed., *Status synodaux*, IV, p. 57).

176 *Handlyng Synne*, pp. 5, 6, ll. 89–90, 120–2, 127–8. See M. Miller, 'Displaced Souls, Idle Talk, Spectacular Scenes: *Handlyng Synne* and the Perspectives of Agency', *Speculum* 71 (1996): 628.

177 *Jacob's Well*, pp. 1–2.

178 *Menagier*, p. 16.

179 Jansen, *Magdalen*, p. 166.

180 R. L. A. Clark, 'Constructing the Female Subject in Late Medieval Devotion', in Ashley and Clark, eds, *Medieval Conduct*, p. 171.

181 S. Salih, 'Margery's Bodies: Piety, Work and Penance', in Arnold and Lewis, eds, *Companion*, pp. 161–76.

182 Jansen, *Magdalen*, p. 114; Bartlett, *Male Authors, Female Readers*, pp. 120–1.

183 Bartlett, *Male Authors, Female Readers*, p. 32.

184 Brown, *Popular Piety*, pp. 207–8; Weissman, 'Cults and Contexts', p. 210.

185 *Handlyng Synne*, pp. 253–5, ll. 10165–256.

6 Dissent

1 P. J. Archambault, trans., *A Monk's Confession: The Memoirs of Guibert de Nogent* (University Park, PA: Pennsylvania State University Press, 1996), p. 196.

See also Wakefield and Evans, *Heresies*, pp. 101–4, for a slightly different translation.

2 Cohn, *Europe's Inner Demons*, pp. 42–59; J. C. Davis, *Fear, Myth and History: The Ranters and the Historians* (Cambridge: Cambridge University Press, 1986).

3 Critical perspectives on eleventh- and twelfth-century sources are given in M. Zerner, ed., *Inventer l'hérésie? Discours polémiques et pouvoirs avant l'inquisition* (Nice: Centre d'Etudes Médiévales, 1998).

4 There are two possible source passages, both occasions of Christ addressing his disciples: John 13:17 ('si haec scitis beati eritis si feceritis ea': 'If you know these things, you are blessed if you do them') or Luke 6:22 ('beati eritis cum vos oderint homines et cum separaverint vos et exprobraverint et eiecerint nomen vestrum tamquam malum propter Filium hominis': 'Blessed are you when men shall hate you, and when they put you apart, and cast out your name as evil, because of the Son of Man').

5 Archambault, *Monk's Confession*, p. 197.

6 Moore, *Formation of a Persecuting Society*, p. 68.

7 The best overview of medieval heresy is Lambert, *Medieval Heresy*.

8 For sources, here and below, see Wakefield and Evans, *Heresies*. On the eleventh-century and twelfth-century phenomena, see particularly R. I. Moore, *The Origins of European Dissent* (1977. Reprint, Toronto: University of Toronto Press, 1994); idem, 'Heresy, Repression and Social Change in the Age of Gregorian Reform', in Waugh and Diehl, eds, *Christendom and its Discontents*, pp. 19–46; Stock, *Implications of Literacy*, pp. 88–240.

9 A. Patschovsky, 'Heresy and Society: On the Political Function of Heresy in the Medieval World', in C. Bruschi and P. Biller, eds, *Texts and the Repression of Medieval Heresy* (York: York Medieval Press, 2003), p. 34.

10 Anonymous chronicle of Laon, translated in Wakefield and Evans, *Heresies*, pp. 200–2.

11 G. Audisio, *The Waldensian Dissent: Persecution and Survival c.1170–c.1570*, trans. C. Davison (Cambridge: Cambridge University Press, 1999); E. Cameron, *Waldenses: Rejections of Holy Church in Medieval Europe* (Oxford: Blackwell, 2000).

12 M. G. Pegg, *The Corruption of Angels: The Great Inquisition of 1245–46* (Princeton, NJ: Princeton University Press, 2001), pp. 15–19; J. Théry, 'L'Hérésie des bons hommes: Comment nommer la dissidence religieuse non vaudoise ni beguine en Languedoc (XIIe–début du XIVe siècle)?', *Hérésis* 36–37 (2002): 75–117.

13 On Cathar theology, see especially Hamilton, 'The Cathars and Christian Perfection', 5–23.

14 Lambert, *The Cathars*; M. Barber, *The Cathars: Dualist Heretics in Languedoc in the High Middle Ages* (Harlow: Longman, 2000).

15 Wakefield and Evans, *Heresies*, p. 413.

16 R. Lerner, *The Heresy of the Free Spirit in the Later Middle Ages* (Berkeley, CA: University of California Press, 1972), pp. 134–41.

17 Hudson, *Premature Reformation*; J. A. F. Thomson, *The Later Lollards* (London: Oxford University Press, 1965).

18 See H. Kaminsky, *A History of the Hussite Revolution* (Berkeley, CA: University of California Press, 1967); Lambert, *Medieval Heresy*, pp. 306–82.

19 Macy, 'Dogma of Transubstantiation', pp. 32–40.

20 Moore, 'Heresy, Repression and Social Change', p. 41: 'The identification of heresy is by definition a political act, requiring both that obedience be demanded and that it be refused.'

21 Moore, *Formation of a Persecuting Society*; Iogna-Prat, *Order and Exclusion*; B. M. Kienzle, *Cistercians, Heresy and Crusade in Occitania, 1145–1229: Preaching in the Lord's Vineyard* (York: York Medieval Press, 2001).

22 B. Hamilton, *The Albigensian Crusade* (London: Historical Association, 1974); J. R. Strayer, *The Albigensian Crusades* (New York: Dial Press, 1971).

23 R. Kieckhefer, 'The Office of Inquisition and Medieval Heresy: The Transition from Personal to Institutional Jurisdiction', *JEH* 46 (1995): 36–61.

24 Given, *Inquisition*.

25 Pegg, *Corruption of Angels*, particularly pp. 35–51.

26 Given, *Inquisition*, pp. 66–92.

27 H. C. Lea, *A History of the Inquisition in the Middle Ages*, 3 vols. (1888. Repr. New York: S. A. Russell, 1955); R. Kieckhefer, *The Repression of Heresy in Medieval Germany* (Liverpool: Liverpool University Press, 1979).

28 J. H. Arnold, 'Lollard Trials and Inquisitorial Discourse', in C. Given-Wilson, ed., *Fourteenth-Century England* II (Woodbridge: Boydell, 2002), pp. 81–94. See also I. Forrest, *The Pursuit of Heresy in Late Medieval England* (Oxford: Oxford University Press, forthcoming).

29 On using inquisitors' records, see the articles by Arnold, Bruschi and Pegg in Bruschi and Biller, eds, *Texts*; Arnold, *Inquisition and Power*.

30 Wakefield and Evans, *Heresies*, p. 83.

31 Wakefield and Evans, *Heresies*, p. 78.

32 Grundmann, *Religious Movements*, particularly pp. 17–21. See Chapter 2, pp. 41–2.

33 Brown, *Popular Piety*, p. 222.

34 Wakefield and Evans, *Heresies*, p. 99. On Tanchelm, see Lambert, *Medieval Heresy*, pp. 57–9.

35 Wakefield and Evans, *Heresies*, p. 115.

36 Arnold, *Inquisition and Power*, pp. 98–107.

37 Pegg, *Corruption of Angels*, pp. 92–103.

38 Duvernoy, 'Les Albigeois', pp. 64–73; Arnold, *Inquisition and Power*, p. 158.

39 Doat 23 fos 121r–4v. See also Roquebert, 'Le Catharisme', pp. 221–42.

40 S. McSheffrey, *Gender and Heresy: Women and Men in Lollard Communities, 1420–1530* (Philadelphia, PA: University of Pennsylvania Press, 1995), pp. 87, 25–7, and 80–107 in general. Similarly on Waldensians, see Audisio, *Waldensian Dissent*, pp. 107–8.

41 McSheffrey, *Gender and Heresy*, p. 99.

42 J. Duvernoy, ed., *L'Inquisition en Quercy: Le registre des pénitences des Pierre Cellan, 1241–1242* (Castelnaud La Chapelle: L'Hydre, 2001), pp. 68, 146 and *passim*. For Italy, see G. G. Merlo, *Eretici e inquisitori nella società Piemontese del Trecento* (Turin: Claudiana, 1977), pp. 20–40.

43 Le Roy Ladurie, *Montaillou*; J. Duvernoy, 'Le Catharisme en Languedoc au début du XIVe siècle', CdF 20 (1985), pp. 27–56.

44 Cameron, *Waldenses*, p. 67; Given, *Inquisition*, pp. 119–20; McSheffrey, *Gender and Heresy*, p. 28.

45 Cameron, *Waldenses*, pp. 133–5.

46 Ibid., p. 136; Doat 24 fos 280v–81r.

47 On class, see Erbstösser, *Heretics in the Middle Ages*, and more subtly R. H. Hilton, *Bond Men Made Free: Medieval Peasant Movements and the English Rising of 1381* (London: Methuen, 1977), pp. 102–9. On gender, B. Bolton, 'Mulieres sanctae', SCH 10 (1973): 77–95; M. Barber, 'Women and Catharism', *Reading Medieval Studies* 3 (1977): 45–62; S. Shahar, *Women in a Medieval Heretical Sect: Agnes and Huguette the Waldensians*, trans. Y. Lotan (Woodbridge: Boydell, 2001).

48 R. Abels and E. Harrison, 'The Participation of Women in Languedocian Catharism', *Mediaeval Studies* 41 (1979): 215–51; McSheffrey, *Gender and Heresy*.

49 Biller, 'Common Woman'; P. Biller, 'Cathars and Material Women', in P. Biller and A. Minnis, eds, *Medieval Theology and the Natural Body* (York: York Medieval Press, 1997), pp. 61–107.

50 One small group – the followers of Guglielma of Milan (d. 1281) – did, however, believe in a female 'pope' who would lead them to salvation. See S. Wessley, 'The Thirteenth-Century Guglielmites: Salvation Through Women', in D. Baker, ed., *Medieval Women*, SCH subsidia 1 (Oxford: Blackwell, 1978), pp. 289–303; J. L. Peterson, 'Social Roles, Gender Inversion, and the Heretical Sect: The Case of the Guglielmites', *Viator* 35 (2004): 203–20.

51 McSheffrey, *Gender and Heresy*, pp. 61–2 and *passim*.

52 Cameron, *Waldenses*, p. 129; Pegg, *Corruption of Angels*, p. 54; McSheffrey, *Gender and Heresy*, p. 148.

53 Audisio, *Waldensian Dissent*, p. 139; Fournier III, p. 120; Tanner, ed., *Norwich Heresy Trials*, p. 147.

54 William of Puylaurens, *Chronicle*, p. 25.

55 Archambault, *Monk's Confession*, p. 198.

56 Kieckhefer, *Repression*, pp. 76–9.

57 Pegg, *Corruption of Angels*, p. 80; Audisio, *Waldensian Dissent*, p. 109.

58 Fournier III, pp. 95–6; Doat 25, fo. 179r.

59 J. Given, 'The Béguins in Bernard Gui's *Liber sententiarum*', in Bruschi and Biller, eds, *Texts*, p. 159; Lansing, *Power and Purity*, p. 15.

60 K. Arnold, ed., *Niklashausen 1476: Quellen und Untersuchengen zur sozialreligiösen Bewegung des Hans Behem und zur Agrarstrukter eines spätmittelalterlichen Dorfes* (Baden-Baden: Koerner, 1980), pp. 214–5; see R. Wunderli, *Peasant Fires: The Drummer of Niklashausen* (Indianapolis, IN: Indiana University Press, 1992).

61 Quoted in Wunderli, *Peasant Fires*, p. 44.

62 Arnold, ed., *Niklashausen 1476*, pp. 195–6.

63 P. Freedman, *Images of the Medieval Peasant* (Stanford, CA: Stanford University Press, 1999), pp. 285, 283.

64 H. J. Cohn, 'Anticlericalism in the German Peasants' War 1525', *P&P* 83 (1979): 5.

65 *Chronique latine de Guillaume de Nangis de 1113 à 1300, avec les continuations de cette chronique de 1300 à 1368*, ed. H. Géraud (Paris: Renouard, 1843), I: 419–20; M. Barber, 'The Pastoureaux of 1320', *JEH* 32 (1981): 163.

66 H. Pirenne, ed., *Le Soulèvement de la Flandre maritime de 1323–1328* (Brussells: Kiessling, 1900), pp. xvi–xxvii; *Corpus Chronicon Flandriae*, in J.-J. de Smet, ed., *Recueil des chroniques de Flandre* (Brussells: Hayez, 1837), I, pp. 201–2.

67 P. Linehan, 'The Mechanization of Ritual: Alfonso XI of Castile in 1332', in Chiffoleau *et al.*, eds, *Riti e rituali*, pp. 309–27.

68 Reynolds, *Kingdoms and Communities*, p. 74; McRee, 'Religious Gilds and Civic Order', p. 73.

69 M. Mullett, *Popular Culture and Popular Protest in Late Medieval and Early Modern Europe* (London: Croom Helm, 1987), pp. 83–4.

70 R. J. Crum and D. G. Wilkins, 'In the Defense of Florentine Republicanism: Saint Anne and Florentine Art, 1343–1575', in Ashley and Sheingorn, eds, *Interpreting Cultural Symbols*, p. 131.

71 *Chroniques des règnes de Jean II et de Charles V*, Les Grandes Chroniques de France (Paris: Renouard, 1910), I: 177–8.

72 P. Strohm, ' "A Revelle!": Chronicle Evidence and the Rebel Voice', in Strohm, *Hochon's Arrow: The Social Imagination of Fourteenth-Century Texts* (Princeton, NJ: Princeton University Press, 1992), p. 53.

73 On 1381, Corpus Christi, and popular politics, see further S. Justice, *Writing and Rebellion: England in 1381* (Berkeley, CA: University of California Press, 1994), pp. 140–92.

74 R. B. Dobson, ed. and trans., *The Peasants' Revolt of 1381*, 2nd edn (Houndmills: Macmillan, 1983), p. 374.

75 A. B. Friedman, ' "When Adam Delved . . .": Contexts of an Historic Proverb', in L. D. Benson, ed., *The Learned and the Lewed: Studies in Chaucer and Medieval Literature* (Cambridge, MA: Harvard University Press, 1974), pp. 213–30.

76 Freedman, *Images*, pp. 60–3.

77 L. Rothkrug, 'Icon and Ideology in Religion and Rebellion 1300–1600: *Bauernfreiheit* and *Religion royale*', in J. M. Bak and G. Benecke, eds, *Religion and Rural Revolt* (Manchester: Manchester University Press, 1984), pp. 31–61.

78 T. Fudge, 'The "Crown" and the "Red Gown": Hussite Popular Religion', in R. W. Scribner, ed., *Popular Religion in Germany and Central Europe 1400–1800* (Houndmills: Macmillan, 1996), pp. 46–7.

79 See anonymous Taborite author in 1420, T. Fudge, ed. and trans., *The Crusade against Heretics in Bohemia 1418–1437: Sources and Documents for the Hussite Crusades* (Aldershot: Ashgate, 2002), pp. 32–3.

80 Friedman, 'When Adam Delved . . .', p. 225.

81 Cohn, 'Anticlericalism', pp. 22–3.

82 Clopper, ed., *REED: Chester*, p. 5.

83 Dobson, ed., *Peasants' Revolt*, p. 81.

84 Lansing, *Power and Purity*, p. 176.

85 Scott, *Domination*, pp. 191–2.

86 Thomas de Cantimpré, *Bonum universale*, II, 47, 3; Arnold, *Inquisition and Power*, p. 188; *Reg. Sutton*, IV, pp. 15–16; III, p. xxxix.

87 Cohn, 'Anticlericalism'; R. W. Scribner, 'Anticlericalism and the Reformation in Germany', in Scribner, *Popular Culture and Popular Movements in Reformation Germany* (London: Hambledon, 1987), pp. 243–56.

88 Thomas de Cantimpré, *Bonum universale*, II, 4, 2.

89 *Historia Episcopum Autissiodorensium, Altera Chronica Lemovicensis* and *Chronicon Anonymi Laudunensis*, all edited in *Recueils des Histoires des Gaules et de la France* 18 (Paris: Victor Palmé, 1879), at pp. 219, 705, 729.

90 Matthew Paris, *Chronica majora*, ed. H. R. Luard, RS 57 (London: Longman, 1880), V, p. 249; *Annals of Burton*, in *Annales Monastici*, ed. H. R. Luard, RS 36 (London: Longman, 1864), p. 292. On the pastoureaux, see W. C. Jordan, *Louis IX and the Challenge of the Crusade* (Princeton, NJ: Princeton University Press, 1979), pp. 113–16.

91 Barber, 'Pastoureaux', p. 146; Nirenberg, *Communities of Violence*, pp. 43–68.

92 D. C. Munro, 'The Children's Crusade', *AHR* 19 (1914): 516–24; G. Dickson, 'The Genesis of the Children's Crusade (1212)', in Dickson, *Religious Enthusiasm in the Medieval West* (Aldershot: Variorum, 2000), essay IV.

93 A. Thompson, *Revival Preachers and Politics in Thirteenth-Century Italy: The Great Devotion of 1233* (Oxford: Clarendon Press, 1992).

94 Dickson, 'Flagellants of 1260': 227–67, though Dickson rejects economic causative factors in this and other movements.

95 D. E. Bornstein, *The Bianchi of 1399: Popular Devotion in Late Medieval Italy* (Ithaca, NY: Cornell University Press, 1993), pp. 43–4, 52, 63–4, 200.

96 J. Hamburger, 'Bosch's Conjuror: An Attack on Magic and Sacramental Heresy', *Simiolus* 14 (1984), pp. 12–13.

97 For example, Hamilton, *Religion*, pp. 189–91; Vauchez, *Laity*, p. 90.

98 See, to varying extents, Murray, 'Piety and Impiety'; Murray, 'Religion among the Poor'; W. L. Wakefield, 'Some Unorthodox Popular Ideas of the Thirteenth Century', *Medievalia et Humanistica* n.s. 4 (1973): 25–35; J. Edwards, 'Religious Faith and Doubt in Late Medieval Spain: Soria c.1450–1500', *P&P* 120 (1988): 3–25; Reynolds, 'Social Mentalities'; Langmuir, *Toward a Definition of Antisemitism*, pp. 100–33. G. Minois, *Histoire de l'athéisme* (Paris: Fayard, 1998), pp. 68–104, places intellectual and popular medieval scepticism within a longer tradition. See also Thomas, *Religion and the Decline of Magic*, pp. 198–206.

99 On theologians' views – but interpreted as covering all possible attitudes – see J.-C. Schmitt, 'Du bon usage de "Credo"', in *Faire croire*, pp. 337–61; J. Wirth, 'La naissance du concept de croyance (XIIe–XVIIe siècles)', *Bibliothèque d'humanisme et renaissance* 45 (1983): 7–58.

100 Reynolds, 'Social Mentalities', p. 29.

101 Goering and Payer, 'Summa', p. 37, ll. 220–1.

102 Shinners and Dohar, eds, *Pastors*, pp. 292, 293, 296; Adam, *Vie paroissiale*, p. 247; Bonet, ed., 'Els processos', p. 62, 75; Brown, *Popular Piety*, p. 212. See also Murray, 'Religion among the Poor', pp. 301–2.

103 Bonet, ed., 'Els processos', pp. 73, 78.

104 O'Sullivan, ed., *Register of Eudes of Rouen*, pp. 425–6, 536; Brown, *Popular Piety*, p. 81; R. K. Marshall, *The Local Merchants of Prato: Small Entrepreneurs in the Late Medieval Economy* (Baltimore, MD: Johns Hopkins University Press, 1999), p. 30.

105 Wenzel, ed., '*Deus est*', p. 250.

106 Thomas de Cantimpré, *Bonum universale*, II, 1, 8.

107 Wakfield, 'Unorthodox Popular Ideas', p. 27.

108 G. Pinto, ed., *Il Libro del Biadaiolo: Carestie e Annona a Firenze dalla Metà del '200 al 1348* (Florence: Olschki, 1978), pp. 316, 367.

109 E. Horodowich, 'Civic Identity and the Control of Blasphemy in Sixteenth-Century Venice', *P&P* 181 (2003): 5–6; C. Leveleux, *La parole interdite: Le blasphème dans la France médiévale (XIIIe–XVIe siècles): Du péché au crime* (Paris: De Boccard, 2001).

110 M. Flynn, 'Blasphemy and the Play of Anger in Sixteenth-Century Spain', *P&P* 149 (1995): 46–7; R. I. Burns, ed., *Las Siete Partidas*, trans. S. P. Scott (Philadelphia, PA: University of Pennsylvania Press, 2001), V, p. 1448 (Part. VII, tit. 28).

111 N. Eymerich, *Le manuel des inquisiteurs*, ed. and trans. L. Sala-Molins (Paris: Albin Michel, 2001), pp. 92–5; Flynn, 'Blasphemy', pp. 35–6.

112 Flynn, 'Blasphemy', p. 32.

113 Flynn, 'Blasphemy', pp. 49–52.

114 Bonet, ed., 'Els processos', p. 56.

115 *Reg. Langton*, p. 80.

116 Jansen, *Magdalen*, p. 310; quoting Salimbene from 1283.

117 Gautier de Coinci, *Les miracles de Notre Dame de Soissons*, ed. L. Lindgren (Helsinki: Suomalainea Tiedeaktemia, 1963), p. 112, ll. 510–5; *AASS* January II, p. 403, col. 2; *AASS* April III, p. 511, col. 1; on earlier periods, see Reynolds, 'Social Mentalities', p. 30; P.-A. Sigal, *L'homme et le miracle dans la France médiévale (XIe–XIIe siècles)* (Paris: CERF, 1985), pp. 210–16.

118 William of Malmesbury, *Gesta pontificum Anglorum*, ed. N. E. S. A. Hamilton RS 52 (London: Longman, 1870), p. 438; quoted in R. Bartlett, *England under the Norman and Angevin Kings 1075–1225* (Oxford: Oxford University Press, 2000), p. 478.

119 See A. Wood, *Riot, Rebellion and Popular Politics in Early Modern England* (Houndmills: Palgrave, 2002), p. 69.

120 J. Robertson, ed., *Materials for the History of Thomas Becket*, RS 67 (London: Longman, 1875), I, pp. 470–1; William of Malmesbury, *Gesta*, pp. 435–6.

121 Murray, 'Piety and impiety', p. 99; Murray, 'Religion among the Poor', p. 301; *Handlyng Synne*, p. 249, ll. 9985–8; Bartlett, *England*, p. 479.

122 *Gesta episcoporum Cameracensium*, MGH VII, pp. 472–3 (III, 22); Mundy, 'Village, Town, and City', p. 157.

123 Wakefield, 'Unorthodox Popular Ideas', pp. 28, 31; Cameron, *Waldenses*, p. 137.

124 Doat 25 fos 231v, 236r, 237v; see also Wakefield, 'Unorthodox Popular Ideas', p. 27.

125 *Reg. Langton*, pp. 50–1.

126 *Reg. Langton*, pp. 82, 72.

127 Walravens, 'Insultes, blasphèmes ou hérésie?', p. 488 n. 6.

128 Brown, *Popular Piety*, p. 214.

129 Alpert of Metz, *De diversitate temporum*, Monumenta Germaniae Historica, Scriptores in folio IV (Hanover, 1841), Book 1, c. 17, p. 709; Thomas de Cantimpré, *Bonum universale*, II, 56, 2; Murray, 'Piety and Impiety', pp. 101–2. See also Murray, 'Religion among the Poor', p. 323.

130 Murray, 'Religion among the Poor', p. 323.

131 H. C. Lea, *A History of the Inquisition in the Middle Ages* (1888. Repr. New York: S. A. Russell, 1965), III, p. 565; Edwards, 'Religious Faith and Doubt', pp. 15, 25.

132 Fournier I, pp. 260–7; II, pp. 129–30.

133 Bartlett, *England*, p. 478; Murray, 'Piety and Impiety', p. 100. My thanks to Barbara Massam for spotting Remigio's biblical reference.

134 Fournier I, p. 166; see Arnold, *Inquisition and Power*, pp. 167–73; Edwards, 'Religious Faith and Doubt', p. 16.

135 Doat 25 fos 24r–26r, 179r.

136 D. L. d'Avray, 'Philosophy in Preaching: The Case of a Franciscan Based in Thirteenth-Century Florence (Servasanto da Faenza)', in R. G. Newhauser and J. Afford, eds, *Literature and Religion in the Later Middle Ages* (Binghamton, NY: Medieval and Renaissance Texts and Studies, 1995), pp. 263–73.

137 Fournier I, p. 206. See J. H. Arnold, 'Inquisition, Texts and Discourse', in Bruschi and Biller, eds, *Texts*. Shinners, ed., *Medieval Popular Religion*, pp. 471–90, provides his own translation of Guillaume's deposition.

138 Doat 25, fos. 20v–23v; Wakefield 'Unorthodox Popular Ideas', pp. 26–7.

139 Fournier II, pp. 118–34. See Le Roy Ladurie, *Montaillou*, p. 144.

140 Doat 25 fo. 232r; Lansing, *Power and Purity*, p. 19; *Handlyng Synne*, p. 238, ll. 9523–6; Edwards, 'Religious Faith and Doubt', pp. 16–17.

141 I am influenced here by various works, including Scribner, ed., *Popular Religion*; Zika, 'Hosts, Processions and Pilgrimage'; H. Kamen, *The Phoenix and the Flame: Catalonia and the Counter Reformation* (New Haven, CT: Yale University Press, 1993); L. Roper, *The Holy Household: Women and Morals in Reformation Augsburg* (Oxford: Clarendon Press, 1989); P. Lake, *The Boxmaker's Revenge* (Manchester: Manchester University Press, 2001).

142 Fournier II, p. 157.

Bibliography

Primary sources

Acta sanctorum, ed. J. Bollandus *et al.* (Antwerp, 1643–1883)

Alan of Lille, *The Art of Preaching*, trans. G. R. Evans (Kalamazoo, MI: Cistercian Studies, 1981)

Alessandra Strozzi, *Selected Letters of Alessandra Strozzi*, ed. and trans. H. Gregory (Berkeley, CA: University of California Press, 1997)

Alpert of Metz, *De diversitate temporum*, Monumenta Germaniae Historica, Scriptores in folio IV (Hanover, 1841), pp. 700–23

Annals of Burton, in *Annales Monastici*, ed. H. R. Luard, Rolls Series 36 (London: Longman, 1864), pp. 290–3

Arnold, K., ed., *Niklashausen 1476: Quellen und Untersuchengen zur sozialreligiösen Bewegung des Hans Behem und zur Agrarstrukter eines spätmittelalterlichen Dorfes* (Baden-Baden: Koerner, 1980)

Avril, J., ed., *Les Statuts synodaux français du XIIIe siècle, t. IV: Les statuts synodaux de l'ancienne province de Reims* (Paris: CTHS, 1995)

Babees Book, ed. F. J. Furnivall, EETS o.s. 32 (London: Trübner, 1868)

Bernard Gui, *Practica inquisitionis heretice pravitatis*, ed. C. Douais (Paris: Alphonse Picard, 1886) [partial translation in W. L. Wakefield and A. P. Evans, eds and trans., *Heresies of the High Middle Ages* (New York: Columbia University Press, 1991), document 55]

Bernard Gui, *Le Livre des sentences de l'inquisiteur Bernard Gui 1308–1323*, ed. A. Pales-Gobilliard, 2 vols (Paris: CNRS, 2002)

Bevington, D., ed., *Medieval Drama* (Boston: Houghton Mifflin, 1975)

Bull, M., ed. and trans., *The Miracles of Our Lady of Rocamadour: Analysis and Translation* (Woodbridge: Boydell, 1999)

Burns, R. I., ed., *Las Siete Partidas*, trans. S. P. Scott, 5 vols (Philadelphia, PA: University of Pennsylvania Press, 2001)

Cadwgan, *De modo confitiendi*, ed. in J. Goering and H. Pryce, 'The *De modo confitiendi* of Cadwgan, bishop of Bangor', *Mediaeval Studies* 62 (2000): 1–27

Caesarius Heisterbacensis, *Dialogus miraculorum*, ed. J. Strange (Cologne: Heberle, 1851), 2 vols [trans. Caesarius of Heisterbach, *The Dialogue on Miracles*, trans. H. von. E. Scott and C. C. Swinton Bland (London: Routledge, 1929)]

Cazelles, B., ed. and trans., *The Lady as Saint: A Collection of French Hagiographic Romances of the Thirteenth Century* (Philadelphia, PA: University of Pennsylvania Press, 1991)

Christine de Pizan, *The Book of the City of Ladies*, trans. R. Brown-Grant (London: Penguin, 1999)

Chronicon Anonymi Laudunensis, in *Recueils des Historiens des Gaules et de la France* 18 (Paris: Victor Palmé, 1879), pp. 702–20

Chroniques des règnes de Jean II et de Charles V, Les Grandes Chroniques de France (Paris: Renouard, 1910)

Clopper, L. M., ed., *Records of Early English Drama: Chester* (Toronto: University of Toronto Press, 1979)

Corpus Chronicon Flandriae, in J.-J. de Smet, ed., *Recueil des chroniques de Flandre* I (Brussells: Hayez, 1837)

Coulton, G. G., ed. and trans., *Social Life in Britain from the Conquest to the Reformation* (Cambridge: Cambridge University Press, 1956)

Debate of Body and Soul, in J. Gardner, ed., *The Alliterative Morte Arthure, The Owl and the Nightingale, and Five Other Middle English Poems* (Carbondale, IL: Southern Illinois University Press, 1971), pp. 161–73

Dives and Pauper, ed. P. H. Barum, EETS o.s. 275, 280 (London: Oxford University Press, 1976–1980)

Dobson, R. B., ed. and trans., *The Peasants' Revolt of 1381*, 2nd edn (Houndmills: Macmillan, 1983)

Douais, C., ed., *Documents sur l'ancienne province de Languedoc*, 2 vols (Toulouse: Privat, 1901–04)

Duvernoy, J., ed., *Le Registre d'inquisition de Jacques Fournier, évêque de Pamiers (1318–1325)*, 3 vols (Toulouse: Privat, 1965)

Duvernoy, J., ed., *L'Inquisition en Quercy: Le registre des pénitences des Pierre Cellan, 1241–1242* (Castelnaud La Chapelle: L'Hydre, 2001)

English Gilds, ed. T. Smith, L. T. Smith and L. Brentano, EETS o.s. 40 (London: Trübner, 1870)

Fossier, R., ed., *Chartes de coutume en Picardie (XI–XIIIe siècle)*, Collection de document inédits sur l'histoire de France, Section de philology et d'histoire jusqu'a 1610, 10 (Paris: Bibliothèque Nationale, 1974)

Foster, K., ed. and trans., *The Life of St Thomas Aquinas: Biographical Documents* (London: Longmans, Green & Co, 1959)

Fudge, T., ed. and trans., *The Crusade against Heretics in Bohemia 1418–1437: Sources and Documents for the Hussite Crusades* (Aldershot: Ashgate, 2002)

Gaufredi Prioris Vosiensis, *Altera Chronica Lemovicensis*, in *Recueils des Histoires des Gaules et de la France* 18 (Paris: Victor Palmé, 1879), pp. 211–13

Gautier de Coinci, *Les Miracles de Nostre Dame*, ed. V. F. Koenig, 3 vols (Geneva: Droz, 1955–1961)

Gautier de Coinci, *Les miracles de Notre Dame de Soissons*, ed. L. Lindgren (Helsinki: Suomalainea Tiedeaktemia, 1963)

Gerald of Wales, *Gemma Ecclesiastica*, in Geraldus Cambrensis, *Opera*, Rolls Series 21, 6 vols (London: Longman, 1862) [trans. Gerald of Wales, *The Jewel of the Church*, ed. John J. Hagen (Leiden: Brill, 1979)]

Gesta episcoporum Cameracensium, Monumenta Germaniae Historica, Scriptores in folio VII (Hanover, 1846), pp. 393–525

Goering, J., and P. J. Payer, 'The *Summa Penitentie Fratrum Predicatorum*: A Thirteenth-Century Confessional Formulary', *Mediaeval Studies* 55 (1993): 1–50

Goodman of Paris, *Le Menagier de Paris*, ed. G. E. Brereton and J. M. Ferrier (Oxford: Clarendon Press, 1981) [trans. E. Power, *The Goodman of Paris: A Treatise on Moral and Domestic Economy by a Citizen of Paris c. 1393* (London: Routledge, 1928)]

Good Wife Taught Her Daughter, and The Good Wyfe Wold A Pylgremage, and The Thewis of Gud Women, ed. T. F. Mustanoja (Helsinki: Annales Academae Scientiarum Fennicae, 1948)

Guibert de Nogent, *A Monk's Confession: The Memoirs of Guibert de Nogent*, trans. P. J. Archambault (University Park, PA: Pennsylvania State University Press, 1996)

Guillaume de Nangis, *Chronique latine de Guillaume de Nangis de 1113 à 1300, avec les continuations de cette chronique de 1300 à 1368*, ed. H. Géraud, 2 vols (Paris: Renouard, 1843)

Grayzel, S., ed., *The Church and the Jews in the Thirteenth Century, Volume II: 1254–1314* (Detroit, MI: Wayne State University Press, 1989)

Haren, M., ed., 'The Interrogatories for Officials, Lawyers and Secular Estates of the *Memoriale presbiterorum*', in P. Biller and A. J. Minnis, eds, *Handling Sin: Confession in the Middle Ages* (York: York Medieval Press, 1998), pp. 123–63

Hefele, C. J., *Histoire des conciles d'après les documents originaux*, trans. H. Leclerq, 10 vols (Paris: Letouzy et Ané, 1907–1938)

Helmholz, R., ed., *Select Cases of Defamation to 1600*, Seldon Society 101 (London: Seldon Society, 1985)

Historia Episcopum Autissiodorensium, in *Recueils des Histoires des Gaules et de la France* 18 (Paris: Victor Palmé, 1879), pp. 725–41

Hudson, A., ed., *Selections from English Wycliffite Writings* (Toronto: University of Toronto Press, 1997)

Hugh of Poitiers, *The Vézelay Chronicle of Hugh of Poitiers*, ed. and trans. J. Scott, R. Thomson and J. Ward (Binghamton, NY: SUNY Press, 1988)

Jacob's Well, ed. A. Brandeis, EETS o.s. 115 (London: Kegan Paul, 1900)

Jacobus de Voragine, *The Golden Legend*, trans. W. G. Ryan, 2 vols (Princeton, NJ: Princeton University Press, 1993)

Jacques de Vitry, *The Exempla, or Illustrative Stories from the* Sermones vulgares *of Jacques de Vitry*, ed. T. F. Crane (London: Folklore Society, 1890)

Jean de Joinville, 'Life of Saint Louis', in *Chronicles of the Crusades*, trans. M. R. B. Shaw (Harmondsworth: Penguin, 1963)

Jean Gerson, *Early Works*, trans. B. P. McGuire (New York: Paulist Press, 1998)

Jocelin of Brakelond, *Chronicle of the Abbey of Bury St Edmunds*, trans. D. Greenway and J. Sayers (Oxford: Oxford University Press, 1989)

John Mirk, *Festial: A Collection of Homilies*, ed. T. Erbe, EETS e.s. 96 (London: Kegan Paul, 1905)

John of God, *Liber penitentiarius*, ed. in P. J. Payer, 'The Origins and Development of the Later Canones Penitentiales', *Mediaeval Studies* 61 (1999): 81–105

Jordan of Saxony, *On the Beginnings of the Order of Preachers*, trans. S. Tugwell (Chicago: Parable, 1982)

Kagay, D. J., trans., *The Usatges of Barcelona* (Philadelphia, PA: University of Pennsylvania Press, 1994)

Knight of La Tour Landry, *The Book of the Knight of La Tour Landry*, ed. T. Wright, EETS o.s. 33 (London: Trübner, 1868)

Liber de laudibus civitatis Ticiensis, ed. R. Maiocchi and F. Quintavalle, Rerum Italicarum Scriptores, new edn 11, i (Citta di Castello, 1903)

Libro del Biadaiolo: Carestie e Annona a Firenze dalla Metà del '200 al 1348, ed. G. Pinto (Florence: Olschki, 1978)

Mansi, G. D., *Sacrorum Conciliorum Nova et Amplissima Collectio*, 53 vols (1759–98. Repr. Graz: Akademische Druck- und Verlagsanstalt, 1961)

Margery Kempe, *The Book of Margery Kempe*, ed. S. B. Leech, EETS o.s. 212 (London: Oxford University Press, 1940)

Matthew Paris, *Chronica majora*, ed. H. R. Luard, Rolls Series 57, 5 vols (London: Longman, 1872–1880)

Meersseman, G. G., *Ordo Fraternitas: confraternite e pietà dei laici nel medioevo* (Rome: Herder, 1977)

Nicholas Eymerich, *Le manuel des inquisiteurs*, ed. and trans. L. Sala-Molins (Paris: Albin Michel, 2001)

Parker, S. L., and L. R. Poos, eds, 'A Consistory Court from the Diocese of Rochester, 1363–4', *English Historical Review* 106 (1991): 652–665

Pearson, F. S., ed., 'Records of a Ruridecanal Court of 1300', in *Collectanea*, Worcestershire Record Society 29 (1912), pp. 69–80

Pontal, O., ed., *Les Statuts synodaux français du XIIIe siècle, t. II: Les statuts de 1230 à 1260* (Paris: CTHS, 1983)

Powicke, F. M. and C. R. Cheney, eds, *Councils and Synods, 1205–1313*, 2 vols (Oxford: Clarendon Press, 1964)

Register of Bernard de Caux and Jean de St-Pierre, inquisitors at Pamiers (1246–1247): Paris, Bibliothèque Nationale, fonds Doat, ms. 24 fos 240–86 (unpublished)

Register of Brother Ferrier, inquisitor (1235–1248): Paris, Bibliothèque Nationale, fonds Doat, ms. 22 fos 108–296; ms. 23; ms. 24 fos 1–237 (unpublished)

Register of Bishop Philip Repingdon, 1405–1419, ed. M. Archer, 3 vols, Lincoln Record Society 57, 58, 74 (1963–1982)

Register of Eudes of Rouen, ed. J. F. O'Sullivan, trans. S. M. Brown (New York: Columbia University Press, 1964)

Register of John de Grandisson, Bishop of Exeter (1327–1369), ed. F. C. Hingeston-Randolph, 3 vols (London: G. Bell, 1894–1899)

Register of John Waltham, Bishop of Salisbury 1388–1395, ed. T. C. B. Timmins (Canterbury & York Society, 1994)

Register of Pons de Gualba, in J. M. Mati i Bonet, ed., 'Els processos de les Visites Pastorals del primer any de pontifical de Ponç de Gualba (a. 1303)', in J. M. Mati i Bonet, L. Niqui i Puigvert and F. Miquel i Mascort, eds, *Processos de l'Arxiu Diocesa de Barcelona* (Barcelona: n. p., 1984), pp. 49–121

Register of Ranulph de Plassac and Pons de Parnac, inquisitors (1273–1278): Paris, Bibliothèque Nationale, fonds Doat ms. 25; ms. 26 fos 1–78 (unpublished)

Register of Thomas Langton, Bishop of Salisbury 1485–93, ed. D. P. Wright, Canterbury and York Society 74 (1985)

Registre de l'officialité de Cerisy 1314–57, ed. G. Dupont, Mémoires de la Société des Antiquaries de Normandie, 3rd ser., 10 (Caen: Le Blanc-Hardel, 1880)

Robert Grosseteste, *Deus est*, ed. S. Wenzel, 'Robert Grosseteste's Treatise on Confession, *Deus est*', *Franciscan Studies* 30 (1970): 218–93

Roberti Grosseteste Epistolae, ed. H. R. Luard, Rolls Series 25 (London: Longman, 1861)

Robert Mannyng of Brunne, *Handlyng Synne*, ed. I. Sullens (Binghamton, NY: Medieval and Renaissance Texts and Studies, 1983)

Robert of Flamborough, *Liber poenitentialis*, ed. J. J. F. Firth (Toronto: PIMS, 1971)

Rolls and Register of Bishop Oliver Sutton, 1280–1299, ed. R. M. T. Hill, Lincoln Record Society 76, 8 vols (Woodbridge: Boydell, 1948–1986)

Rothwell, H., ed., *English Historical Documents, Volume III: 1189–1327* (London: Eyre and Spottiswoode, 1975)

Serlo, *Summa de Penitentia*, ed. in J. Goering, 'The *Summa de Penitentia* of Magister Serlo', *Mediaeval Studies* 38 (1976): 1–53

Shinners, J., ed. and trans., *Medieval Popular Religion 1000–1500: A Reader* (Peterborough, ON: Broadview Press, 1997)

Shinners, J. and W. Dohar, eds and trans., *Pastors and the Care of Souls in Medieval England* (Notre Dame, IN: University of Notre Dame Press, 1998)

Tale of Beryn, ed. F. J. Furnivall and W. G. Store, EETS e.s. 105 (London: Kegan Paul, 1909)

Tanner, N., ed., *Norwich Heresy Trials 1428–31*, Camden Society 4th series, 20 (London: Royal Historical Society, 1977)

Teulet, A., ed., *Layettes du Trésor des Chartes*, 5 vols (Paris: Plon, 1863–1909)

Thomas Becket, *Materials for the History of Thomas Becket*, ed. J. Robertson, Rolls Series 67, 7 vols (London: Longman, 1875–85)

Thomas de Cantimpré, *Bonum universale de apibus*, ed. G. Colvenere (Douais, 1627)

Tugwell, S., ed. and trans., *Early Dominicans: Selected Writings* (New York: Paulist Press, 1982)

Wakefield, W. L., and A. P. Evans, eds and trans., *Heresies of the High Middle Ages* (New York: Columbia University Press, 1991)

Weaver, J. R. H., and A. Beardwood, eds, *Some Oxfordshire Wills, Proved in the Prerogative Court of Canterbury, 1393–1550*, Oxfordshire Record Society 39 (1958)

Webb, D., ed. and trans., *Pilgrims and Pilgrimage in the Medieval West* (London: I.B. Tauris, 2001)

William of Malmesbury, *Gesta pontificum Anglorum*, ed. N. E. S. A. Hamilton, Rolls Series 52 (London: Longman, 1870)

William of Newburgh, *Historia rerum anglicarum*, in *Chronicles of the Reigns of Stephen, Henry II and Richard I*, ed. R. Howlett, Rolls Series 82, 2 vols (London: Longman, 1884–1885) [translation in J. Stevenson, ed. and trans., *The Church Historians of England* (London: Seeleys, 1866), vol. IV, pt. 2]

William of Puylaurens, *The Chronicle of William of Puylaurens: The Albigensian Crusade and its Aftermath*, ed. and trans. W. A. Sibly and M. D. Sibly (Woodbridge: Boydell, 2003)

Zanella, G., *Itinerari ereticali: Patari e catari tra Rimini e Verona*, Istituto Storico Italiano per il medio evo, Studi storici fasc. 153 (Rome: Nella Sede dell'Istituto, 1986), appendix I

Secondary texts

Abels, R., and E. Harrison, 'The Participation of Women in Languedocian Catharism', *Mediaeval Studies* 41 (1979): 215–51

Abou-El Haj, B., 'The Urban Setting for Late Medieval Church Building: Reims and its Cathedral Between 1210 and 1240', *Art History* 11 (1988): 17–41

Abou-el-Haj, B., 'The Audiences for the Medieval Cult of Saints', *Gesta* 30, 1 (1991): 3–15

Adam, P., *La vie paroissiale en France au XIVe siècle* (Paris: Sirey, 1964)

Alexandre-Bidou, D., 'Une foi en deux ou trois dimensions? Images et objets du faire croire à l'usage des laïcs', *Annales: Histoire, Sciences Sociales* 53.6 (1998): 1155–90

Arnold, J. H., 'The Historian as Inquisitor', *Rethinking History* 2 (1998): 379–86

Arnold, J. H., 'The Preaching of the Cathars', in C. Muessig, ed., *Medieval Monastic Preaching* (Leiden: Brill, 1998), pp. 183–205

Arnold, J. H., *Inquisition and Power: Catharism and the Confessing Subject in Medieval Languedoc* (Philadelphia, PA: University of Pennsylvania Press, 2001)

Arnold, J. H., 'Lollard Trials and Inquisitorial Discourse', in C. Given-Wilson, ed., *Fourteenth-Century England* II (Woodbridge: Boydell, 2002), pp. 81–94

Arnold, J. H., ' "A Man Takes an Ox by the Horn and a Peasant by the Tongue": Literacy, Orality and Inquisition in Medieval Languedoc', in S. Rees-Jones, ed., *Learning and Literacy in Medieval England and Abroad* (Turnhout: Brepols, 2003), pp. 42–3

Arnold, J. H., 'Inquisition, Texts and Discourse', in C. Bruschi and P. Biller, eds, *Texts and the Repression of Medieval Heresy* (York: York Medieval Press, 2003), pp. 63–80

Arnold, J. H., 'The Labour of Continence: Masculinity and Clerical Virginity', in A. Bernau, R. Evans and S. Salih, eds, *Medieval Virginities* (Cardiff: University of Wales Press, 2003), pp. 102–18

Arnold, J. H., and K. J. Lewis, eds, *A Companion to the Book of Margery Kempe* (Cambridge: Brewer, 2004)

Asad, T., 'Anthropological Conceptions of Religions: Reflections on Geertz', *Man* 18 (1983): 237–59

Asad, T., 'On Ritual and Discipline in Medieval Christian Monasticism', *Economy and Society* 16 (1987): 159–203

Asad, T., *Genealogies of Religion: Discipline and Reasons of Power in Christianity and Islam* (Baltimore, MD: Johns Hopkins University Press, 1993)

Ashley, K., and R. L. A. Clark, eds, *Medieval Conduct* (Minneapolis, MN: University of Minnesota Press, 2001).

Aston, M., *Lollards and Reformers: Images and Literacy in Late Medieval Religion* (London: Hambledon, 1984)

Aston, M., 'Segregation in Church', in W. J. Sheils and D. Wood, eds, *Women in the Church*, Studies in Church History 27 (Oxford: Blackwell, 1990), pp. 237–94

Aston, M., 'Death', in R. Horrox, ed., *Fifteenth-Century Attitudes: Perceptions of Society in Late Medieval England* (Cambridge: Cambridge University Press, 1994), pp. 202–28

Audisio, G., *The Waldensian Dissent: Persecution and Survival c.1170–c. 1570*, trans. C. Davison (Cambridge: Cambridge University Press, 1999)

Bailey, M. D., *Battling Demons: Witchcraft, Heresy, and Reform in the Late Middle Ages* (University Park, PA: Pennsylvania State University Press, 2003).

Bainbridge, V. R., *Gilds in the Medieval Countryside: Social and Religious Change in Cambridgeshire c.1350–1558* (Woodbridge: Boydell, 1996)

Baldwin, J. W., *Masters, Princes and Merchants: The Social Views of Peter the Chanter and His Circle*, 2 vols (Princeton, NJ: Princeton University Press, 1970)

Baldwin, J. W., 'From the Ordeal to Confession: In Search of Lay Religion in Early Thirteenth-Century France', in P. Biller and A. J. Minnis, eds, *Handling Sin: Confession in the Middle Ages* (York: York Medieval Press, 1998), pp. 191–209

Banker, J. R., *Death in the Community: Memorialization and Confraternities in an Italian Commune in the Late Middle Ages* (Athens, GA: University of Georgia Press, 1988)

Barber, M., 'Women and Catharism', *Reading Medieval Studies* 3 (1977): 45–62

Barber, M., 'The Pastoureaux of 1320', *Journal of Ecclesiastical History* 32 (1981): 143–66

Barber, M., *The Cathars: Dualist Heretics in Languedoc in the High Middle Ages* (Harlow: Longman, 2000)

Bardsley, S., 'Sin, Speech and Scolding in Late Medieval England', in T. Fenster and D. L. Smail, eds, *Fama: The Politics of Talk and Reputation in Medieval Europe* (Ithaca, NY: Cornell University Press, 2003), pp. 145–64

Bartlett, A. C., *Male Authors, Female Readers: Representation and Subjectivity in Middle English Devotional Reading* (Ithaca, NY: Cornell University Press, 1995)

Bartlett, R., *England under the Norman and Angevin Kings 1075–1225* (Oxford: Oxford University Press, 2000)

Bastard-Fournié, M., 'Le purgatoire dans la région Toulousaine au XIVe et au début du XVe siècles', *Annales du Midi* 92 (1980): 5–34

Beattie, C., 'The Problem of Women's Work Identities in Post Black Death England', in J. Bothwell, P. J. P. Goldberg and W. M. Ormrod, eds, *The Problem of Labour in Fourteenth-Century England* (York: York Medieval Press, 2000), pp. 1–19

Beckwith, S., *Signifying God: Social Relation and Symbolic Act in the York Corpus Christi Plays* (Chicago: University of Chicago Press, 2001)

Bennett, J. M., 'Conviviality and Charity in Medieval and Early Modern England', *Past and Present* 134 (1992): 19–41

Bennett, J. M., 'England: Women and Gender', in S. H. Rigby, ed., *A Companion to Britain in the Later Middle Ages* (Oxford: Blackwell, 2003), pp. 87–106

Bennett, J. M., 'Writing Fornication: Medieval Leyrwite and its Historians', *Transactions of the Royal Historical Society* 6th ser., 13 (2003): 131–62

Benson, R. L., and G. Constable, eds, *Renaissance and Renewal in the Twelfth Century* (Cambridge, MA: Harvard University Press, 1982)

Benton, J. F., 'Consciousness of Self and Perceptions of Individuality', in R. L. Benson and G. Constable, eds, *Renaissance and Renewal in the Twelfth Century* (Cambridge, MA: Harvard University Press, 1982), pp. 263–95

Bériou, N., 'Autour de Latran IV (1215): La naissance de la confession moderne et sa diffusion', in Groupe de la Bussière, *Pratiques de la confession: Des pères du désert à Vatican II* (Paris: CERF, 1983), pp. 73–92

Bériou, N., *L'Avènement des maîtres de la parole: La prédication à Paris au XIIIe siècle*, 2 vols (Paris: Institut d'Etudes Augustiniennes, 1998)

Bériou, N., 'Les Sermons latins après 1200', in B. M. Kienzle, ed., *The Sermon*, Typologie des Sources du Moyen Âge Occidental 81–83 (Turnhout: Brepols, 2000), pp. 363–448

Bernstein, A., 'Theology between Heresy and Folklore: William of Auvergne on Punishment after Death', *Studies in Medieval and Renaissance History* 5 (1982): 1–44

Biller, P., 'Birth-control in the West in the Thirteenth and Early Fourteenth Centuries', *Past and Present* 94 (1982): 3–26

Biller, P., 'The Common Woman in the Western Church in the Thirteenth and Fourteenth Centuries', in W. J. Sheils and D. Wood, eds, *Women in the Church*, Studies in Church History 27 (Oxford: Blackwell, 1990), pp. 127–57

Biller, P., 'Marriage Patterns and Women's Lives: A Sketch of a Pastoral Geography', in P. J. P. Goldberg, ed., *Woman is a Worthy Wight: Women in Medieval English Society c.1200–1500* (Stroud: Sutton, 1992), pp. 60–107

Biller, P., 'The Cathars of Languedoc and Written Materials', in P. Biller and A. Hudson, eds, *Heresy and Literacy, 1000–1530* (Cambridge: Cambridge University Press, 1994), pp. 61–82

Biller, P., 'Cathars and Material Women', in P. Biller and A. Minnis, eds, *Medieval Theology and the Natural Body* (York: York Medieval Press, 1997), pp. 61–107

Biller, P., 'Popular Religion in the Central and Later Middle Ages', in M. Bentley, ed., *Companion to Historiography* (London: Routledge, 1997), pp. 221–46

Biller, P., 'Confession in the Middle Ages: Introduction', in P. Biller and A. J. Minnis, eds, *Handling Sin: Confession in the Middle Ages* (York: York Medieval Press, 1998), pp. 3–33

Biller, P., *The Measure of Multitude: Population in Medieval Thought* (Oxford: Oxford University Press, 2000)

Biller, P., 'Cathar Peace-Making', in S. Ditchfield, ed., *Christianity and Community in the West: Essays for John Bossy* (Aldershot: Ashgate, 2001), pp. 1–23

Biller, P., '*Multum ieiunantes et se castigantes*: medieval Waldensian Asceticism', in idem, *The Waldenses, 1170–1530*, Variorum reprints (Aldershot: Ashgate, 2001), pp. 69–79

Biller, P., and A. J. Minnis, eds, *Handling Sin: Confession in the Middle Ages* (York: York Medieval Press, 1998)

Billington, S., *Midsummer: A Cultural Sub-Text from Chrétien de Troyes to Jean Michel* (Turnhout: Brepols, 2000)

Binski, P., *Medieval Death: Ritual and Representation* (London: British Museum Press, 1996)

Binski, P., 'The Crucifixion and the Censorship of Art around 1300', in P. Linehan and J. Nelson, eds, *The Medieval World* (London: Routledge, 2001), pp. 342–60

Binz, L., 'Les confréries dans le diocèse de Genève à la fin du moyen âge', in *Le Mouvement confraternel au moyen âge: France, Italie, Suisse* (Rome: Ecole Française de Rome, 1987), pp. 233–61

Bitel, L., *Isle of the Saints: Monastic Settlement and Christian Community in Early Ireland* (Ithaca, NY: Cornell University Press, 1990)

Blumenfeld-Kosinski, R., and T. Szell, eds, *Images of Sainthood in Medieval Europe* (Ithaca, NY: Cornell University Press, 1991)

Bolton, B., '*Mulieres sanctae*', in D. Baker, ed., *Sanctity and Secularity: The Church and the World*, Studies in Church History 10 (Oxford: Blackwell, 1973), pp. 77–95

Bolton, B., 'Message, Celebration, Offering: The Place of Twelfth- and early Thirteenth-Century Liturgical Drama as "Missionary Theatre"', in R. N. Swanson, *Continuity and Change in Christian Worship*, Studies in Church History 35 (Woodbridge: Boydell, 1999), p. 97

Bolzoni, L., *The Web of Images: Vernacular Preaching from its Origins to St Bernardino da Siena*, trans. C. Preston and L. Chien (2001. Aldershot: Ashgate, 2004)

Bornstein, D. E., *The Bianchi of 1399: Popular Devotion in Late Medieval Italy* (Ithaca, NY: Cornell University Press, 1993)

Bossy, J., 'Blood and Baptism: Kinship, Community and Christianity in Western Europe from the Fourteenth to the Seventeenth Centuries', in D. Baker, ed., *Sanctity and Secularity: The Church and the World*, Studies in Church History 10 (Oxford: Blackwell, 1973), pp. 129–43

Bossy, J., 'The Social History of Confession in the Age of the Reformation', *Transactions of the Royal Historical Society* 5th ser., 25 (1975): 21–38

Bossy, J., 'The Mass as a Social Institution 1200–1700', *Past and Present* 100 (1983): 29–61

Bossy, J., *Christianity in the West 1400–1700* (Oxford: Oxford University Press, 1985)

Bossy, J., 'Moral Arithmetic: Seven Sins into Ten Commandements', in E. Leites, ed., *Conscience and Casuistry in Early Modern Europe* (Cambridge: Cambridge University Press, 1988), pp. 214–34

Boulton, M., 'Anti-Jewish Attitudes in Twelfth-Century French Literature', in M. A. Signer and J. Van Engen, eds, *Jews and Christians in Twelfth-Century Europe* (Notre Dame, IN: University of Notre Dame Press, 2001), pp. 234–54

Bourdieu, P., *Outline of a Theory of Practice*, trans. R. W. Nice (Cambridge: Cambridge University Press, 1977)

Boyle, L. E., 'The Summa for Confessors as a Genre, and its Religious Intent', in C. Trinkaus and H. A. Oberman, eds, *The Pursuit of Holiness in Late Medieval and Renaissance Religion* (Leiden: Brill, 1974), pp. 126–30

Boyle, L. E., 'Popular Piety in the Middle Ages: What is Popular?', *Florilegium* 4 (1982): 184–93

Boyle, L. E., 'The Fourth Lateran Council and Manuals of Popular Theology', in T. Heffernan, ed., *The Popular Literature of Medieval England* (Knoxville, TN: University of Tennessee Press, 1985), 30–43

Boyle, L. E., 'Innocent III and Vernacular Versions of Scripture', in K. Walsh and D. Wood, eds, *The Bible in the Medieval World: Essays in Memory of Beryl Smalley*, Studies in Church History subsidia 4 (Oxford: Basil Blackwell, 1985), pp. 97–107

Branner, R., 'Historical Aspects of the Reconstruction of Reims Cathedral, 1210–1241', *Speculum* 36 (1961): 23–37

Brentano, R., *Two Churches: England and Italy in the Thirteenth Century*, 2nd edn (Berkeley, CA: University of California Press, 1988)

Brolis, M. T., 'A Thousand and More Women: The Register of Women for the Confraternity of Misericordia Maggiore in Bergamo, 1265–1339', *Catholic Historical Review* 88 (2002): 231–46

Brown, A., *Popular Piety in Late Medieval England: The Dioceses of Salisbury, c.1250–c.1550* (Oxford: Oxford University Press, 1995)

Brown, P., 'The Rise and Function of the Holy Man in Late Antiquity', in idem, *Society and the Holy in Late Antiquity* (Berkeley, CA: University of California Press, 1982), pp. 103–52

Brown, P., *The Body and Society: Men, Women and Sexual Renunciation in Early Christianity* (London: Faber & Faber, 1989)

Brown, P., 'Arbiters of the Holy: The Christian Holy Man in Late Antiquity', in idem, *Authority and the Sacred: Aspects of the Christianization of the Roman World* (Cambridge: Cambridge University Press, 1995), pp. 55–78

Brundage, J. A., *Medieval Canon Law* (Harlow: Longman, 1995)

Bruschi, C., ' "Magna diligentia est habenda per inquisitorem": Precautions before Reading Doat 21–26', in C. Bruschi and P. Biller, eds, *Texts and the Repression of Medieval Heresy* (York: York Medieval Press, 2003), pp. 81–110

Bull, M., *Knightly Piety and the Lay Response to the First Crusade: The Limousin and Gascony, c.970–c.1130* (Oxford: Clarendon Press, 1993)

Burgess, C., ' "A Fond Thing Vainly Invented": An Essay on Purgatory and Pious Motive in Later Medieval England', in S. J. Wright, ed., *Parish, Church and People: Local Studies in Lay Religion 1350–1750* (London: Hutchinson, 1988), pp. 56–84

Burgess, C., 'Late Medieval Wills and Pious Convention: Testamentary Evidence Reconsidered', in M. Hicks, ed., *Profit, Piety, and the Professions in Later Medieval England* (Gloucester: Alan Sutton, 1990), pp. 14–33

Burke, P., *History and Social Theory* (Cambridge: Polity, 1992)

Bynum, C. W., *Jesus as Mother: Studies in the Spirituality of the High Middle Ages* (Berkeley, CA: University of California Press, 1982), pp. 82–109

Bynum, C. W., *Fragmentation and Redemption: Essays on Gender and the Human Body in Medieval Religion* (New York: Zone, 1992)

Bynum, C. W., *Metamorphosis and Identity* (New York: Zone, 2001)

Caciola, N., 'Wraiths, Revenants and Rituals in Medieval Culture', *Past and Present* 152 (1996): 3–45

Caciola, N., 'Spirits Seeking Bodies: Death, Possession and Communal Memory in the Middle Ages', in B. Gordon and P. Marshall, eds, *The Place of the Dead: Death and Remembrance in Late Medieval and Early Modern Europe* (Cambridge: Cambridge University Press, 2000), pp. 66–86

Caciola, N., *Discerning Spirits: Divine and Demonic Possession in the Middle Ages* (Ithaca, NY: Cornell University Press, 2003)

Caldwell, C., 'Doctors of Souls: Inquisition and the Dominican Order, 1231–1331', unpublished PhD thesis, University of Notre Dame, Ind., 2002

Cameron, E., *Waldenses: Rejections of Holy Church in Medieval Europe* (Oxford: Blackwell, 2000)

Camille, M., 'Seeing and Reading: Some Visual Implications of Medieval Literacy and Illiteracy', *Art History* 8: 1 (1985): 26–49

Camille, M., *Image on the Edge: The Margins of Medieval Art* (London: Reaktion, 1992)

Camille, M., *Gothic Art: Visions and Revelations of the Medieval World* (London: Weidenfeld & Nicolson, 1996)

Camille, M., 'At the Sign of the "Spinning Sow": The "Other" Chartres and Images of Everyday Life of the Medieval Street', in A. Bolvig and P. Lindley, eds, *History and Images: Toward a New Iconology* (Turnhout: Brepols, 2003), pp. 249–76

Carrasco, M., 'Sanctity and Experience in Pictorial Hagiography: Two Illustrated Lives of Saints from Romanesque France', in R. Blumenfeld-Kosinski and T. Szell, eds, *Images of Sainthood in Medieval Europe* (Ithaca, NY: Cornell University Press, 1991), pp. 33–66

Carruthers, L., ' "Know Thyself": Criticism, Reform and the Audience of *Jacob's Well*', in J. Hamesse, B. M. Kienzle, D. L. Stoudt and A. T. Thayer, eds, *Medieval Sermons and Society: Cloister, City, University*, Textes et Etudes du Moyen Âge 9 (Louvain-La-Neuve: Fédération Internationale des Instituts d'Etudes Médiévales, 1998), pp. 219–40

Carruthers, M., *The Book of Memory: A Study of Memory in Medieval Culture* (Cambridge: Cambridge University Press, 1990)

Casagrande, C., 'The Protected Woman', in C. Klapisch-Zuber, ed., *A History of Women in the West II: Silences of the Middle Ages* (Cambridge, MA: Harvard University Press, 1992), pp. 70–104

Casagrande, G., 'Women in Confraternities between the Middle Ages and the Modern Age', *Confraternitas* 5, 2 (1994): 3–13

Casagrande, G., 'Confraternities and Lay Female Religiosity in Late Medieval and Renaissance Umbria', in Nicholas Terpstra, ed., *The Politics of Ritual Kinship: Confraternities and Social Order in Early Modern Italy* (Cambridge: Cambridge University Press, 2000), pp. 48–66

Casenave, A., 'Langage catholique et discours cathare: Les Ecoles du Montpellier', in A. Casenave and J.-F. Lyotard, eds, *L'Art des confins: Mélanges offerts à Maurice de Gandillac* (Paris: Presses Universitaires de France, 1985), pp. 139–52

Cazelles, B., 'Introduction', in R. Blumenfeld-Kosinski and T. Szell, eds, *Images of Sainthood in Medieval Europe* (Ithaca, NY: Cornell University Press, 1991), pp. 1–17

Charon, V., 'The Knowledge of Herbs', in L. Milis, ed., *The Pagan Middle Ages* (Woodbrige: Boydell, 1998), pp. 109–28

Chazan, R., 'From the First Crusade to the Second: Evolving Perceptions of the Christian-Jewish Conflict', in M. A. Signer and J. Van Engen, eds, *Jews and Christians in Twelfth-Century Europe* (Notre Dame, IN: University of Notre Dame Press, 2001), pp. 46–62

Chazelle, C. M., 'Pictures, Books, and the Illiterate: Pope Gregory I's Letters to Serenus of Marseilles', *Word and Image* 6: 2 (1990): 138–53

Chenu, M.-D., 'The Symbolist Mentality', in idem, *Nature, Man and Society in the*

Twelfth Century, ed. and trans. J. Taylor and L. K. Little (Toronto: University of Toronto Press, 1997), pp. 99–145

Chickering, H., and T. H. Seiler, eds, *The Study of Chivalry: Resources and Approaches* (Kalamazoo, MI: Medieval Institute Publications, 1988)

Chiffoleau, J., *La comptabilité de l'au delà: Les hommes, la mort et la religion dans la région d'Avignon à la fin du moyen-âge* (Rome: Ecole Française de Rome, 1980)

Chojnacki, S., 'The Power of Love: Wives and Husbands in Late Medieval Venice', in M. Erler and M. Kowaleski, eds, *Women and Power in the Middle Ages* (Athens, GA: University of Georgia Press, 1988), pp.126–148

Clanchy, M. T., *From Memory to Written Record: England, 1066–1307*, 2nd edn (Oxford: Blackwell, 1993)

Clanchy, M. T., 'Images of Ladies with Prayer Books: What Do They Mean?', in R. N. Swanson, ed., *The Church and the Book*, Studies in Church History 38 (Woodbridge: Boydell, 2004), pp. 106–22

Clark, R. L. A., 'Community versus Subject in Late Medieval French Confraternity Drama and Ritual', in A. Hindley, ed., *Drama and Community: People and Plays in Medieval Europe* (Turnhout: Brepols, 1999), pp. 34–56

Clark, R. L. A., 'Constructing the Female Subject in Late Medieval Devotion', in K. Ashley and R. L. A. Clark, eds, *Medieval Conduct* (Minneapolis, MN: University of Minnesota Press, 2001), pp. 160–82

Clifford, J. and G. E. Marcus, eds, *Writing Culture: The Poetics and Politics of Ethnography* (Berkeley, CA: University of California Press, 1986)

Cohen, J., *The Friars and the Jews: The Evolution of Medieval Anti-Judaism* (London: Cornell University Press, 1982)

Cohen, J., 'A 1096 Complex? Constructing the First Crusade in Jewish Historical Memory, Medieval and Modern', in M. A. Signer and J. Van Engen, eds, *Jews and Christians in Twelfth-Century Europe* (Notre Dame, IN: University of Notre Dame Press, 2001), pp. 9–26

Cohn, H. J., 'Anticlericalism in the German Peasants' War, 1525', *Past and Present* 83 (1979): 3–31

Cohn, N., *Europe's Inner Demons: An Inquiry Inspired by the Great Witch Hunt* (St Albans: Paladin, 1976)

Cohn, S. K., *The Cult of Remembrance and the Black Death: Six Renaissance Cities in Central Italy* (Baltimore, MD: Johns Hopkins University Press, 1992)

Cohn, S. K., 'The Place of the Dead in Flanders and Tuscany: Towards a Comparative History of the Black Death', in B. Gordon and P. Marshall, eds, *The Place of the Dead: Death and Remembrance in Late Medieval and Early Modern Europe* (Cambridge: Cambridge University Press, 2000), pp. 17–43

Coleman, J., *Public Reading and the Reading Public in Late Medieval England and France* (Cambridge: Cambridge University Press, 1996)

Collette, C. P., 'Chaucer and the French Tradition Revisited: Philippe de Mézières and the Good Wife', in J. Wogan-Browne *et al.*, eds, *Medieval Women: Texts and Contexts in Late Medieval Britain. Essays for Felicity Riddy* (Turnhout: Brepols, 2000), pp. 151–68

Constable, G., 'Resistance to Tithes in the Middle Ages', *Journal of Ecclesiastical History* 13 (1962): 172–85

Crane, S., *The Performance of Self: Ritual, Clothing and Identity During the Hundred Years War* (Philadelphia, PA: University of Pennsylvania Press, 2002)

Crum, R. J., and D. G. Wilkins, 'In the Defense of Florentine Republicanism: Saint Anne and Florentine Art, 1343–1575', in K. Ashley and P. Sheingorn, eds, *Interpreting Cultural Symbols: Saint Anne in Late Medieval Society* (Athens, GA: University of Georgia Press, 1990), pp. 131–68

Cullum, P., and P. J. P. Goldberg, 'How Margaret Blackburn Taught Her Daughters: Reading Devotional Instruction in a Book of Hours', in J. Wogan-Browne *et al.*, eds, *Medieval Women: Texts and Contexts in Late Medieval Britain. Essays for Felicity Riddy* (Turnhout: Brepols, 2000), pp. 217–36

Dalarun, J., 'The Clerical Gaze', in C. Klapisch-Zuber, ed., *A History of Women in the West II: Silences of the Middle Ages* (Cambridge, MA: Harvard University Press, 1992), pp. 15–42

Davis, J. C., *Fear, Myth and History: The Ranters and the Historians* (Cambridge: Cambridge University Press, 1986)

Davis, N. Z., 'Some Tasks and Themes in the Study of Popular Religion', in C. Trinkaus and H. A. Oberman, eds, *The Pursuit of Holiness in Late Medieval and Renaissance Religion* (Leiden: Brill, 1974), pp. 307–36

D'Avray, D. L., *The Preaching of the Friars: Sermons Diffused from Paris before 1300* (Oxford: Clarendon Press, 1985)

D'Avray, D. L., 'Philosophy in Preaching: The Case of a Franciscan based in Thirteenth-Century Florence (Servasanto da Faenza)', in R. G. Newhauser and J. Afford, eds, *Literature and Religion in the Later Middle Ages: Philological Studies in Honor of Siegfried Wenzel* (Binghamton, NY: Medieval and Renaissance Texts and Studies, 1995), pp. 263–73

D'Avray, D. L., *Medieval Marriage Sermons: Mass Communication in a Culture Without Print* (Oxford: Oxford University Press, 2001)

D'Avray, D. L., 'Symbolism and Medieval Religious Thought', in P. Linehan and J. Nelson, eds, *The Medieval World* (London: Routledge, 2001), pp. 267–78

Dedieu, H., 'Quelques traces de religion populaire autour des Frères Mineurs de la province d'Aquitaine', in *La Religion Populaire en Languedoc du XIIIe siècle à la moitié du XIVe siècle*, Cahiers de Fanjeaux 11 (Toulouse: Privat, 1976), pp. 227–49

Delcorno, C., 'Medieval Preaching in Italy (1200–1500)' in B. M. Kienzle, ed., *The Sermon*, Typologie des Sources du Moyen Âge Occidental 81–83 (Turnhout: Brepols, 2000), pp. 449–560

Delumeau, J., *Sin and Fear: The Emergence of a Western Guilt Culture, 13th–18th Centuries*, trans. E. Nicholson (1983. New York: St Martin's Press, 1990)

Delumeau, J., ed., *L'Historien et la foi* (Paris: Fayard, 1996)

Deregnaucourt, J.-P., 'L'élection de sépulture d'après les testaments douaisiens (1295–1500)', *Revue du Nord* 65 (1983): 343–52

Derwich, M., 'Les Bénédictins et la christianisation des campagnes en Pologne', in J.-P. Massaut and M.-E. Henneau, eds, *La Christianisation des campagnes: Actes du colloque du C.I.H.E.C. (25–27 août)* (Brussels: Institut Historique Belge de Rome, 1996), pp. 103–16

Dickson, G., 'The Flagellants of 1260 and the Crusades', *Journal of Medieval History* 15 (1989): 227–67

Dickson, G., 'The Genesis of the Children's Crusade (1212)', in idem, *Religious Enthusiasm in the Medieval West* (Aldershot: Variorum, 2000), essay IV

Dinn, R., ' "Monuments Answerable to Men's Worth": Burial Patterns, Social Status and Gender in Late Medieval Bury St Edmunds', *Journal of Ecclesiastical History* 46 (1995): 237–55

Douglas, M., *Natural Symbols* (London: Barrie & Rockliff, 1970)

Dronke, P., *Women Writers of the Middle Ages* (Cambridge: Cambridge University Press, 1984)

Duby, G., 'Solitude', in G. Duby, ed., *A History of Private Life, II: Revelations of the Medieval World*, trans. A. Goldhammer (Cambridge, MA: Belknap Press, 1988), p. 528

Duffy, E., *The Stripping of the Altars: Traditional Religion in England 1400–1580* (New Haven, CT: Yale University Press, 1992)

Duffy, E., *The Voices of Morebath: Reformation and Rebellion in an English Village* (New Haven, CT: Yale University Press, 2001)

Duggan, L. G., 'Was Art Really the "Book of the Illiterate"?', *Word and Image* 5: 3 (1989): 227–51

Dupont, A., 'La Religion – anthropologie religieuse', in J. Le Goff and P. Nora, eds, *Faire de l'histoire: Nouvelle approches*, 3 vols (Paris: Gallimard, 1974), 2, pp. 105–36

Durkheim, E., *The Elementary Forms of the Religious Life*, trans. J. W. Swain (London: George Allen & Unwin, 1915)

Duvernoy, J., 'Les Albigeois dans la vie sociale et économique de leurs temps', *Annales de l'Institut d'Etudes Occitanes* (1962–63): 64–73

Duvernoy, J., 'Le Catharisme en Languedoc au début du XIVe siècle', in *Effacement du Catharisme (XIII–XIVe siècles)?*, Cahiers de Fanjeaux 20 (Toulouse: Privat, 1985), pp. 27–56

Dyer, C., *Standards of Living in the Later Middle Ages: Social Change in England c.1200–1520* (Cambridge: Cambridge University Press, 1989)

Dymond, D., 'God's Disputed Acre', *Journal of Ecclesiastical History* 50 (1999): 464–97

Edgren, H., ' "Primitive" Paintings: The Visual World of *Populus rusticus*', in A. Bolvig and P. Lindley, eds, *History and Images: Towards a New Iconology* (Turnhout: Brepols, 2003), pp. 301–22

Edwards, G., 'Purgatory: Birth or Evolution?', *Journal of Ecclesiastical History* 36 (1985): 634–46

Edwards, J., 'Religious Faith and Doubt in Late Medieval Spain: Soria c.1450–1500', *Past and Present* 120 (1988): 3–25

Eisenbichler, K., 'Introduction', in K. Eisenbichler, ed., *Crossing the Boundaries: Christian Piety and the Arts in Italian Medieval and Renaissance Confraternities* (Kalamazoo, MI: Medieval Institute Publications, 1991), pp. 1–9

Elliott, D., 'Dress as Mediator between Inner and Outer Self: The Pious Matron of the High and Later Middle Ages', *Mediaeval Studies* 53 (1991): 279–308

Elliott, D., *Spiritual Marriage: Sexual Abstinence in Medieval Wedlock* (Princeton, NJ: Princeton University Press, 1993)

Elliott, D., *Fallen Bodies: Pollution, Sexuality and Demonology in the Middle Ages* (Philadelphia, PA: University of Pennsylvania Press, 1999)

Elliott, D., 'Seeing Double: John Gerson, the Discernment of Spirits, and Joan of Arc', *American Historical Review* 107 (2002): 26–54

Elliott, D., 'Marriage', in C. Dinshaw and D. Wallace, eds, *The Cambridge Companion to Medieval Women's Writing* (Cambridge: Cambridge University Press, 2003), pp. 40–57

Elliott, D., 'Women and Confession: From Empowerment to Pathology', in M. C. Erler and M. Kowaleski, eds, *Gendering the Master Narrative: Women and Power in the Middle Ages* (Ithaca, NY: Cornell University Press, 2003), pp. 31–51

Engels, F., *The Peasant War in Germany* (1850. Repr., Moscow: Progress, 1956) pp. 42–52

Engen, J. van, 'The Christian Middle Ages as an Historiographical Problem', *American Historical Review* 91 (1986): 519–52

Engen, J. van, 'The Sayings of the Fathers: An Inside Look at the New Devout in Deventer', in R. J. Bast and A. C. Gow, eds, *Continuity and Change: The Harvest of Late Medieval and Reformation History. Essays Presented to Heiko A. Oberman* (Leiden: Brill, 2000), 279–320

Erbstösser, M., *Heretics in the Middle Ages*, trans. Janet Fraser (Leipzig: Edition Leipzig, 1984)

Erler, M., 'Palm Sunday Prophets and Processions, and Eucharistic Controversy', *Renaissance Quarterly* 48 (1995): 58–81

Evans, R., 'The Book of Margery Kempe', in P. Brown, ed., *A Companion to Medieval Literature and Culture* (Oxford: Blackwell, 2004)

Falvey, K., 'Early Italian Dramatic Traditions and Comforting Rituals: Some Initial Considerations', in K. Eisenbichler, ed., *Crossing the Boundaries: Christian Piety and the Arts in Italian Medieval and Renaissance Confraternities* (Kalamazoo, MI: Medieval Institute Publications, 1991), pp. 32–55

Farmer, S., 'Persuasive Voices: Clerical Images of Medieval Wives', *Speculum* 61 (1986): 517–43

Farmer, S., *Surviving Poverty in Medieval Paris: Gender, Ideology, and the Daily Lives of the Poor* (Ithaca, NY: Cornell University Press, 2002)

Finch, A., 'The Disciplining of the Laity in Late Medieval Normandy', *French History* 10 (1996): 163–81

Finucane, R. C., *Miracles and Pilgrims: Popular Beliefs in Medieval England* (1977. London: Macmillan, 1995)

Fisher, J. D. C., *Christian Initiation: Baptism in the Medieval West* (London: SPCK, 1965)

Fletcher, A. J., *Preaching, Politics and Poetry in Late Medieval England* (Dublin: Four Courts Press, 1998)

Fletcher, R., *The Conversion of Europe: From Paganism to Christianity 371–1386 AD* (London: Fontana, 1998)

Flint, V. I. J., *The Rise of Magic in Early Medieval Europe* (Oxford: Clarendon Press, 1991)

Flint, V. I. J., 'The Saint and the Operation of the Law: Reflections Upon the Miracles of St Thomas Cantilupe', in R. Gameson and H. Leyser, eds, *Belief and Culture in the Middle Ages: Studies Presented to Henry Mayr-Harting* (Oxford: Oxford University Press, 2001), pp. 342–57

Flynn, M., *Sacred Charity: Confraternities and Social Welfare in Spain 1400–1700* (Houndmills: Macmillan, 1989)

Flynn, M., 'Blasphemy and the Play of Anger in Sixteenth-Century Spain', *Past and Present* 149 (1995): 29–56

Forrest, I., *The Pursuit of Heresy in Late Medieval England* (Oxford: Oxford University Press, forthcoming)

Foucault, M., *Power/Knowledge: Selected Interviews and Other Writings, 1972–1977*, ed. C. Gordon (London: Harvester Wheatsheaf, 1980)

Frassetto, M., 'Heretics and Jews in the Writings of Adémar of Chabannes and the Origins of Medieval Anti-Semitism', *Church History* 71 (2002): 1–15

Freedman, P., *Images of the Medieval Peasant* (Stanford, CA: Stanford University Press, 1999)

French, K. L., ''Maidens' Lights and Wives' Stores: Women's Parish Guilds in Late Medieval England', *Sixteenth Century Journal* 29 (1998): 399–425

French, K. L., *The People of the Parish: Community Life in a Late Medieval English Diocese* (Philadelphia, PA: University of Pennsylvania Press, 2001)

Friedman, A. B., ' "When Adam Delved . . .": Contexts of an Historic Proverb', in L. D. Benson, ed., *The Learned and the Lewed: Studies in Chaucer and Medieval Literature* (Cambridge, MA: Harvard University Press, 1974), pp. 213–30

Friesen, A., 'Medieval Heretics or Forerunners of the Reformation: the Protestant Rewriting of the History of Medieval Heresy', in A. Ferreiro, ed., *The Devil, Heresy and Witchcraft in the Middle Ages: Essays in Honor of Jeffrey B. Russell* (Leiden: Brill, 1998), pp. 165–189

Fudge, T., 'The "Crown" and the "Red Gown": Hussite Popular Religion', in R. W. Scribner, ed., *Popular Religion in Germany and Central Europe 1400–1800* (Houndmills: Macmillan, 1996), pp. 38–57

Fulton, R., *From Judgment to Passion: Devotion to Christ and the Virgin Mary, 800–1200* (New York: Columbia University Press, 2002)

Ganshof, F. L., 'Pèlerinages expiatoires flamands à Saint-Gilles pendant le XIVe siècle', *Annales du Midi* 78 (1966): 391–407

Geary, P., 'Humiliation of Saints', in S. Wilson, ed., *Saints and Their Cults: Studies in Religious Sociology, Folklore and History* (Cambridge: Cambridge University Press, 1983), pp. 123–40

Geertz, C., *The Interpretation of Cultures* (London: Fontana, 1993)

Gellrich, J. M., *The Idea of the Book in the Middle Ages: Language Theory, Mythology and Fiction* (Ithaca, NY: Cornell University Press, 1985)

Gentilcore, D., *Healers and Healing in Early Modern Italy* (Manchester: Manchester University Press, 1998)

Georgianna, L., *The Solitary Self: Individuality in the* Ancrene Wisse (Cambridge, MA: Harvard University Press, 1981)

Gibbs, M., and J. Lang, *Bishops and Reform 1215–1272* (Oxford: Oxford University Press, 1934)

Gibson, G. M., 'Saint Anne and the Religion of Childbed: Some East Anglian Texts and Talismans', in K. Ashley and P. Sheingorn, eds, *Interpreting Cultural Symbols: Saint Anne in Late Medieval Society* (Athens, GA: University of Georgia Press, 1990), pp. 95–110

Gibson, G. M., 'Blessing from Sun and Moon: Churching as Women's Theater', in B. A. Hanawalt and D. Wallace, eds, *Bodies and Disciplines: Intersections of Literature and History in Fifteenth-Century England* (Minneapolis, MN: University of Minnesota Press, 1999), pp. 139–154

Gillingham, J., 'The Historian as Judge: William of Newburgh and Hubert Walter', *English Historical Review* 119 (2004): 1275–87

Given, J. B., 'Factional Politics in a Medieval Society: A Case from Fourteenth-Century Foix', *Journal of Medieval History* 14 (1988): 233–50

Given, J. B., *Inquisition and Medieval Society: Power, Discipline and Resistance in Medieval Languedoc* (Ithaca, NY: Cornell University Press, 1997)

Given, J. B., 'The Béguins in Bernard Gui's *Liber sententiarum*', in C. Bruschi and P. Biller, eds, *Texts and the Repression of Medieval Heresy* (York: York Medieval Press, 2003), pp. 147–61

Gold, P. S., *The Lady and the Virgin: Image, Attitude and Experience in Twelfth-Century France* (Chicago: University of Chicago Press, 1985)

Goldberg, P. J. P., 'The Public and the Private: Women in the Pre-Plague Economy', in P. R. Coss and S. D. Lloyd, eds, *Thirteenth-Century England III* (Woodbridge: Boydell, 1991), pp. 75–89

Goldberg, P. J. P., 'Masters and Men in Later Medieval England', in D. M. Hadley, ed., *Masculinity in Medieval Europe* (London: Longman, 1999), pp. 56–70

Goodich, M., 'The Politics of Canonization in the Thirteenth Century: Lay and Mendicant Saints', *Church History* 44 (1975): 294–307

Goodich, M., 'Battling the Devil in Rural Europe: Late Medieval Miracle Collections', in J.-P. Massaut and M.-E. Henneau, eds, *La Christianisation des campagnes: Actes du colloque du C.I.H.E.C. (25–27 août)* (Brussels: Institut Historique Belge de Rome, 1996), pp. 139–52

Goodman, A., *Margery Kempe and Her World* (London: Longman, 2002)

Graves, C. P., 'Social Space in the English Medieval Parish Church', *Economy and Society* 18 (1989): 297–322

Greenfield, P. H., 'Festive Drama at Christmas in Aristocratic Households', in M. Twycross, ed., *Festive Drama* (Cambridge: Brewer, 1996), pp. 34–40

Grundmann, H., *Religious Movements in the Middle Ages: The Historical Links between Heresy, the Mendicant Orders, and the Women's Religious Movement in the Twelfth and Thirteenth Century*, trans. S. Rowan (1935. Revised 1961. Notre Dame, IN: University of Notre Dame Press, 1995)

Gurevich, A., 'Popular and Scholarly Medieval Cultural Traditions: Notes in the Margin of Jacques Le Goff's Book', *Journal of Medieval History* 9 (1983): 71–90

Gurevich, A., *Categories of Medieval Culture*, trans. G. L. Campbell (1972. London: Routledge, 1985)

Gurevich, A., *Medieval Popular Culture: Problems of Belief and Practice* trans. J. M. Bak and P. A. Hollingsworth (Cambridge: Cambridge University Press, 1988)

Hall, T. N., 'The Early Medieval Sermon', in B. M. Kienzle, ed., *The Sermon*, Typologie des Sources du Moyen Age Occidental 81–83 (Turnhout: Brepols, 2000), pp. 203–69

Hamburger, J., 'Bosch's Conjuror: An Attack on Magic and Sacramental Heresy', *Simiolus* 14 (1984): 5–23

Hamilton, B., *The Albigensian Crusade* (London: Historical Association, 1974)

Hamilton, B., *Religion in the Medieval West* (London: Arnold, 1986)

Hamilton, B., 'The Cathars and Christian Perfection', in P. Biller and B. Dobson, eds, *The Medieval Church: Universities, Heresy, and the Religious Life. Essays in Honour of Gordon Leff*, Studies in Church History subsidia 11 (Woodbridge: Boydell, 1999)

Hamilton, S., *The Practice of Penance 900–1050* (Woodbridge: Royal Historical Society, 2001)

Hamilton, S., 'The Unique Favour of Penance: The Church and the People c.800–c.1100', in P. Linehan and J. L. Nelson, eds, *The Medieval World* (London: Routledge, 2001), pp. 229–45

Hanawalt, B. A., 'At the Margins of Women's Space in Medieval Europe', in eadem, *Of Good and Ill Repute: Gender and Social Control in Medieval England* (Oxford: Oxford University Press, 1998), pp. 70–87

Hanawalt, B. A., 'Violence in the Domestic Milieu of Late Medieval England', in R. Kaeuper, ed., *Violence in Medieval Society* (Woodbridge: Boydell, 2000), pp. 197–214

Harrod, H., 'Extracts from Early Wills in the Norwich Registries', *Norfolk Archaeology* 4 (1855): 317–39

Haywood, P. A., 'Demystifying the Role of Sanctity', in J. Howard-Johnston and P.A. Haywood, eds, *The Cult of Saints in Late Antiquity and the Middle Ages* (Oxford: Oxford University Press, 1999), pp. 115–42

Hebdige, D., 'From Culture to Hegemony', in Hebdige, *Subculture: The Meaning of Style* (London: Routledge, 1979), pp. 5–19

Henderson, J., 'Confraternities and the Church in Late Medieval Florence', in W. J. Sheils and D. Wood, eds, *Voluntary Religion*, Studies in Church History 23 (Oxford: Blackwell, 1986), pp. 69–83

Henderson, J., *Piety and Charity in Late Medieval Florence* (Oxford: Clarendon Press, 1994)

Herlihy, D., 'Tuscan Names, 1200–1530', in D. Herlihy, *Women, Family and Society in Medieval Europe* (Providence, RI: Berghahn, 1995), pp. 330–52

Heslop, T. A., 'Attitudes to the Visual Arts: The Evidence from Written Sources', in J. Alexander and P. Binski, eds, *Age of Chivalry: Art in Plantagenet England 1200–1400* (London: RCA, 1987), pp. 26–32

Hilton, R. H., *Bond Men Made Free: Medieval Peasant Movements and the English Rising of 1381* (London: Methuen, 1977)

Hilton, R. H., *English and French Towns in Feudal Society: A Comparative Study* (Cambridge: Cambridge University Press, 1992)

Homans, G. C., *English Villagers of the Thirteenth Century* (Cambridge, MA: Harvard University Press, 1942)

Horodowich, E., 'Civic Identity and the Control of Blasphemy in Sixteenth-Century Venice', *Past and Present* 181 (2003): 3–33

Hudson, A., *The Premature Reformation: Wycliffite Texts and Lollard History* (Oxford: Clarendon Press, 1988)

Hughes, D. O., 'Mourning Rites, Memory, and Civilization in Premodern Italy', in J. Chiffoleau, L. Martines and A. P. Bagliani, eds, *Riti e Rituali: nelle Società Medievali* (Spoleto: Centro Italiano di Studi Sull'Alto Medioevo, 1994), pp. 23–38

Huizinga, J., *The Waning of the Middle Ages* (1924. Harmondsworth: Penguin, 1955)

Humphrey, C., *The Politics of Carnival: Festive Misrule in Medieval England* (Manchester: Manchester University Press, 2001)

Hunter, M., 'The Problem of "Atheism" in Early Modern England', *Transactions of the Royal Historical Society* 5th ser., 35 (1985): 135–57

Hutton, R., *The Rise and Fall of Merry England: The Ritual Year 1400–1700* (Oxford: Oxford University Press, 1994)

Hyde, J. K., 'Italian Pilgrim Literature in the Late Middle Ages', in I. K. Hyde, *Literacy and Its Uses: Studies on Late Medieval Italy*, ed. D. Waley (Manchester: Manchester University Press, 1993), pp. 136–61

Hyde, J. K., 'Some Uses of Literacy in Venice and Florence in the Thirteenth and Fourteenth centuries', in J. K. Hyde, *Literacy and Its Uses: Studies on Late Medieval Italy*, ed. D. Waley (Manchester: Manchester University Press, 1993), pp. 112–35

Innes, M., *State and Society in the Early Middle Ages: The Middle Rhine Valley 400–1000* (Cambridge: Cambridge University Press, 2000)

Iogna-Prat, D., *Order and Exclusion: Cluny and Christendom Face Heresy, Judaism, and Islam (1000–1150)*, trans. G. R. Edwards (Ithaca, NY: Cornell University Press, 2002)

James, M., 'Ritual, Drama and Social Body in the Late Medieval English Town', *Past and Present* 98 (1983): 3–29

Jansen, K. L., *The Making of the Magdalen: Preaching and Popular Devotion in the Later Middle Ages* (Princeton, NJ: Princeton University Press, 2000)

Jenkins, J., 'Reading and *The Book of Margery Kempe*', in J. H. Arnold and K. J. Lewis, eds, *A Companion to the Book of Margery Kempe* (Cambridge: Brewer, 2004), pp. 113–28

Jolly, K. L., *Popular Religion in Late Saxon England: Elf Charms in Context* (Chapel Hill, NC: University of North Carolina Press, 1996)

Jong, M. de, 'What was *Public* About Public Penance? *Paenitentia Publica* and Justice in the Carolingian World', in *La Giustizia nell'alto medioevo (secoli IX–XI)*, Settimane di Studio 44 (Spoleto: Presso Sede del Centro, 1997), II: 863–902

Jordan, M. D., *The Invention of Sodomy in Christian Theology* (Chicago: University of Chicago Press, 1998)

Jordan, W. C., *Louis IX and the Challenge of the Crusade* (Princeton, NJ: Princeton University Press, 1979)

Julia, D., 'Religion', in Jacques Le Goff, Roger Chartier and Jacques Revel, eds, *La Nouvelle Histoire* (Paris: CEPL, 1978), pp. 488–94

Justice, S., *Writing and Rebellion: England in 1381* (Berkeley, CA: University of California Press, 1994)

Justice, S., 'Inquisition, Speech, and Writing: A Case from Late-Medieval Norwich', *Representations* 48 (1994): 1–29

Kaeuper, R., *Chivalry and Violence in Medieval Europe* (Oxford: Oxford University Press, 1999)

Kahrl, S. J., 'Secular Life and Popular Piety in Medieval English Drama', in T. Heffernan, ed., *The Popular Literature of Medieval England* (Knoxville, TN: University of Tennessee Press, 1985), pp. 85–107

Kamen, H., *The Phoenix and the Flame: Catalonia and the Counter Reformation* (New Haven, CT: Yale University Press, 1993)

Kamerick, K., *Popular Piety and Art in the Later Middle Ages: Image Worship and Idolatry in England 1350–1500* (Houndmills: Palgrave, 2002)

Kaminsky, H., *A History of the Hussite Revolution* (Berkeley, CA: University of California Press, 1967)

Kan, F. J. W. van, 'Around St George: Integration and Precedence during the Meetings of the Civic Militia of The Hague', in W. Blockman and A. Janse, eds, *Showing Status: Representations of Social Positions in the Late Middle Ages* (Turnhout: Brepols, 1999), pp. 177–95

Karras, R. M., 'Gendered Sin and Misogyny in John of Bromyard's *Summa Predicantium*', *Traditio* 47 (1992): 233–57

Karras, R. M., *Common Women: Prostitution and Sexuality in Medieval England* (Oxford: Oxford University Press, 1996)

Karras, R. M., *From Boys to Men: Formations of Masculinity in Late Medieval Europe* (Philadelphia, PA: University of Pennsylvania Press, 2002)

Karras, R. M., ' "Because the Other is a Poor Woman She Shall Be Called His Wench": Gender, Sexuality and Social Status in Late Medieval England', in S. Farmer and C. B. Pasternack, eds, *Gender and Difference in the Middle Ages* (Minneapolis, MN: University of Minnesota Press, 2003), pp. 210–29

Keen, M., *Chivalry* (New Haven, CT: Yale University Press, 1984)

Kemp, W., *The Narratives of Stained Glass Windows* (Cambridge: Cambridge University Press, 1997)

Kieckhefer, R., *The Repression of Heresy in Medieval Germany* (Liverpool: Liverpool University Press, 1979)

Kieckhefer, R., *Magic in the Middle Ages* (Cambridge: Cambridge University Press, 1989)

Kieckhefer, R., 'The Office of Inquisition and Medieval Heresy: The Transition from Personal to Institutional Jurisdiction', *Journal of Ecclesiastical History* 46 (1995): 36–61

Kieckhefer, R., 'The Holy and the Unholy: Sainthood, Witchcraft, and Magic in Late Medieval Europe', in S. L. Waugh and P. D. Diehl, eds, *Christendom and its Discontents: Exclusion, Persecution, and Rebellion, 1000–1500* (Cambridge: Cambridge University Press, 1996), pp. 310–37

Kienzle, B. M., *Cistercians, Heresy and Crusade in Occitania, 1145–1229: Preaching in the Lord's Vineyard* (York: York Medieval Press, 2001)

Klaniczay, G., 'Fashionable Beards and Herevics' Rags', in idem, *The Uses of Supernatural Power: The Transformation of Popular Religion in Medieval and Early Modern Europe*, trans. S. Singerman (Princeton, NJ: Princeton University Press, 1990)

Kleinberg, A., *Prophets in Their Own Country: Living Saints and the Making of Sainthood in the Later Middle Ages* (Chicago: University of Chicago Press, 1992)

Kloczowski, J., 'Les Paroisses en Bohème, en Hongrie et en Pologne (X–XIII siècles)', in *Le Istituzioni ecclesiastiche della 'societàs christiana' dei secoli XI–XII: Diocesi, pievi, parrochie*, Miscellanea del Centro di Studi Mediovali, VIII (Milan: Università Catholica del Sacro Cuore, 1977), pp. 187–98

Koziol, G., 'The Dangers of Polemic: Is Ritual Still an Interesting Topic of Historical Study?', *Early Medieval Europe* 11 (2002): 367–88

Kruger, R. L., ' "Nouvelles choses": Social Instability and the Problem of Fashion in the *Livre du Chevalier de la Tour Landry*, the *Ménagier de Paris*, and Christine de Pisan's

Livre des Trois Vertus', in K. Ashley and R. L. A. Clark, eds, *Medieval Conduct* (Minneapolis, MN: University of Minnesota Press, 2001), pp. 49–85

Kupfer, M., *Romanesque Wall Painting in Central France: The Politics of Narrative* (New Haven, CT: Yale University Press, 1993)

Kuster, H. J., and R. J. Cormier, 'Old Views and New Trends: Observations on the Problem of Homosexuality in the Middle Ages', *Studi Medievali* 25 (1984): 587–610

Lake, P., *The Boxmaker's Revenge* (Manchester: Manchester University Press, 2001)

Lambert, M. D., *The Cathars* (Oxford: Blackwell, 1998)

Lambert, M. D., *Medieval Heresy: Popular Movements from the Gregorian Reform to the Reformation*, 3rd edn (Oxford: Blackwell, 2002)

Langmuir, G. I., 'Thomas of Monmouth: Detector of Ritual Murder', *Speculum* 59 (1984): 820–46

Langmuir, G. I., *Toward a Definition of Antisemitism* (Berkeley, CA: University of California Press, 1990)

Lansing, C., *Power and Purity: Cathar Heresy in Medieval Italy* (Oxford: Oxford University Press, 1998)

Lauwers, M., *La mémoire des ancêtres, le souci des morts: Morts, rites et société au moyen âge (Diocèse de Liège, XIe–XIIIe siècles)* (Paris: Beauchesne, 1997)

Lavanchy, L., *Ecrire sa mort, décrire sa vie: Testaments de laïcs lausannois (1400–1450)* (Lausanne: Université de Lausanne, 2003)

Lawrence, C. H., *The Friars: The Impact of the Early Mendicant Movement on Western Society* (Harlow: Longman, 1994)

Lea, H. C., *A History of the Inquisition in the Middle Ages*, 3 vols (1888. Repr. New York: S. A. Russell, 1965)

Le Goff, J., *Time, Work and Culture in the Middle Ages*, trans. A. Goldhammer (Chicago: University of Chicago Press, 1980)

Le Goff, J., *The Birth of Purgatory*, trans. A. Goldhammer (London: Scolar Press, 1984)

Lerner, R. E., *The Heresy of the Free Spirit in the Later Middle Ages* (Notre Dame, IN: University of Notre Dame Press, 1972)

Lerner, R. E., 'The Black Death and European Eschatological Mentalities', *American Historical Review* 86 (1981): 533–52

Le Roy Ladurie, E., *Montaillou: Cathars and Catholics in a French Village, 1294–1324*, trans. B. Bray (1978. London: Penguin, 1980)

Leveleux, C., *La parole interdite: Le blasphème dans la France médiévale (XIIIe–XVIe siécles): Du péché au crime* (Paris: De Boccard, 2001)

Lewis, A. W., 'Forest Rights and the Celebration of May: Two Documents from the French Vexin, 1311–1318', *Mediaeval Studies* 53 (1991): 259–77

Lewis, K. J., 'Model Girls? Virgin-Martyrs and the Training of Young Women in Late Medieval England', in K. J. Lewis, N. James Menuge and K. M. Phillips, eds, *Young Medieval Women* (Stroud: Sutton, 1999), pp. 25–46

Lewis, K. J., 'Pilgrimage and the Cult of St Katherine of Alexandria in the Later Middle Ages', in J. Stopford, ed., *Medieval Pilgrimage* (York: York Medieval Press, 1999), pp. 145–60

Lewis, K. J., *The Cult of St Katherine of Alexandria in Late Medieval England* (Woodbridge: Boydell, 2000)

Lewis, K. J., 'Margery Kempe and Saint-Making in Later Medieval England', in J. H. Arnold and K. J. Lewis, eds, *A Companion to the Book of Margery Kempe* (Cambridge: Brewer, 2004), pp. 195–215

Leyser, H., *Hermits and the New Monasticism: A Study of Religious Communities in Western Europe, 1000–1150* (London: Macmillan, 1984)

Leyser, H., *Medieval Women: A Social History of Women in England 450–1500* (London: Weidenfeld & Nicolson, 1995)

Lindenbaum, S., 'Rituals of Exclusion: Feasts and Plays of the English Religious Fraternities', in M. Twycross, ed., *Festive Drama* (Cambridge: Brewer, 1996), pp. 54–65

Linehan, P., 'The Mechanization of Ritual: Alfonso XI of Castile in 1332' in J. Chiffoleau, L. Martines and A. P. Bagliani, eds, *Riti e Rituali: nelle Società Medievali* (Spoleto: Centro Italiano di Studi Sull'Alto Medioevo, 1994), pp. 309–27

Lipman, V. D., *The Jews of Medieval Norwich* (London: Jewish Historical Society of England, 1967)

Little, L. K., *Religious Poverty and the Profit Economy in Medieval Europe* (Ithaca, NY: Cornell University Press, 1978)

Little, L. K., 'Les techniques de la confession et la confession comme technique', in *Faire croire: Modalités de la diffusion et de la réception des messages religieux de XIIe au XVe siècle* (Rome: Ecole Française de Rome, 1981), pp. 87–99

Lochrie, K., *Covert Operations: The Medieval Uses of Secrecy* (Philadelphia, PA: University of Pennsylvania Press, 1999)

Logan, R. D., 'A Conception of the Self in the Later Middle Ages', *Journal of Medieval History* 12 (1986): 253–68

Lorcin, M.-T., 'Les clauses religieuses dans les testaments du plat pays lyonnais aux XIVe et XVe siècles', *Moyen Âge* 78 (1972): 287–323

Mackay, A., 'The Hispanic-*Converso* Predicament', *Transactions of the Royal Historical Society* 5th ser., 35 (1985): 159–79

MacKenney, R., 'Devotional Confraternities in Renaissance Venice', in W. J. Sheils and D. Wood, eds, *Voluntary Religion*, Studies in Church History 23 (Oxford: Blackwell, 1986), pp. 85–96

Macy, G., 'The Dogma of Transubstantiation in the Middle Ages', *Journal of Ecclesiastical History* 45 (1994): 32–40

Macy, G., 'Was there a "the Church" in the Middle Ages?', in R. Swanson, ed., *Unity and Diversity in the Church*, Studies in Church History 52 (Oxford: Blackwell, 1996), pp. 107–16

Macy, G., 'Nicolas Eymeric and the Condemnation of Orthodoxy', in A. Ferreiro, ed., *The Devil, Heresy and Witchcraft in the Middle Ages: Essays in Honor of Jeffrey B. Russell* (Leiden: Brill, 1998), pp. 369–81

Male, E., *Religious Art in France in the Thirteenth Century*, 3rd edn, trans. D. Nussey (London: Dent, 1913)

Manselli, R., 'Les Approches matérialistes de l'histoire du catharisme', in *Historiographie du catharisme*, Cahiers du Fanjeaux 14 (Toulouse: Privat, 1979), pp. 229–48

Mansfield, M. C., *The Humiliation of Sinners: Public Penance in Thirteenth-Century France* (Ithaca, NY: Cornell University Press, 1995)

Marandat, M.-C., *Le souci de l'au-delà: La pratique testamentaire dans la région*

Toulousaine (1300–1450), 2 vols (Perpignan: Presses Universitaires du Perpignan, 1998)

Marshall, P., *Beliefs and the Dead in Reformation England* (Oxford: Oxford University Press, 2002)

Marshall, R. K., *The Local Merchants of Prato: Small Entrepreneurs in the Late Medieval Economy* (Baltimore, MD: Johns Hopkins University Press, 1999)

Martin, H., *Les Ordres mendiants en Bretagne, vers 1230–vers 1530: Pauvreté volontaire et prédication à la fin du moyen-âge* (Paris: CNRS, 1975)

Martin, H., 'Confession et contrôle social à la fin du moyen âge', in Groupe de la Bussière, eds, *Pratiques de la confession: Des pères du desert à Vatican II* (Paris: CERF, 1983), pp. 117–34

McCulloh, J. M., 'Jewish Ritual Murder: William of Norwich, Thomas of Monmouth, and the Early Dissemination of the Myth', *Speculum* 72 (1997): 698–740

McGuire, B., 'Purgatory, the Communion of Saints, and Medieval Change', *Viator* 20 (1989): 61–84

McHardy, A. K., 'Careers and Disappointments in the Late-Medieval Church: Some English Evidence', in W. J. Sheils and D. Wood, eds, *The Ministry: Clerical and Lay*, Studies in Church History 26 (Oxford: Blackwell, 1989), pp. 111–30

McNamara, J. A., 'The *Herrenfrage*: The Restructuring of the Gender System, 1050–1150', in Clare A. Lees, ed., *Medieval Masculinities: Regarding Men in the Middle Ages* (Minneapolis, MN: University of Minnesota Press, 1994), pp. 3–29

McRee, B. R., 'Religious Gilds and Civic Order: The Case of Norwich in the Late Middle Ages', *Speculum* 67 (1992): 69–97

McRee, B. R., 'Charity and Gild Solidarity in Late Medieval England', *Journal of British Studies* 32 (1993): 195–225

McRee, B. R., 'Unity or Division? The Social Meaning of Guild Ceremony in Urban Communities', in B. Hanawalt and K. Reyerson, eds, *City and Spectacle in Medieval Europe* (Minneapolis, PA, MN: University of Minnesota Press, 1994), pp. 189–207

McSheffrey, S., *Gender and Heresy: Women and Men in Lollard Communities 1420–1530* (Philadelphia: University of Pennsylvania Press, 1995)

McSheffrey, S., 'Heresy, Orthodoxy and English Vernacular Religion, 1480–1525', *Past and Present* (forthcoming)

Meens, R., 'The Frequency and Nature of Early Medieval Penance', in P. Biller and A. J. Minnis, eds, *Handling Sin: Confession in the Middle Ages* (York: York Medieval Press, 1998), pp. 35–62

Menarche, S., *The Vox Dei: Communication in the Middle Ages* (Oxford: Oxford University Press, 1990)

Merlo, G. G., *Eretici e inquisitori nella società Piemontese del Trecento* (Turin: Claudiana, 1977)

Milis, L. J. R., *Angelic Monks and Earthly Men: Monasticism and its Meaning to Medieval Society* (Woodbridge: Boydell, 1992)

Miller, M., 'Displaced Souls, Idle Talk, Spectacular Scenes: *Handlyng Synne* and the Perspectives of Agency', *Speculum* 71 (1996): 606–32

Millett, B., 'Women in No Man's Land: English Recluses and the Development of Vernacular Literature in the Twelfth and Thirteenth Centuries', in C. M. Meale, ed.,

Women and Literature in Britain 1150–1500 (Cambridge: Cambridge University Press), pp. 86–103

Milway, M., 'Forgotten Best-Sellers from the Dawn of the Reformation', in R. J. Bast and A. C. Gow, eds, *Continuity and Change: The Harvest of Late Medieval and Reformation History. Essays Presented to Heiko A. Oberman* (Leiden: Brill, 2000), pp. 113–42

Minois, G., *Histoire de l'athéisme* (Paris: Fayard, 1998)

Moore, R. I., *The Formation of a Persecuting Society: Power and Deviance in Western Europe, 950–1250* (Oxford: Blackwell, 1987)

Moore, R. I., *The Origins of European Dissent* (1977. Repr, Toronto: University of Toronto Press, 1994)

Moore, R. I., 'Heresy, Repression and Social Change in the Age of Gregorian Reform', in S. L. Waugh and P. D. Diehl, eds, *Christendom and its Discontents: Exclusion, Persecution and Rebellion 1000–1500* (Cambridge: Cambridge University Press, 1996), pp. 19–46

Moos, P. von, '*Occulta cordis*: Contrôle de soi et confession au moyen âge', *Médiévales* 29 (1995): 131–40; 30 (1996): 117–37

Morris, C., *The Discovery of the Individual: 1050–1200* (New York: SPCK, 1973)

Muchembled, R., 'Witchcraft, Popular Culture, and Christianity in the Sixteenth Century, with Emphasis upon Flanders and Artois', in R. Foster and O. Ranum, eds, *Ritual, Religion and the Sacred*, Selections from *Annales ESC* 7, trans. E. Forster and P. Ranum (Baltimore, MD: Johns Hopkins University Press, 1982), pp. 213–36 [first publ. *Annales: Economie, Société, Civilisation* 28 (1973): 264–84]

Muessig, C. A., 'Audience and Sources in Jacques de Vitry's *Sermons feriales et communes*', in J. Hamesse, B. M. Kienzle, D. L. Stoudt and A. T. Thayer, eds, *Medieval Sermons and Society: Cloister, City, University*, Textes et Etudes du Moyen Âge 9 (Louvain-La-Neuve: Fédération Internationale des Instituts d'Etudes Médiévales, 1998), pp. 183–202

Muldoon, J., *Popes, Lawyers and Infidels: The Church and the Non-Christian World 1250–1550* (Liverpool: Liverpool University Press, 1979)

Mullett, M., *Popular Culture and Popular Protest in Late Medieval and Early Modern Europe* (London: Croom Helm, 1987)

Mundy, J. H., 'Village, Town, and City in the Region of Toulouse', in J. A. Raftis, ed., *Pathways to Medieval Peasants* (Toronto: Pontifical Institute of Medieval Studies, 1981), pp. 141–90

Mundy, J. H., 'The Parishes of Toulouse from 1150 to 1250', *Traditio* 46 (1991): 171–204

Munro, D. C., 'The Children's Crusade', *American Historical Review* 19 (1914): 516–24

Murray, A., 'Piety and Impiety in Thirteenth-Century Italy', in G. J. Cuming and D. Baker, eds, *Popular Belief and Practice*, Studies in Church History 8 (Cambridge: Cambridge University Press, 1972), pp. 83–106

Murray, A., 'Religion among the Poor in Thirteenth-Century France: The Testimony of Humbert de Romans', *Traditio* 30 (1974): 285–324

Murray, A., 'Confession as an Historical Source in the Thirteenth Century', in R. H. C. Davis and J. M. Wallace-Hadrill, eds, *The Writing of History in the Middle Ages: Essays Presented to R. W. Southern* (Oxford: Clarendon Press, 1981), pp. 275–322

Murray, A., 'Medieval Christmas', *History Today* 36: 12 (December 1986): 31–9

Murray, A., 'Confession Before 1215', *Transactions of the Royal Historical Society* 6th ser., (1993): 51–81

Murray, A., 'Counselling in Medieval Confession', in P. Biller and A. J. Minnis, eds, *Handling Sin: Confession in the Middle Ages* (York: York Medieval Press, 1998), pp. 63–77

Murray, J., 'The Absent Penitent: The Cure of Women's Souls and Confessor's Manuals in Thirteenth-Century England', in L. Smith and J. H. M. Taylor, eds, *Women, the Book and the Godly* (Cambridge: Brewer, 1995), pp. 13–25

Murray, J., 'Gendered Souls in Sexed Bodies: The Male Construction of Female Sexuality in Some Medieval Confessors' Manuals', in P. Biller and A. J. Minnis, eds, *Handling Sin: Confession in the Middle Ages* (York: York Medieval Press, 1998), pp. 79–93

Murray, J., ' "The Law of Sin That is in My Members": The Problem of Male Embodiment', in S. J. E. Riches and S. Salih, eds, *Gender and Holiness: Men, Women and Saints in Late Medieval Europe* (London: Routledge, 2002), pp. 9–22

Needham, R., *Belief, Language and Experience* (Oxford: Blackwell, 1972)

Newman, B., 'Possessed by the Spirit: Devout Women, Demoniacs, and the Apostolic Life in the Thirteenth Century', *Speculum* 73 (1998): 733–70

Nilsén, A., 'Man and Picture: On the Function of Wall Paintings in Medieval Churches', in A. Bolvig and P. Lindley, eds, *History and Images: Toward a New Iconology* (Turnhout: Brepols, 2003), pp. 323–40

Nirenberg, D., *Communities of Violence: Persecution of Minorities in the Middle Ages* (Princeton, NJ: Princeton University Press, 1996)

Nirenberg, D., 'Religious and Sexual Boundaries in the Medieval Crown of Aragon', in M. D. Meyerson and E. D. English, eds, *Christians, Muslims, and Jews in Medieval and Early Modern Spain: Interaction and Cultural Change* (Notre Dame, IN: University of Notre Dame Press, 2000), pp. 141–60

Nirenberg, D., 'Conversion, Sex, and Segregation: Jews and Christians in Medieval Spain', *American Historical Review* 107 (2002): 1065–93

Nirenberg, D., 'Mass Conversion and Genealogical Mentalities: Jews and Christians in Fifteenth-Century Spain', *Past and Present* 174 (2002): 3–41

Orme, N., 'Children and the Church in Medieval England', *Journal of Ecclesiastical History* 45 (1994): 563–87

Otis, L. L., *Prostitution in Medieval Society: The History of an Urban Institution in Languedoc* (Chicago: University of Chicago Press, 1985)

Owst, G. R., *Preaching in Medieval England* (Cambridge: Cambridge University Press, 1926)

Owst, G. R., '*Sortilegium* in English Homilectic Literature of the Fourteenth Century', in J. Conway Davies, ed., *Studies Presented to Sir Hilary Jenkinson* (London: Oxford University Press, 1957), pp. 272–303

Parker, K., 'Lynn and the Making of a Mystic', in J. H. Arnold and K. L. Lewis, eds, *A Companion to the Book of Margery Kempe* (Woodbridge: Boydell, 2004), pp. 55–73

Parkes, M. B., 'The Literacy of the Laity', in Parkes, *Scribes, Scripts and Readers: Studies in the Communication, Presentation and Dissemination of Medieval Texts* (London: Hambledon, 1991), pp. 275–97

Pasche, V., *'Pour le salut de mon âme'*: *Les Lausannois face à la mort (XIVe siècle)* (Lausanne: Université de Lausanne, 1989)

Patschovsky, A., 'Heresy and Society: On the Political Function of Heresy in the Medieval World', in C. Bruschi and P. Biller, eds, *Texts and the Repression of Medieval Heresy* (York: York Medieval Press, 2003), pp. 23–41

Paul, J., 'Miracles et mentalité religieuse populaire à Marseille au début du XIVe siècle', *La Religion Populaire en Languedoc du XIIIe siècle à la moitié du XIVe siècle*, Cahiers de Fanjeaux 11 (Toulouse: Privat, 1976), pp. 61–90

Payer, P. J., 'The Origins and Development of the Later *Canones penitentiales*', *Mediaeval Studies* 61 (1999): 81–105

Pederson, F., *Marriage Disputes in Medieval England* (London: Hambledon, 2000)

Pegeot, P., 'Un Exemple de parenté baptismale à la fin du Moyen Âge: Porrentruy 1482–1500', *Annales de l'Est*, 5th series, 34 (1982): 53–70

Pegg, M. G., *The Corruption of Angels: The Great Inquisition of 1245–46* (Princeton, NJ: Princeton University Press, 2001)

Pegg, M. G., 'Questions about Questions: Toulouse 609 and the Great Inquisition of 1245–6', in C. Bruschi and P. Biller, eds, *Texts and the Repression of Medieval Heresy* (York: York Medieval Press, 2003), pp. 111–26

Pellegrini, L., 'Female Religious Experience and Society in Thirteeth-Century Italy', in S. Farmer and B. H. Rosenwein, eds, *Monks and Nuns, Saints and Outcasts: Religion in Medieval Society. Essays in Honor of Lester K. Little* (Ithaca, NY: Cornell University Press, 2000), 97–122

Peterson, J. L., 'Social Roles, Gender Inversion, and the Heretical Sect: The Case of the Guglielmites', *Viator* 35 (2004): 203–20

Phillips, K. M., 'Maidenhood as the Perfect Age of Woman's Life', in K. J. Lewis, N. J. Menuge and K. M. Phillips, eds, *Young Medieval Women* (Stroud: Sutton, 1999), pp. 1–24

Phillips, K. M., 'Four Virgins' Tales: Sex and Power in Medieval Law', in A. Bernau, R. Evans and S. Salih, eds, *Medieval Virginities* (Cardiff: University of Wales Press, 2003), pp. 80–101

Phillips, K. M., *Medieval Maidens: Young Women and Gender in England, 1270–1540* (Manchester: Manchester University Press, 2003)

Phythian-Adams, C., 'Ceremony and the Citizen: The Communal Year at Coventry, 1450–1550', in P. Clark and P. Slack, eds, *Crisis and Order in English Towns, 1500–1700* (London: Routledge, 1972), pp. 57–85

Pirenne, H., ed., *Le Soulèvement de la Flandre maritime de 1323–1328* (Brussells: Kiessling, 1900)

Platt, C., *The Parish Churches of Medieval England* (London: Secker & Warburg, 1981)

Poos, L. R., 'Social History and the Book of Hours', in R. S. Wieck, ed, *The Book of Hours in Medieval Art and Life* (London: Sotheby's, 1988), pp. 33–8

Poos, L. R., 'Sex, Lies and the Church Courts of Pre-Reformation England', *Journal of Interdisciplinary History* 25 (1995): 585–607

Populer, M., 'La culture religieuse des laïcs à la fin du Moyen Âge: le carnet des notes d'un bourgeois de Francfort (ca. 1470–1482)', *Moyen Âge* 102 (1996): 479–527

Pullan, B., *Rich and Poor in Renaissance Venice: The Social Institutions of a Catholic State* (Oxford: Blackwell, 1971)

Reinburg, V., 'Liturgy and the Laity in Late Medieval and Reformation France', *Sixteenth-Century Journal* 23 (1992): 526–47

Reinburg, V., 'Praying to Saints in the Late Middle Ages', in Sandro Sticca, ed., *Saints: Studies in Hagiography* (Binghamton, NY: Medieval and Renaissance Texts and Studies, 1996), pp. 269–82

Remensnyder, A. G.,'The Colonization of Sacred Architecture: The Virgin Mary, Mosques, and Temples in Medieval Spain and Early Sixteenth-Century Mexico', in S. Farmer and B.H. Rosenwein, eds, *Monks and Nuns, Saints and Outcasts: Religion in Medieval Society. Essays in Honor of Lester K. Little* (Ithaca, NY: Cornell University Press, 2000), pp. 189–219

Reynolds, S., *Kingdoms and Communities in Western Europe 900–1300* (Oxford: Clarendon Press, 1984)

Reynolds, S., 'Social Mentalities and the Case of Medieval Scepticism', *Transactions of the Royal Historical Society* 6th ser., 1 (1991): 21–41

Richards, P., *The Medieval Leper and His Northern Heirs* (Cambridge: Brewer, 1977)

Richter, M., 'Latina lingua – sacra seu vulgaris?', in W. Lourdaux and D. Verhelst, eds, *The Bible and Medieval Culture* (Leuven: Leuven University Press, 1979), pp. 16–34

Riddy, F., ' "Women Talking About the Things of God": A Late Medieval Subculture', in C. M. Meale, ed., *Women and Literature in Britain, 1100–1500* (Cambridge: Cambridge University Press, 1993), pp. 104–27

Riddy, F., 'Mother Knows Best: Reading Social Change in a Courtesy Text', *Speculum* 71 (1996): 66–86

Ridyard, S. J., 'Functions of a Twelfth-Century Recluse Revisited: The Case of Godric of Finchale', in R. Gameson and H. Leyser, eds, *Belief and Culture in the Middle Ages: Studies Presented to Henry Mayr-Harting* (Oxford: Oxford University Press, 2001), pp. 236–50

Rivers, K., 'Memory and Medieval Preaching: Mnemonic Advice in the *Ars praedicandi* of Francesc Eiximenis (ca 1327–1409)', *Viator* 30 (1999): 253–84

Roach, A., 'The Cathar Economy', *Reading Medieval Studies* 12 (1986): 51–71

Roberts, P. B., 'Preaching in/and the Medieval City', in J. Hamesse, B. M. Kienzle, D. L. Stoudt and A. T. Thayer, eds, *Medieval Sermons and Society: Cloister, City, University*, Textes et Etudes du Moyen Âge, 9 (Louvain-La-Neuve: Fédération Internationale des Instituts d'Etudes Médiévales, 1998), pp. 151–64

Robertson Jr., D. W., 'Frequency of Preaching in Thirteenth-Century England', *Speculum* 24 (1949): 376–88

Robertson, E., *Early English Devotional Prose and the Female Audience* (Knoxville, TN: University of Tennessee Press, 1990)

Rodgers, E. C., *Discussions of Holidays in the Later Middle Ages* (New York: Columbia University Press, 1940)

Roper, L., *The Holy Household: Women and Morals in Reformation Augsburg* (Oxford: Clarendon Press, 1989)

Roquebert, M., 'Le Catharisme comme tradition dans la "familia" languedocienne', in *Effacement du Catharisme (XIIIe–XIVe siècles)?* Cahiers de Fanjeaux 20 (Toulouse: Privat, 1985), pp. 221–42

Rosser, G., 'The Cure of Souls in English Towns before 1000', in John Blair and Richard Sharpe, eds, *Pastoral Care Before the Parish* (Leicester: Leicester University Press, 1992), pp. 267–84

Rosser, G., 'Going to the Fraternity Feast: Commensality and Social Relations in Late Medieval England', *Journal of British Studies* 33 (1994): 430–46

Rosser, G., 'Crafts, Guilds and the Negotiation of Work in the Medieval Town', *Past and Present* 154 (1997): 3–31

Rossiaud, J., 'Les Rituels de la fête civique à Lyon, XIIe–XVIe siècles', in J. Chiffoleau, L. Martines and A. P. Bagliani, eds, *Riti e Rituali: nelle Società Medievali* (Spoleto: Centro Italiano di Studi Sull'Alto Medioevo, 1994), pp. 285–308

Rothkrug, L., 'Icon and Ideology in Religion and Rebellion 1300–1600: *Bauernfreiheit* and *Religion royale*', in J. M. Bak and G. Benecke, eds, *Religion and Rural Revolt* (Manchester: Manchester University Press, 1984), pp. 31–61

Rubellin, M., 'Entrée dans la vie, entrée dans la chrétienté, entrée dans la société: Autour du baptême à l'époque carolingienne', *Annales de l'Est* 5th ser., 34 (1982): 31–51

Rubin, M., *Charity and Community in Medieval Cambridge* (Cambridge: Cambridge University Press, 1987)

Rubin, M., *Corpus Christi: The Eucharist in Late Medieval Culture* (Cambridge: Cambridge University Press, 1991)

Rubin, M., 'Small Groups: Identity and Solidarity in the Late Middle Ages', in J. Kermode, ed., *Enterprise and Individuals in Fifteenth-Century England* (Gloucester: Sutton, 1991), pp. 132–50

Rubin, M., 'What did the Eucharist mean to Thirteenth-Century Villagers?', in P. R. Coss and S. D. Lloyd, eds, *Thirteenth-Century England* IV (Woodbridge: Boydell, 1992), pp. 47–55

Rubin, M., *Gentile Tales: The Narrative Assault on Late Medieval Jews* (New Haven, CT: Yale University Press, 1999)

Rubin, M., and S. Kay, eds, *Framing Medieval Bodies* (Manchester: Manchester University Press, 1994)

Ruggiero, G., *The Boundaries of Eros: Sex Crime and Sexuality in Renaissance Venice* (Oxford: Oxford University Press, 1985)

Rusconi, R., 'De la prédication à la confession: Transmission et contrôle de modèles de comportement au XIIIe siècle', in *Faire croire: Modalités de la diffusion et de la réception des messages religieux du XIIe au XVe siècle* (Rome: Ecole Française de Rome, 1981), pp. 67–85

Rusconi, R., '*Ordinate confiteri*: La confessione dei peccati nelle *summae de casibus* e nei manuali per i confessori (metà XII–inizi XIV secolo)', in *L'Aveu: Antiquité et moyen-âge*, Actes de la table ronde organisée par l'Ecole Française de Rome avec le concours du CNRS et de l'Université de Trieste, Rome 28–30 Mars 1984 (Rome: Ecole Française de Rome, 1986), pp. 297–313

Rusconi, R., *L'ordine dei peccati: La confessione tra Medioevo ed età moderna* (Bologna: Il Mulino, 2002)

Salih, S., 'Margery's Bodies: Piety, Work and Penance', in J. H. Arnold and K. J. Lewis, eds, *A Companion to the Book of Margery Kempe* (Cambridge: Brewer, 2004), pp. 161–76

Schemmann, U., *Confessional Literature and Lay Education: The* Manuel de Pechez *as a Book of Good Conduct and Guide to Personal Religion* (Düsseldorf: Droste, 2000)

Schiferl, E., 'Italian Confraternity Art Contracts: Group Consciousness and Corporate Patronage, 1400–1525', in K. Eisenbichler, ed., *Crossing the Boundaries: Christian Piety and the Arts in Italian Medieval and Renaissance Confraternities* (Kalamazoo, MI: Medieval Institute Publications, 1991), pp. 121–40

Schmitt, J.-C., ' "Religion Populaires" et culture folklorique', *Annales: Economie, Sociétés, Civilisations* 31 (1976): 941–53

Schmitt, J.-C., 'Du bon usage de "Credo" ', in *Faire croire: Modalités de la diffusion et de la réception des messages religieux du XIIe au XVe siècle* (Rome: Ecole Française de Rome, 1981), pp. 337–61

Schmitt, J.-C., *The Holy Greyhound: Guinefort, Healer of Children since the Thirteenth Century*, trans. M. Thom (1979. Cambridge: Cambridge University Press, 1983)

Schmitt, J.-C., *Ghosts in the Middle Ages: The Living and the Dead in Medieval Society*, trans. T. L. Fagan (1994. Chicago: University of Chicago Press, 1998)

Schmitt, J.-C., 'Religion, Folklore and Society in the Medieval West', in B. Rosenwein and L. K. Little, eds, *Debating the Middle Ages* (Oxford: Blackwell, 1998), pp. 376–87

Schmitt, J.-C., *Le corps, les rites, les rêves, le temps: Essais d'anthropologies médiévales* (Paris: Gallimard, 2001)

Schnell, R., 'The Discourse on Marriage in the Middle Ages', *Speculum* 73 (1998): 771–86

Scott, J. C., *Domination and the Arts of Resistance: Hidden Transcripts* (New Haven, CT: Yale University Press, 1990)

Scribner, R. W., 'Ritual and Popular Religion in Catholic Germany at the Time of the Reformation', *Journal of Ecclesiastical History* 35 (1984): 47–77

Scribner, R. W., 'Anticlericalism and the Reformation in Germany', in idem, *Popular Culture and Popular Movements in Reformation Germany* (London: Hambledon, 1987), pp. 243–56

Scribner, R. W., ed., *Popular Religion in Germany and Central Europe 1400–1800* (Houndmills: Macmillan, 1996)

Sekules, V., *Medieval Art* (Oxford: Oxford University Press, 2001)

Shahar, S., *Childhood in the Middle Ages*, trans. C. Galai (London: Routledge, 1990)

Shahar, S., 'The Boy Bishop's Feast: A Case-Study in Church Attitudes towards Children in the High and Late Middle Ages', in D. Wood, ed., *The Church and Childhood*, Studies in Church History 31 (Oxford: Blackwell, 1994), pp. 243–60

Shahar, S., *Women in a Medieval Heretical Sect: Agnes and Huguette the Waldensians*, trans. Y. Lotan (Woodbridge: Boydell Press, 2001)

Shatzmiller, J., *Shylock Reconsidered: Jews, Moneylending and Medieval Society* (Berkeley, CA: University of California Press, 1990)

Shaw, D. G., *The Creation of a Community: The City of Wells in the Middle Ages* (Oxford: Clarendon Press, 1993)

Shaw, J., 'The Influence of Canonical and Episcopal Reform on Popular Books of Instruction', in T. Heffernan, ed., *The Popular Literature of Medieval England* (Knoxville, TN: University of Tennessee Press, 1985), pp. 44–60

Shemek, D., 'Circular Definitions: Configuring Gender in Italian Renaissance Festival', *Renaissance Quarterly* 48 (1995): 1–40

Sigal, P. A., 'Un aspect du culte des saints: le châtiment divin aux XIe et XIIe siècles d'après la littérature hagiographique du Midi de la France', in *La Religion Populaire en Languedoc du XIIIe siècle à la moitié du XIVe siècle*, Cahiers de Fanjeaux 11 (Toulouse: Privat, 1976), pp. 39–59

Sigal, P.-A., *L'homme et le miracle dans la France médiévale (XIe–XIIe siècles)* (Paris: CERF, 1985)

Simons, W., *Cities of Ladies: Beguine Communities in the Medieval Low Countries, 1200–1565* (Philadelphia, PA: University of Pennsylvania Press, 2001)

Smith, J. M. H., 'Oral and Written: Saints, Miracles, and Relics in Brittany, c. 850–1250', *Speculum* 65 (1990): 309–43

Smoller, L., 'Defining the Boundaries of the Natural in Fifteenth-Century Brittany: The Inquest into the Miracles of Saint Vincent Ferrer (d. 1419)', *Viator* 28 (1997): 333–59

Sneddon, C. R., 'The "Bible du XIIIe siècle": Its Medieval Public in the Light of its Manuscript Tradition', in W. Lourdaux and D. Verhelst, eds, *The Bible and Medieval Culture* (Leuven: Leuven University Press, 1979), pp. 127–40

Spencer, H. L., *English Preaching in the Late Middle Ages* (Oxford: Clarendon Press, 1993)

Sperling, J. G., *Convents and the Body Politic in late Renaissance Venice* (Chicago: University of Chicago Press, 1999)

Sponsler, C., 'Festive Profit and Ideological Production: *Le Jeu de Saint Nicolas*', in M. Twycross, ed., *Festive Drama* (Cambridge: Brewer, 1996), pp. 66–79

Sponsler, C., 'Drama and Piety: Margery Kempe', in J. H. Arnold and K. J. Lewis, eds, *A Companion to the Book of Margery Kempe* (Cambridge: Brewer, 2004), pp. 129–43

Stacey, R. C., 'Anti-Semitism and the Medieval English State', in J. R. Maddicott and D. M. Palliser, eds, *The Medieval State: Essays Presented to James Campbell* (London: Hambledon, 2000), pp. 163–77

Stacey, R. C., 'Jews and Christians in Twelfth-Century England: Some Dynamics of a Changing Relationship', in M. A. Signer and J. Van Engen, eds, *Jews and Christians in Twelfth-Century Europe* (Notre Dame, IN: University of Notre Dame Press, 2001), pp. 340–54

Stephens, W., *Demon Lovers: Witchcraft, Sex, and the Crisis of the Belief* (Chicago: University of Chicago Press, 2002)

Stock, B., *The Implications of Literacy: Written Language and Models of Interpretation in the Eleventh and Twelfth Centuries* (Princeton, NJ: Princeton University Press, 1983)

Strayer, J. R., *The Albigensian Crusades* (New York: Dial Press, 1971)

Strickland, D. H., *Saracens, Demons, and Jews: Making Monsters in Medieval Art* (Princeton, NJ: Princeton University Press, 2003)

Strohm, P., ' "A Revelle!": Chronicle Evidence and the Rebel Voice', in idem, *Hochon's Arrow: The Social Imagination of Fourteenth-Century Texts* (Princeton, NJ: Princeton University Press, 1992), pp. 33–56

Swanson, H., *Medieval Artisans: An Urban Class in Late Medieval England* (Oxford: Blackwell, 1989)

Swanson, R. N., 'Medieval Liturgy and Theatre: The Props', in D. Wood, ed., *The Church and the Arts*, Studies in Church History 28 (Oxford: Blackwell, 1992), pp. 239–54

Swanson, R. N., *Religion and Devotion in Europe, c.1215–c.1515* (Cambridge: Cambridge University Press, 1995)

Sweet, J., 'Some Thirteenth-Century Sermons and Their Authors', *Journal of Ecclesiastical History* 4 (1953): 27–36

Symes, C., 'The Appearance of Early Vernacular Plays: Forms, Functions, and the Future of Medieval Theater', *Speculum* 77 (2002): 778–831

Tambling, J., *Confession: Sin, Sexuality, the Subject* (Manchester: Manchester University Press, 1995)

Tanner, N., 'The Cathedral and the City', in I. Atherton, E. Fernie, C. Harper-Bill and H. Smith, eds, *Norwich Cathedral: Church, City and Diocese, 1096–1996* (London: Hambledon, 1996), pp. 255–80

Taylor, L., 'French Sermons 1215–1535', in B. M. Kienzle, ed., *The Sermon*, Typologie des Sources du Moyen Âge Occidental 81–83 (Turnhout: Brepols, 2000), pp. 711–58

Tentler, T. N., 'The Summa for Confessors as an Instrument of Social Control', in C. Trinkaus and H. A. Oberman, eds, *The Pursuit of Holiness in Late Medieval and Renaissance Religion* (Leiden: Brill, 1974), pp. 103–26

Tentler, T. N., *Sin and Confession on the Eve of the Reformation* (Princeton, NJ: Princeton University Press, 1977)

Tentler, T. N., 'Seventeen Authors in Search of Two Religious Cultures' [review of *Faire croire*], *Catholic Historical Review* 71 (1985): 248–57

Terpstra, N., 'Death and Dying in Renaissance Confraternities', in K. Eisenbichler, ed., *Crossing the Boundaries: Christian Piety and the Arts in Italian Medieval and Renaissance Confraternities* (Kalamazoo, MI: Medieval Institute Publications, 1991), pp. 179–200

Terpstra, N., *Lay Confraternities and Civic Religion in Renaissance Bologna* (Cambridge: Cambridge University Press, 1995)

Teunis, H., 'Negotiating Secular and Ecclesistical Power in the Central Middle Ages: A Historiographical Introduction', in H. Teunis, A. Wareham and A.-J. A. Bijsterveld, eds, *Negotiating Secular and Ecclesiastical Power* (Turnhout: Brepols, 1999), pp. 1–16

Theilmann, J. M., 'Political Canonization and Political Symbolism in Medieval England', *Journal of British Studies* 29 (1990): 241–66

Théry, J., 'L'Hérésie des bons hommes: Comment nommer la dissidence religieuse non vaudoise ni beguine en Languedoc (XIIe–début du XIVe siècle)?', *Heresis* 36–37 (2002): 75–117

Thomas, K., *Religion and the Decline of Magic* (London: Penguin, 1973)

Thompson, A., *Revival Preachers and Politics in Thirteenth-Century Italy: The Great Devotion of 1233* (Oxford: Clarendon Press, 1992)

Thompson, E. P., *The Making of the English Working Class* (Harmondsworth: Penguin, 1968)

Thompson, J. A. F., *The Later Lollards* (London: Oxford University Press, 1965)

Trexler, R. C., 'Ritual in Florence: Adolescence and Salvation in the Renaissance', in C. Trinkaus and H. A. Oberman, eds, *The Pursuit of Holiness in Late Medieval and Renaissance Religion* (Leiden: Brill, 1974), pp. 200–64

Trexler, R. C., *Public Life in Renaissance Florence* (New York: Academic Press, 1980)

Turner, R. V., 'The *Miles Literatus* in Twelfth- and Thirteenth-Century England: How Rare a Phenomenon?', *American Historical Review* 83 (1978): 928–45

Turner, V., *The Ritual Process: Structure and Anti-Structure* (London: Routledge, 1969)

Twycross, M., 'Some Approaches to Dramatic Festivity, especially Processions', in M. Twycross, ed., *Festive Drama* (Cambridge: Brewer, 1996), pp. 1–33

Ullmann, W., 'Public Welfare and Social Legislation in the Early Medieval Councils', in G.J. Cuming and D. Baker, eds, *Councils and Assemblies*, Studies in Church History 7 (Cambridge: Cambridge University Press, 1971), pp. 1–39

Vauchez, A., 'La religion populaire dans la France méridionale au XIVe siècle, d'après les procès de canonisation', in *La Religion Populaire en Languedoc du XIIIe siècle à la moitié du XIVe siècle*, Cahiers de Fanjeaux 11 (Toulouse: Privat, 1976), pp. 91–107

Vauchez, A., 'Présentation', in *Faire croire: Modalités de la diffusion et de la réception des messages religieux du XIIe au XVe siècle* (Rome: Ecole Française de Rome, 1981), pp. 7–16

Vauchez, A., 'Conclusion', in *Le Mouvement confraternel au moyen âge: France, Italie, Suisse* (Rome: Ecole Française de Rome, 1987), pp. 395–405

Vauchez, A., *The Laity in the Middle Ages: Religious Beliefs and Devotional Practices*, trans. M. J. Schneider (1987. Notre Dame, IN: University of Notre Dame Press, 1993)

Vauchez, A., 'Lay People's Sanctity in Western Europe: Evolution of a Pattern (Twelfth and Thirteenth Centuries)', in R. Blumenfeld-Kosinski and T. Szell, eds, *Images of Sainthood in Medieval Europe* (Ithaca, NY: Cornell University Press, 1991), pp. 21–32

Vauchez, A., 'Saints admirables et saints imitables: Les functions de l'hagiographie ont-elles changé aux derniers siècles du moyen âge?', in *Les Fonctions des saints dans le monde occidental (IIIe–XIIe siècle)* (Palas Farnèse: Ecole Française de Rome, 1991), pp. 161–72

Vauchez, A., *Sainthood in the Later Middle Ages*, trans. J. Birrell (1988. Cambridge: Cambridge University Press, 1997)

Vecchio, S., 'The Good Wife', in C. Klapisch-Zuber, ed., *A History of Women in the West II: Silences of the Middle Ages* (Cambridge, MA: Harvard University Press, 1992), pp. 105–35

Vincent, C., *Des Charités biens ordonnées: Les confréries Normandes de la fin du XIIIe siècle au début du XIVe siècle* (Paris: Ecole Normale Supérieure, 1988)

Vincent, C., *Les Confréries médiévales dans le royaume de France XIIIe–XVe siècle* (Paris: Albin Michel, 1994)

Vodola, E., *Excommunication in the Middle Ages* (Berkeley, CA: University of California Press, 1986)

Wakefield, W. L., 'Some Unorthodox Popular Ideas of the Thirteenth Century', *Medievalia et Humanistica* n.s. 4 (1973): 25–35

Walravens, C., 'Insultes, blasphèmes ou hérésie? Un procès à l'officialité épiscopale de Troyes en 1445', *Bibliothèques de l'Ecole des Chartres* 154: 2 (1996): 485–507

Warren, N. B., *Spiritual Economies: Female Monasticism in Later Medieval England* (Philadelphia, PA: University of Pennsylvania Press, 2001)

Watkins, C., 'Sin, Penance and Purgatory in the Anglo-Norman Realm: The Evidence of Visions and Ghost Stories', *Past and Present* 175 (2002): 3–33

Watson, N., 'Censorship and Cultural Change in Late-Medieval England: Vernacular

Theology, the Oxford Translation Debate, and Arundel's Constitutions of 1409', *Speculum* 70 (1990): 821–64

Watt, D., *Secretaries of God: Women Prophets in Late Medieval and Early Modern England* (Cambridge: Boydell, 1997)

Webb, D., *Patrons and Defenders: The Saints in the Italian City States* (London: I.B. Tauris, 1996)

Webb, D., *Pilgrimage in Medieval England* (London: Hambledon and London, 2000)

Webb, D., *Medieval European Pilgrimage* (Houndmills: Palgrave, 2002)

Weinstein, D., and R. M. Bell, *Saints and Society: The Two Worlds of Latin Christendom, 1000–1700* (Chicago: University of Chicago Press, 1987)

Weissman, R. F. E., *Ritual Brotherhood in Renaissance Florence* (New York: Academic Press, 1982)

Weissman, R. F. E., 'Cults and Contexts: In Search of the Renaissance Confraternity', in K. Eisenbichler, ed., *Crossing the Boundaries: Christian Piety and the Arts in Italian Medieval and Renaissance Confraternities* (Kalamazoo, MI: Medieval Institute Publications, 1991), pp. 201–20

Welch, E., *Art and Society in Italy, 1350–1500* (Oxford: Oxford University Press, 1997)

Wessley, S., 'The Thirteenth-Century Guglielmites: Salvation Through Women', in D. Baker, ed., *Medieval Women*, Studies in Church History subsidia 1 (Oxford: Blackwell, 1978), pp. 289–303

Williamson, B., 'Liturgical Image or Devotional Image? The London *Madonna of the Firescreen*', in C. Hourihan, ed., *Objects, Images and the Word: Art in the Service of the Liturgy* (Princeton, NJ: Princeton University Press, 2003), pp. 298–318

Williamson, B., 'Altarpieces, Liturgy and Devotion', *Speculum* 79 (2004): 341–406

Wilson, S., *The Magical Universe: Everyday Ritual and Magic in Pre-Modern Europe* (London: Hambledon and London, 2000)

Wirth, J., 'La naissance du concept de croyance (XIIe–XVIIe siècles)', *Bibliothèque d'humanisme et renaissance* 45 (1983): 7–58

Wood, A., *Riot, Rebellion and Popular Politics in Early Modern England* (Houndmills: Palgrave, 2002)

Wootton, D., 'Lucien Febvre and the Problem of Unbelief in the Early Modern Period', *Journal of Modern History* 60 (1988): 695–730

Wunderli, R., *Peasant Fires: The Drummer of Niklashausen* (Indianapolis: Indiana University Press, 1992)

Zerner, M., ed., *Inventer l'hérésie? Discours polémiques et pouvoirs avant l'inquisition* (Nice: Centre d'Etudes Médiévales, 1998)

Zika, C., 'Hosts, Processions and Pilgrimages: Controlling the Sacred in Fifteenth-Century Germany', *Past and Present* 118 (1988): 25–64

Zink, M., 'Les destinaires des recueils de sermons en langue vulgaire au XIIe et XIII siècles. Prédication effective et prédication dans un fauteuil', in *La Piété populaire au Moyen Âge*, Actes du 99e Congrès National des Sociétés Savantes, Besançon 1974 (Paris: Bibliothèque Nationale, 1977), pp. 59–74

Index